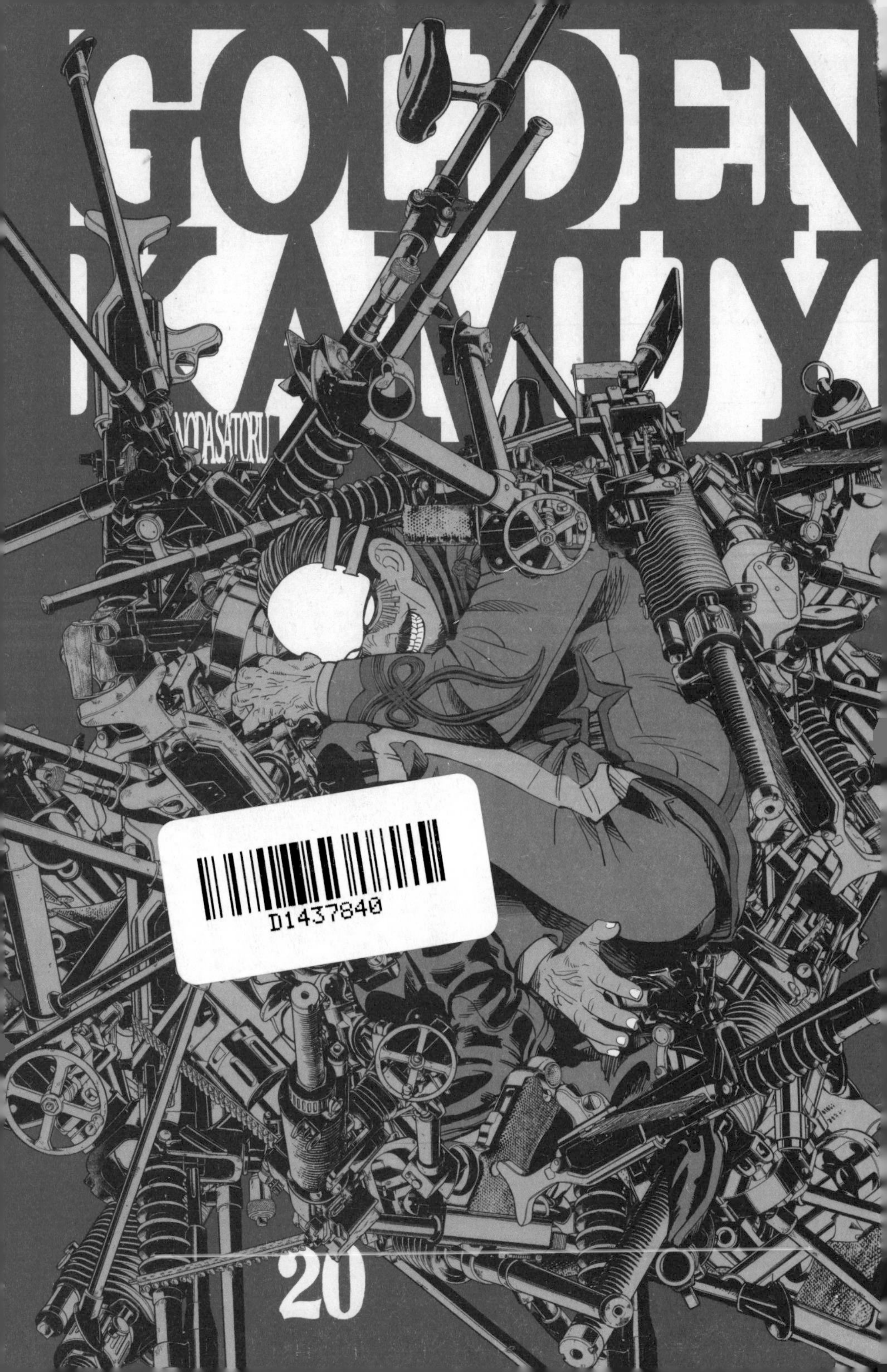
GOLDEN
KAMUY
NODA SATORU
20

The Story So Far

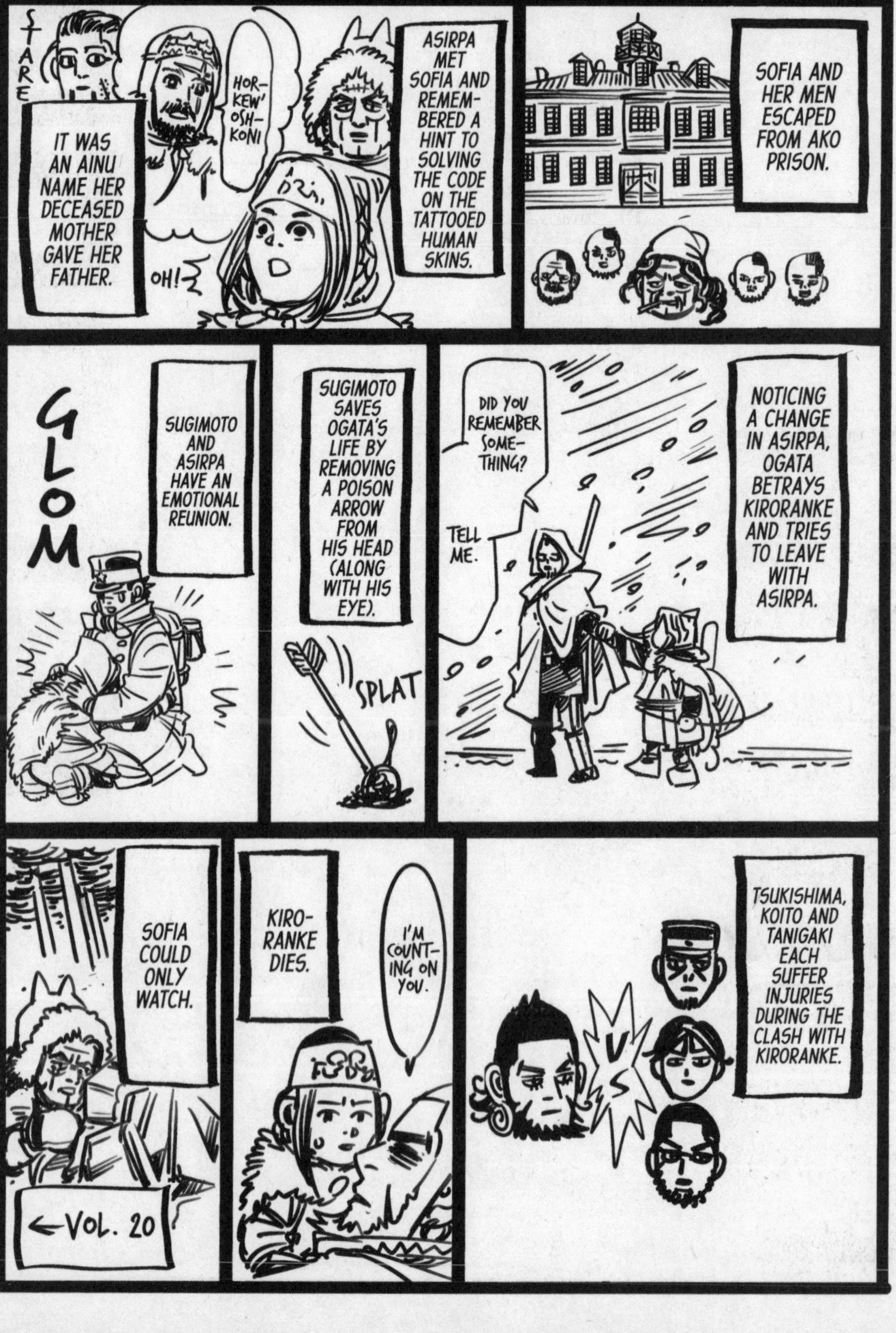
SOFIA AND HER MEN ESCAPED FROM AKO PRISON.
ASIRPA MET SOFIA AND REMEMBERED A HINT TO SOLVING THE CODE ON THE TATTOOED HUMAN SKINS.
HORKEW' OSHKONI
STARE
IT WAS AN AINU NAME HER DECEASED MOTHER GAVE HER FATHER.
OH!
NOTICING A CHANGE IN ASIRPA, OGATA BETRAYS KIRORANKE AND TRIES TO LEAVE WITH ASIRPA.
DID YOU REMEMBER SOMETHING?
TELL ME.
SUGIMOTO SAVES OGATA'S LIFE BY REMOVING A POISON ARROW FROM HIS HEAD (ALONG WITH HIS EYE).
SPLAT
SUGIMOTO AND ASIRPA HAVE AN EMOTIONAL REUNION.
GLOM
TSUKISHIMA, KOITO AND TANIGAKI EACH SUFFER INJURIES DURING THE CLASH WITH KIRORANKE.
VS
I'M COUNTING ON YOU.
KIRORANKE DIES.
SOFIA COULD ONLY WATCH.
←VOL. 20

CONTENTS

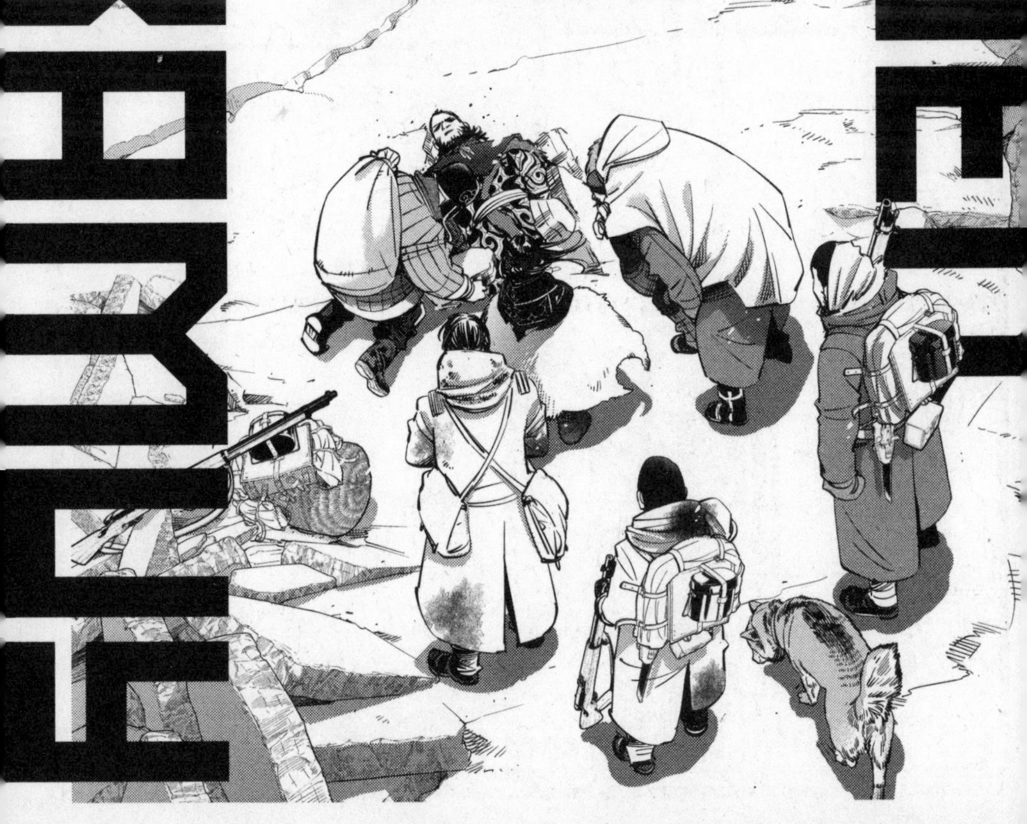

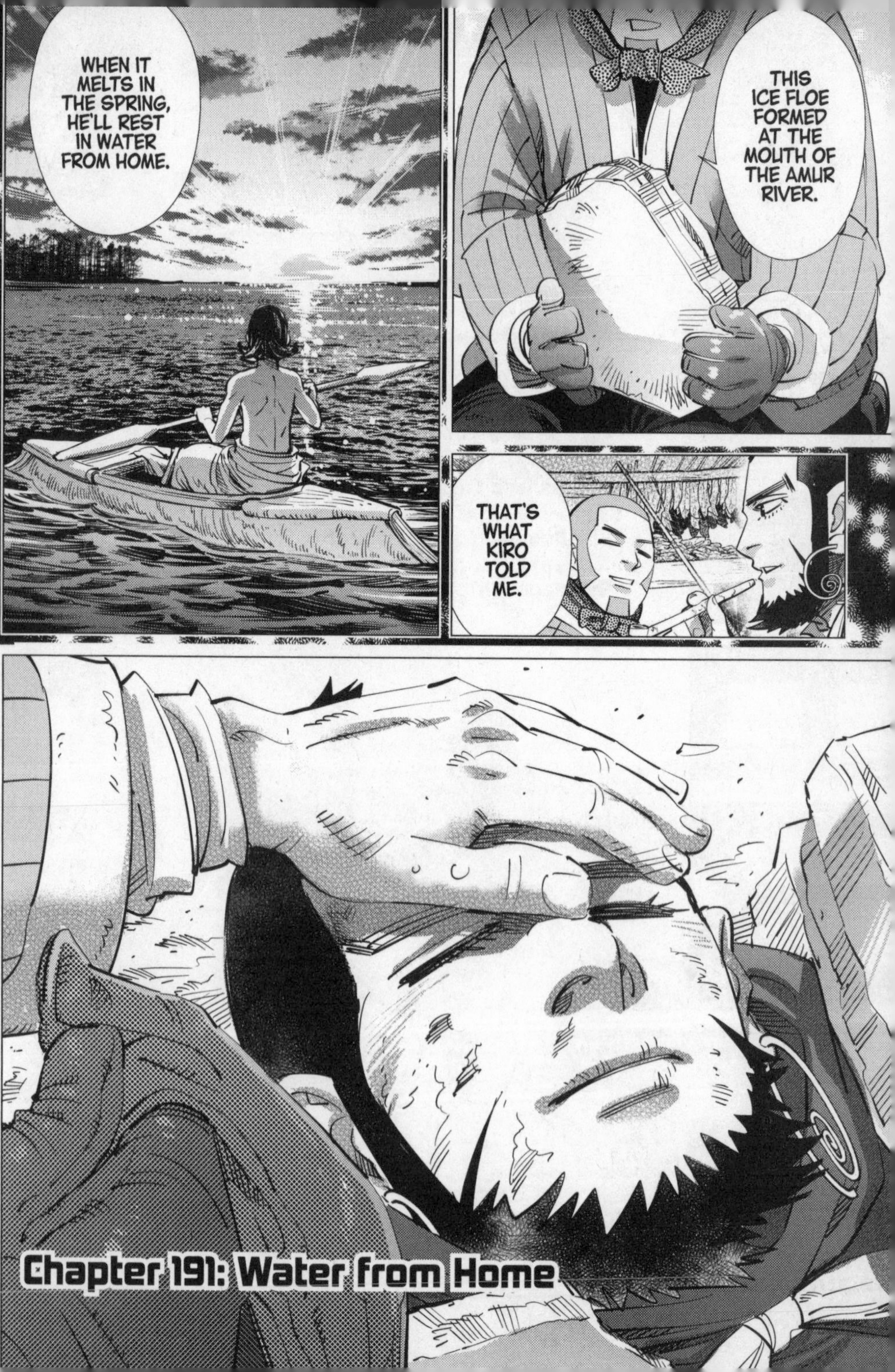
THIS ICE FLOE FORMED AT THE MOUTH OF THE AMUR RIVER.
THAT'S WHAT KIRO TOLD ME.
WHEN IT MELTS IN THE SPRING, HE'LL REST IN WATER FROM HOME.
Chapter 191: Water from Home

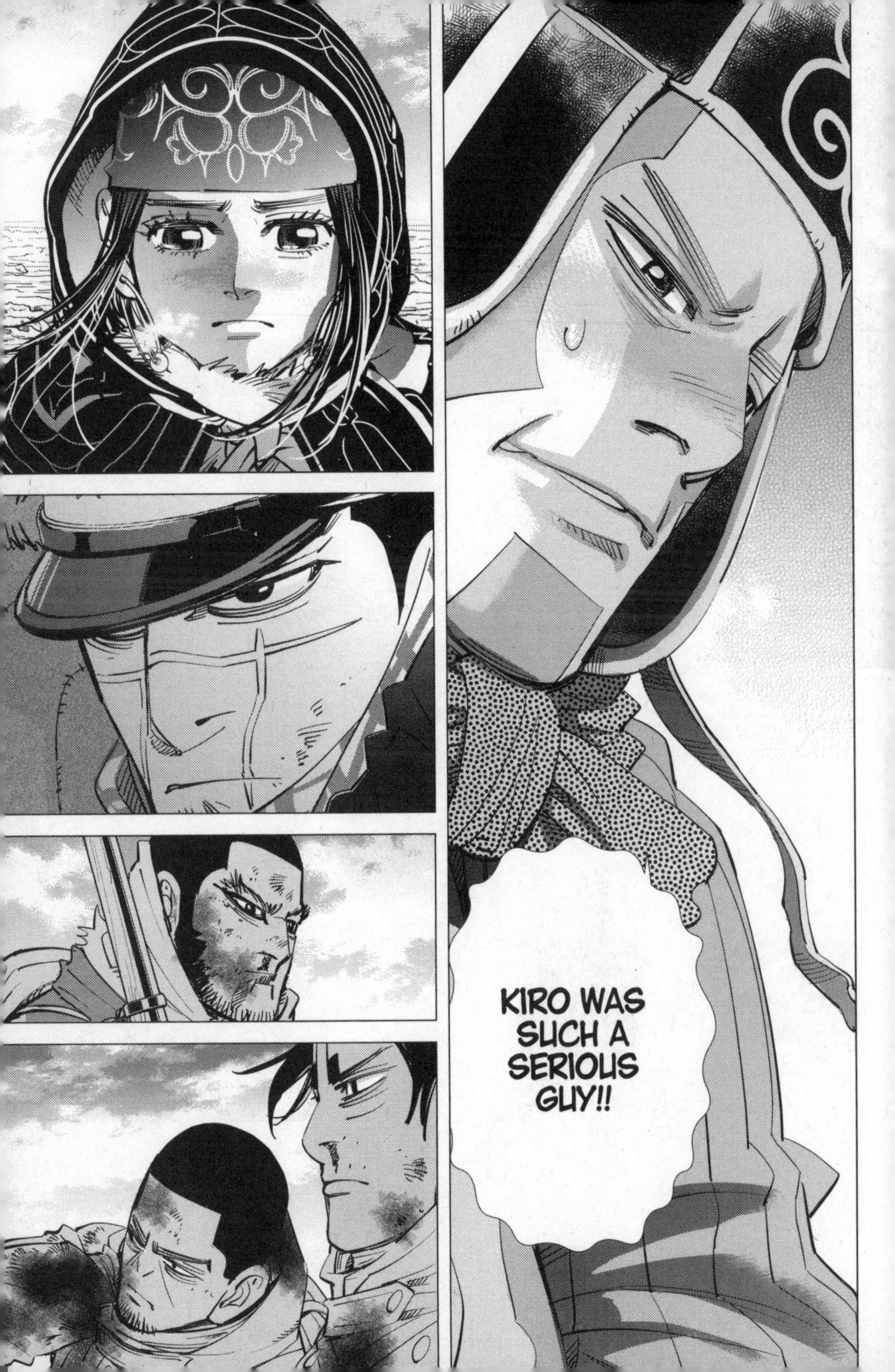
KIRO WAS SUCH A SERIOUS GUY!!

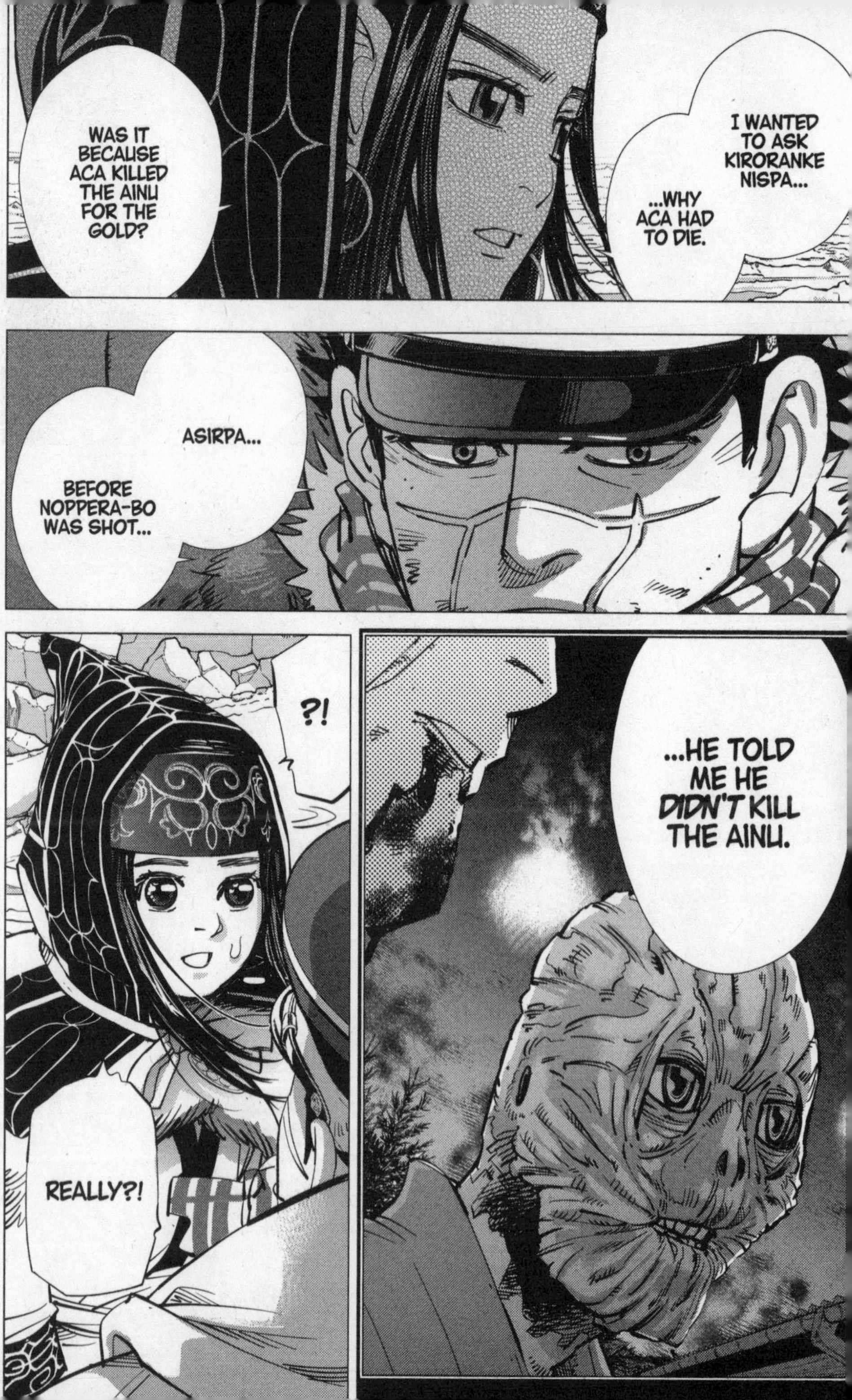
I WANTED TO ASK KIRORANKE NISPA...
...WHY ACA HAD TO DIE.
WAS IT BECAUSE ACA KILLED THE AINU FOR THE GOLD?
ASIRPA...
BEFORE NOPPERA-BO WAS SHOT...
...HE TOLD ME HE *DIDN'T* KILL THE AINU.
?!
REALLY?!

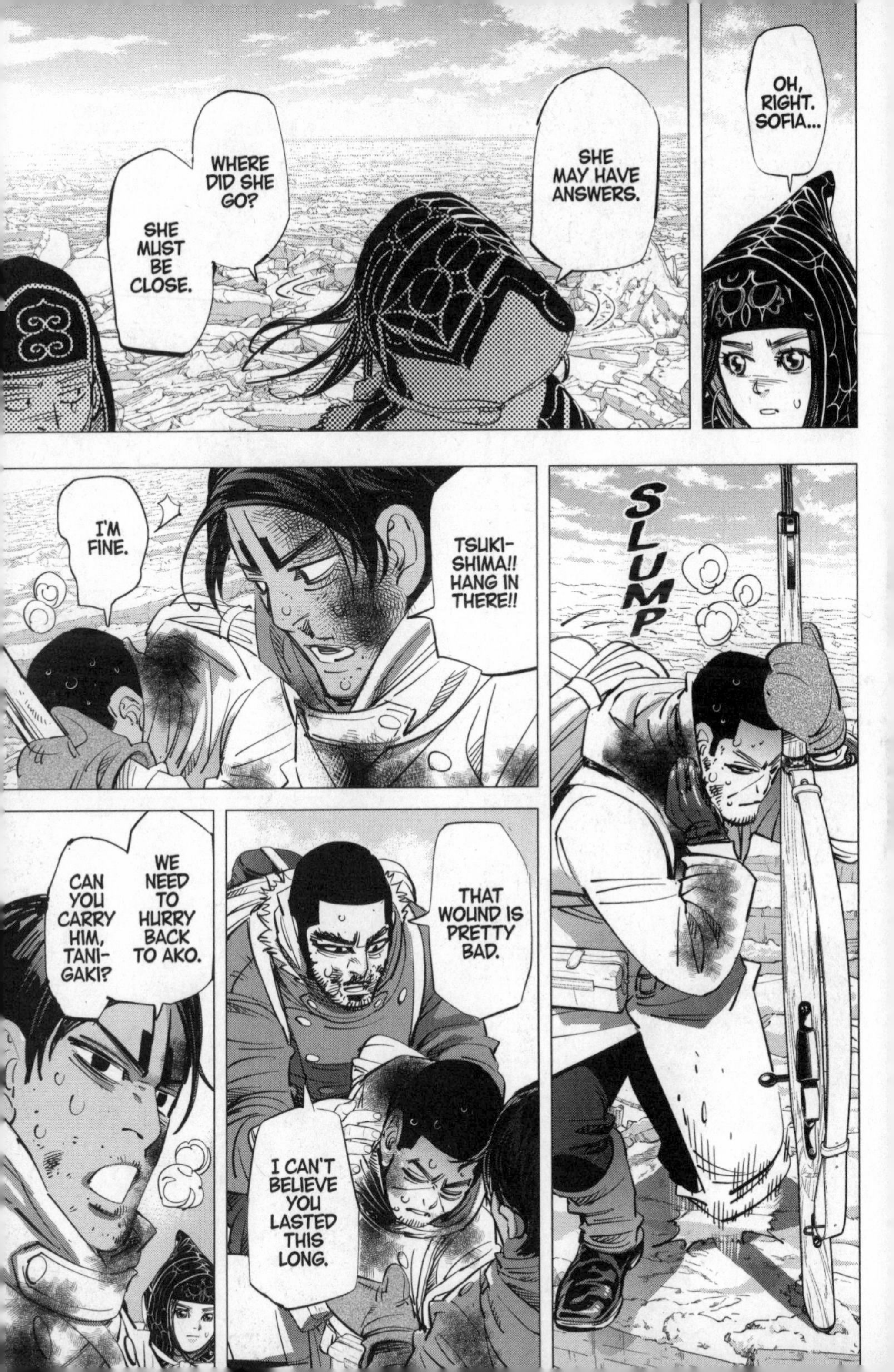
OH, RIGHT. SOFIA...
SHE MAY HAVE ANSWERS.
WHERE DID SHE GO?
SHE MUST BE CLOSE.
SLUMP
TSUKI-SHIMA!! HANG IN THERE!!
I'M FINE.
THAT WOUND IS PRETTY BAD.
I CAN'T BELIEVE YOU LASTED THIS LONG.
WE NEED TO HURRY BACK TO AKO.
CAN YOU CARRY HIM, TANI-GAKI?

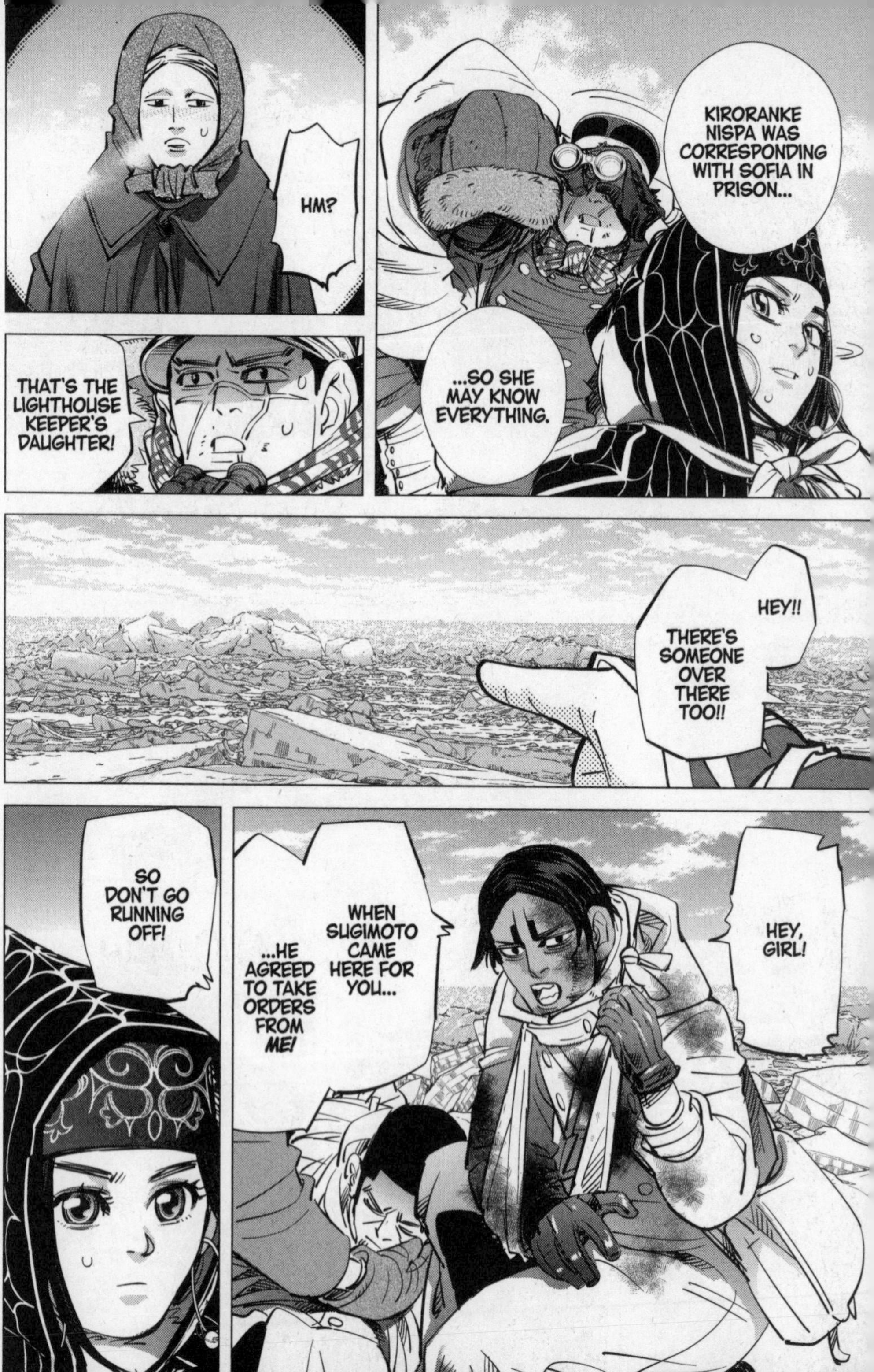
KIRORANKE NISPA WAS CORRESPONDING WITH SOFIA IN PRISON...
...SO SHE MAY KNOW EVERYTHING.
HM?
THAT'S THE LIGHTHOUSE KEEPER'S DAUGHTER!
HEY!!
THERE'S SOMEONE OVER THERE TOO!!
HEY, GIRL!
WHEN SUGIMOTO CAME HERE FOR YOU...
...HE AGREED TO TAKE ORDERS FROM ME!
SO DON'T GO RUNNING OFF!

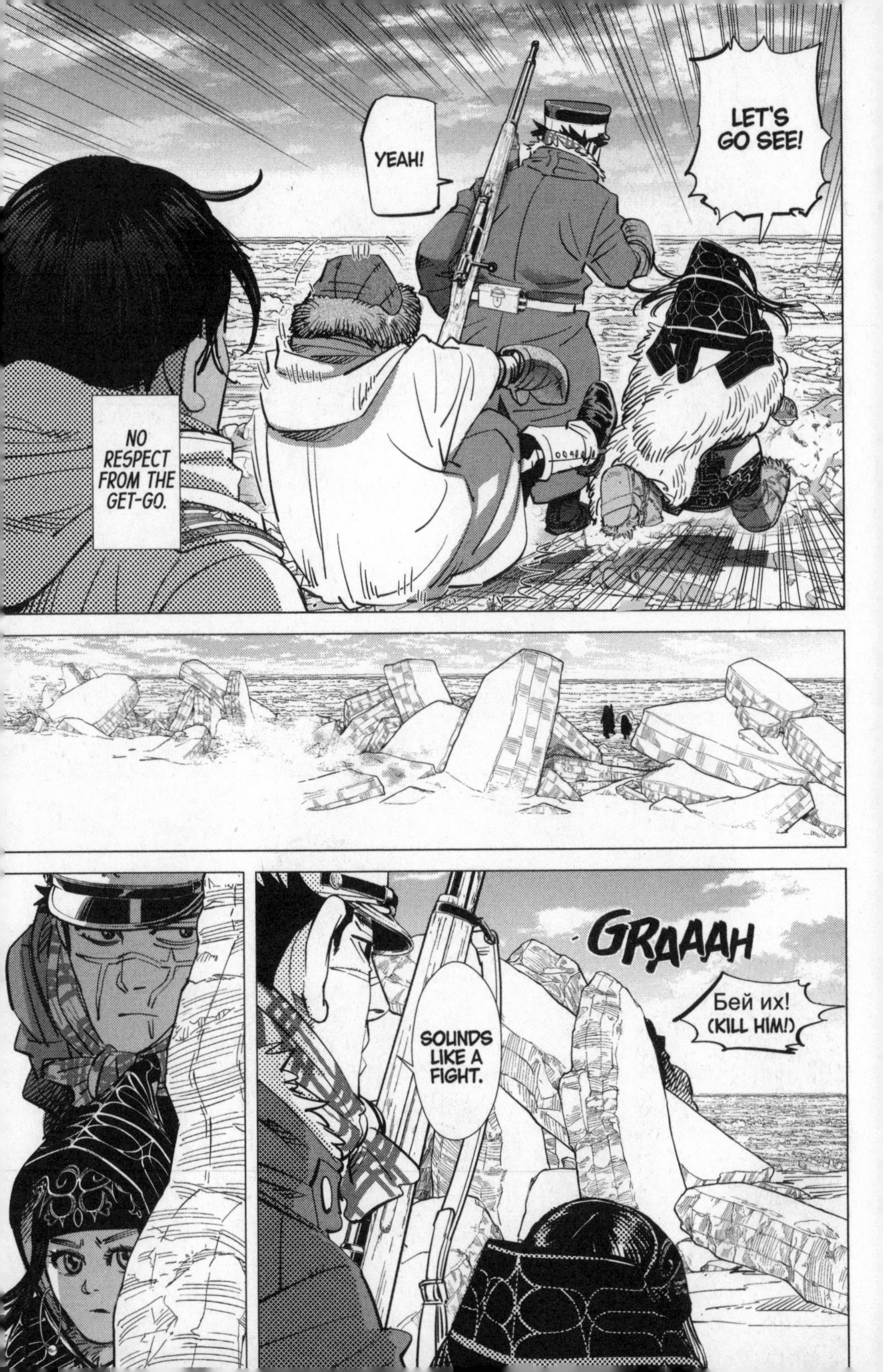
LET'S GO SEE!
YEAH!
NO RESPECT FROM THE GET-GO.
GRAAAH
Бей их! (KILL HIM!)
SOUNDS LIKE A FIGHT.

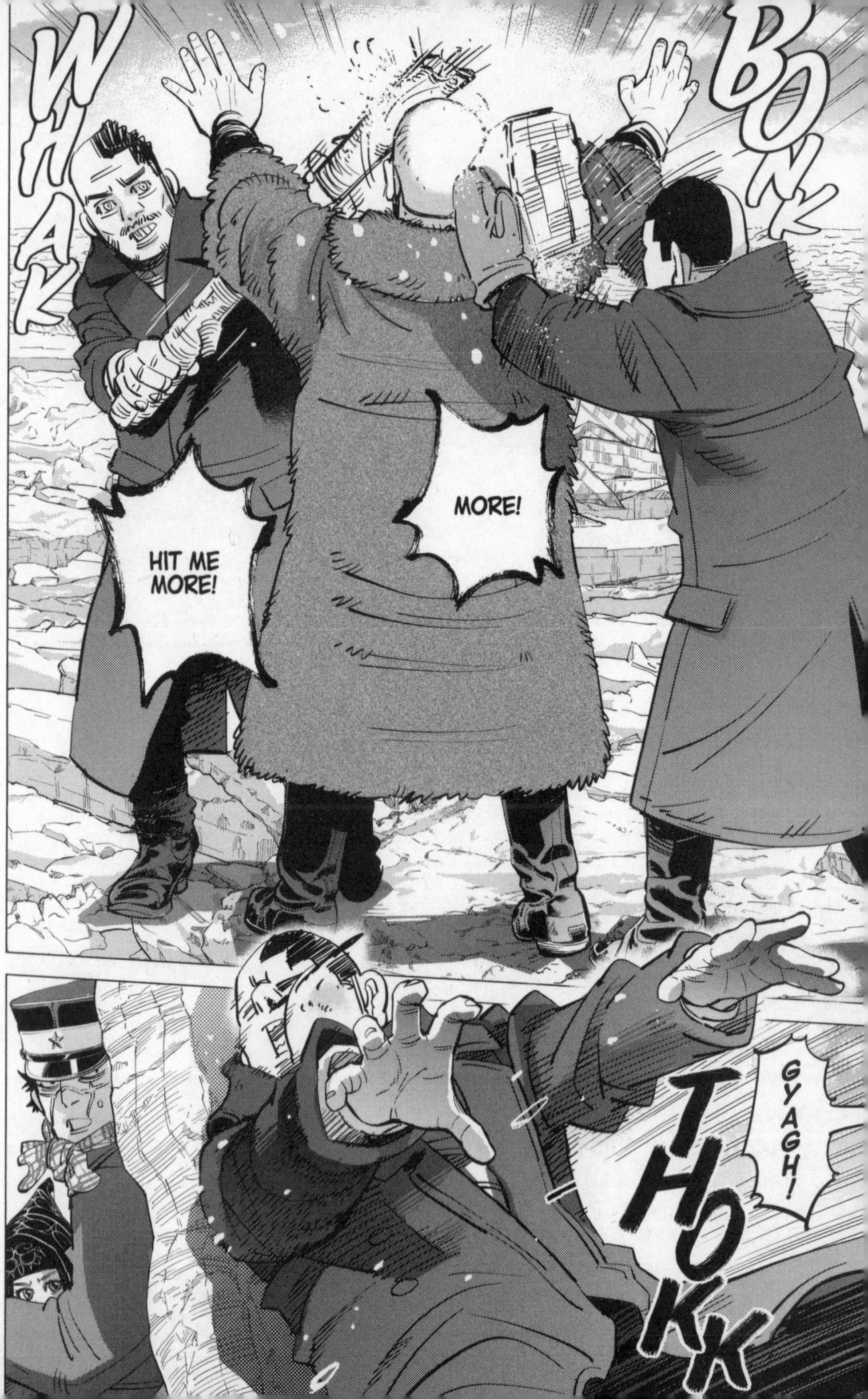
BONK
WHAK
MORE!
HIT ME MORE!
GYAGH!
THOKK

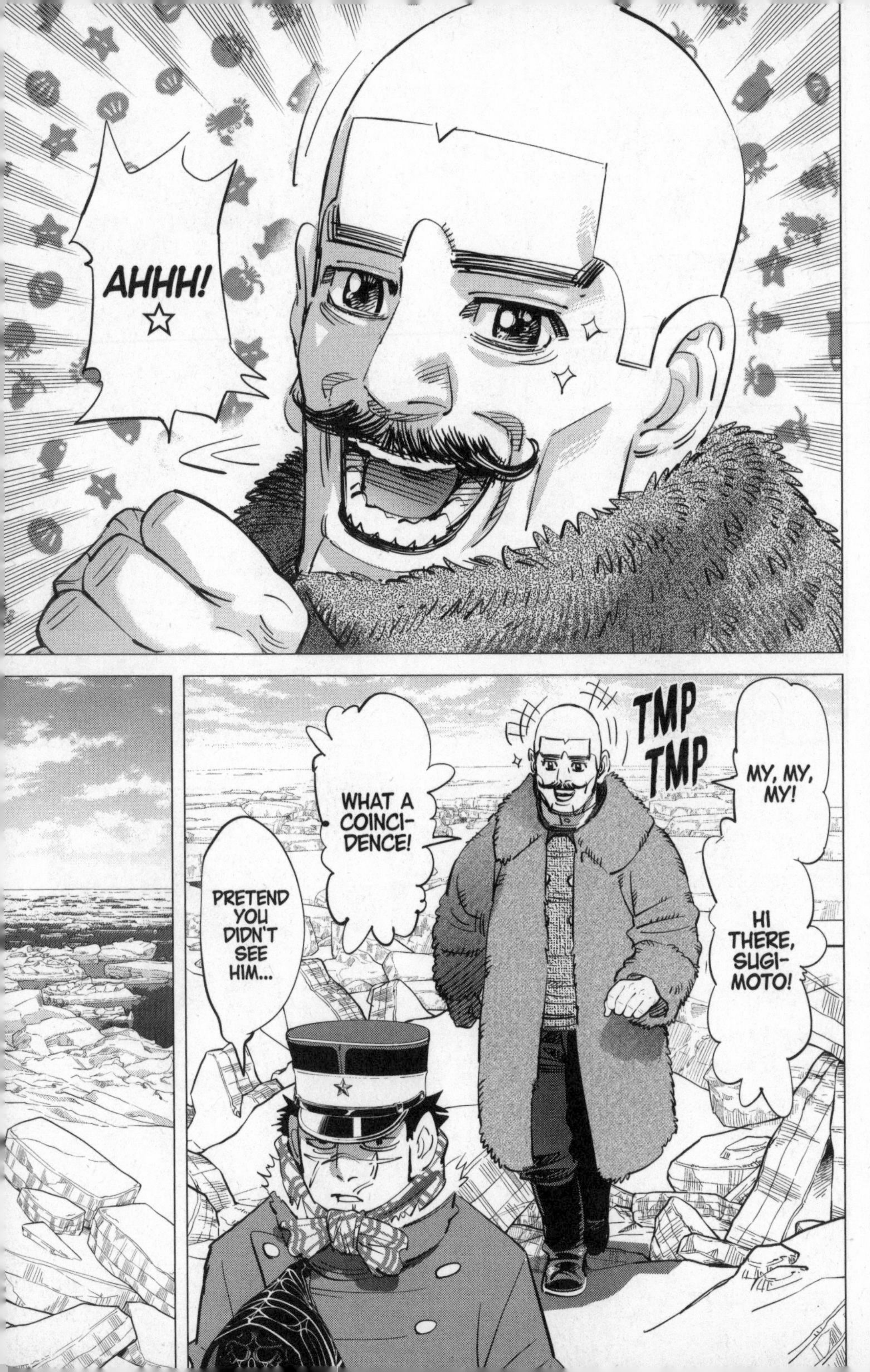
AHHH! ☆
TMP TMP
MY, MY, MY!
HI THERE, SUGIMOTO!
WHAT A COINCIDENCE!
PRETEND YOU DIDN'T SEE HIM...

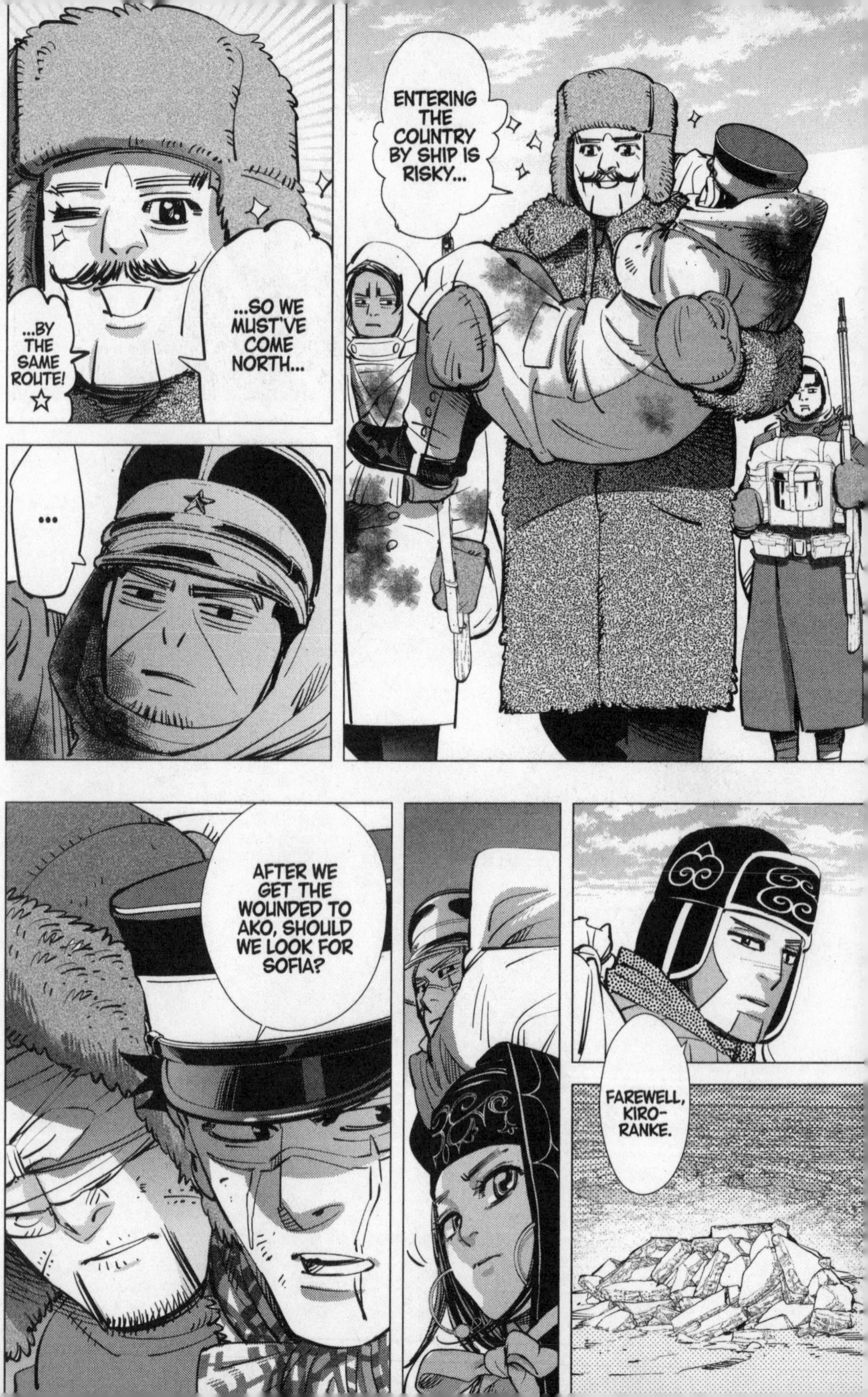
ENTERING THE COUNTRY BY SHIP IS RISKY...
...SO WE MUST'VE COME NORTH...
...BY THE SAME ROUTE! ☆
...
FAREWELL, KIRO-RANKE.
AFTER WE GET THE WOUNDED TO AKO, SHOULD WE LOOK FOR SOFIA?

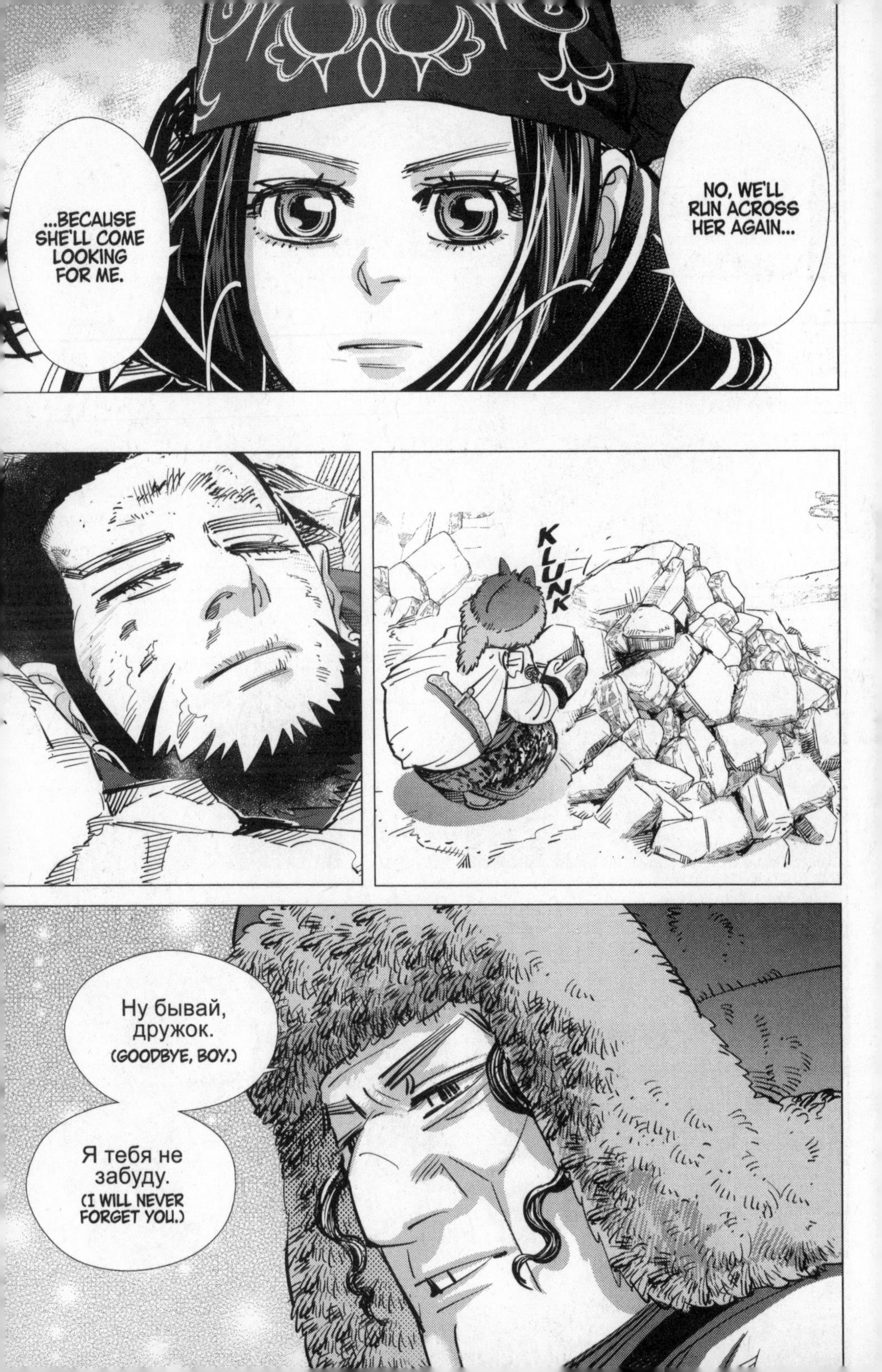
NO, WE'LL RUN ACROSS HER AGAIN...
...BECAUSE SHE'LL COME LOOKING FOR ME.
KLUNK
Ну бывай, дружок.
(GOODBYE, BOY.)
Я тебя не забуду.
(I WILL NEVER FORGET YOU.)

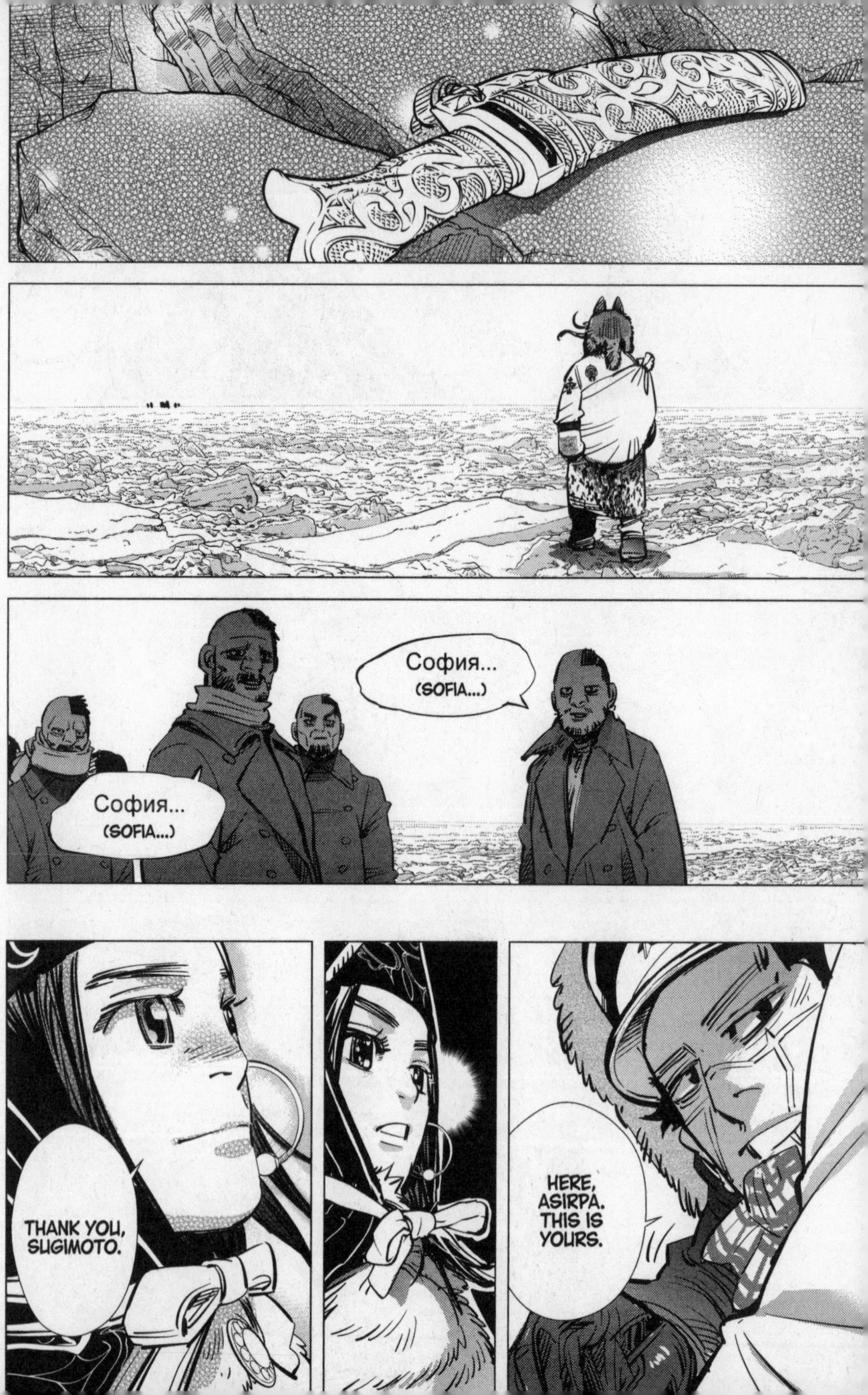
София... (SOFIA...)
София... (SOFIA...)
HERE, ASIRPA. THIS IS YOURS.
THANK YOU, SUGIMOTO.

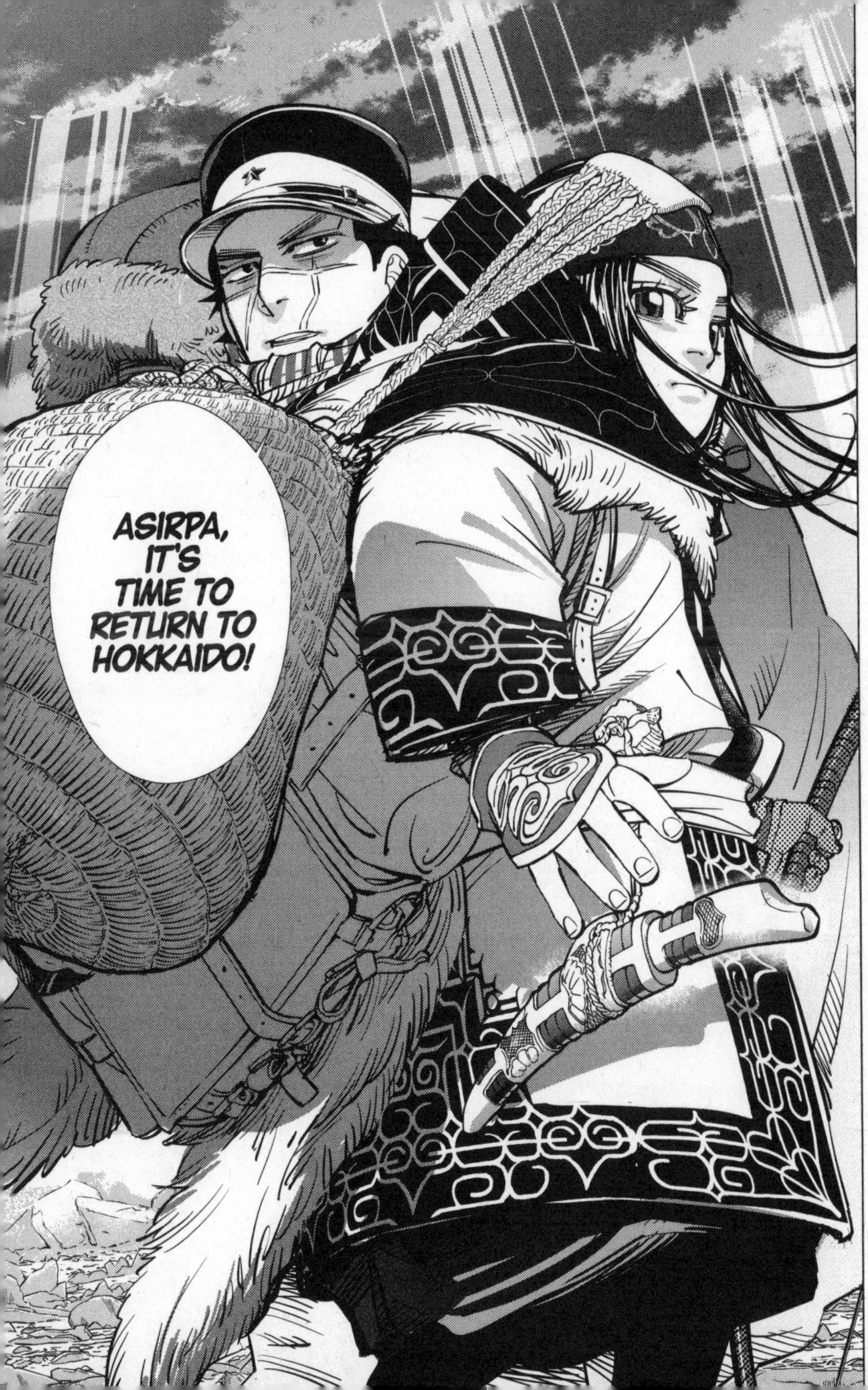
ASIRPA, IT'S TIME TO RETURN TO HOKKAIDO!

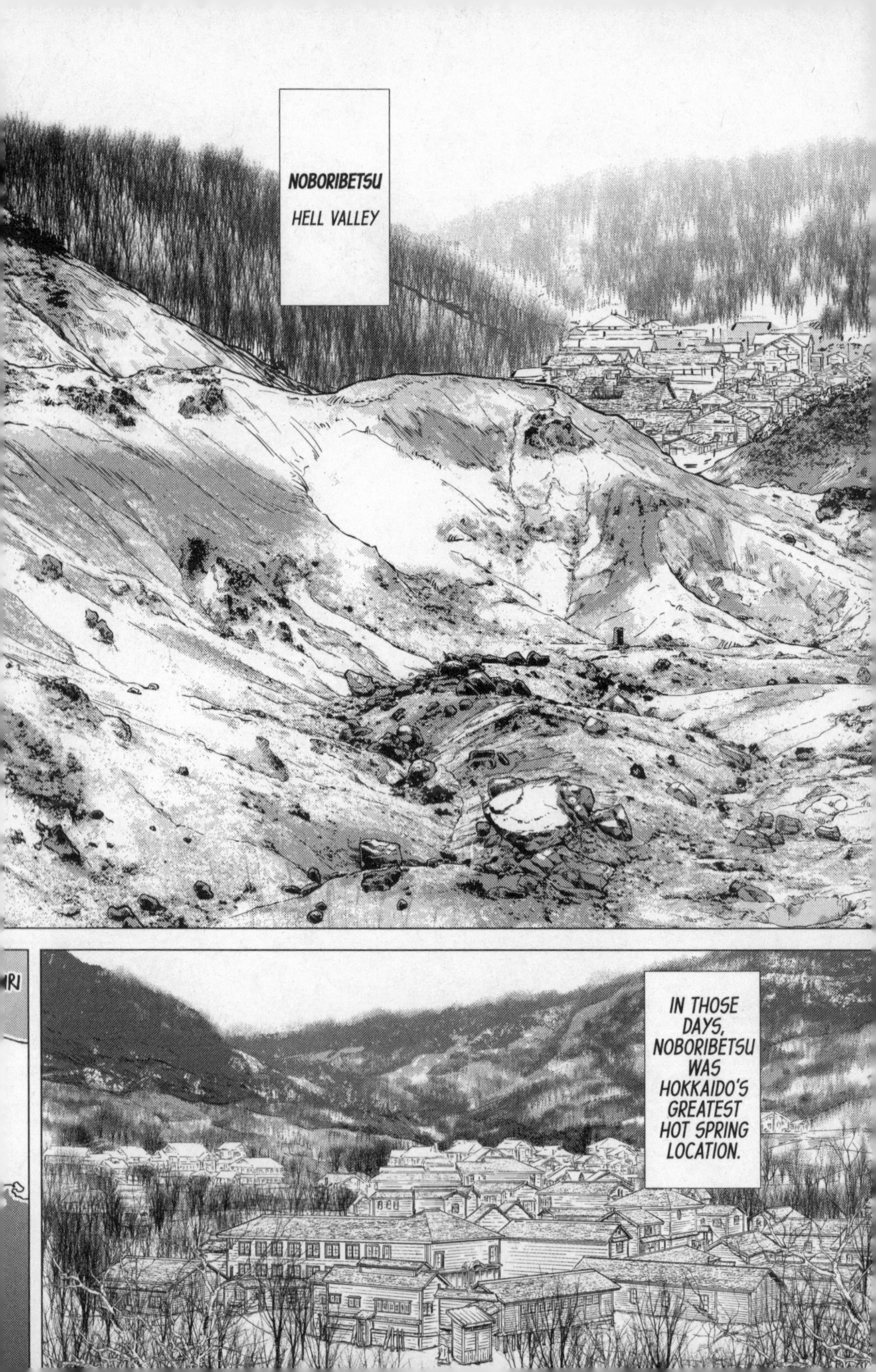
NOBORIBETSU
HELL VALLEY
IN THOSE DAYS, NOBORIBETSU WAS HOKKAIDO'S GREATEST HOT SPRING LOCATION.

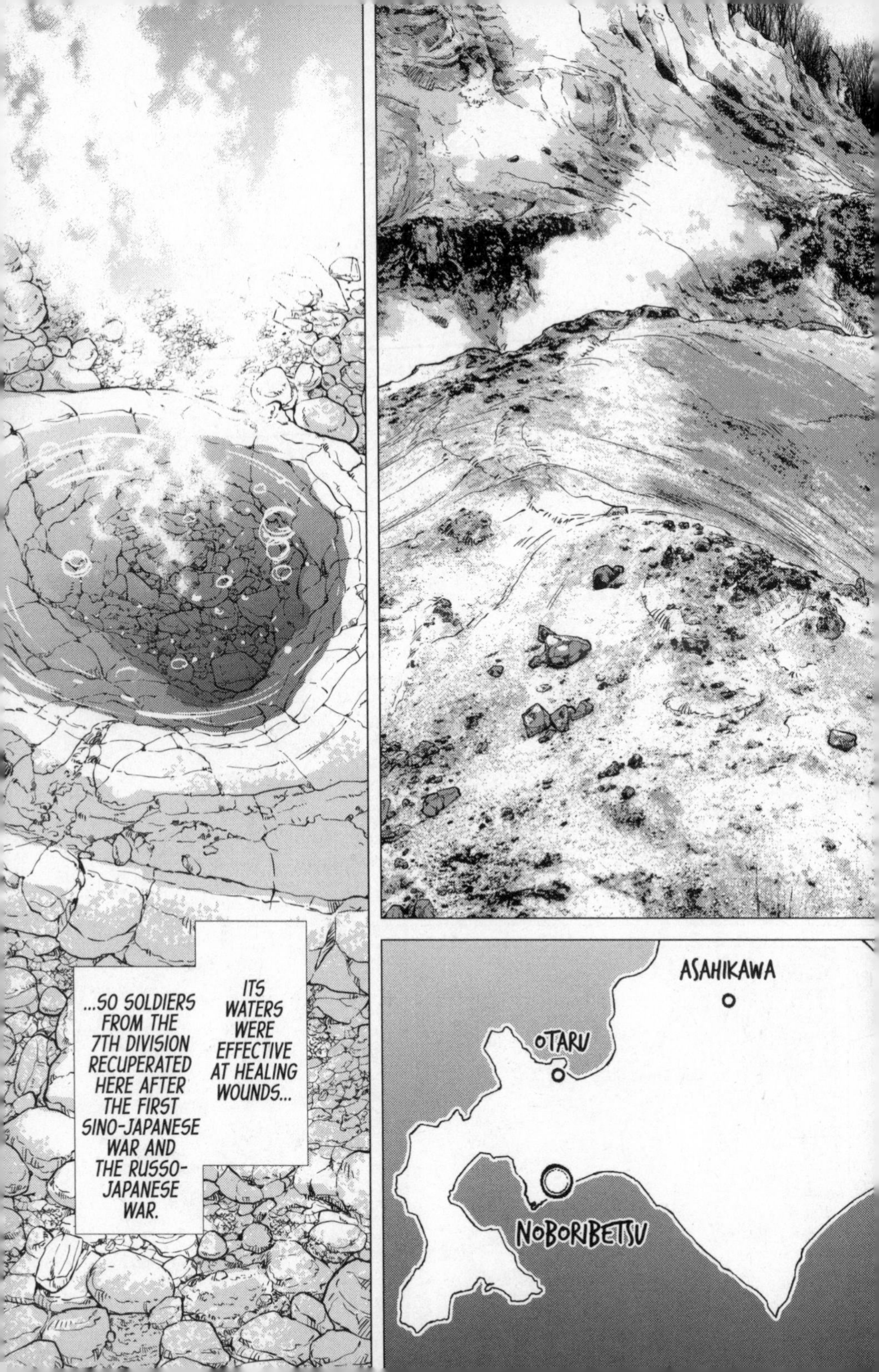
ASAHIKAWA
OTARU
NOBORIBETSU
ITS WATERS WERE EFFECTIVE AT HEALING WOUNDS...
...SO SOLDIERS FROM THE 7TH DIVISION RECUPERATED HERE AFTER THE FIRST SINO-JAPANESE WAR AND THE RUSSO-JAPANESE WAR.

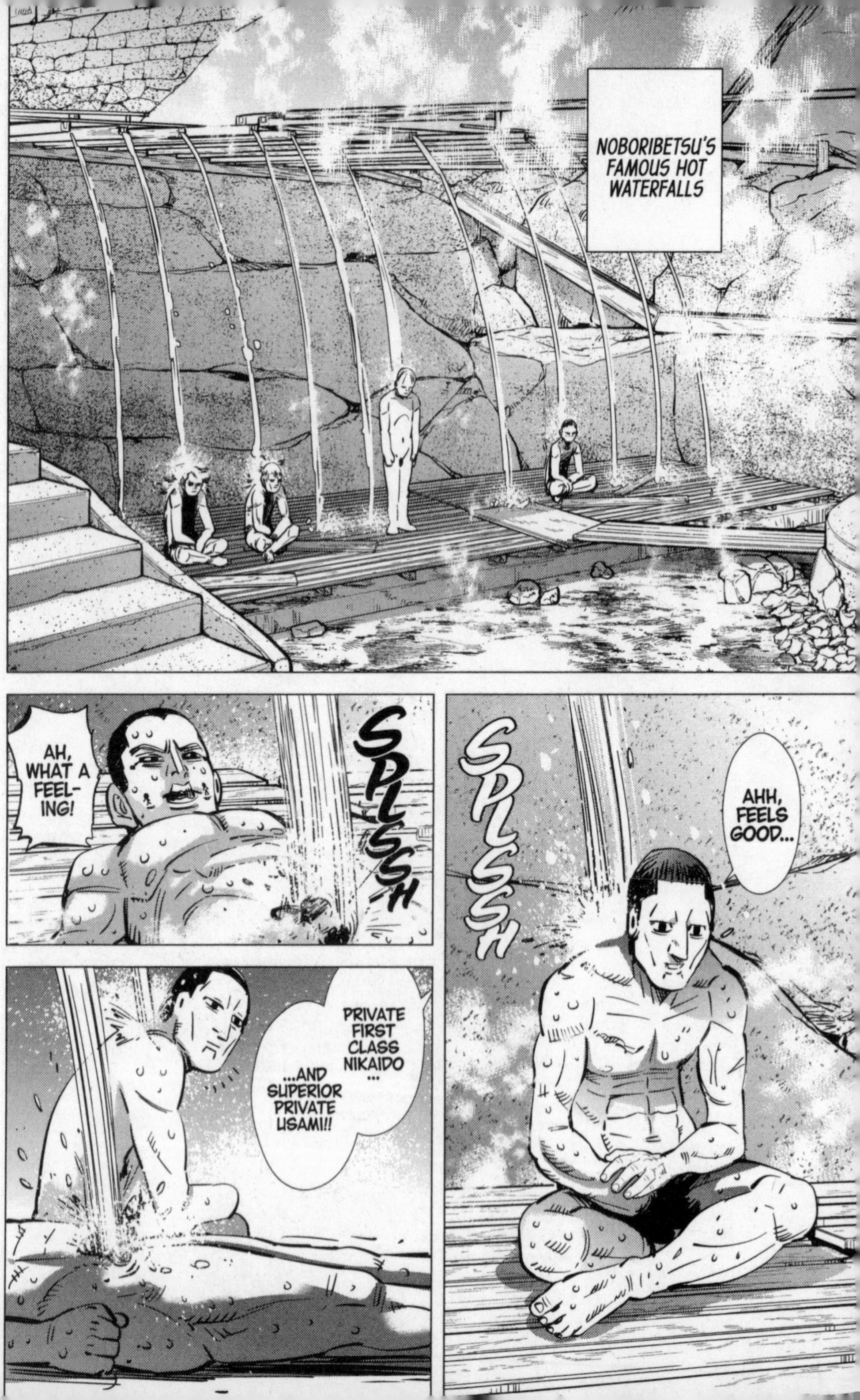
NOBORIBETSU'S FAMOUS HOT WATERFALLS
SPLSSH
AHH, FEELS GOOD...
AH, WHAT A FEEL-ING!
SPLSSH
PRIVATE FIRST CLASS NIKAIDO ...
...AND SUPERIOR PRIVATE USAMI!!

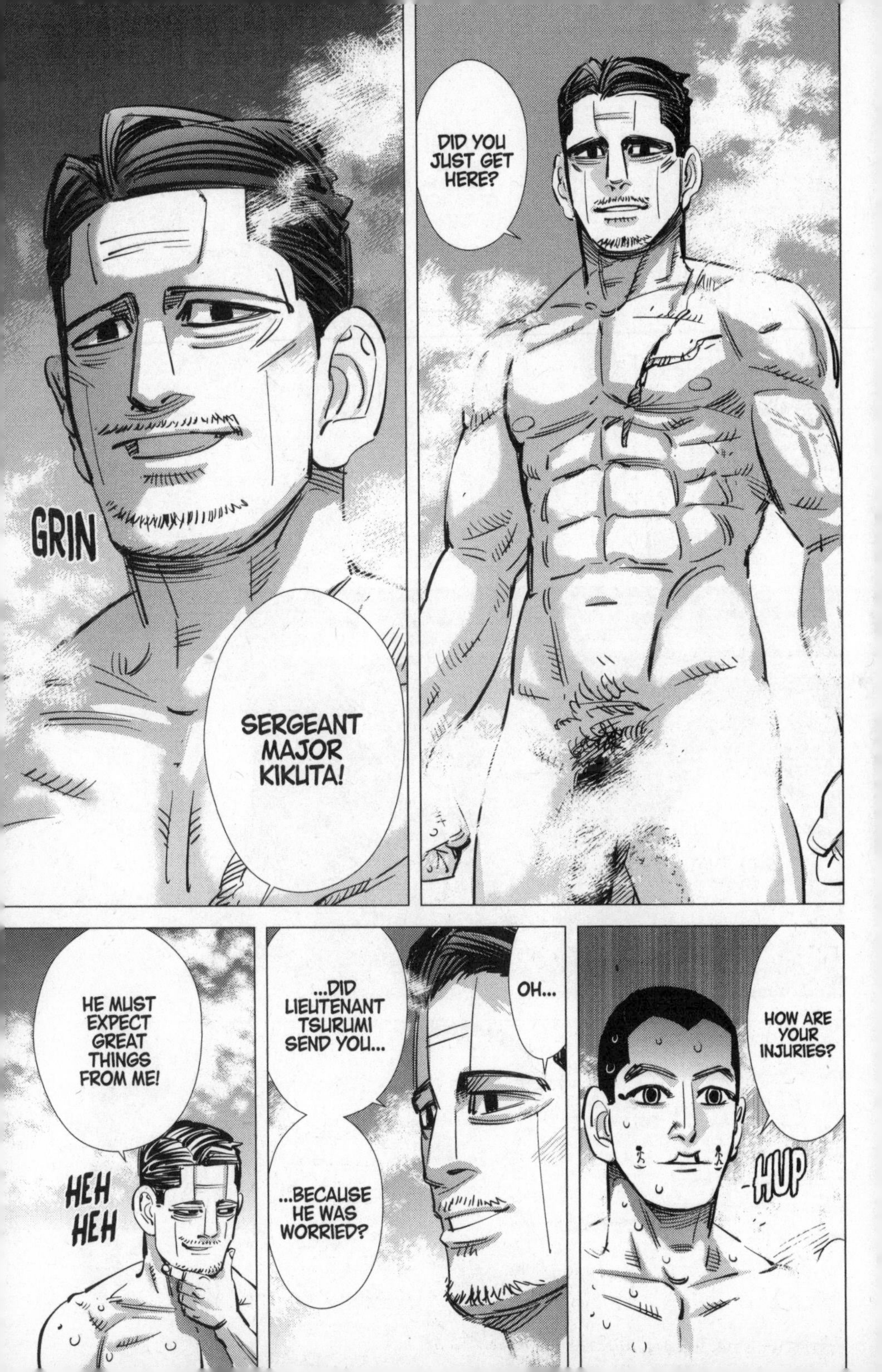
DID YOU JUST GET HERE?
GRIN
SERGEANT MAJOR KIKUTA!
HOW ARE YOUR INJURIES?
HUP
OH...
...DID LIEUTENANT TSURUMI SEND YOU...
...BECAUSE HE WAS WORRIED?
HE MUST EXPECT GREAT THINGS FROM ME!
HEH HEH

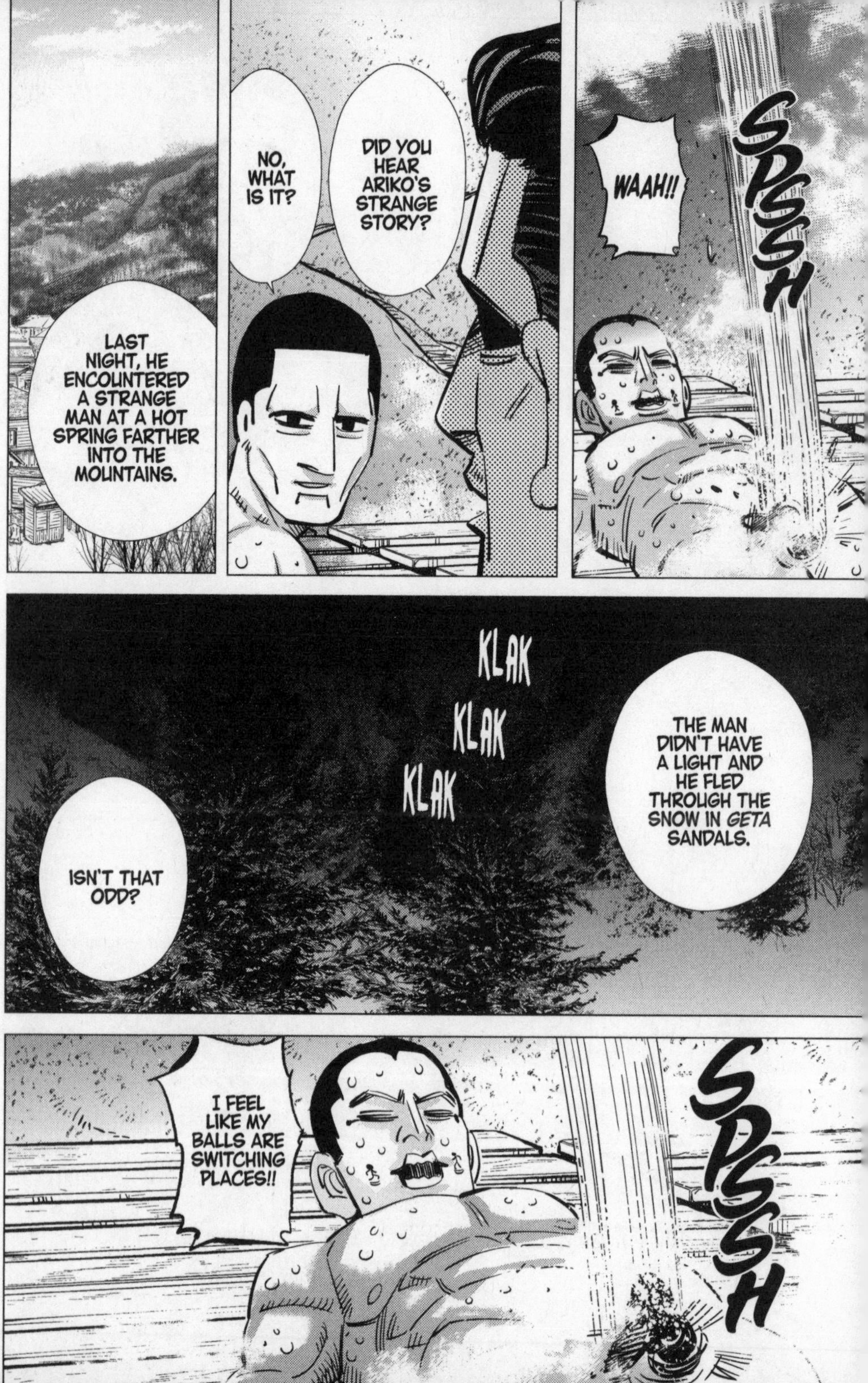
SPSSH
WAAH!!
DID YOU HEAR ARIKO'S STRANGE STORY?
NO, WHAT IS IT?
LAST NIGHT, HE ENCOUNTERED A STRANGE MAN AT A HOT SPRING FARTHER INTO THE MOUNTAINS.
THE MAN DIDN'T HAVE A LIGHT AND HE FLED THROUGH THE SNOW IN *GETA* SANDALS.
KLAK
KLAK
KLAK
ISN'T THAT ODD?
SPSSH
I FEEL LIKE MY BALLS ARE SWITCHING PLACES!!

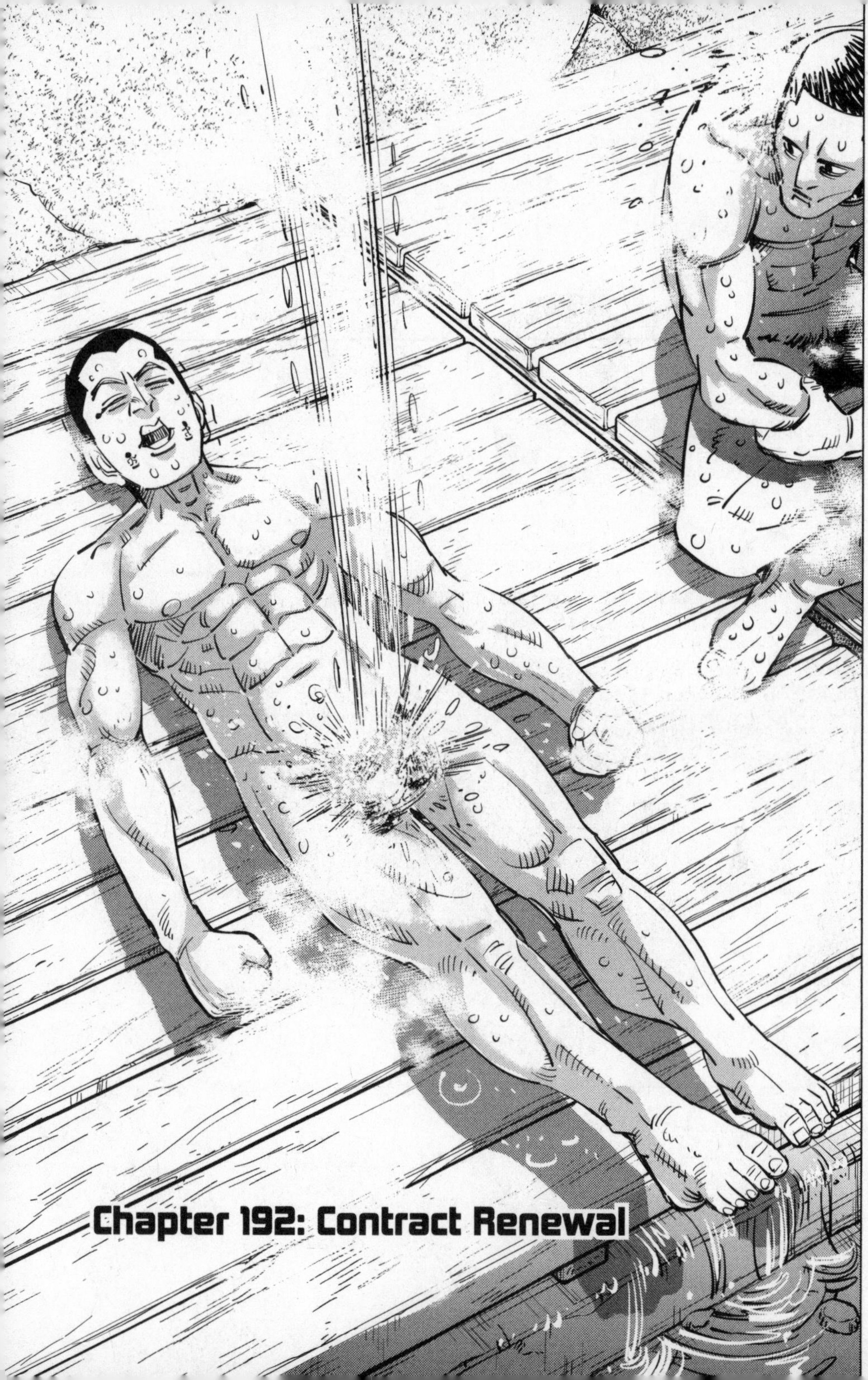
Chapter 192: Contract Renewal

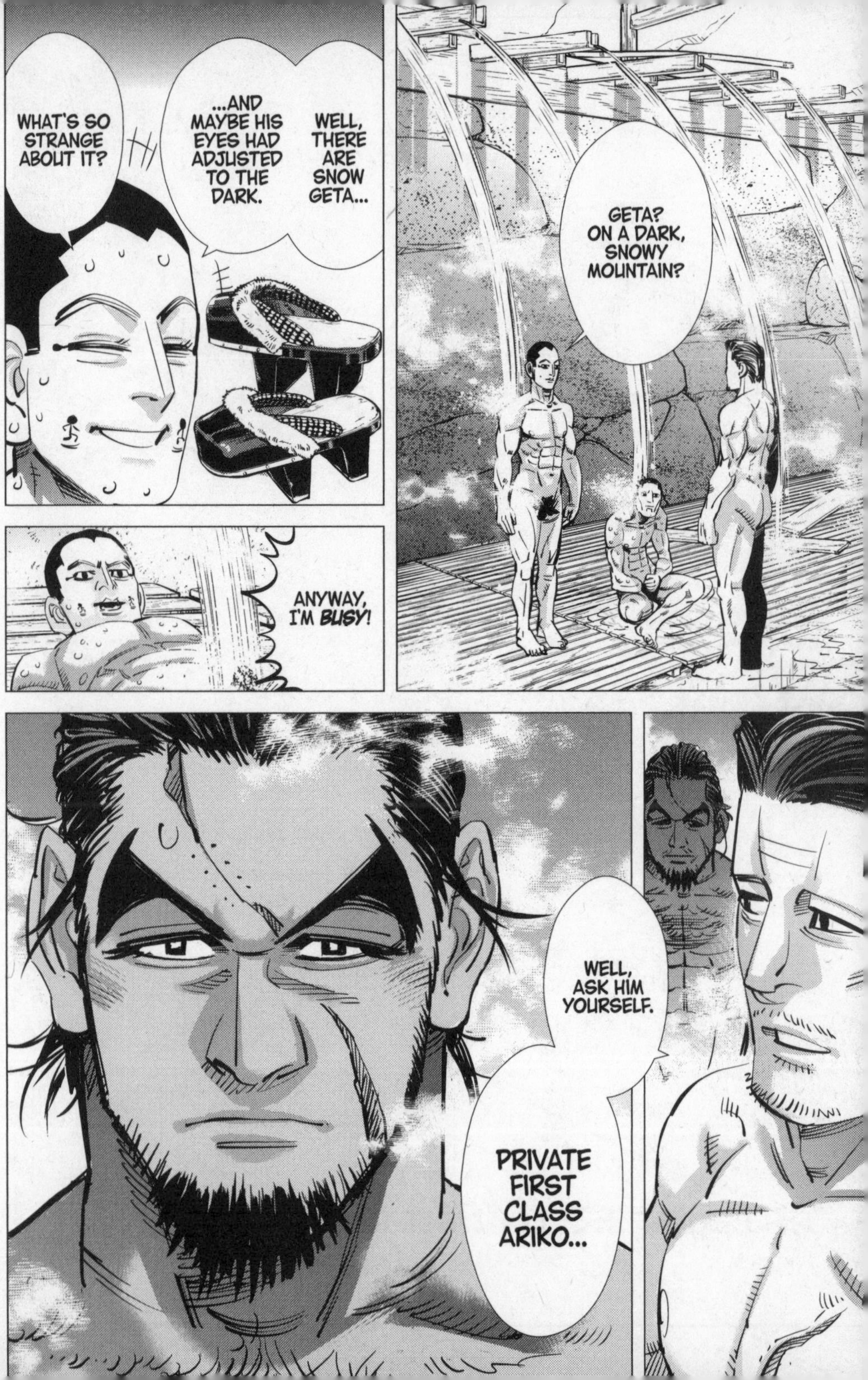
GETA? ON A DARK, SNOWY MOUNTAIN?
WELL, THERE ARE SNOW GETA...
...AND MAYBE HIS EYES HAD ADJUSTED TO THE DARK.
WHAT'S SO STRANGE ABOUT IT?
ANYWAY, I'M *BUSY*!
WELL, ASK HIM YOURSELF.
PRIVATE FIRST CLASS ARIKO...

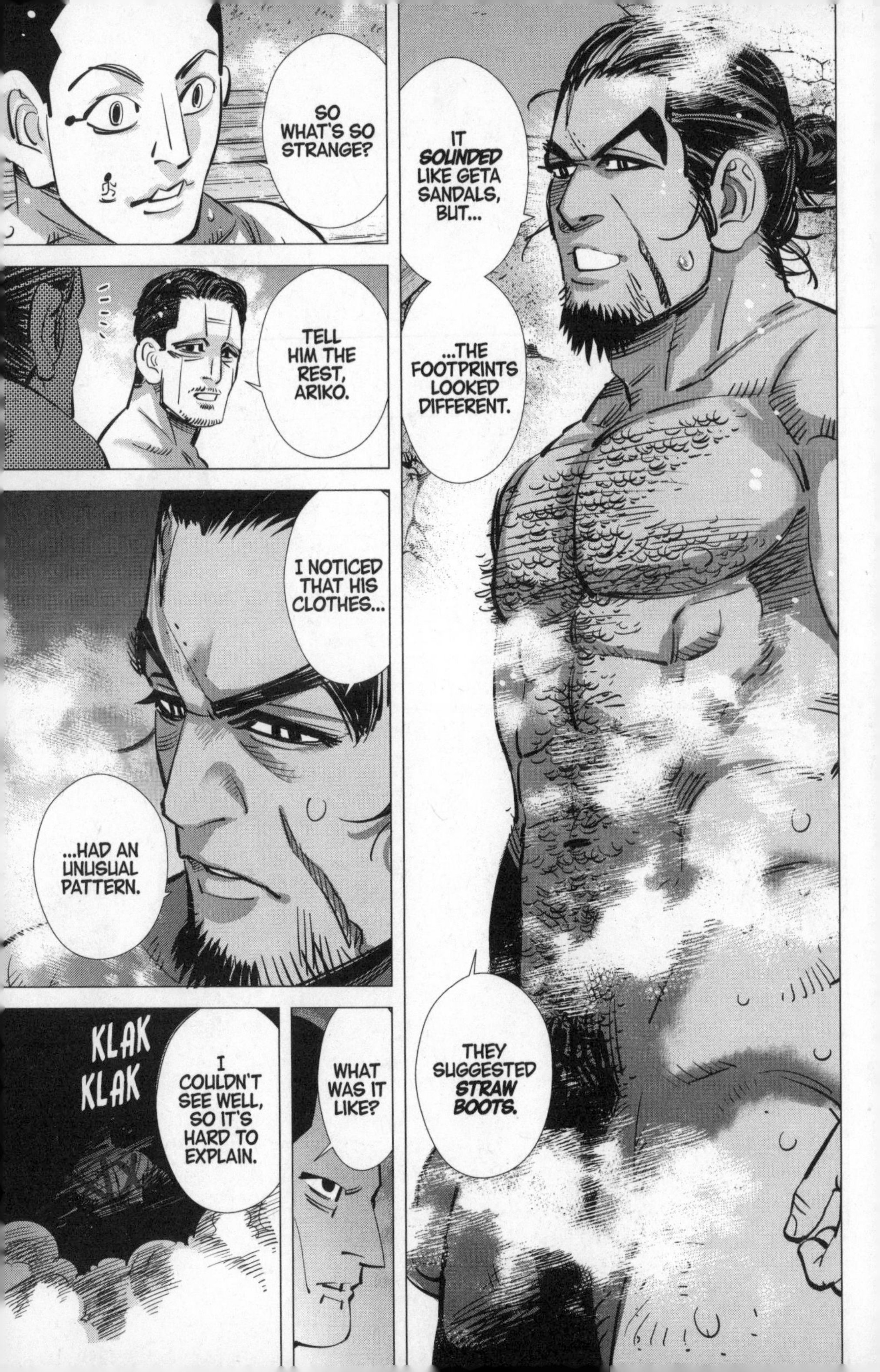
IT SOUNDED LIKE GETA SANDALS, BUT...
...THE FOOTPRINTS LOOKED DIFFERENT.
THEY SUGGESTED STRAW BOOTS.
SO WHAT'S SO STRANGE?
TELL HIM THE REST, ARIKO.
I NOTICED THAT HIS CLOTHES...
...HAD AN UNUSUAL PATTERN.
WHAT WAS IT LIKE?
KLAK KLAK
I COULDN'T SEE WELL, SO IT'S HARD TO EXPLAIN.

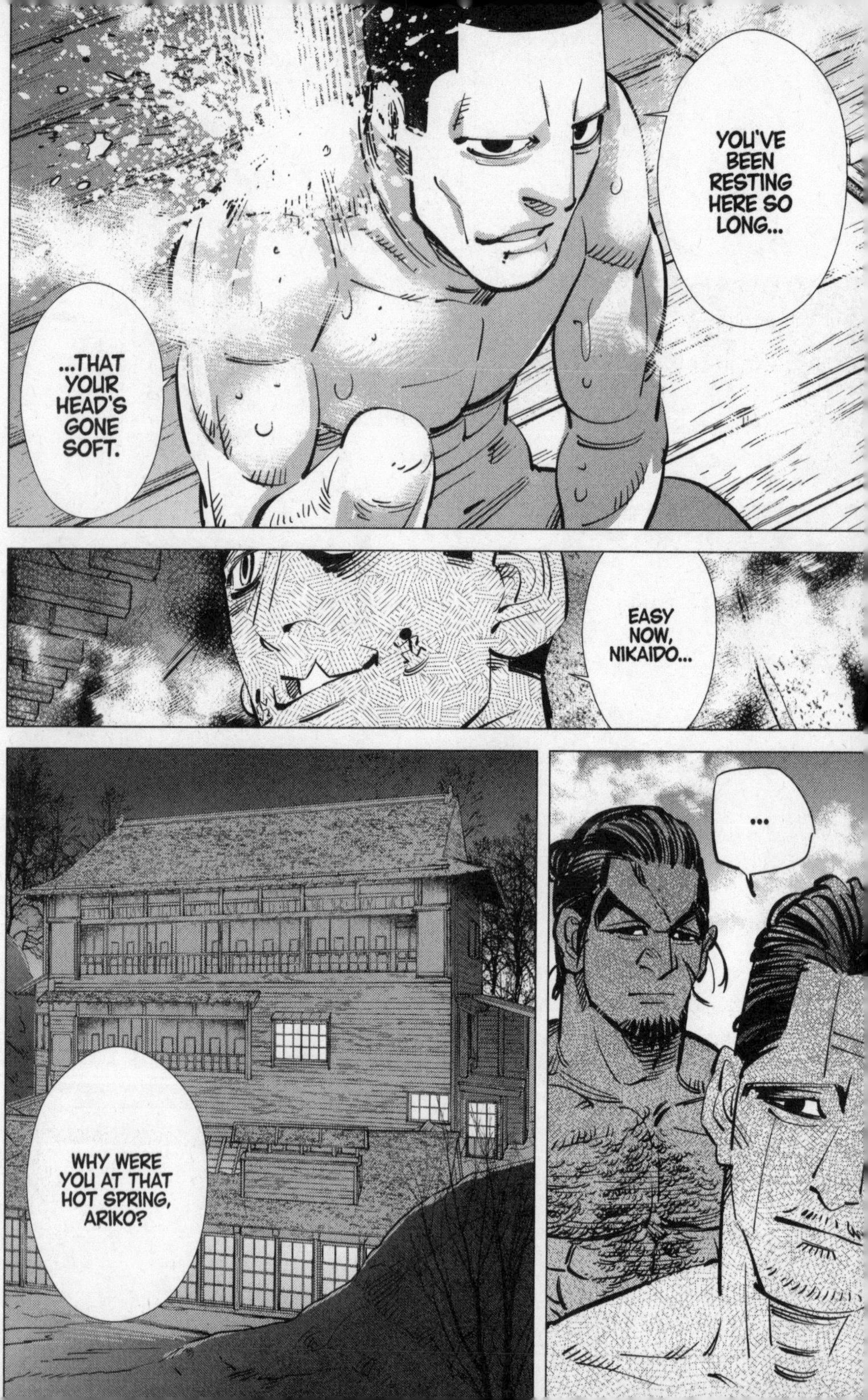
YOU'VE BEEN RESTING HERE SO LONG...
...THAT YOUR HEAD'S GONE SOFT.
EASY NOW, NIKAIDO...
...
WHY WERE YOU AT THAT HOT SPRING, ARIKO?

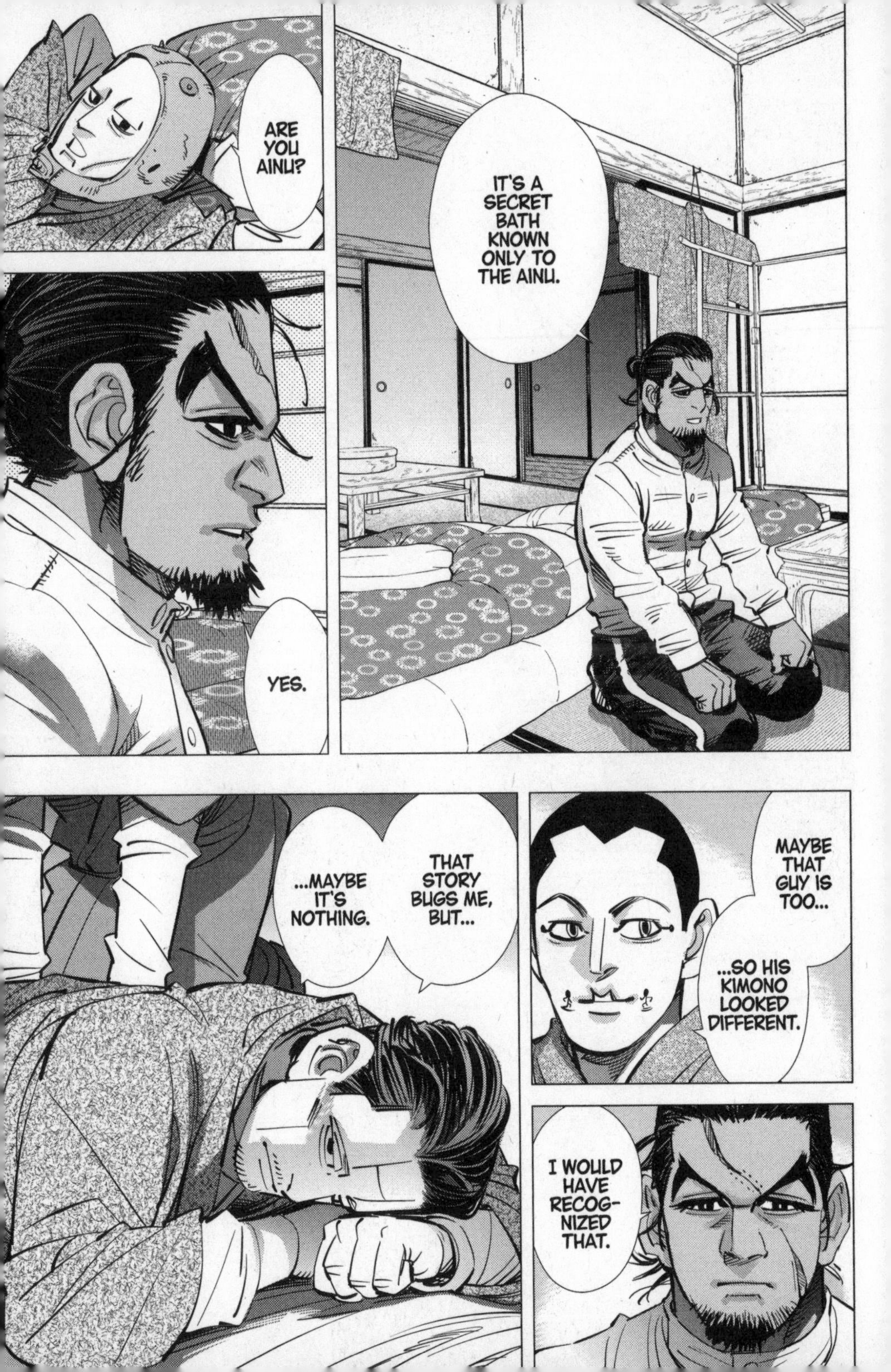

IT'S A SECRET BATH KNOWN ONLY TO THE AINU.
ARE YOU AINU?
YES.
MAYBE THAT GUY IS TOO...
...SO HIS KIMONO LOOKED DIFFERENT.
I WOULD HAVE RECOG-NIZED THAT.
THAT STORY BUGS ME, BUT...
...MAYBE IT'S NOTHING.

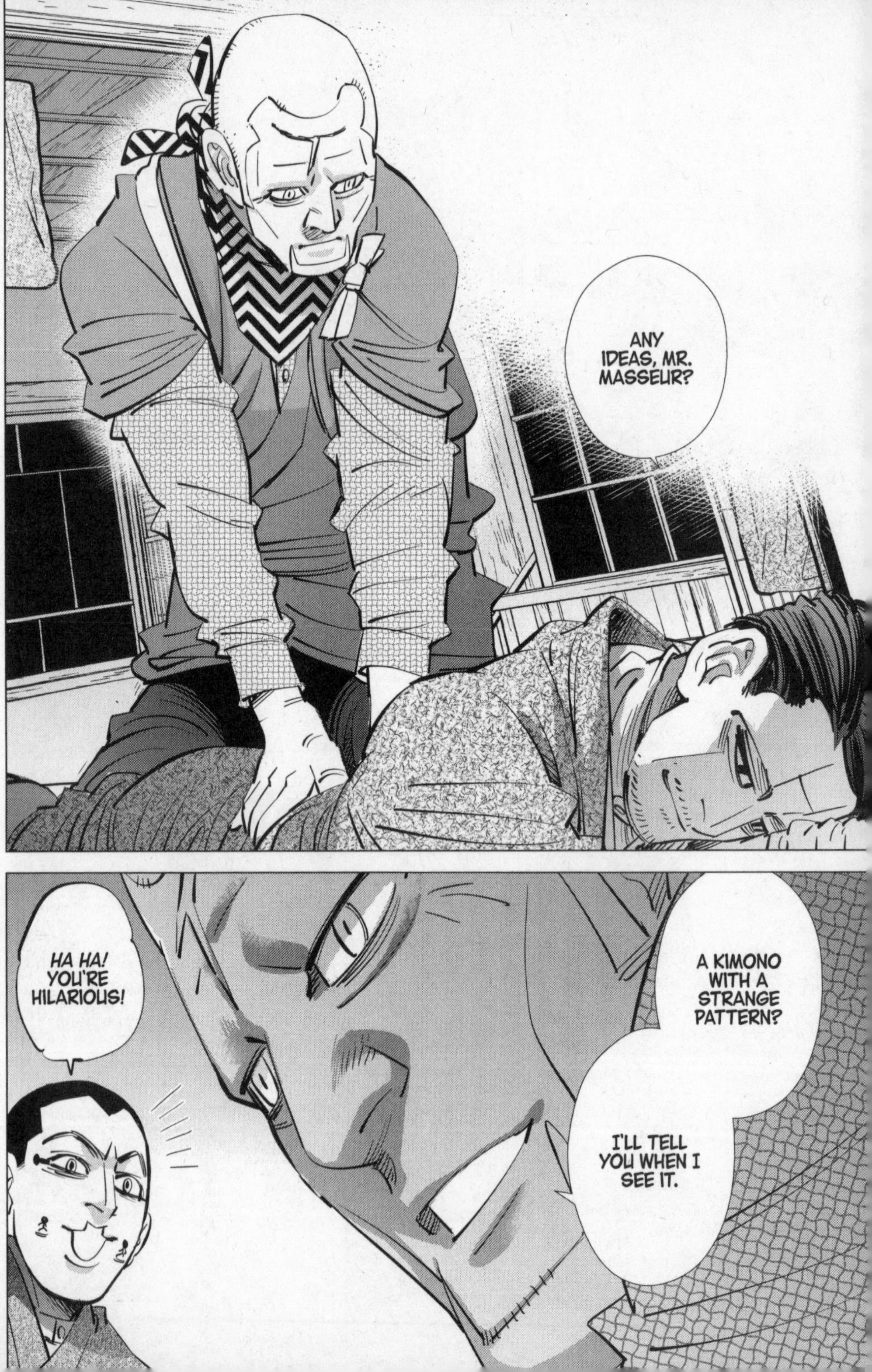
ANY IDEAS, MR. MASSEUR?
A KIMONO WITH A STRANGE PATTERN?
I'LL TELL YOU WHEN I SEE IT.
HA HA! YOU'RE HILARIOUS!

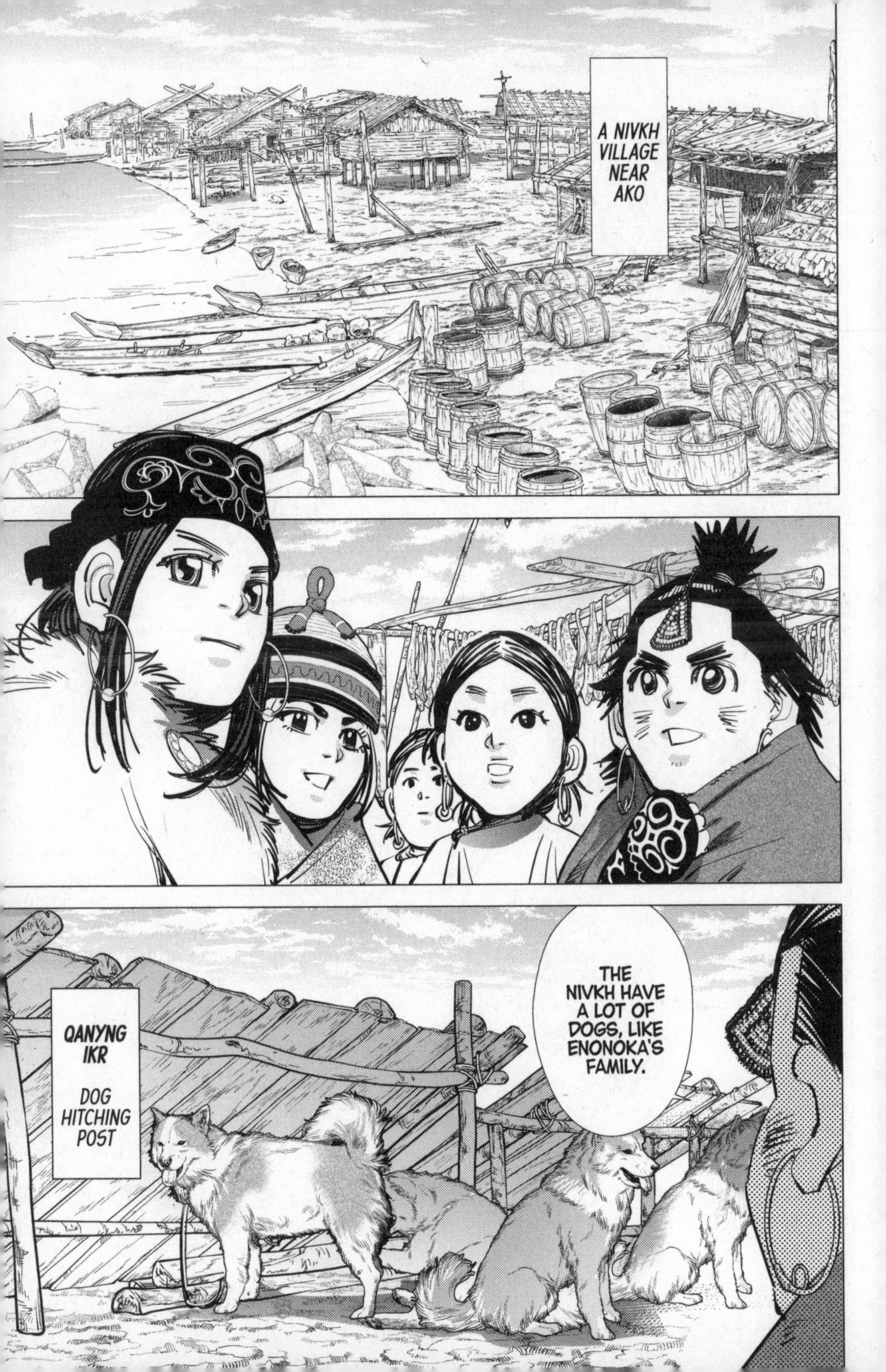
A NIVKH VILLAGE NEAR AKO
THE NIVKH HAVE A LOT OF DOGS, LIKE ENONOKA'S FAMILY.
QANYNG IKR
DOG HITCHING POST

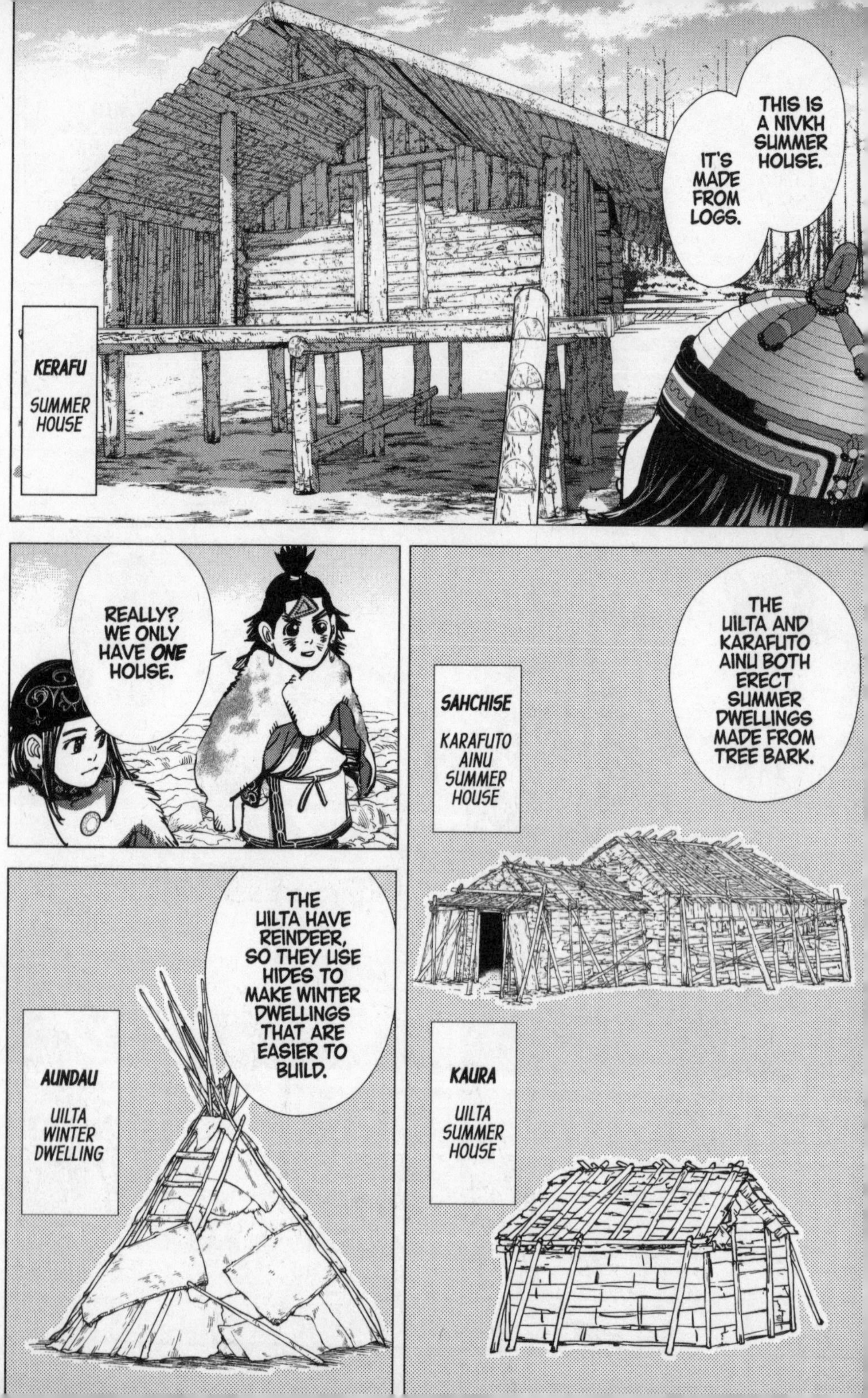
THIS IS A NIVKH SUMMER HOUSE.
IT'S MADE FROM LOGS.
KERAFU
SUMMER HOUSE
THE UILTA AND KARAFUTO AINU BOTH ERECT SUMMER DWELLINGS MADE FROM TREE BARK.
SAHCHISE
KARAFUTO AINU SUMMER HOUSE
KAURA
UILTA SUMMER HOUSE
REALLY? WE ONLY HAVE **ONE** HOUSE.
THE UILTA HAVE REINDEER, SO THEY USE HIDES TO MAKE WINTER DWELLINGS THAT ARE EASIER TO BUILD.
AUNDAU
UILTA WINTER DWELLING

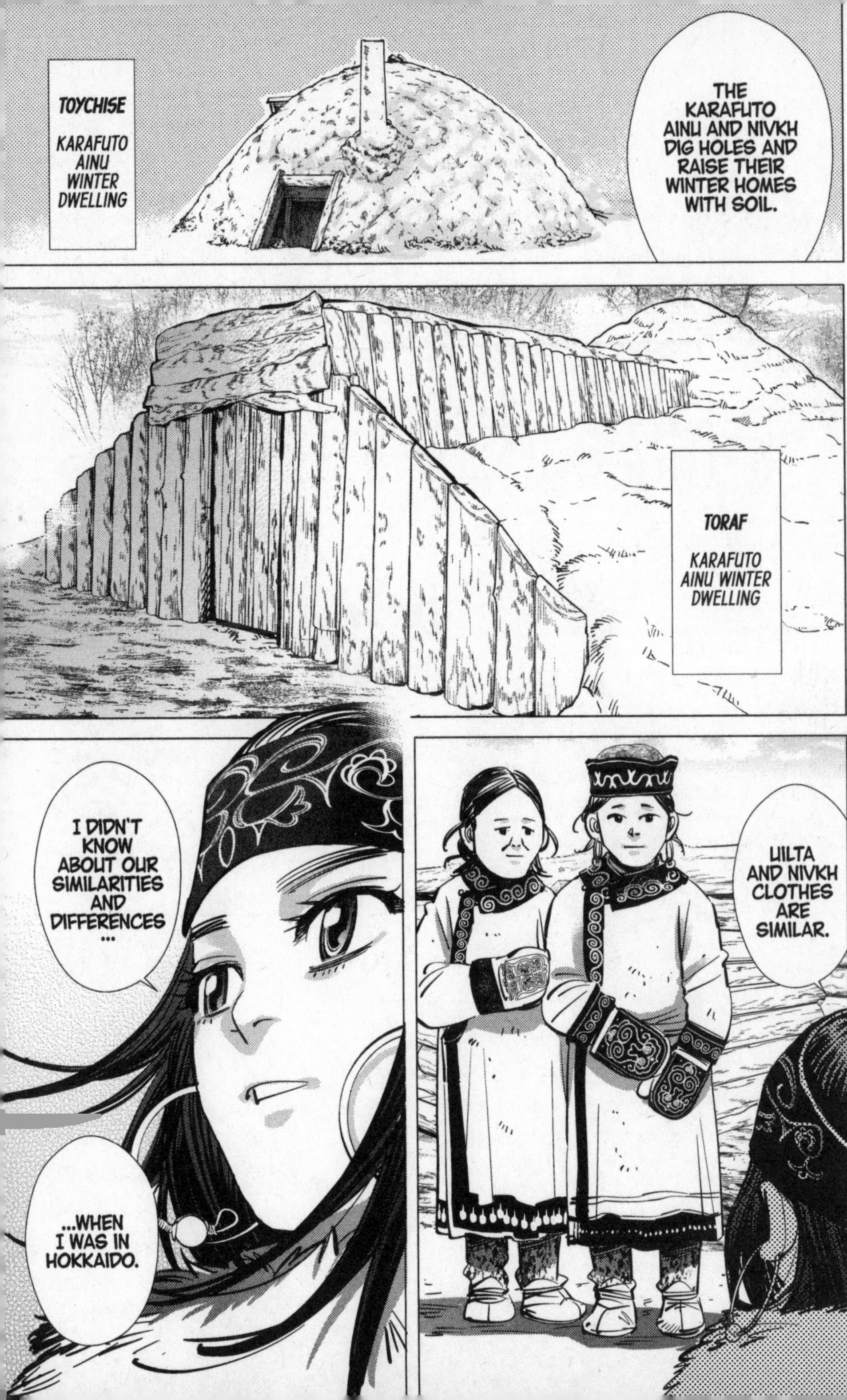
THE KARAFUTO AINU AND NIVKH DIG HOLES AND RAISE THEIR WINTER HOMES WITH SOIL.
TOYCHISE
KARAFUTO AINU WINTER DWELLING
TORAF
KARAFUTO AINU WINTER DWELLING
UILTA AND NIVKH CLOTHES ARE SIMILAR.
I DIDN'T KNOW ABOUT OUR SIMILARITIES AND DIFFERENCES ...
...WHEN I WAS IN HOKKAIDO.

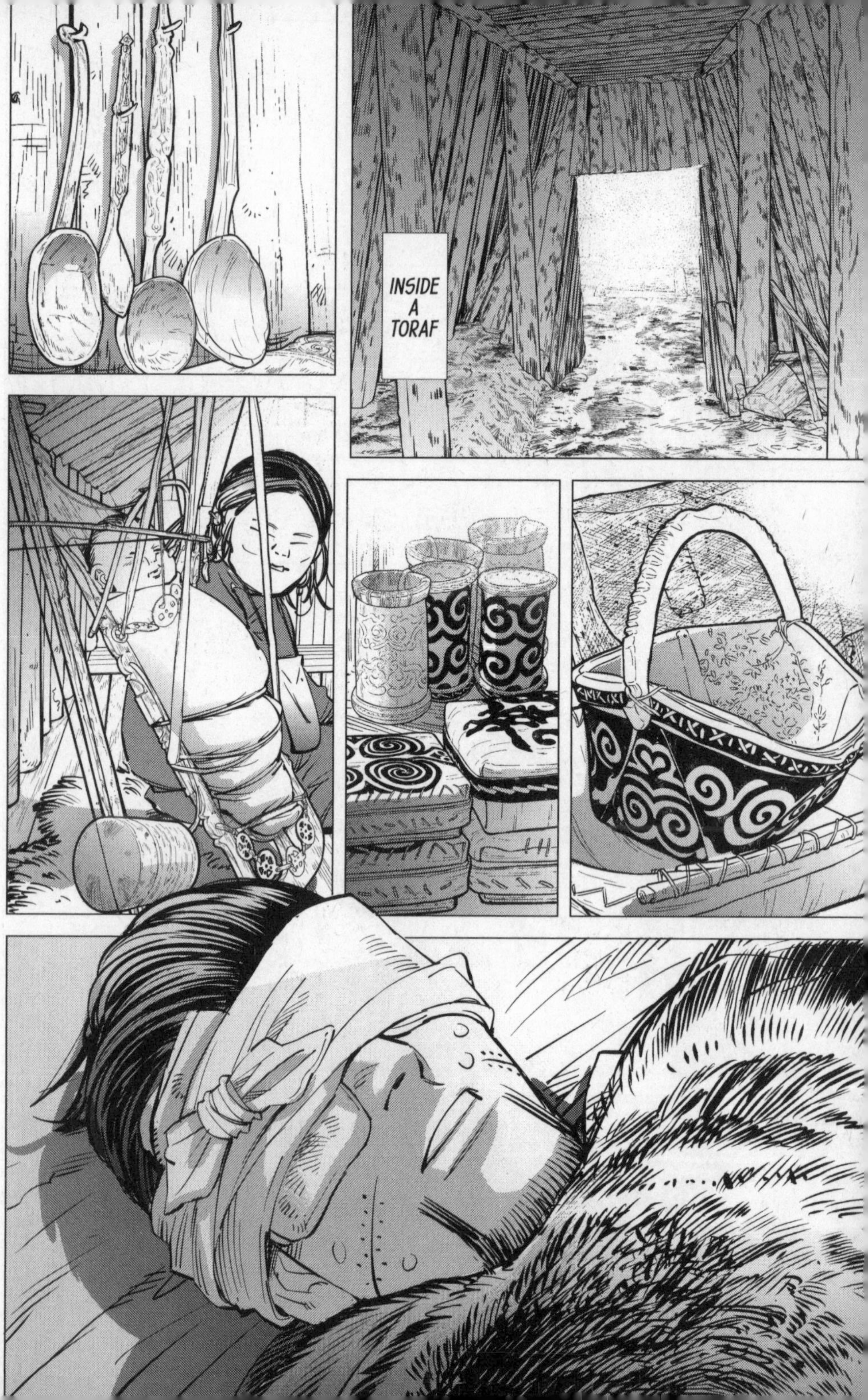
INSIDE A TORAF

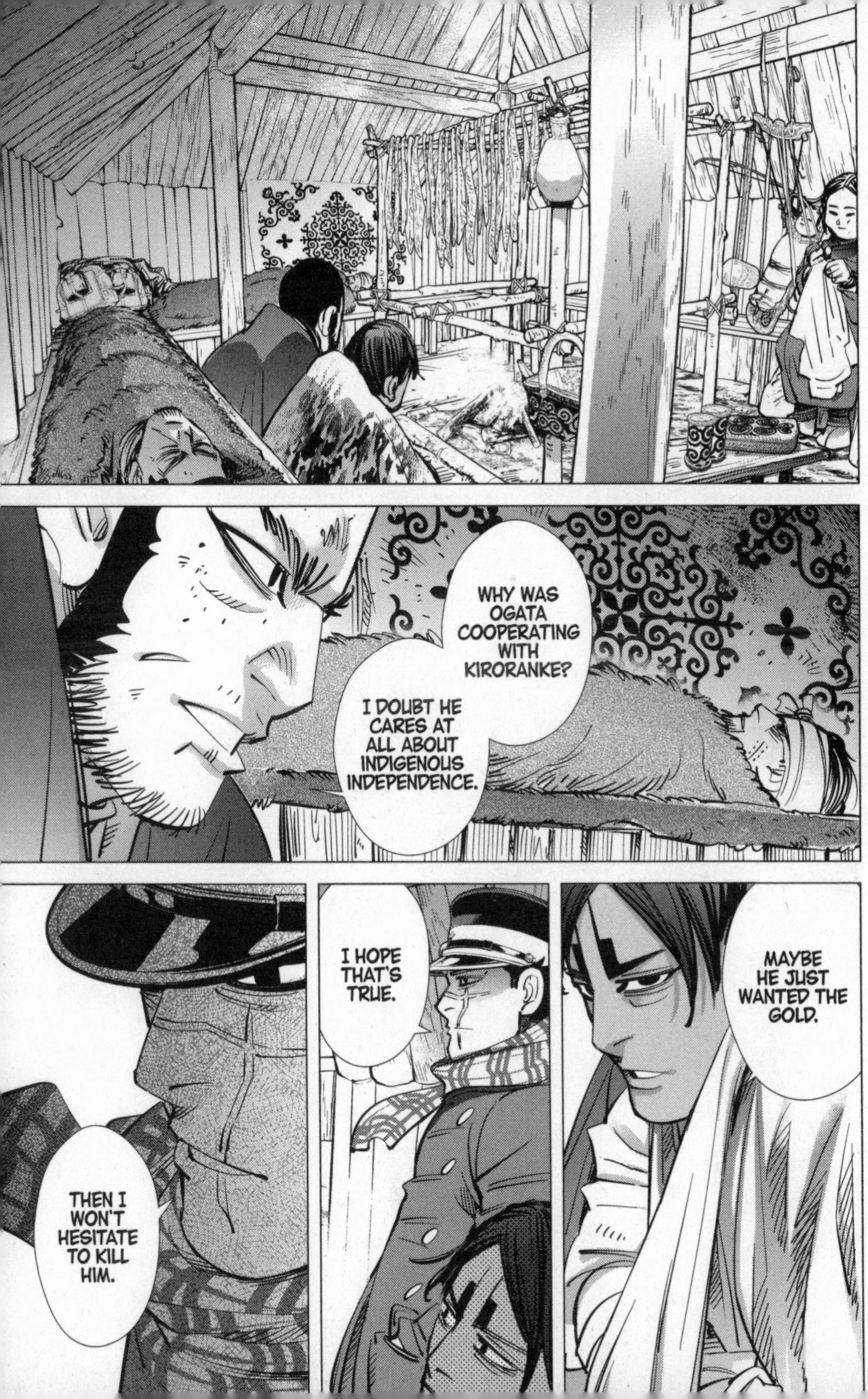
WHY WAS OGATA COOPERATING WITH KIRORANKE?
I DOUBT HE CARES AT ALL ABOUT INDIGENOUS INDEPENDENCE.
MAYBE HE JUST WANTED THE GOLD.
I HOPE THAT'S TRUE.
THEN I WON'T HESITATE TO KILL HIM.

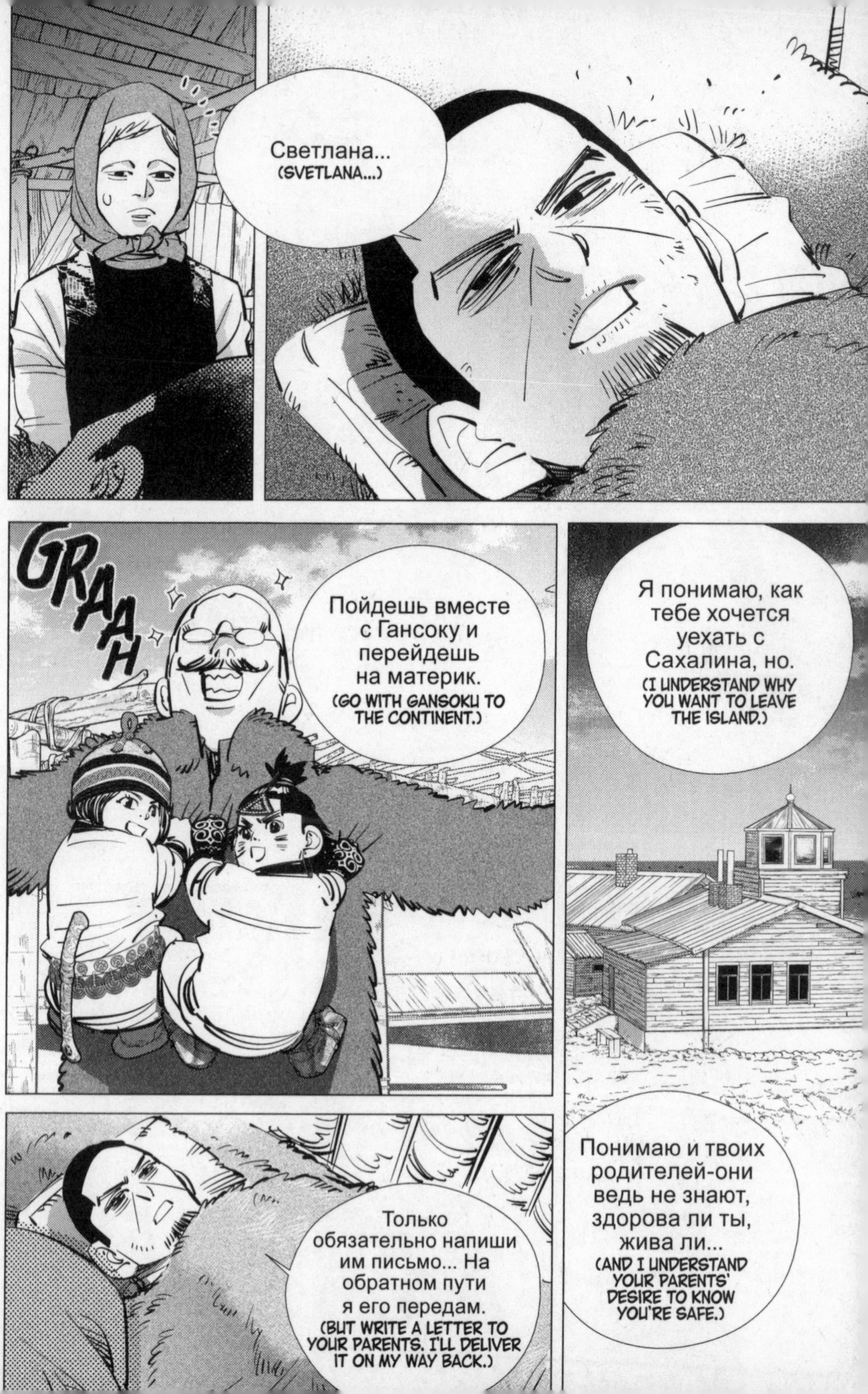
Светлана...
(SVETLANA...)
Я понимаю, как тебе хочется уехать с Сахалина, но.
(I UNDERSTAND WHY YOU WANT TO LEAVE THE ISLAND.)
Понимаю и твоих родителей-они ведь не знают, здорова ли ты, жива ли...
(AND I UNDERSTAND YOUR PARENTS' DESIRE TO KNOW YOU'RE SAFE.)
Пойдешь вместе с Гансоку и перейдешь на материк.
(GO WITH GANSOKU TO THE CONTINENT.)
GRAAH
Только обязательно напиши им письмо... На обратном пути я его передам.
(BUT WRITE A LETTER TO YOUR PARENTS. I'LL DELIVER IT ON MY WAY BACK.)

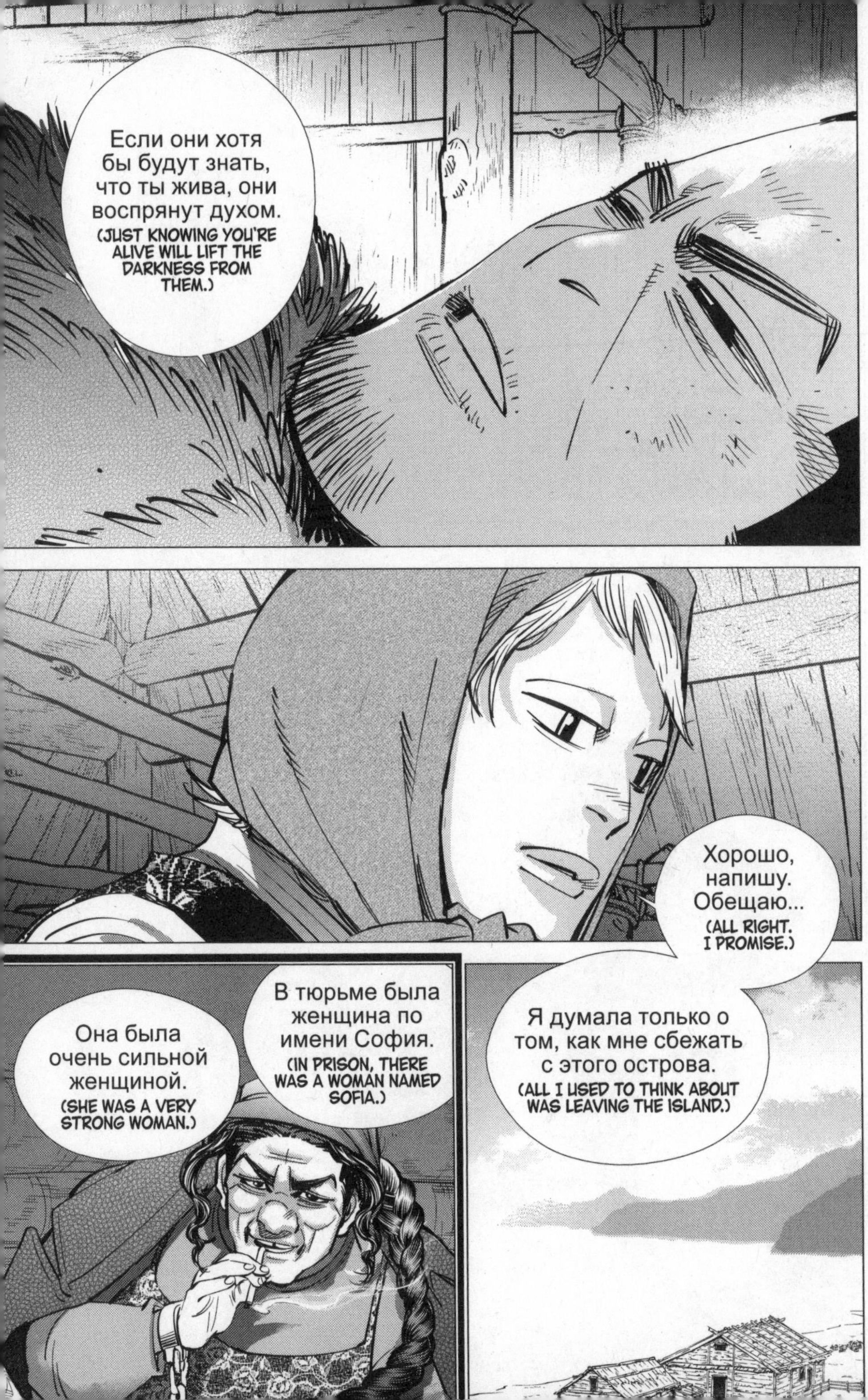
Если они хотя бы будут знать, что ты жива, они воспрянут духом.
(JUST KNOWING YOU'RE ALIVE WILL LIFT THE DARKNESS FROM THEM.)
Хорошо, напишу. Обещаю...
(ALL RIGHT. I PROMISE.)
Я думала только о том, как мне сбежать с этого острова.
(ALL I USED TO THINK ABOUT WAS LEAVING THE ISLAND.)
В тюрьме была женщина по имени София.
(IN PRISON, THERE WAS A WOMAN NAMED SOFIA.)
Она была очень сильной женщиной.
(SHE WAS A VERY STRONG WOMAN.)

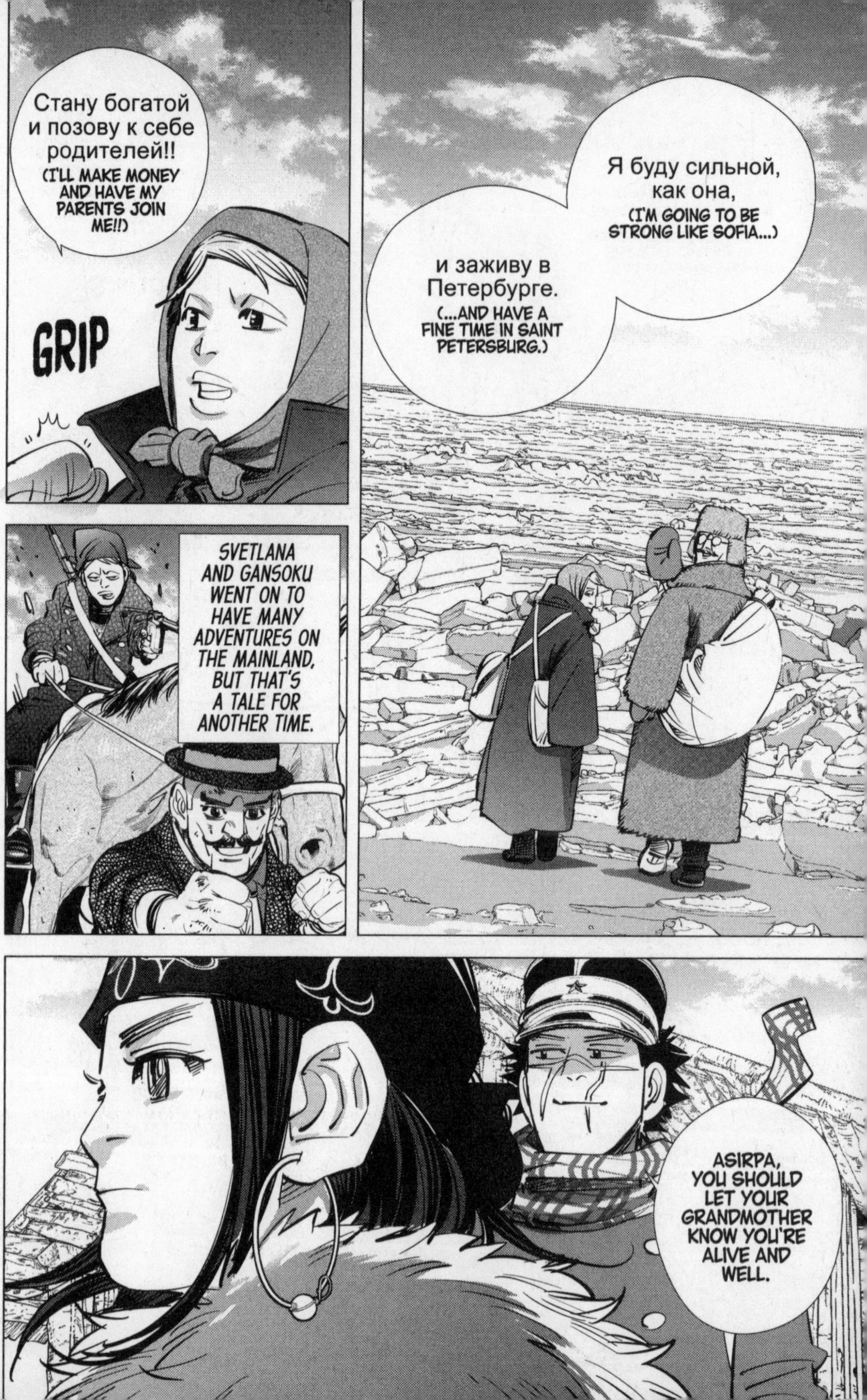

Я буду сильной, как она,
(I'M GOING TO BE STRONG LIKE SOFIA...)
и заживу в Петербурге.
(...AND HAVE A FINE TIME IN SAINT PETERSBURG.)
Стану богатой и позову к себе родителей!!
(I'LL MAKE MONEY AND HAVE MY PARENTS JOIN ME!!)
GRIP
SVETLANA AND GANSOKU WENT ON TO HAVE MANY ADVENTURES ON THE MAINLAND, BUT THAT'S A TALE FOR ANOTHER TIME.
ASIRPA, YOU SHOULD LET YOUR GRANDMOTHER KNOW YOU'RE ALIVE AND WELL.

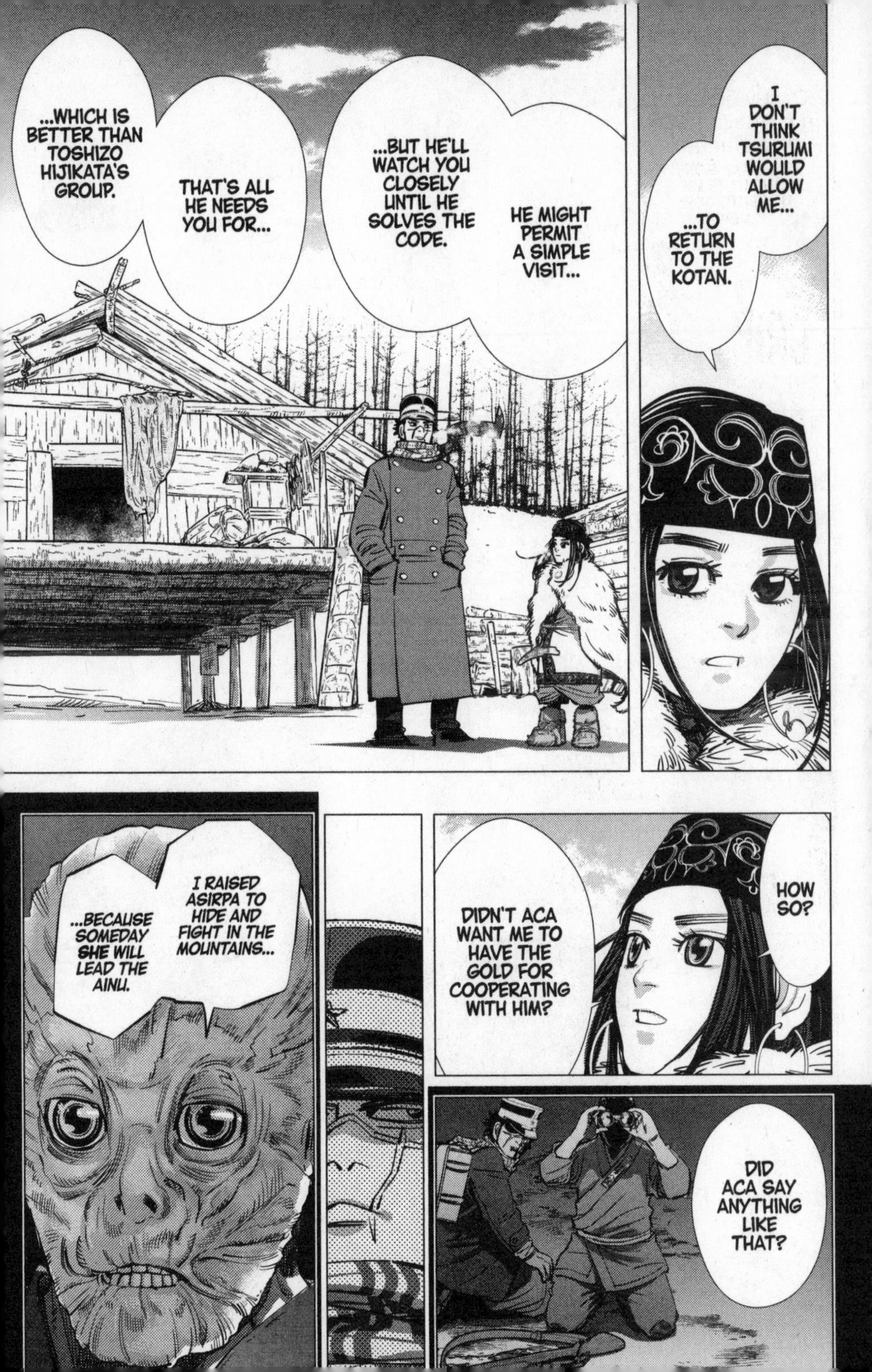
I DON'T THINK TSURUMI WOULD ALLOW ME...
...TO RETURN TO THE KOTAN.
HE MIGHT PERMIT A SIMPLE VISIT...
...BUT HE'LL WATCH YOU CLOSELY UNTIL HE SOLVES THE CODE.
THAT'S ALL HE NEEDS YOU FOR...
...WHICH IS BETTER THAN TOSHIZO HIJIKATA'S GROUP.
HOW SO?
DIDN'T ACA WANT ME TO HAVE THE GOLD FOR COOPERATING WITH HIM?
DID ACA SAY ANYTHING LIKE THAT?
I RAISED ASIRPA TO HIDE AND FIGHT IN THE MOUNTAINS...
...BECAUSE SOMEDAY SHE WILL LEAD THE AINU.

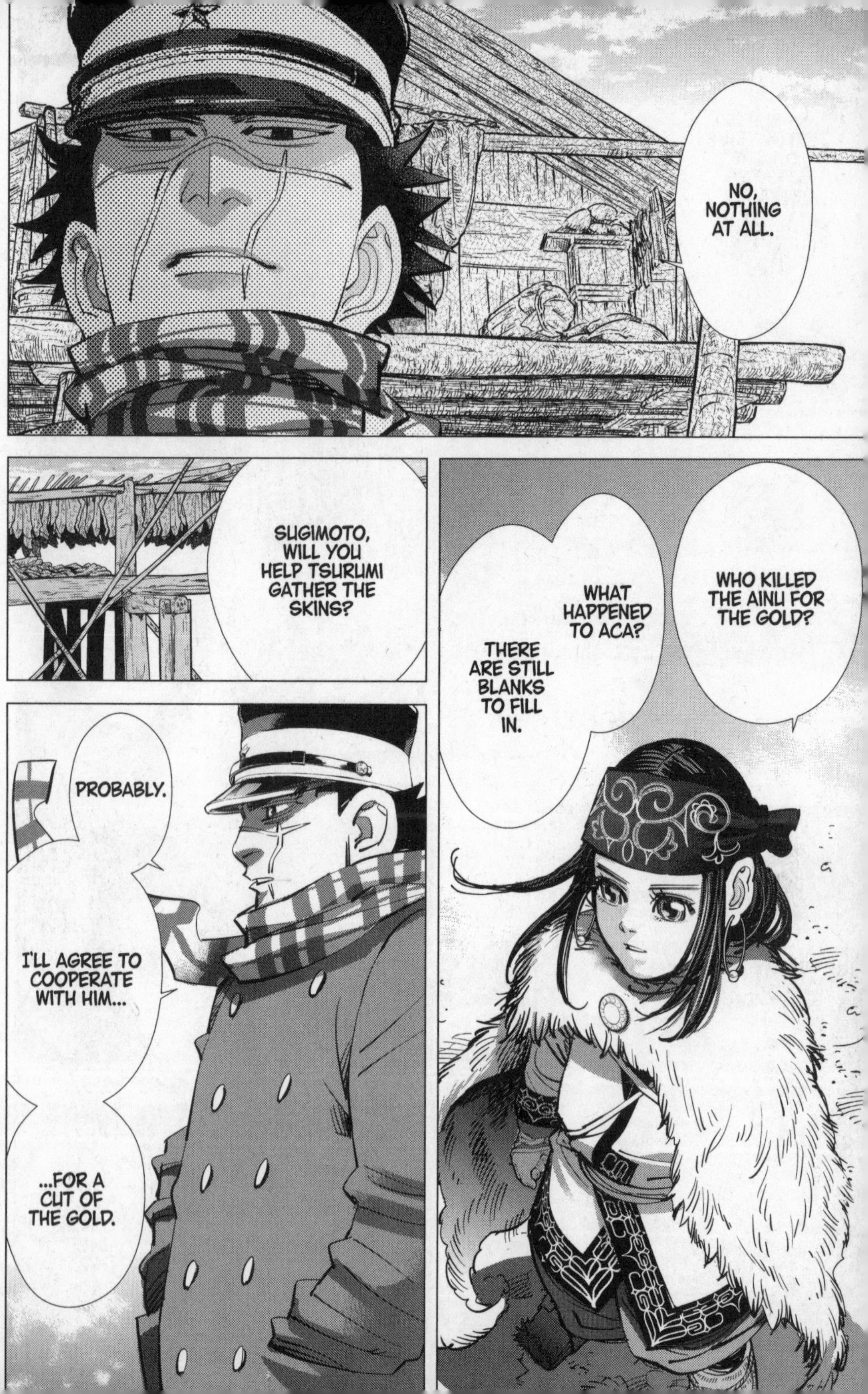
NO, NOTHING AT ALL.
WHO KILLED THE AINU FOR THE GOLD?
WHAT HAPPENED TO ACA?
THERE ARE STILL BLANKS TO FILL IN.
SUGIMOTO, WILL YOU HELP TSURUMI GATHER THE SKINS?
PROBABLY.
I'LL AGREE TO COOPERATE WITH HIM...
...FOR A CUT OF THE GOLD.

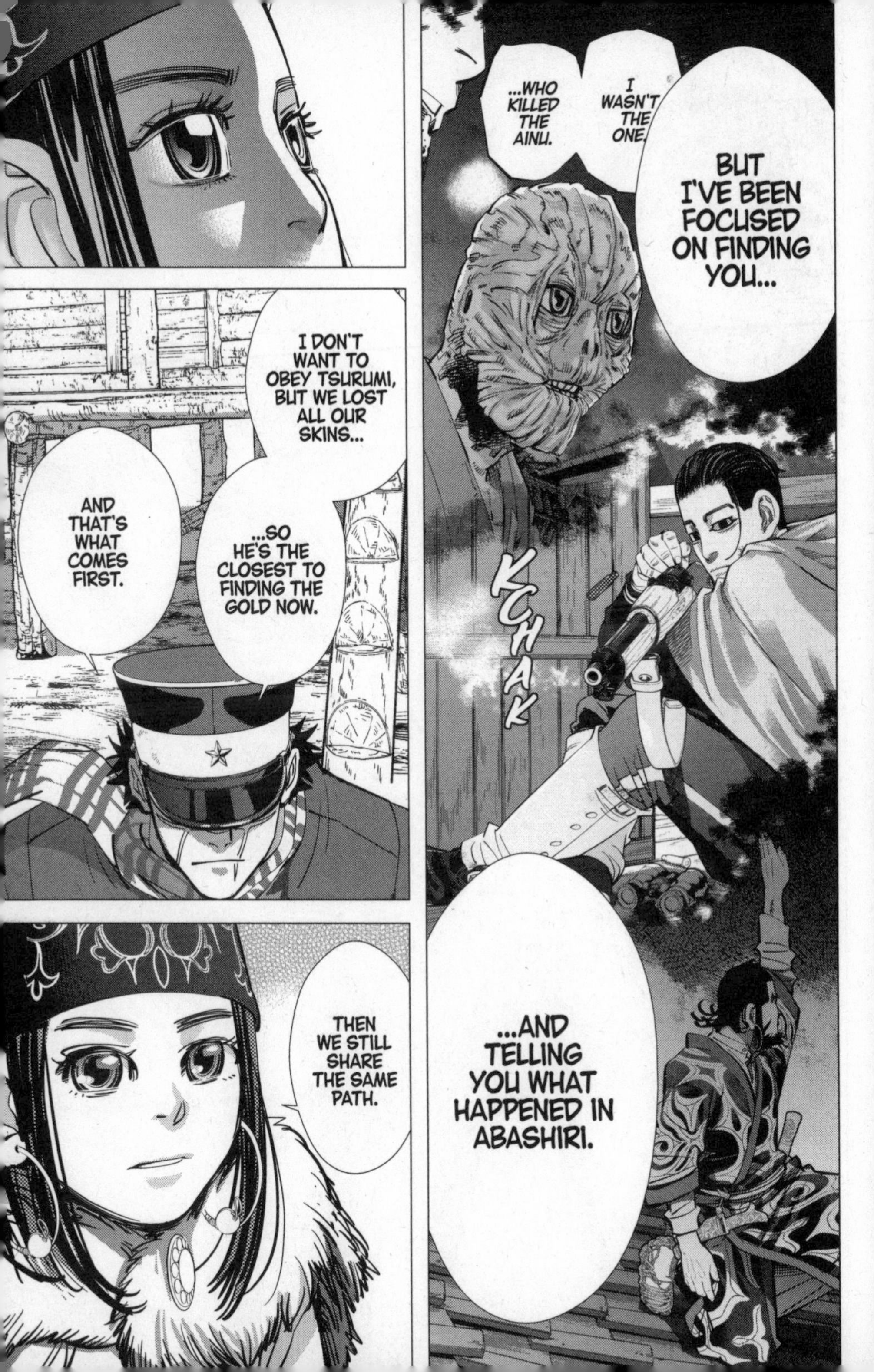
I WASN'T THE ONE...
...WHO KILLED THE AINU.
BUT I'VE BEEN FOCUSED ON FINDING YOU...
KCHAK
...AND TELLING YOU WHAT HAPPENED IN ABASHIRI.
I DON'T WANT TO OBEY TSURUMI, BUT WE LOST ALL OUR SKINS...
...SO HE'S THE CLOSEST TO FINDING THE GOLD NOW.
AND THAT'S WHAT COMES FIRST.
THEN WE STILL SHARE THE SAME PATH.

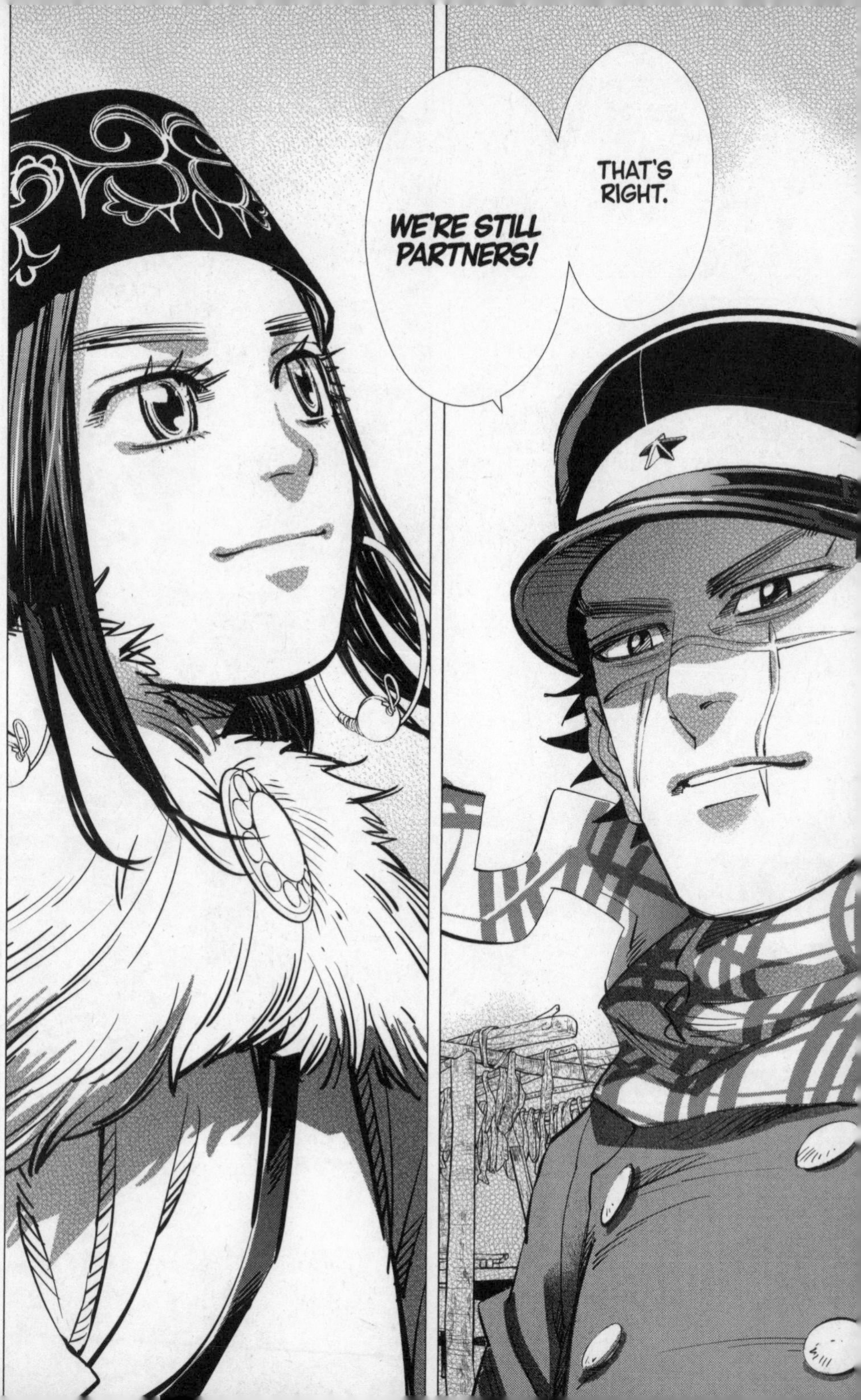
THAT'S RIGHT.
WE'RE STILL PARTNERS!

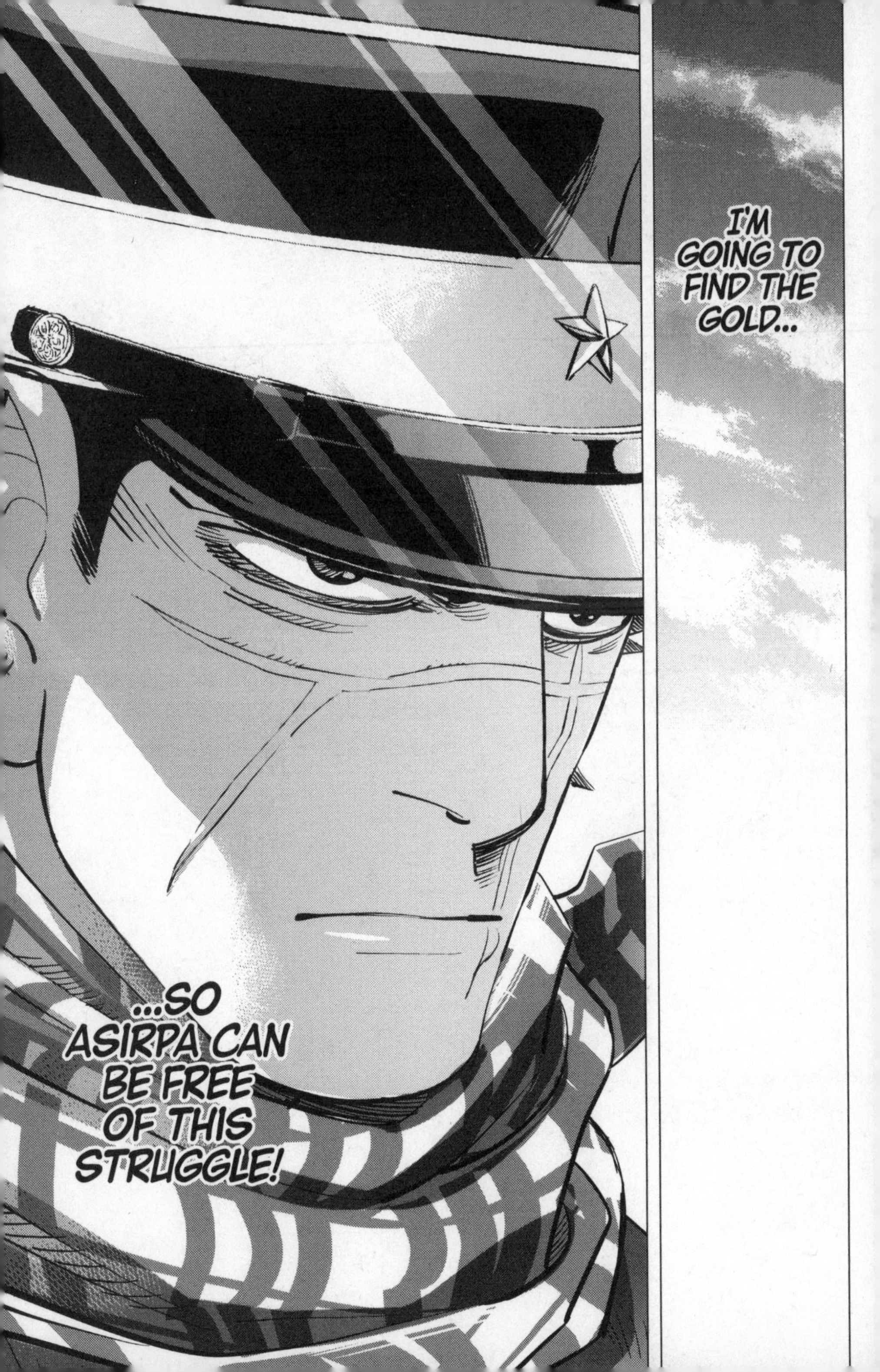
I'M GOING TO FIND THE GOLD...
...SO ASIRPA CAN BE FREE OF THIS STRUGGLE!

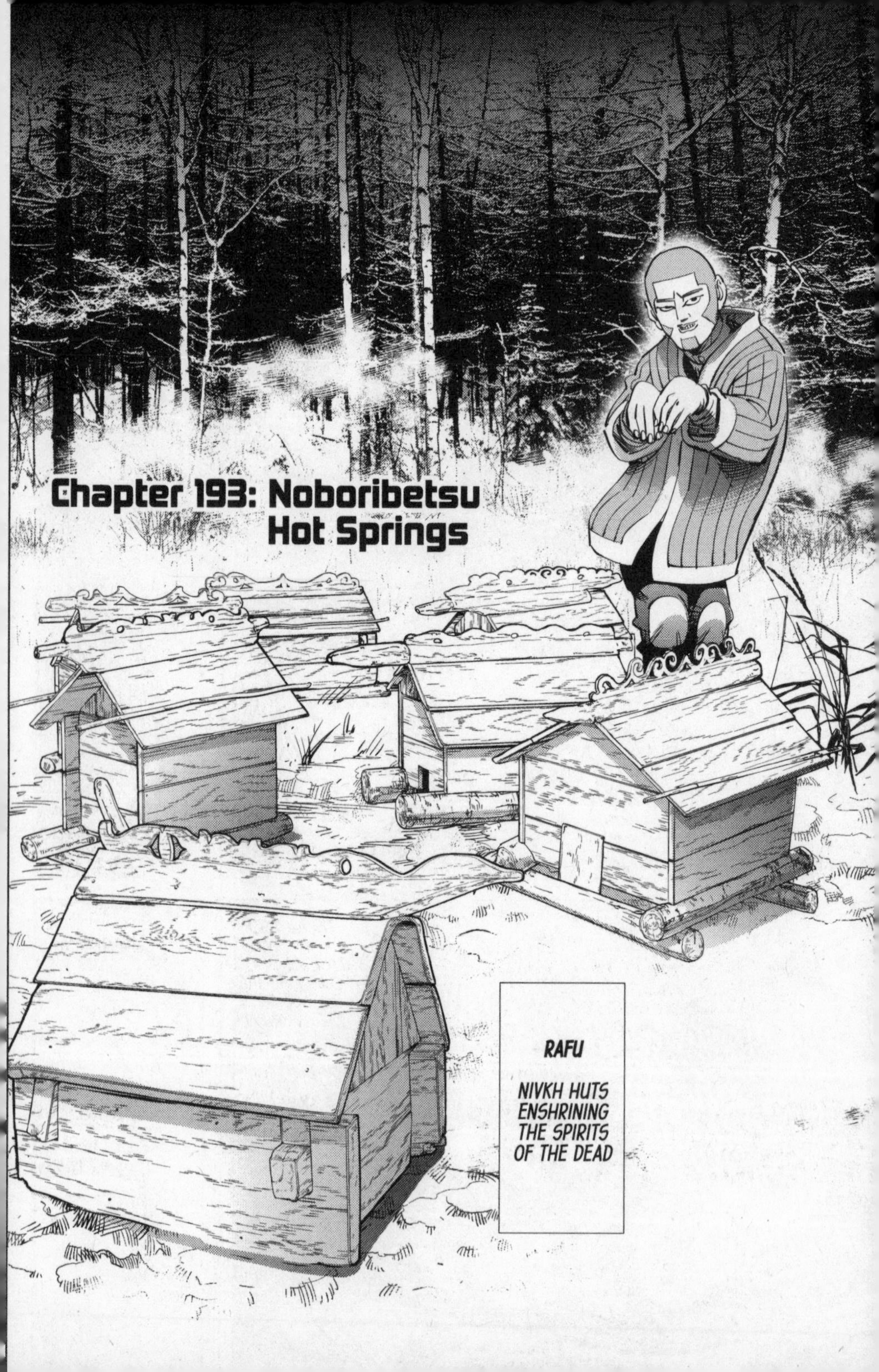
Chapter 193: Noboribetsu Hot Springs
RAFU
NIVKH HUTS ENSHRINING THE SPIRITS OF THE DEAD

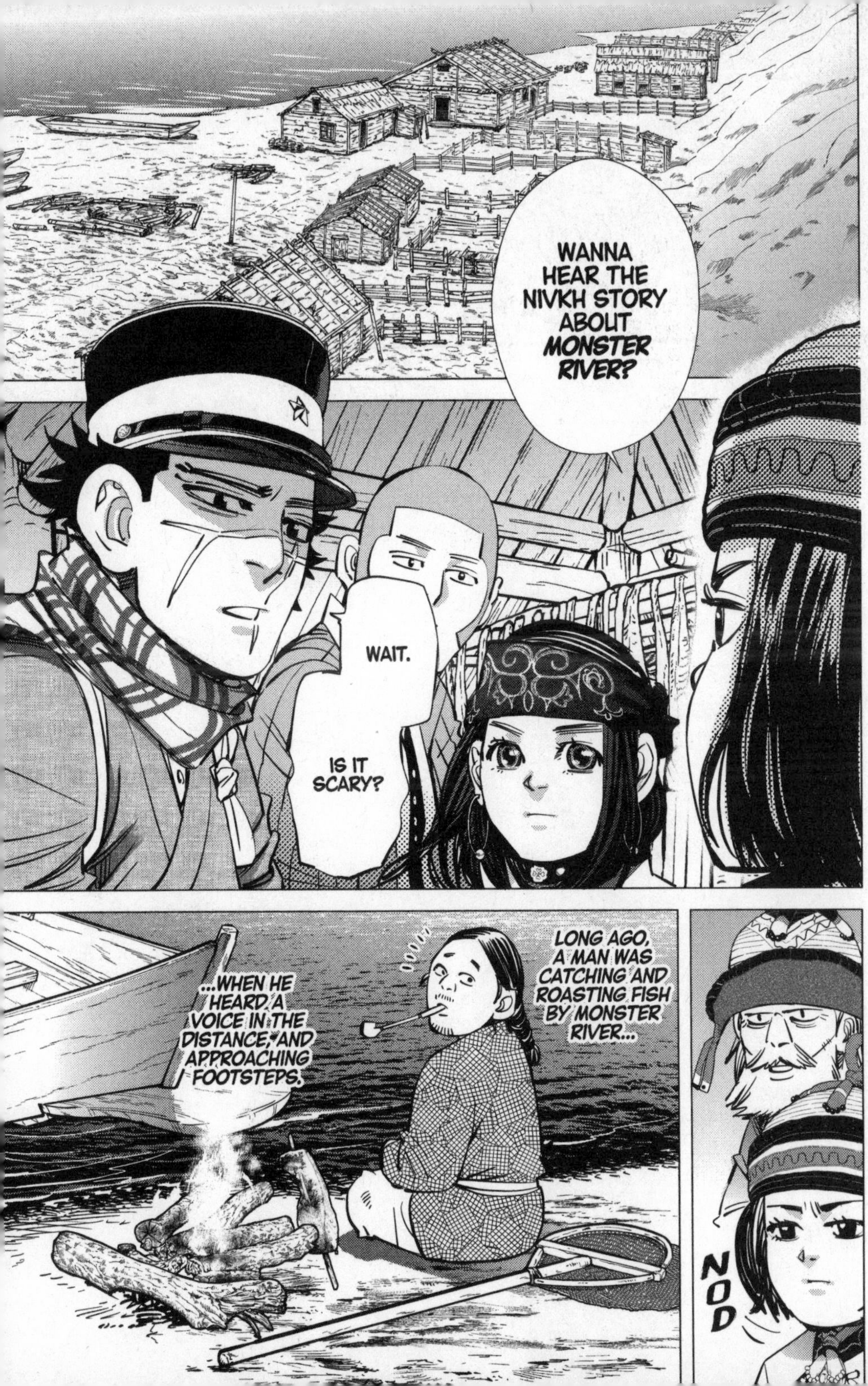
WANNA HEAR THE NIVKH STORY ABOUT *MONSTER RIVER?*
WAIT.
IS IT SCARY?
NOD
LONG AGO, A MAN WAS CATCHING AND ROASTING FISH BY MONSTER RIVER...
...WHEN HE HEARD A VOICE IN THE DISTANCE, AND APPROACHING FOOTSTEPS.

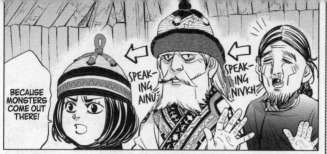

SO HE STRIPPED NAKED.
WHY?!
SPEAKING NIVKH
SPEAKING AINU
BECAUSE MONSTERS COME OUT THERE!
HE USED CHARCOAL FROM HIS FIRE TO DRAW LARGE EYES ON HIS BUTTOCKS...
...THEN BENT OVER AND LOOKED THROUGH HIS LEGS IN THE DIRECTION OF THE SOUND.
WHAT IF IT WAS A NEIGHBOR?!
WHEN THE MONSTER SAW THOSE EYES, IT GOT SCARED AND RAN AWAY.

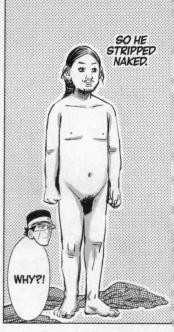

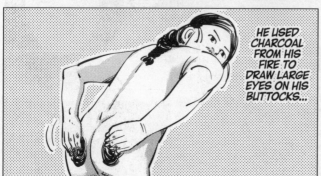

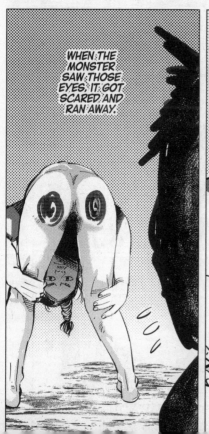

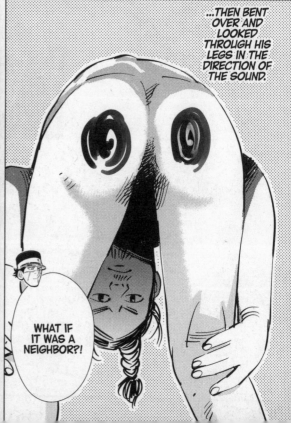

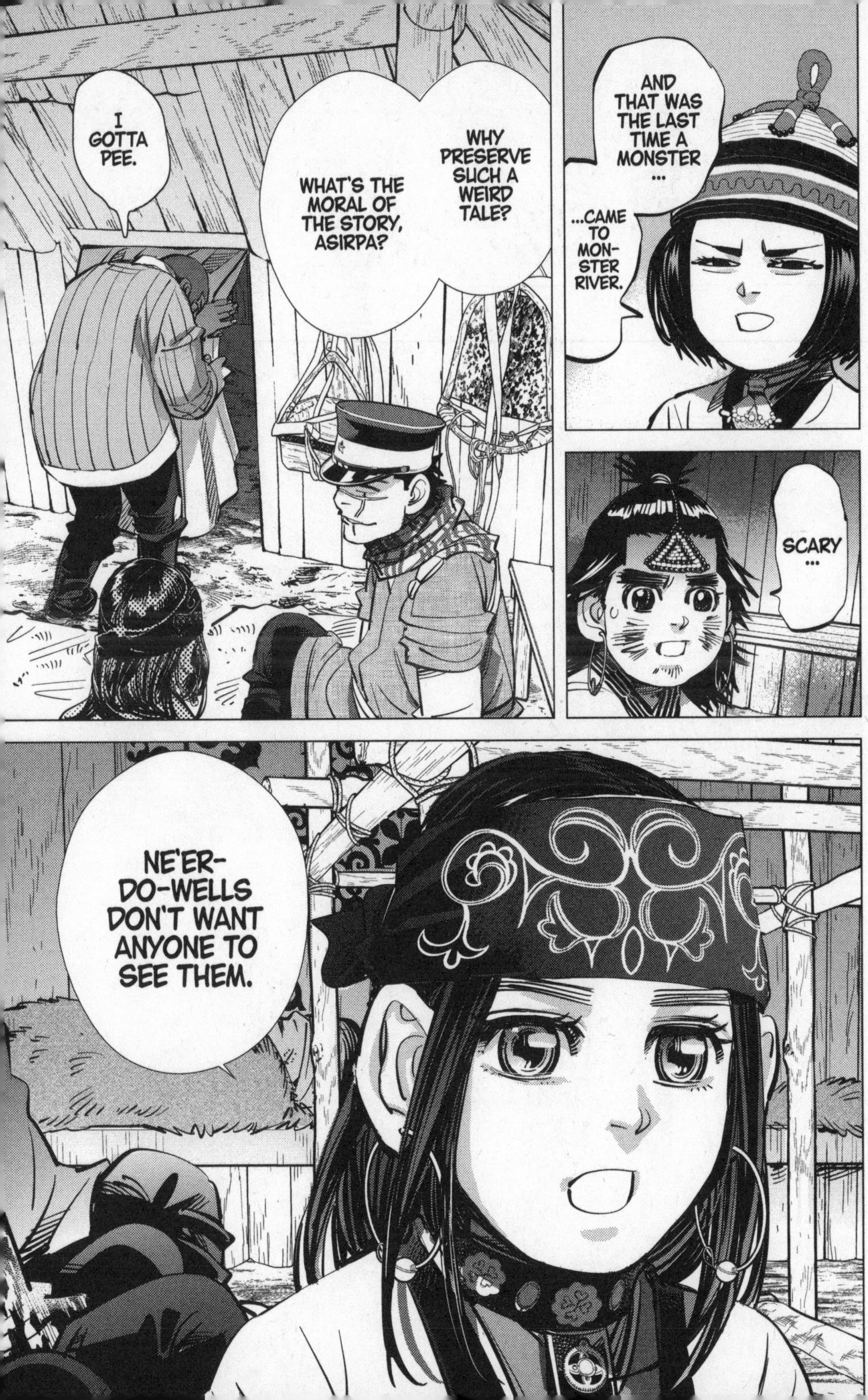
AND THAT WAS THE LAST TIME A MONSTER ...
...CAME TO MON-STER RIVER.
SCARY ...
WHY PRESERVE SUCH A WEIRD TALE?
WHAT'S THE MORAL OF THE STORY, ASIRPA?
I GOTTA PEE.
NE'ER-DO-WELLS DON'T WANT ANYONE TO SEE THEM.

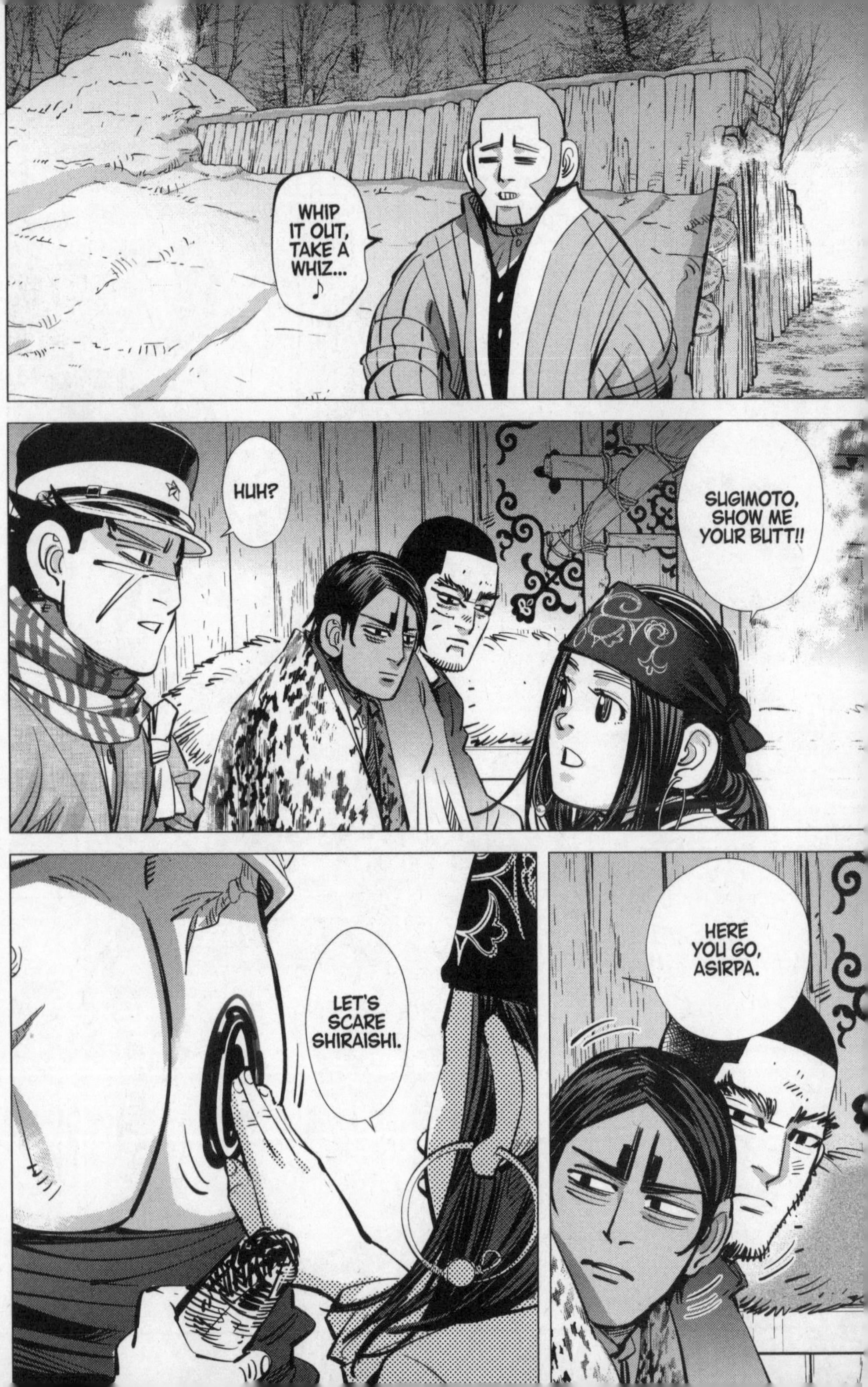
WHIP IT OUT, TAKE A WHIZ... ♪
SUGIMOTO, SHOW ME YOUR BUTT!!
HUH?
HERE YOU GO, ASIRPA.
LET'S SCARE SHIRAISHI.

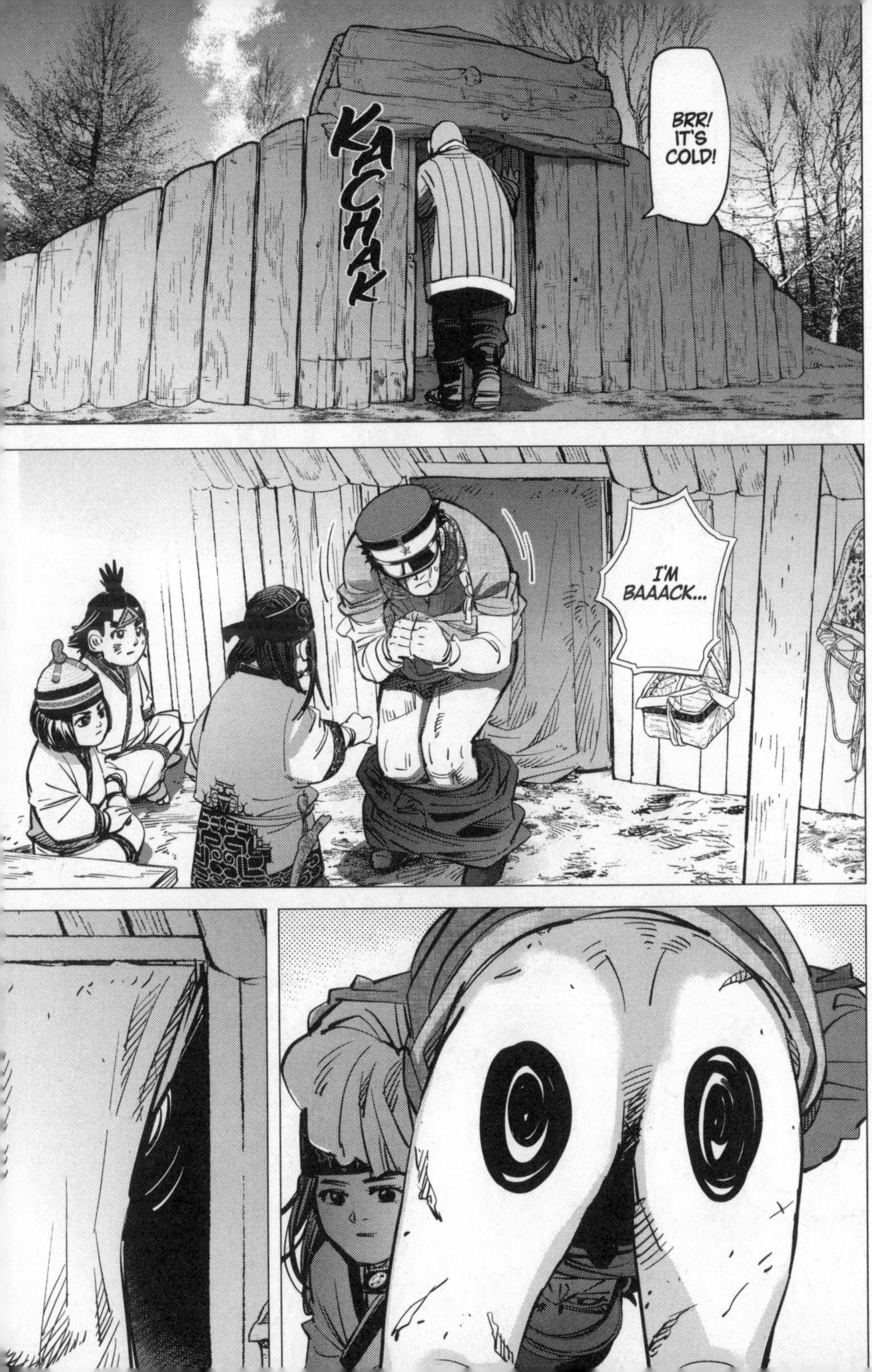
BRR! IT'S COLD!
KACHAK
I'M BAAACK...

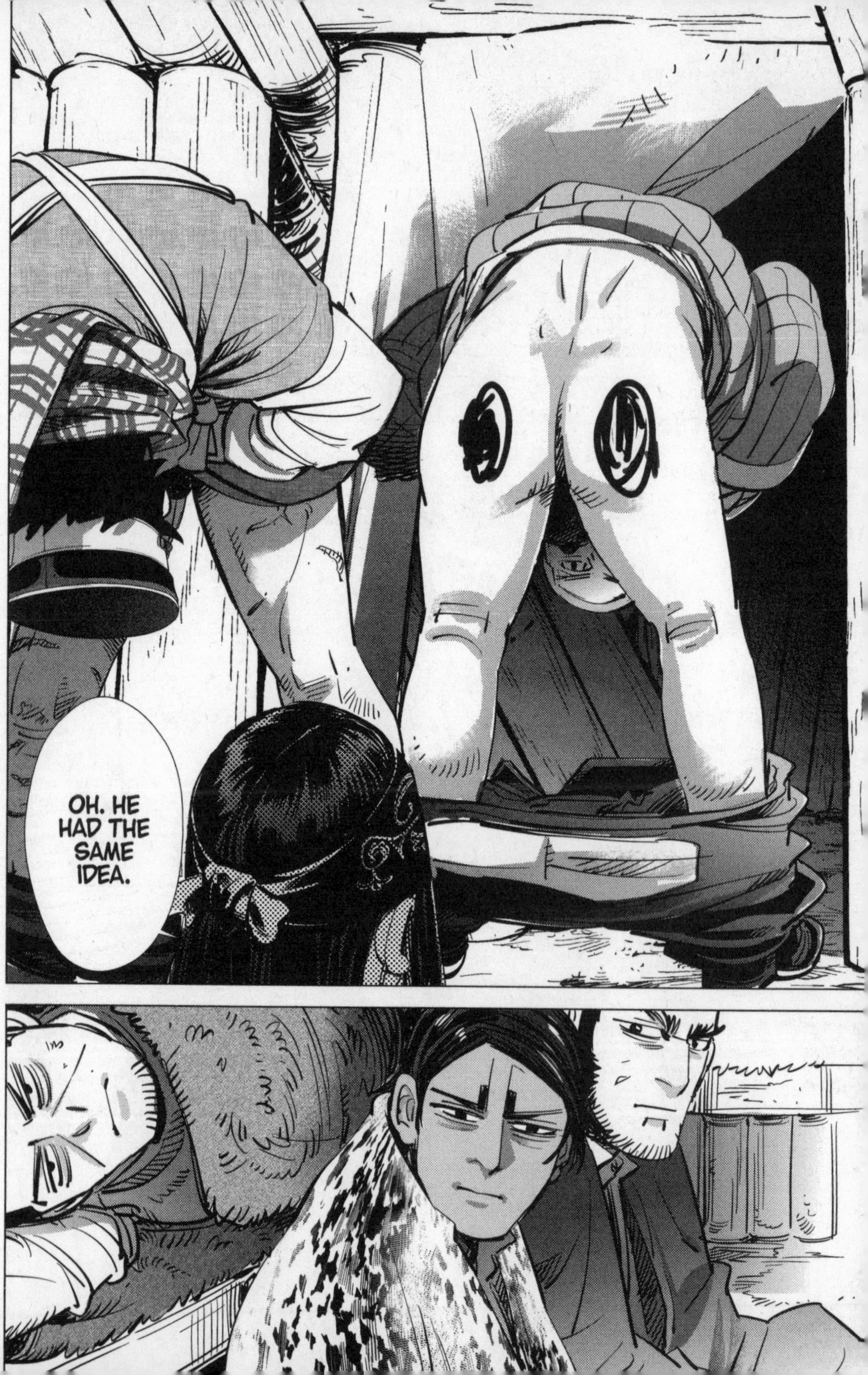
OH. HE HAD THE SAME IDEA.

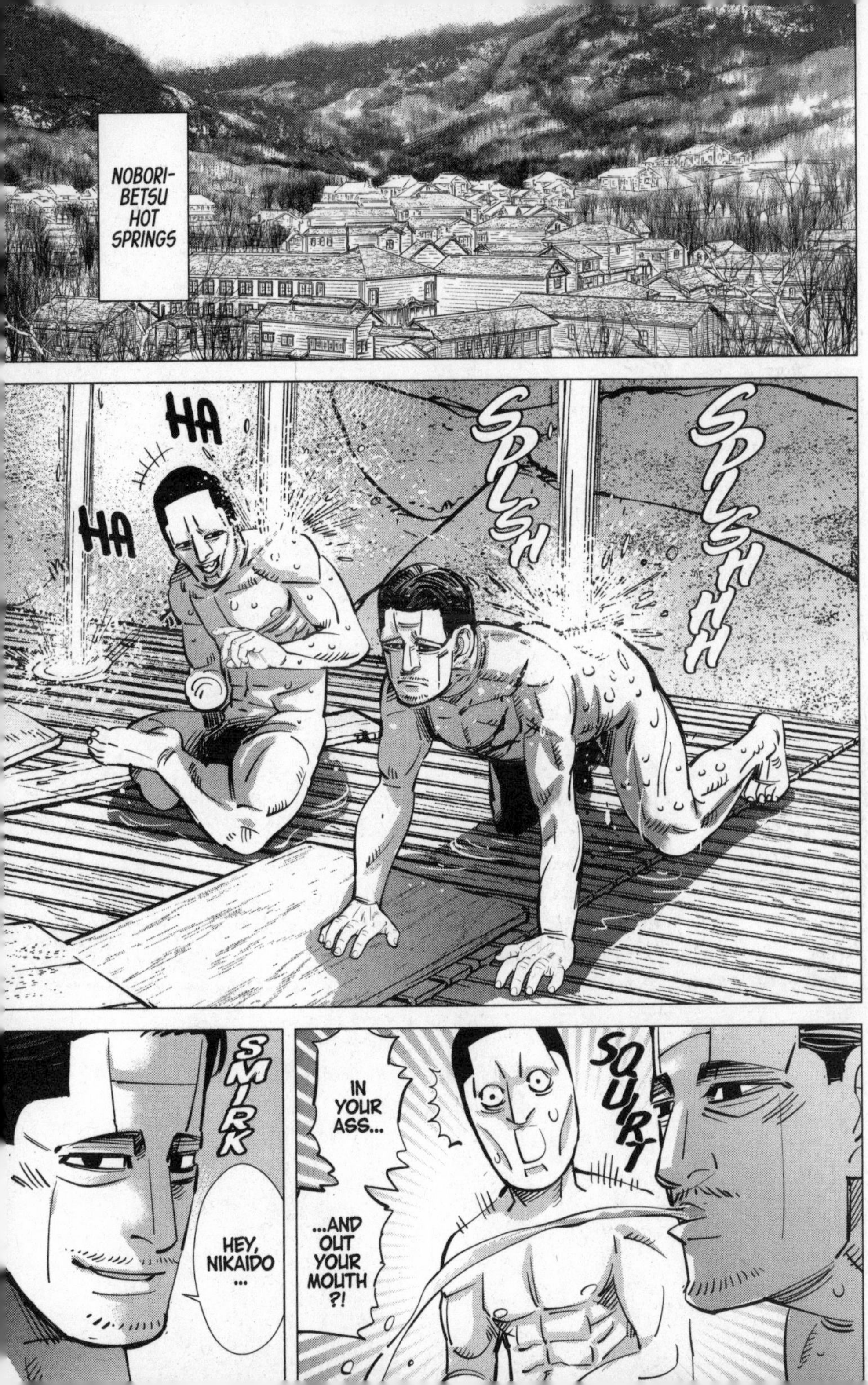
NOBORI-
BETSU
HOT
SPRINGS
SPLSHHHH
SPLSH
HA
HA
SQUIRT
IN YOUR ASS...
...AND OUT YOUR MOUTH ?!
SMIRK
HEY, NIKAIDO ...

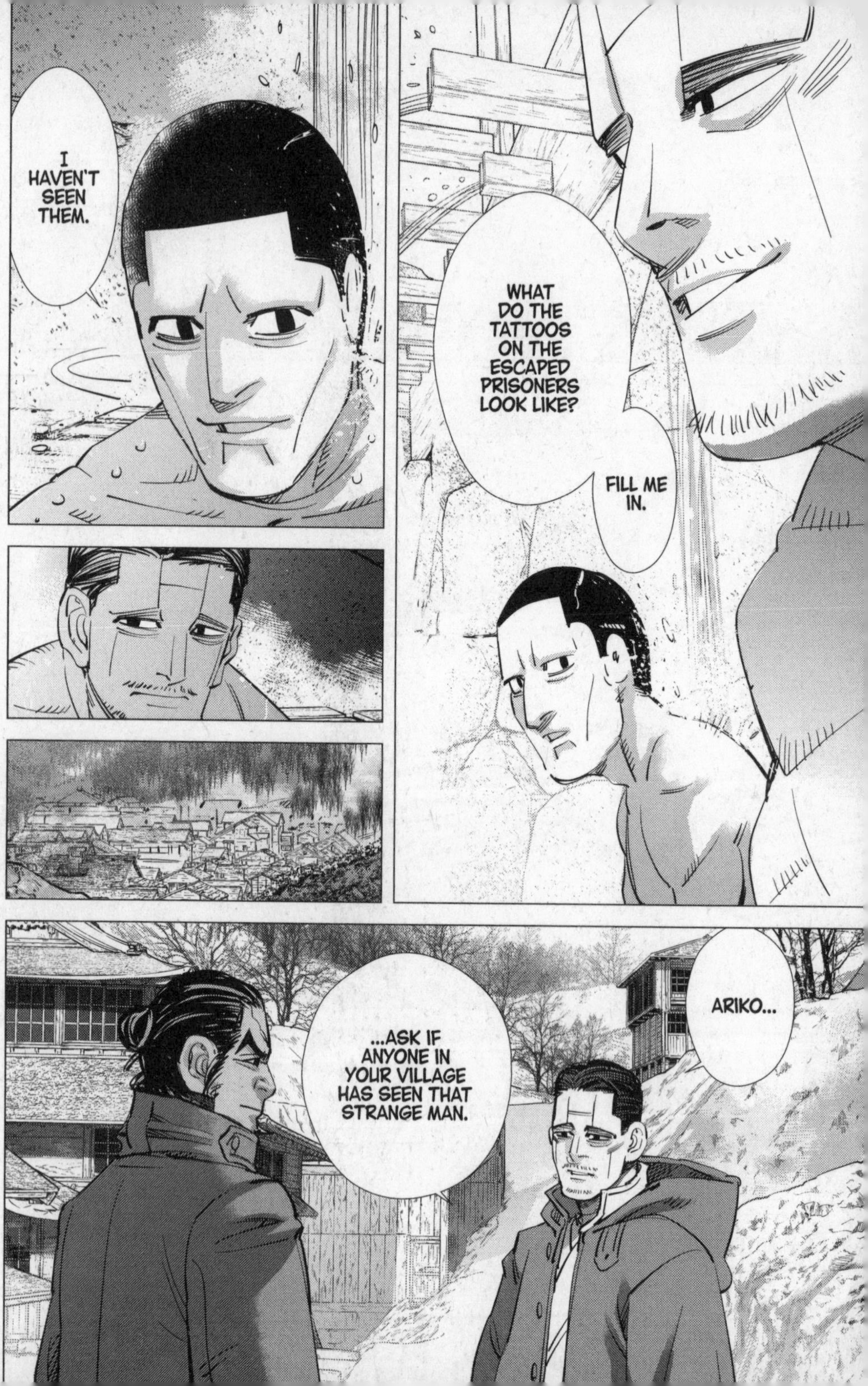
WHAT DO THE TATTOOS ON THE ESCAPED PRISONERS LOOK LIKE?
FILL ME IN.
I HAVEN'T SEEN THEM.
ARIKO...
...ASK IF ANYONE IN YOUR VILLAGE HAS SEEN THAT STRANGE MAN.

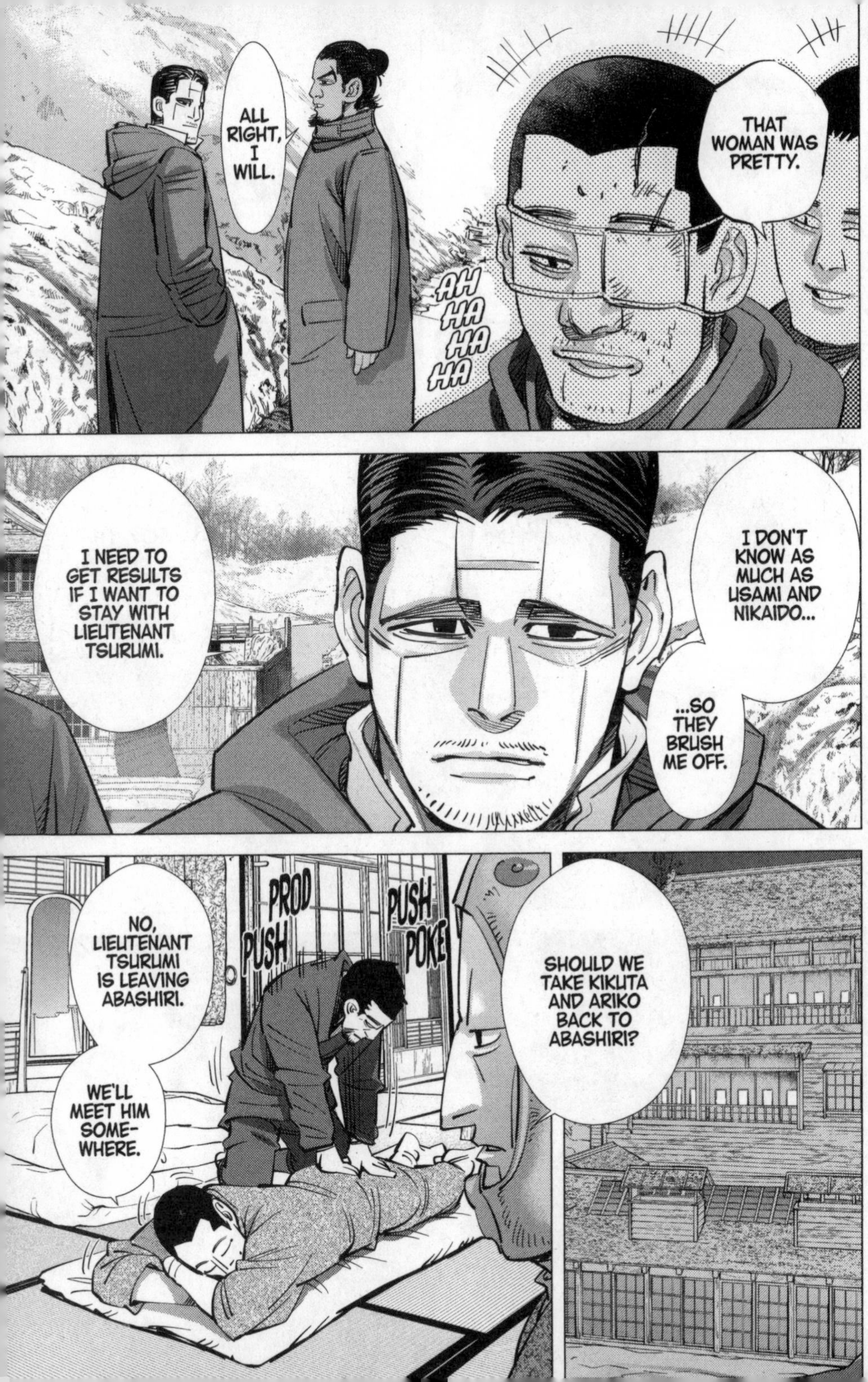
THAT WOMAN WAS PRETTY.
AH HA HA HA
ALL RIGHT, I WILL.
I DON'T KNOW AS MUCH AS USAMI AND NIKAIDO...
...SO THEY BRUSH ME OFF.
I NEED TO GET RESULTS IF I WANT TO STAY WITH LIEUTENANT TSURUMI.
SHOULD WE TAKE KIKUTA AND ARIKO BACK TO ABASHIRI?
PUSH POKE
PROD PUSH
NO, LIEUTENANT TSURUMI IS LEAVING ABASHIRI.
WE'LL MEET HIM SOME-WHERE.

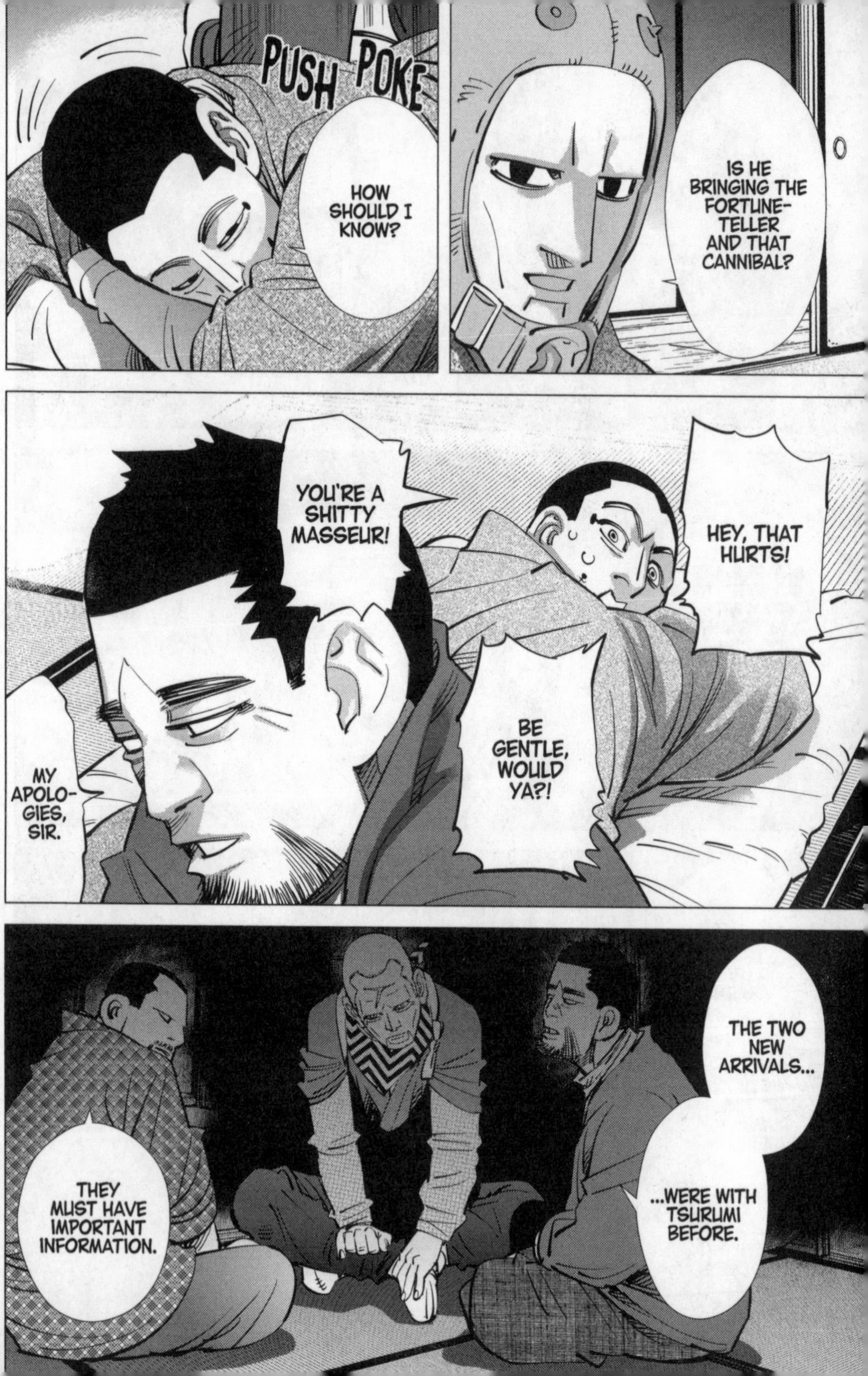
IS HE BRINGING THE FORTUNE-TELLER AND THAT CANNIBAL?
PUSH POKE
HOW SHOULD I KNOW?
HEY, THAT HURTS!
BE GENTLE, WOULD YA?!
YOU'RE A SHITTY MASSEUR!
MY APOLOGIES, SIR.
THE TWO NEW ARRIVALS...
...WERE WITH TSURUMI BEFORE.
THEY MUST HAVE IMPORTANT INFORMATION.

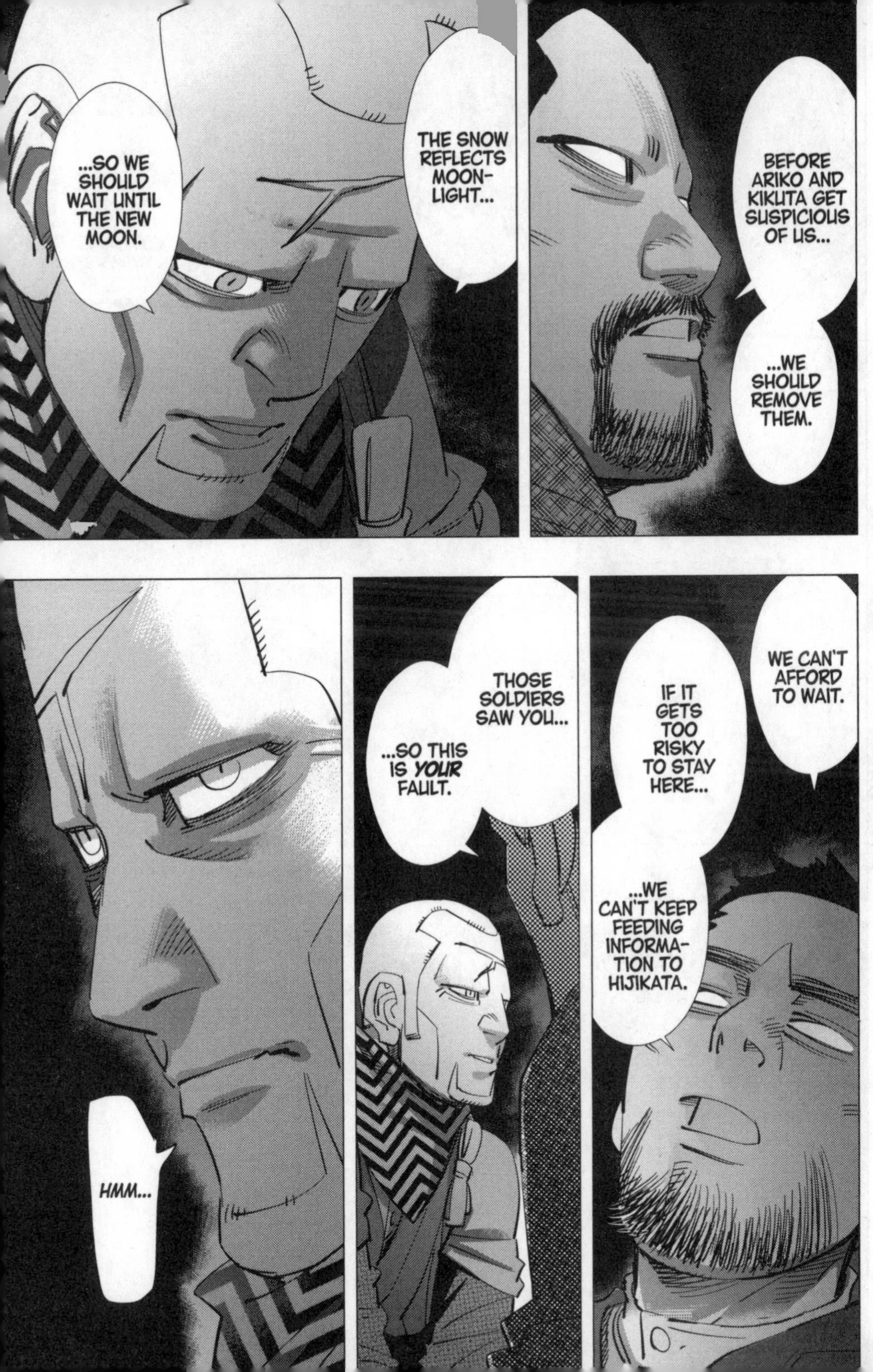
BEFORE ARIKO AND KIKUTA GET SUSPICIOUS OF US...
...WE SHOULD REMOVE THEM.
THE SNOW REFLECTS MOON-LIGHT...
...SO WE SHOULD WAIT UNTIL THE NEW MOON.
WE CAN'T AFFORD TO WAIT.
IF IT GETS TOO RISKY TO STAY HERE...
...WE CAN'T KEEP FEEDING INFORMA-TION TO HIJIKATA.
THOSE SOLDIERS SAW YOU...
...SO THIS IS *YOUR* FAULT.
HMM...

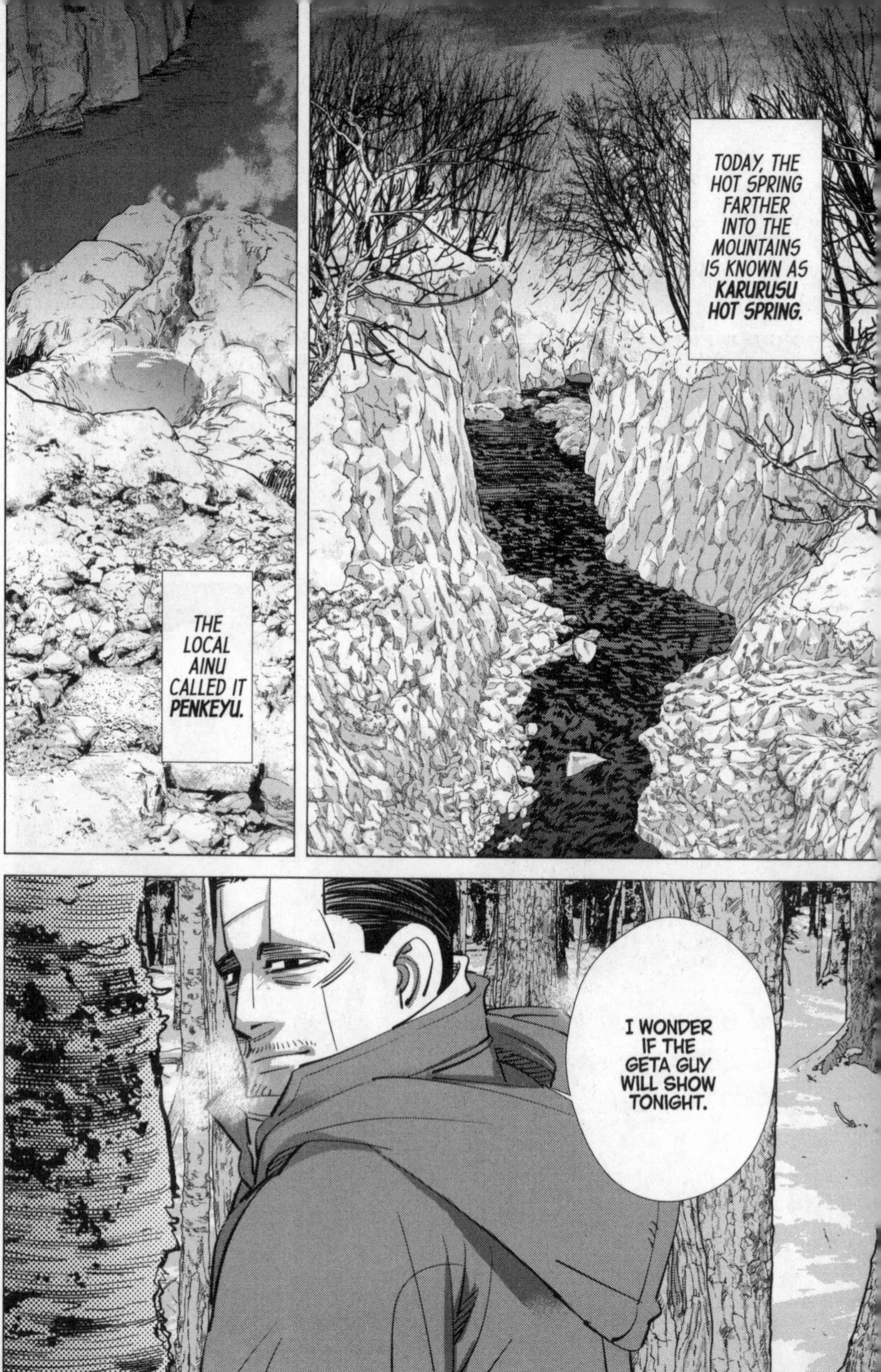
TODAY, THE HOT SPRING FARTHER INTO THE MOUNTAINS IS KNOWN AS **KARURUSU HOT SPRING.**
THE LOCAL AINU CALLED IT **PENKEYU.**
I WONDER IF THE GETA GUY WILL SHOW TONIGHT.

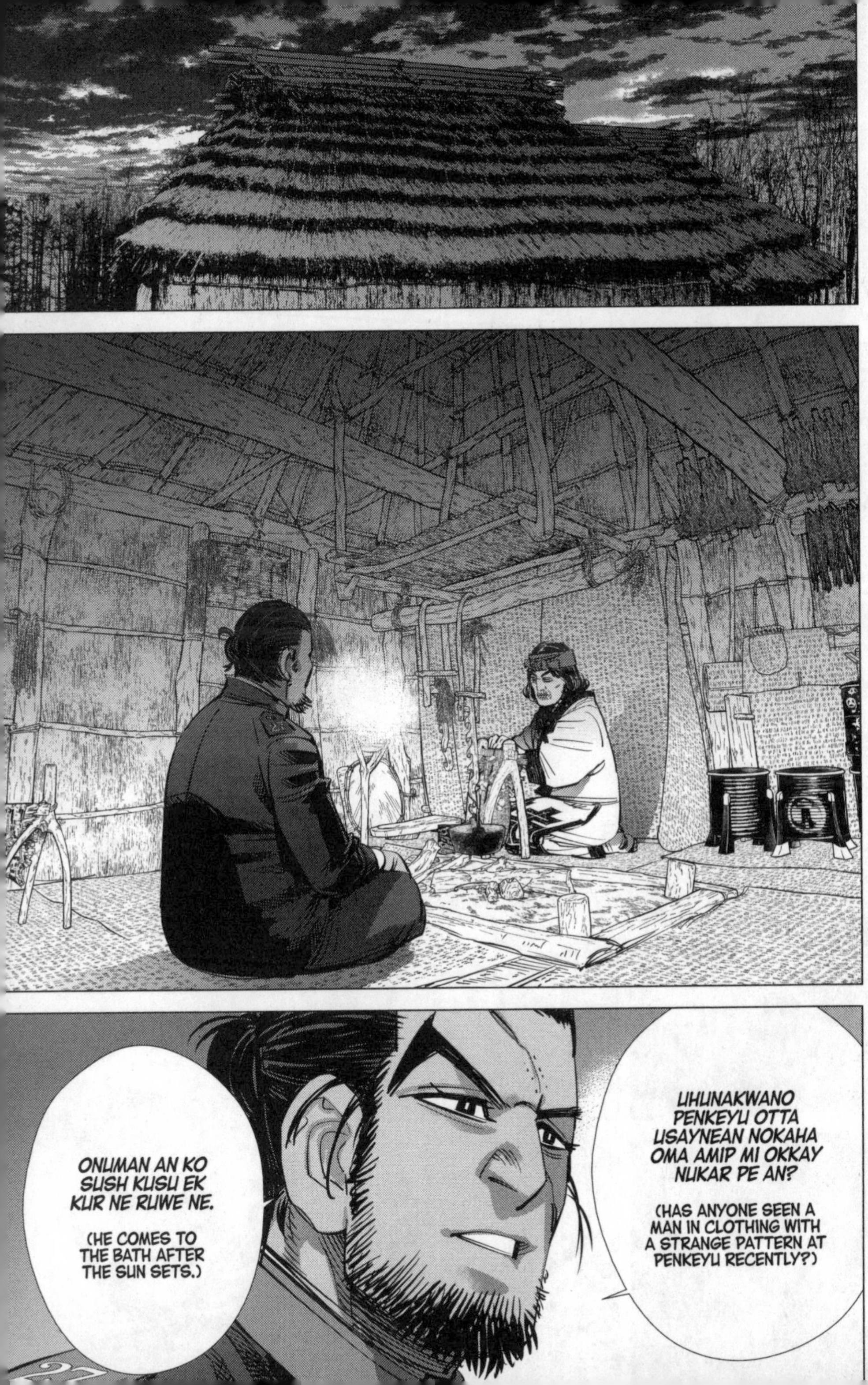
UHUNAKWANO PENKEYU OTTA USAYNEAN NOKAHA OMA AMIP MI OKKAY NUKAR PE AN?
(HAS ANYONE SEEN A MAN IN CLOTHING WITH A STRANGE PATTERN AT PENKEYU RECENTLY?)
ONUMAN AN KO SUSH KUSU EK KUR NE RUWE NE.
(HE COMES TO THE BATH AFTER THE SUN SETS.)

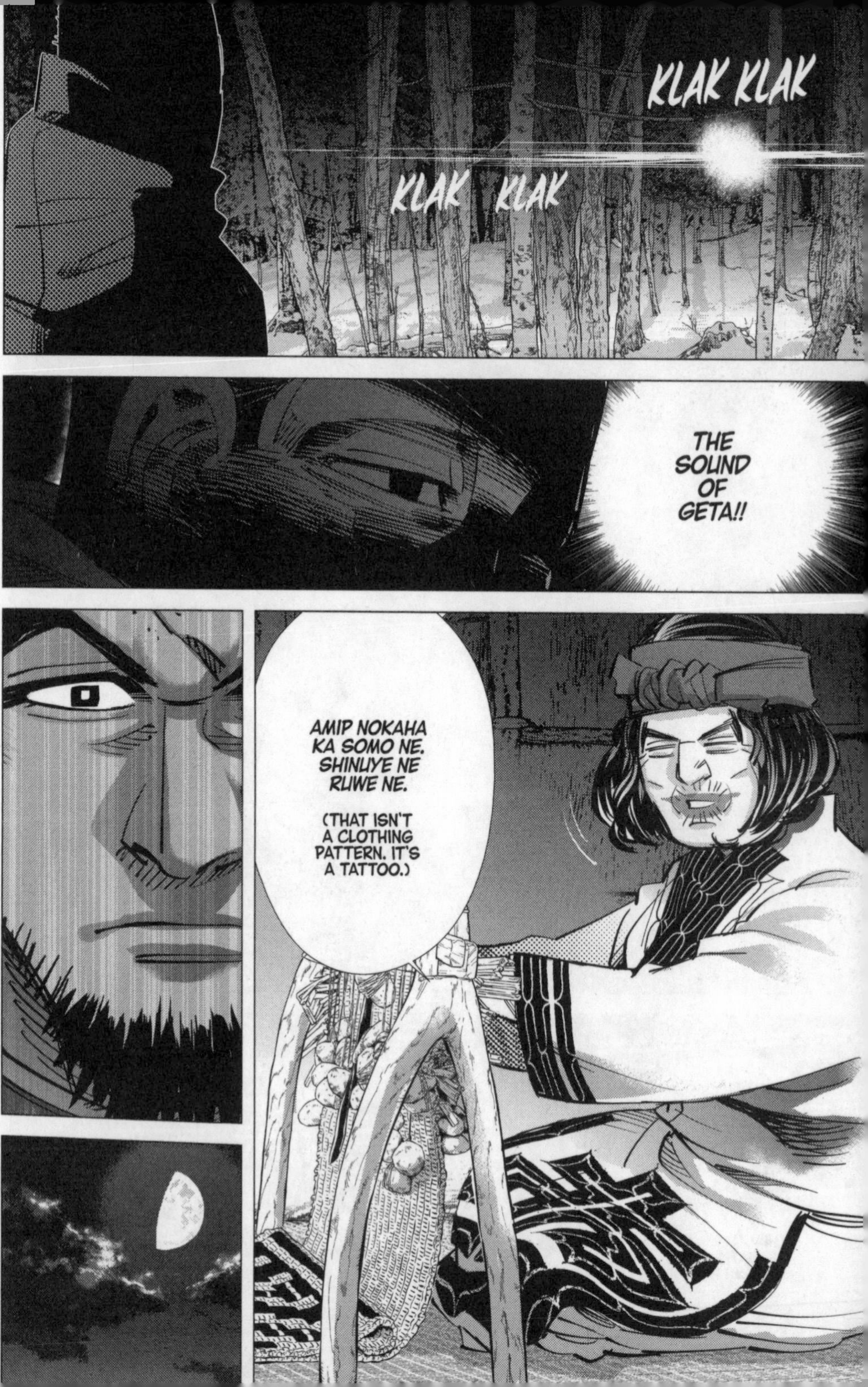
KLAK KLAK
KLAK KLAK
THE SOUND OF GETA!!
AMIP NOKAHA KA SOMO NE. SHINUYE NE RUWE NE.
(THAT ISN'T A CLOTHING PATTERN. IT'S A TATTOO.)

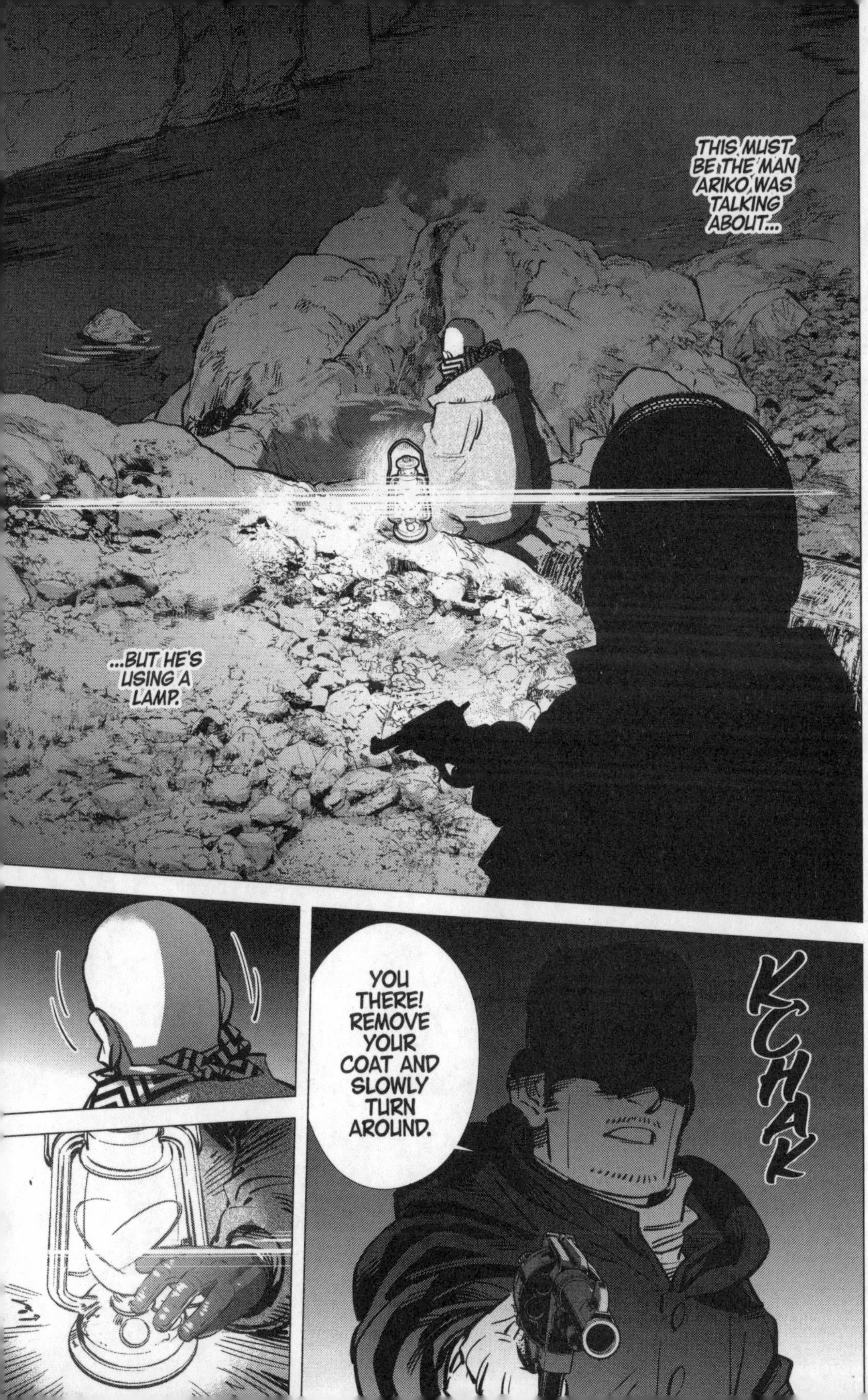
THIS MUST BE THE MAN ARIKO WAS TALKING ABOUT...
...BUT HE'S USING A LAMP.
KCHAK
YOU THERE! REMOVE YOUR COAT AND SLOWLY TURN AROUND.

FWSH

SHUF

SWIP

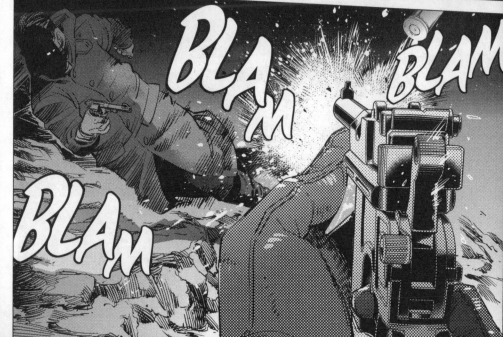

BLAM

BLAM

BLAM

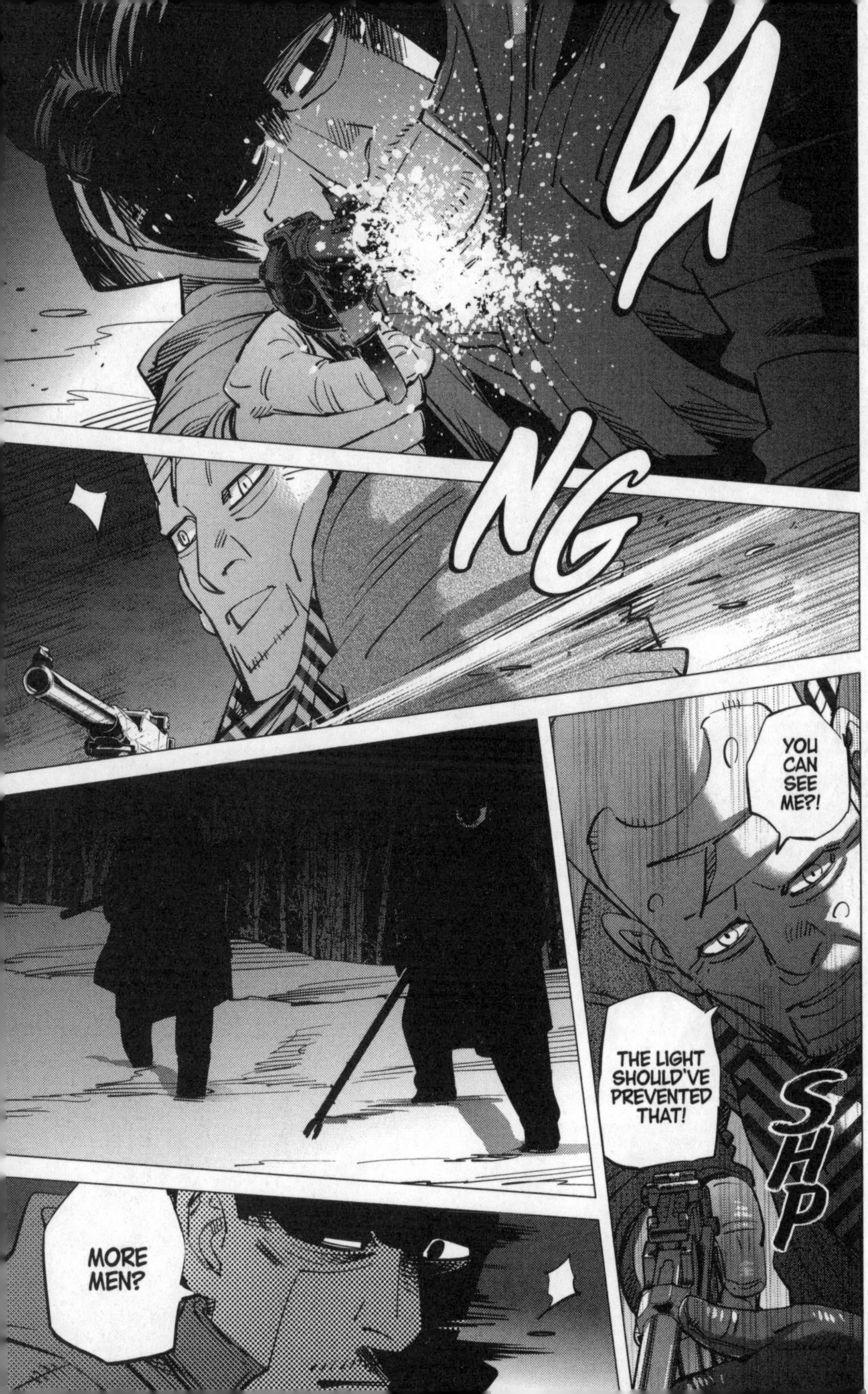
BANG
YOU CAN SEE ME?!
THE LIGHT SHOULD'VE PREVENTED THAT!
SHP
MORE MEN?

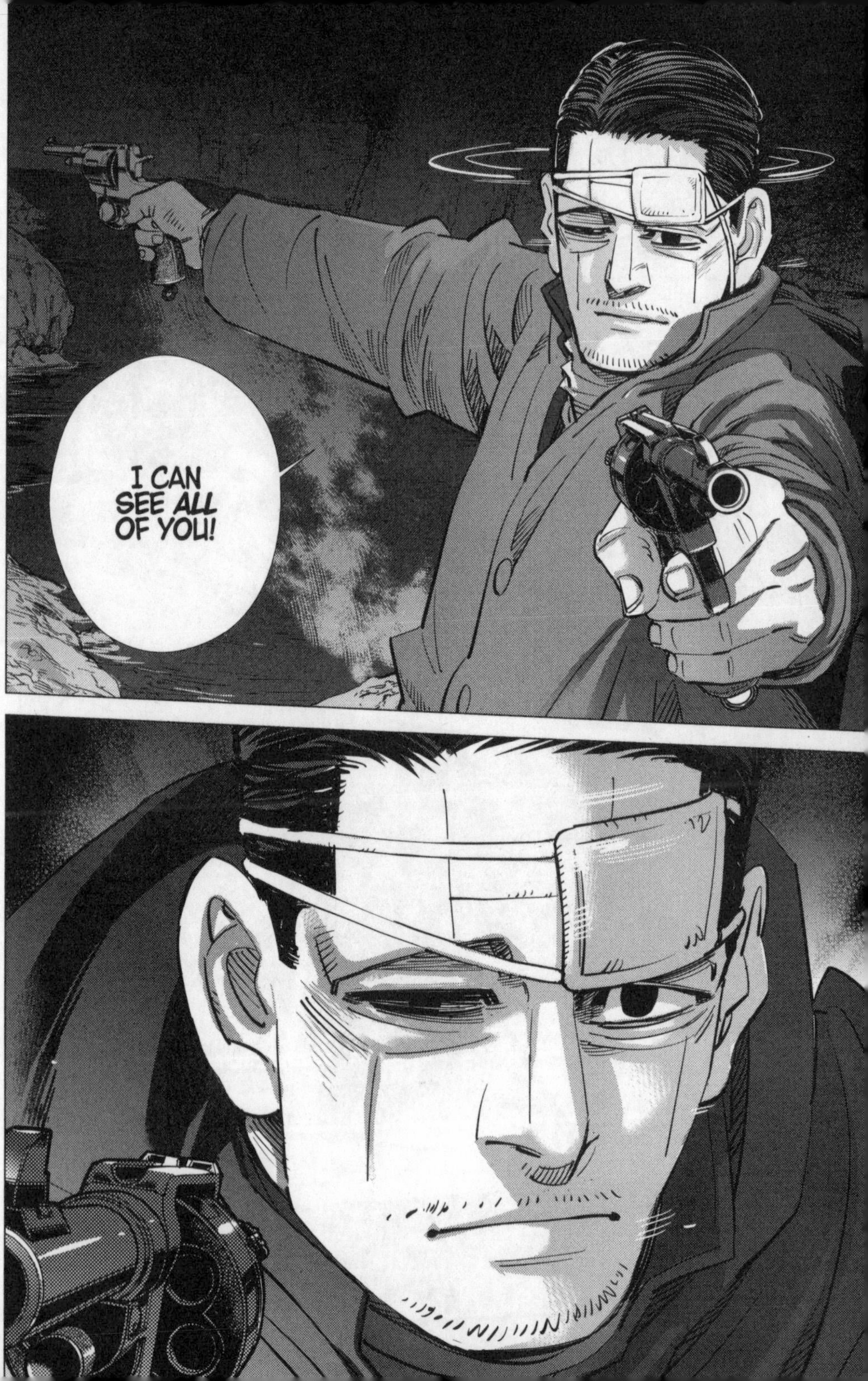
I CAN SEE ALL OF YOU!

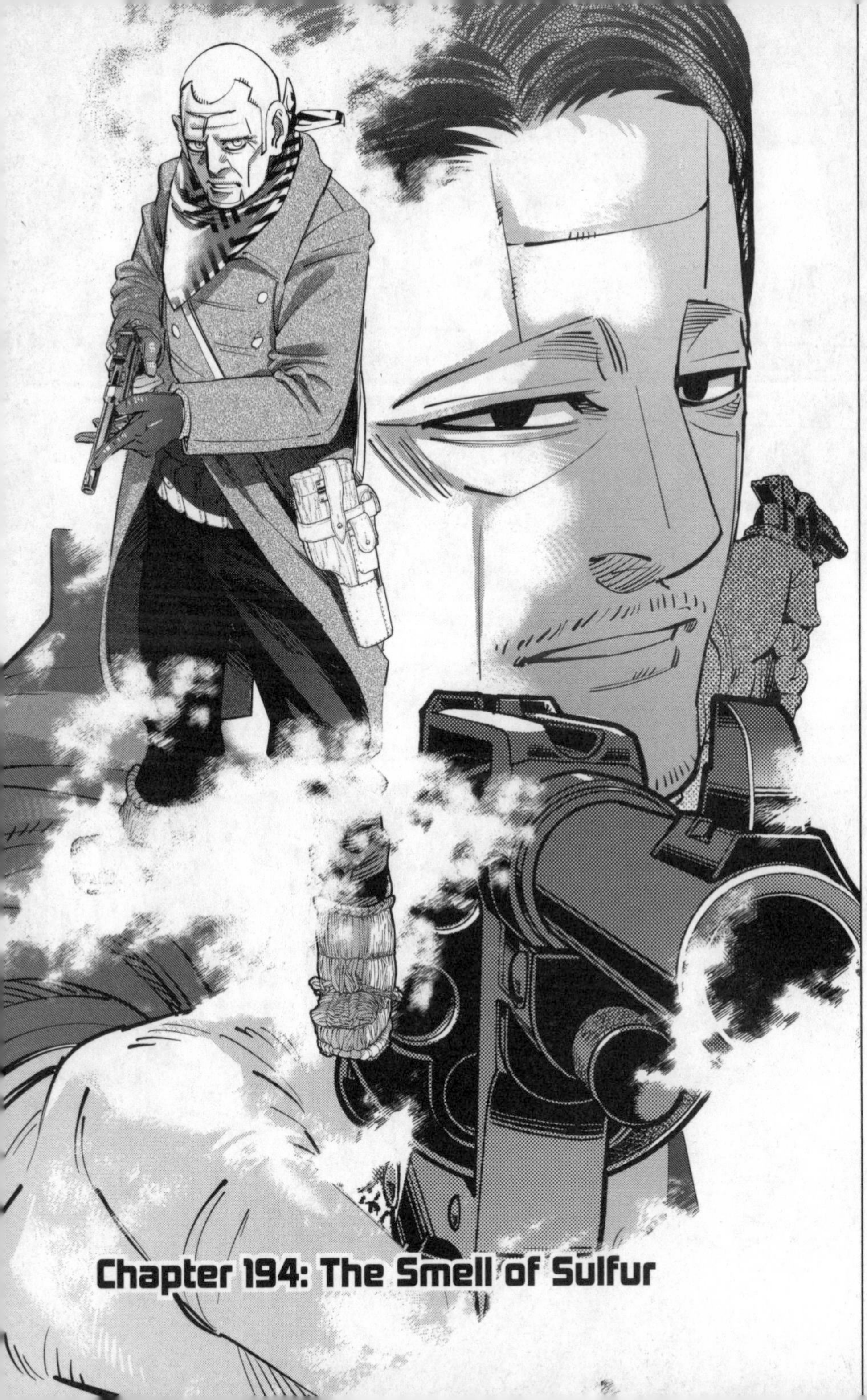
Chapter 194: The Smell of Sulfur

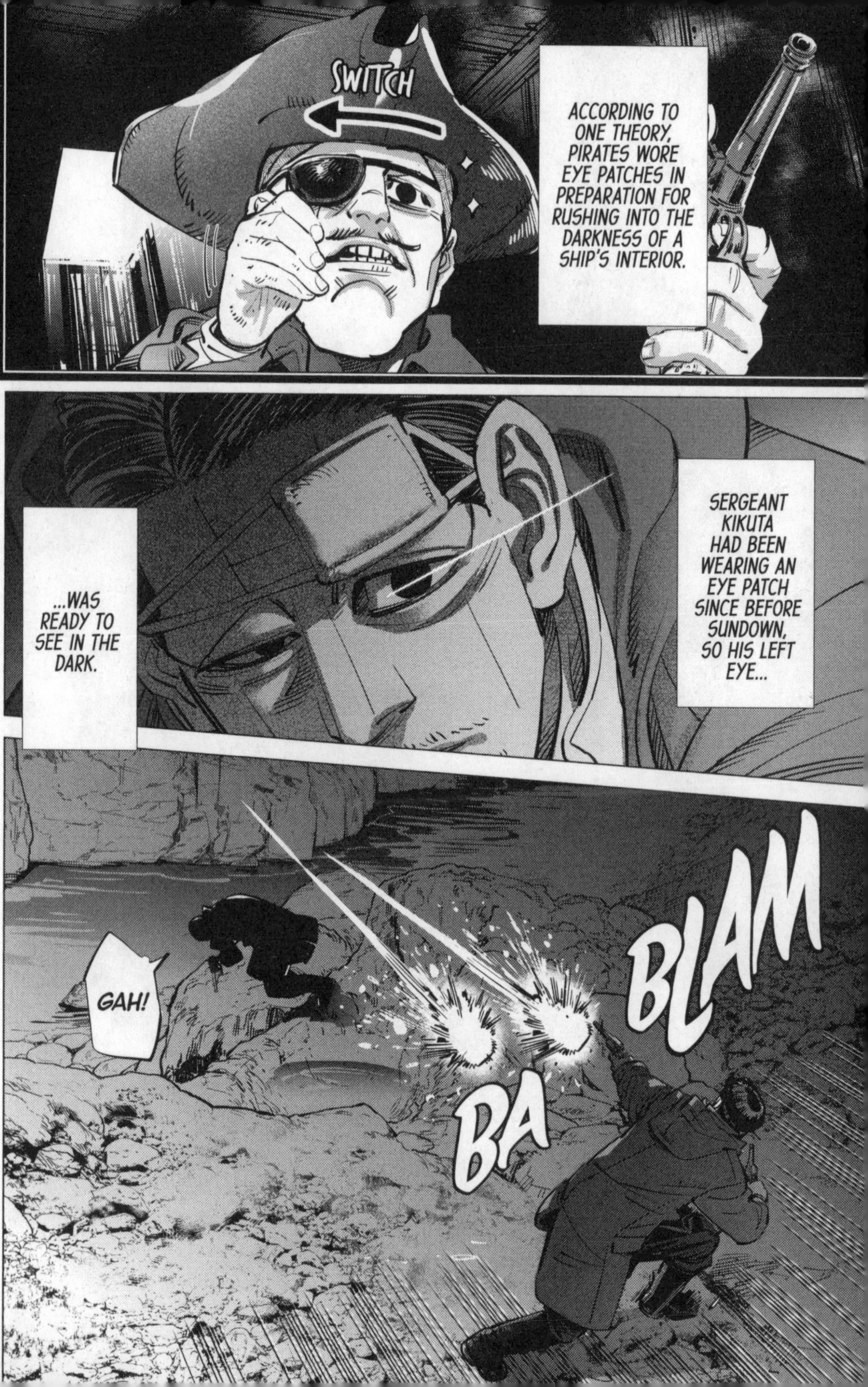
SWITCH
ACCORDING TO ONE THEORY, PIRATES WORE EYE PATCHES IN PREPARATION FOR RUSHING INTO THE DARKNESS OF A SHIP'S INTERIOR.
SERGEANT KIKUTA HAD BEEN WEARING AN EYE PATCH SINCE BEFORE SUNDOWN, SO HIS LEFT EYE...
...WAS READY TO SEE IN THE DARK.
BLAM
BA
GAH!

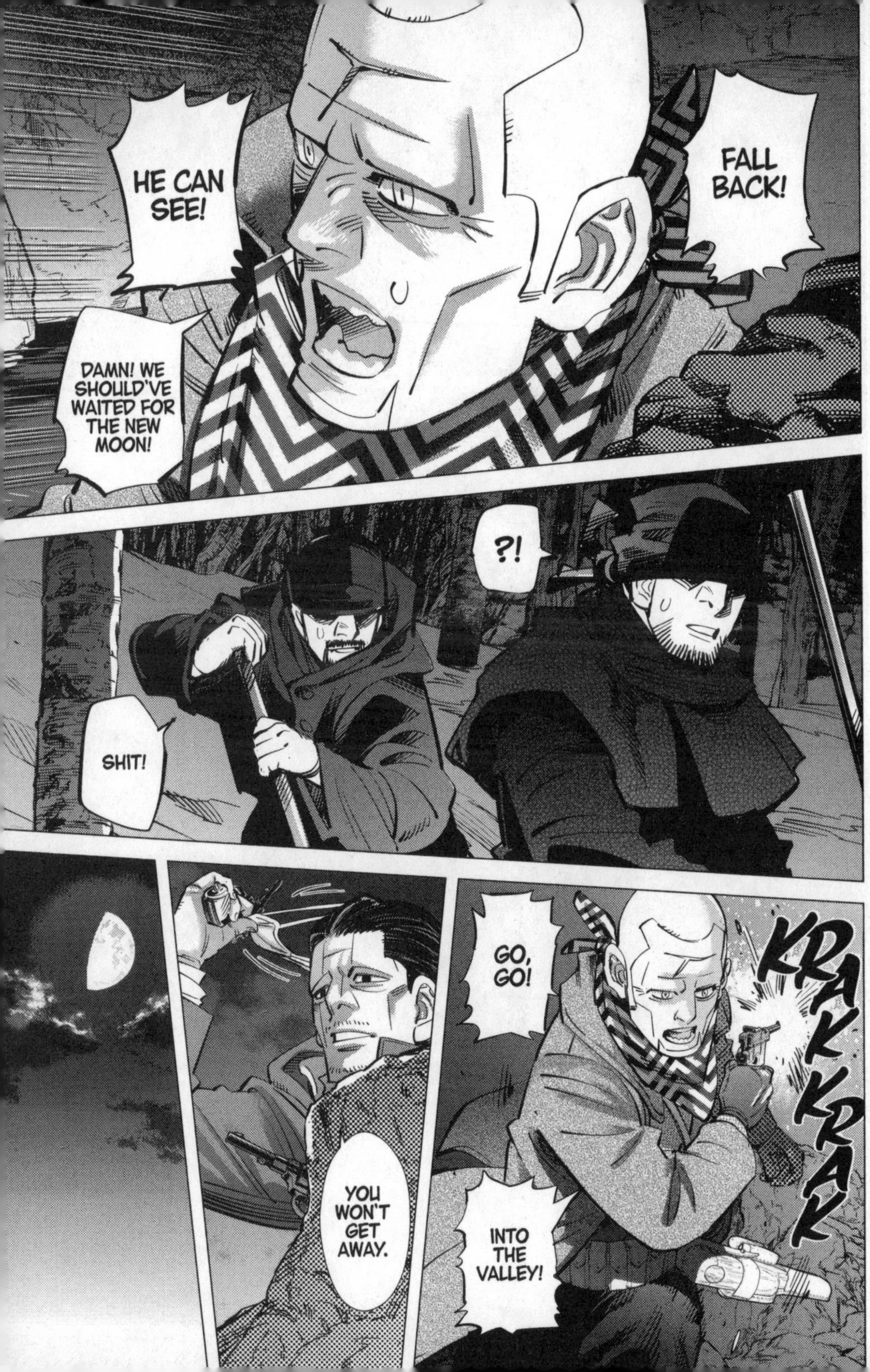
FALL BACK!
HE CAN SEE!
DAMN! WE SHOULD'VE WAITED FOR THE NEW MOON!
?!
SHIT!
GO, GO!
KRAK KRAK KRAK
INTO THE VALLEY!
YOU WON'T GET AWAY.

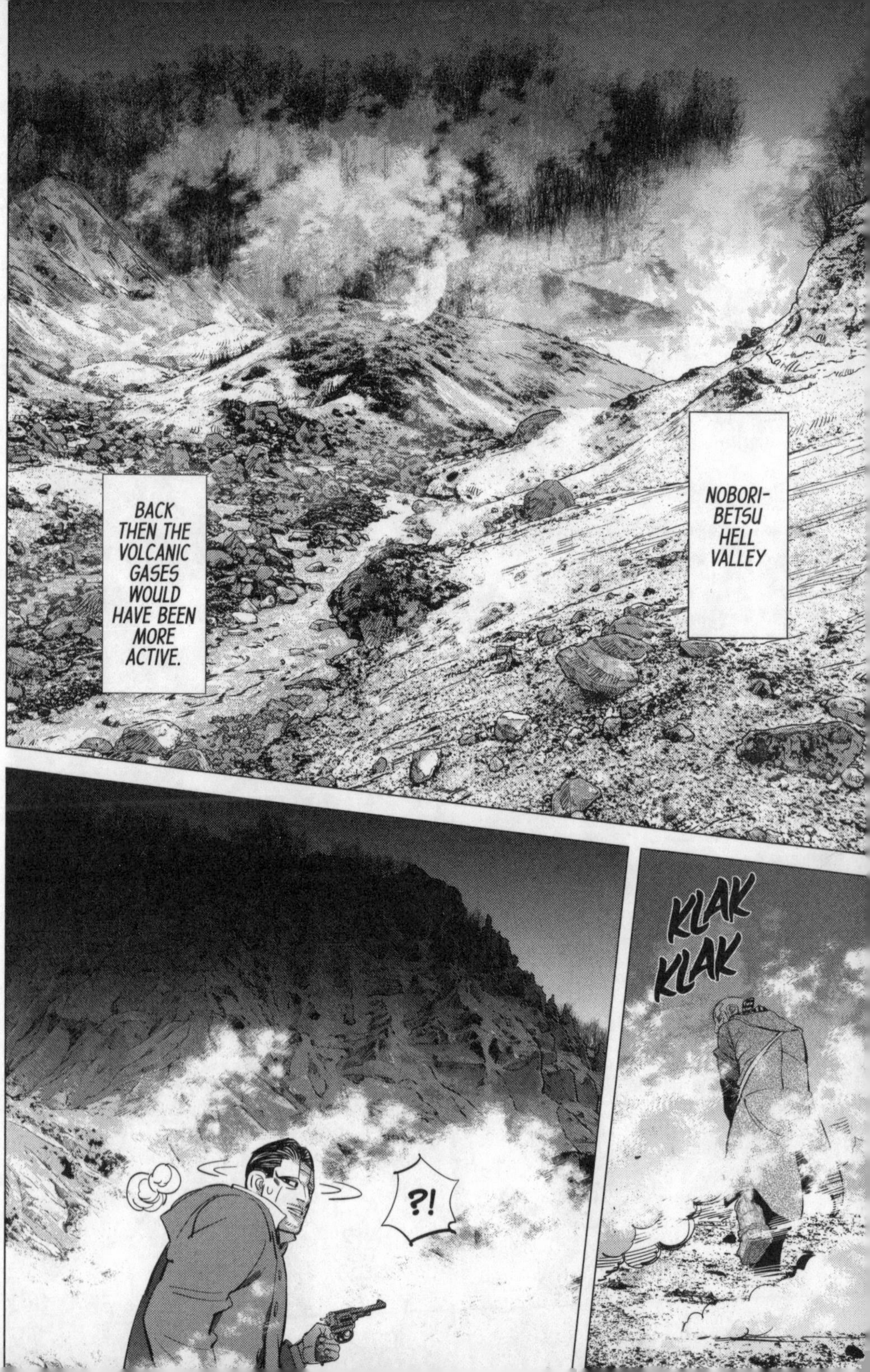
NOBORI-BETSU HELL VALLEY
BACK THEN THE VOLCANIC GASES WOULD HAVE BEEN MORE ACTIVE.
KLAK KLAK
?!

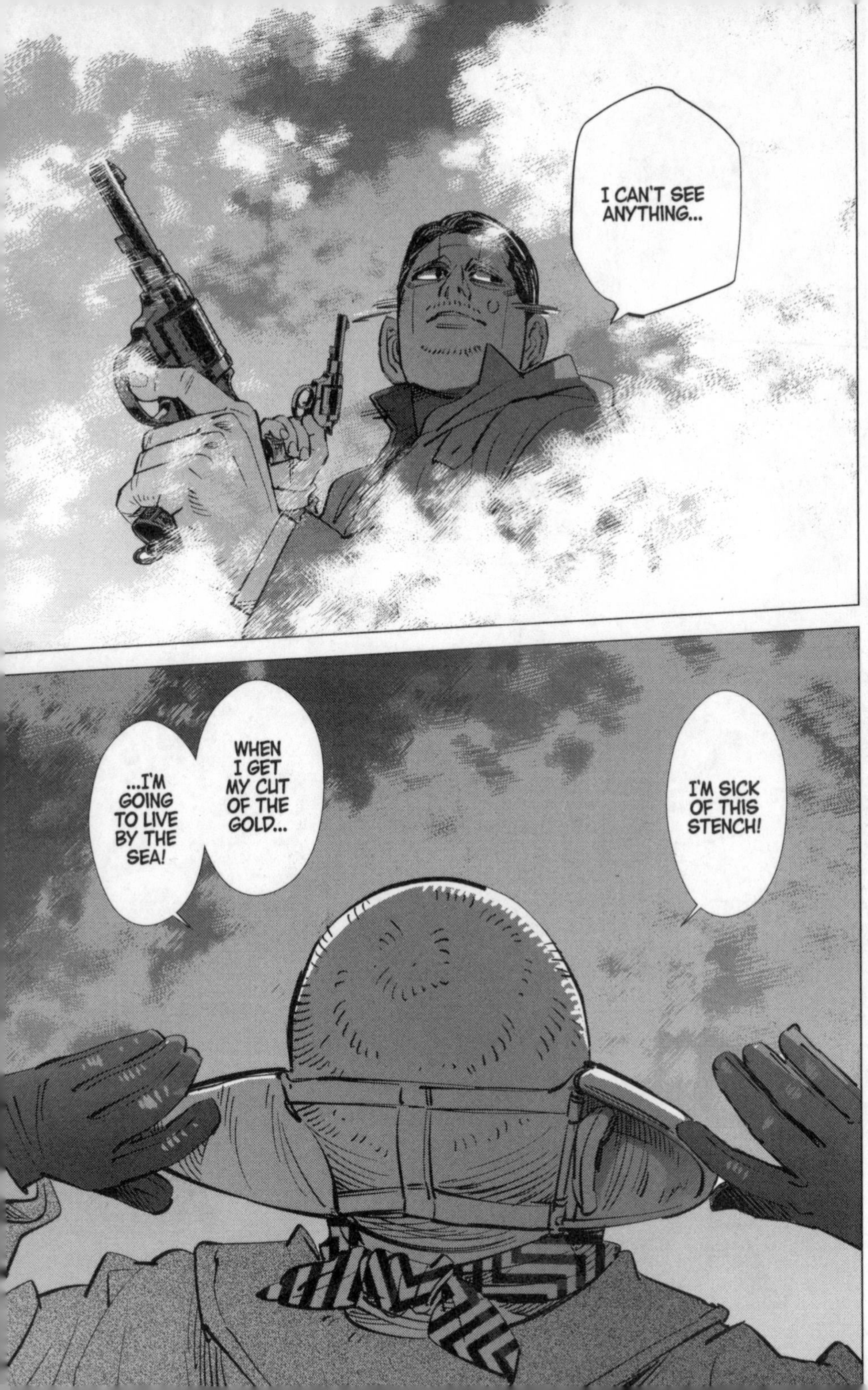
I CAN'T SEE ANYTHING...
I'M SICK OF THIS STENCH!
WHEN I GET MY CUT OF THE GOLD...
...I'M GOING TO LIVE BY THE SEA!

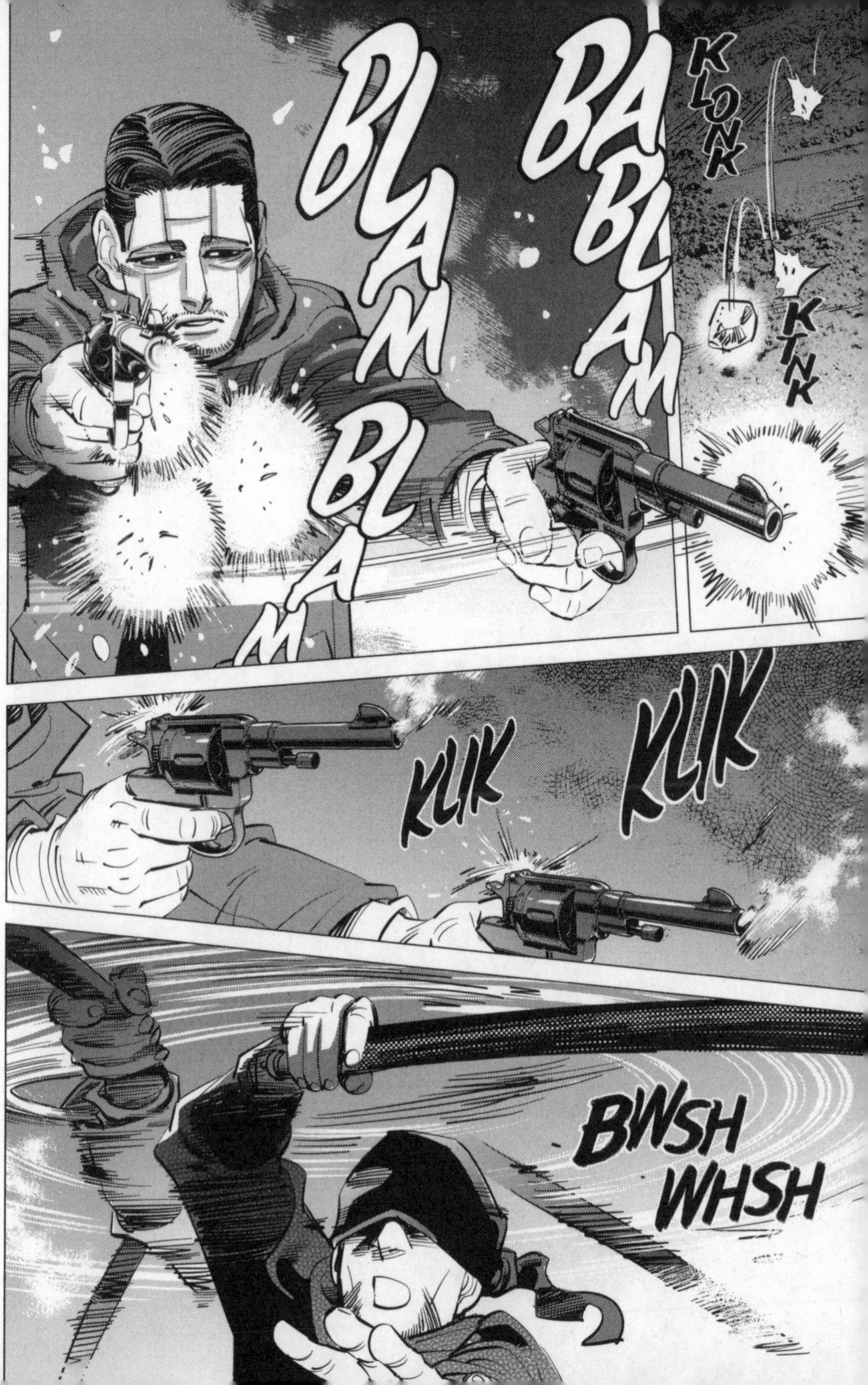
KLONK
KTINK
BABLAM
BLAM
BLAM
KLIK
KLIK
BWSH
WHSH

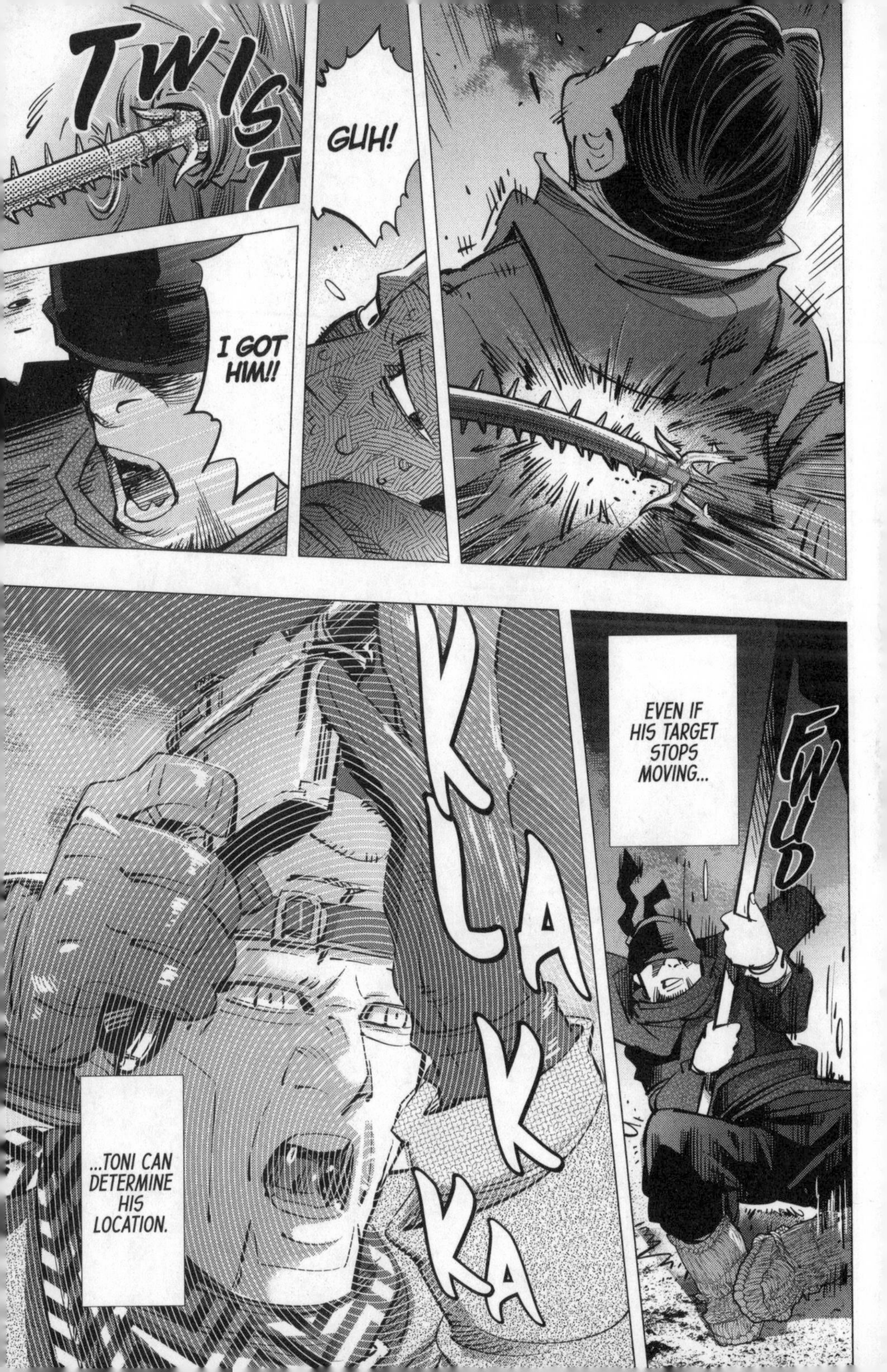
GUH!
TWIST
I GOT HIM!!
EVEN IF HIS TARGET STOPS MOVING...
FWUD
KLAKKA
...TONI CAN DETERMINE HIS LOCATION.

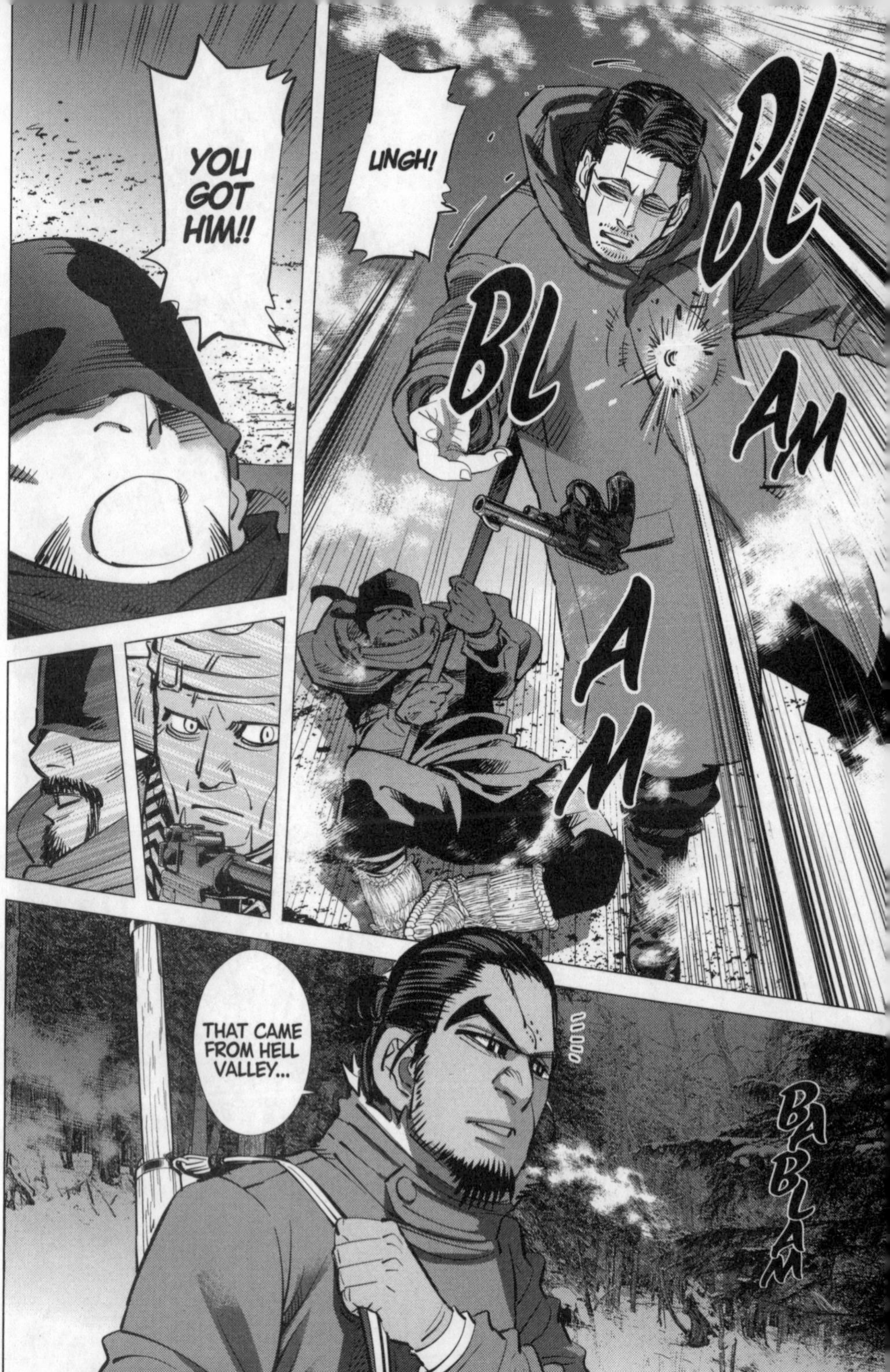
UNGH!
BLAM
BLAM
YOU GOT HIM!!
THAT CAME FROM HELL VALLEY...
BABLAM

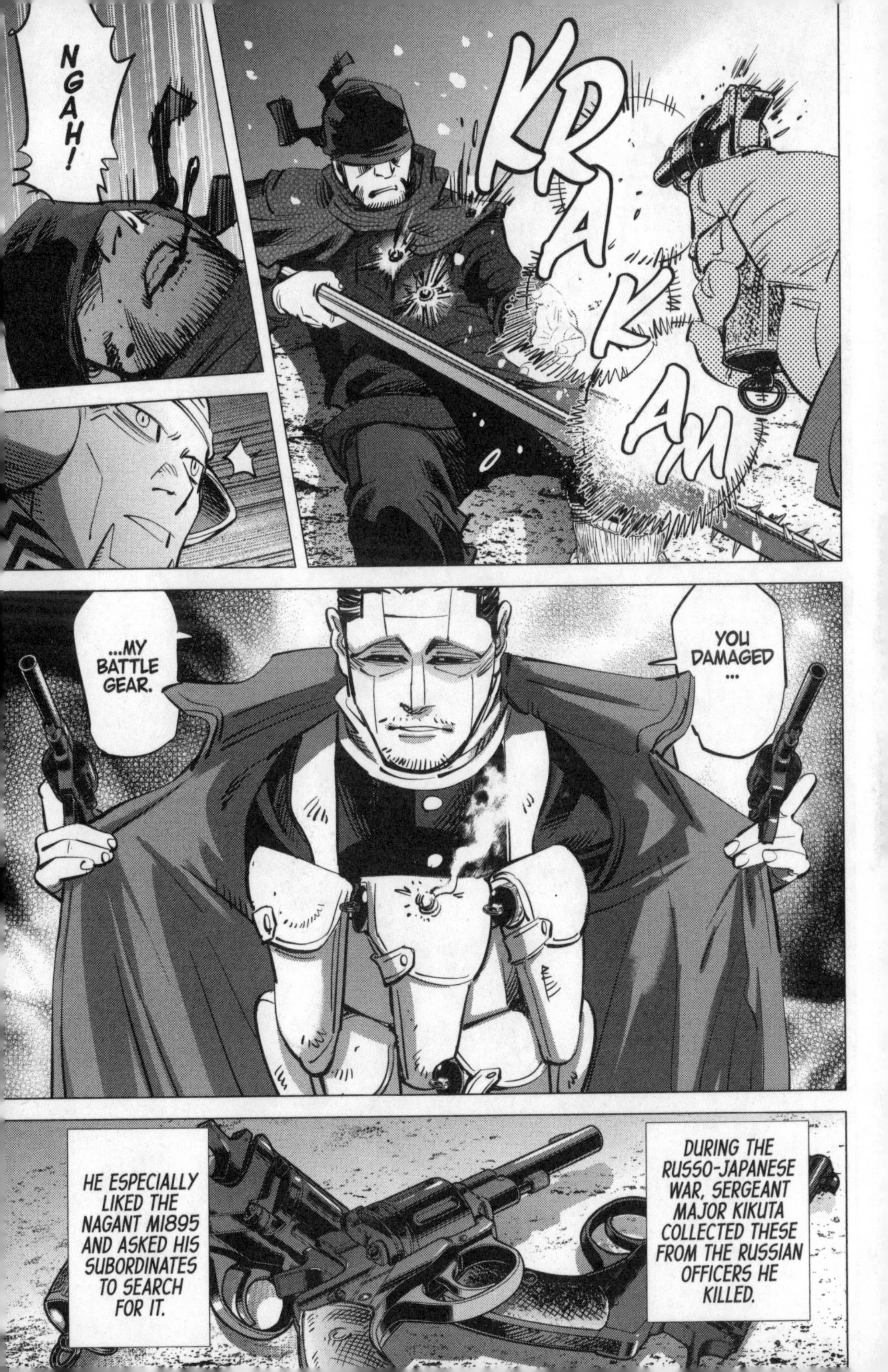
KRAKAM
NGAH!
YOU DAMAGED...
...MY BATTLE GEAR.
DURING THE RUSSO-JAPANESE WAR, SERGEANT MAJOR KIKUTA COLLECTED THESE FROM THE RUSSIAN OFFICERS HE KILLED.
HE ESPECIALLY LIKED THE NAGANT M1895 AND ASKED HIS SUBORDINATES TO SEARCH FOR IT.

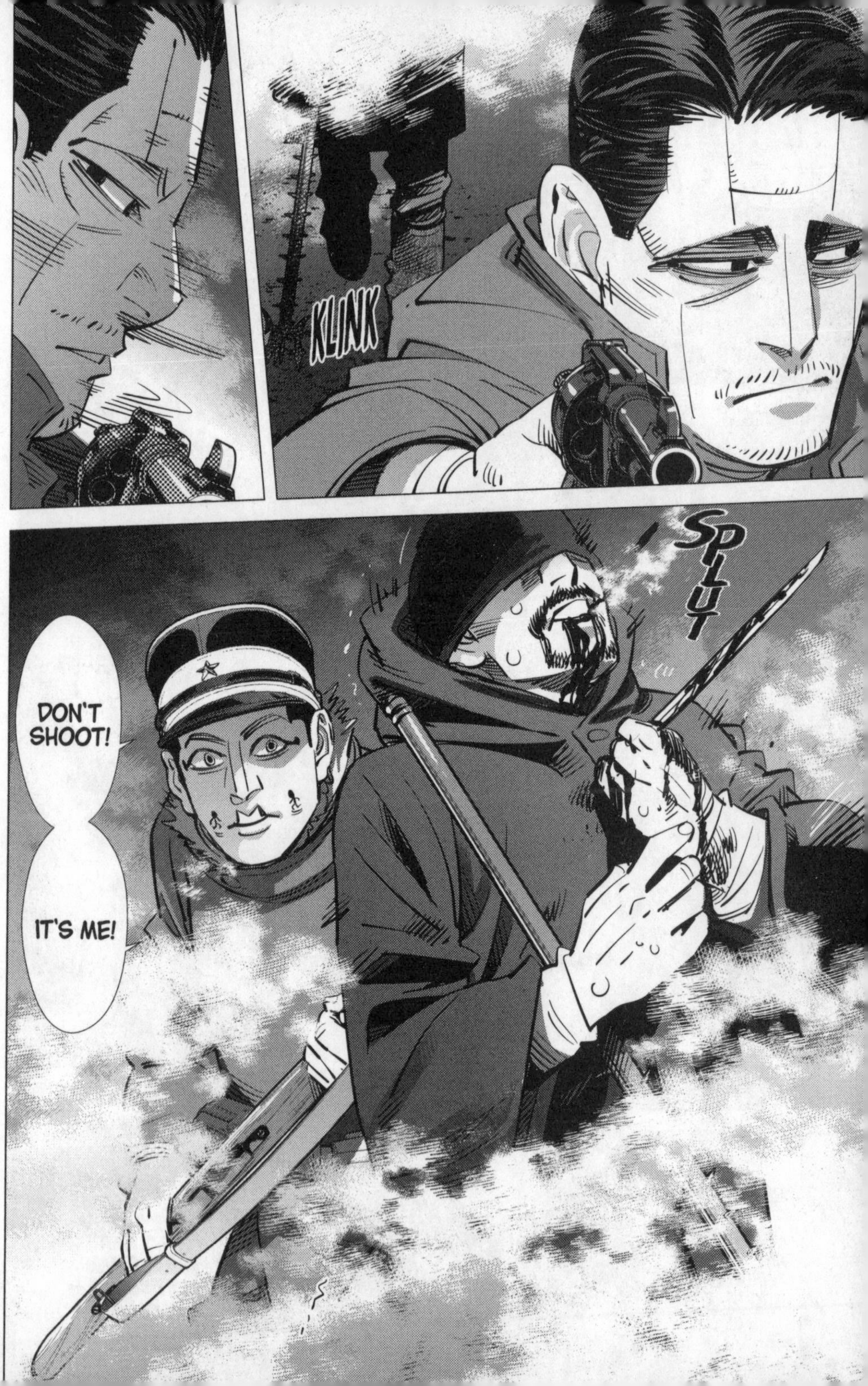
KLINK
SPLUT
DON'T SHOOT!
IT'S ME!

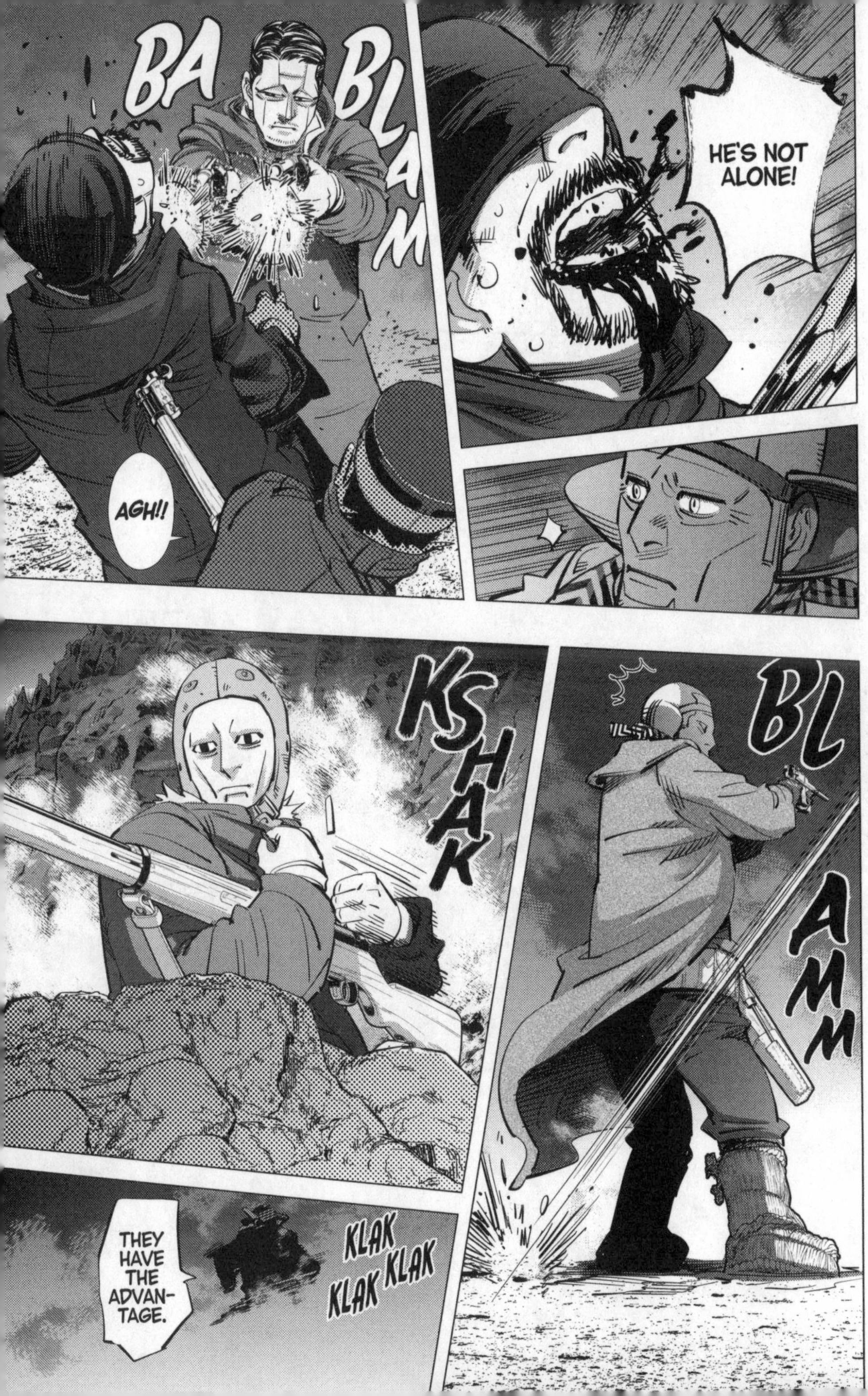
HE'S NOT ALONE!
BA BLAM M
AGH!!
BL AMM
KSHAK
THEY HAVE THE ADVAN-TAGE.
KLAK KLAK KLAK

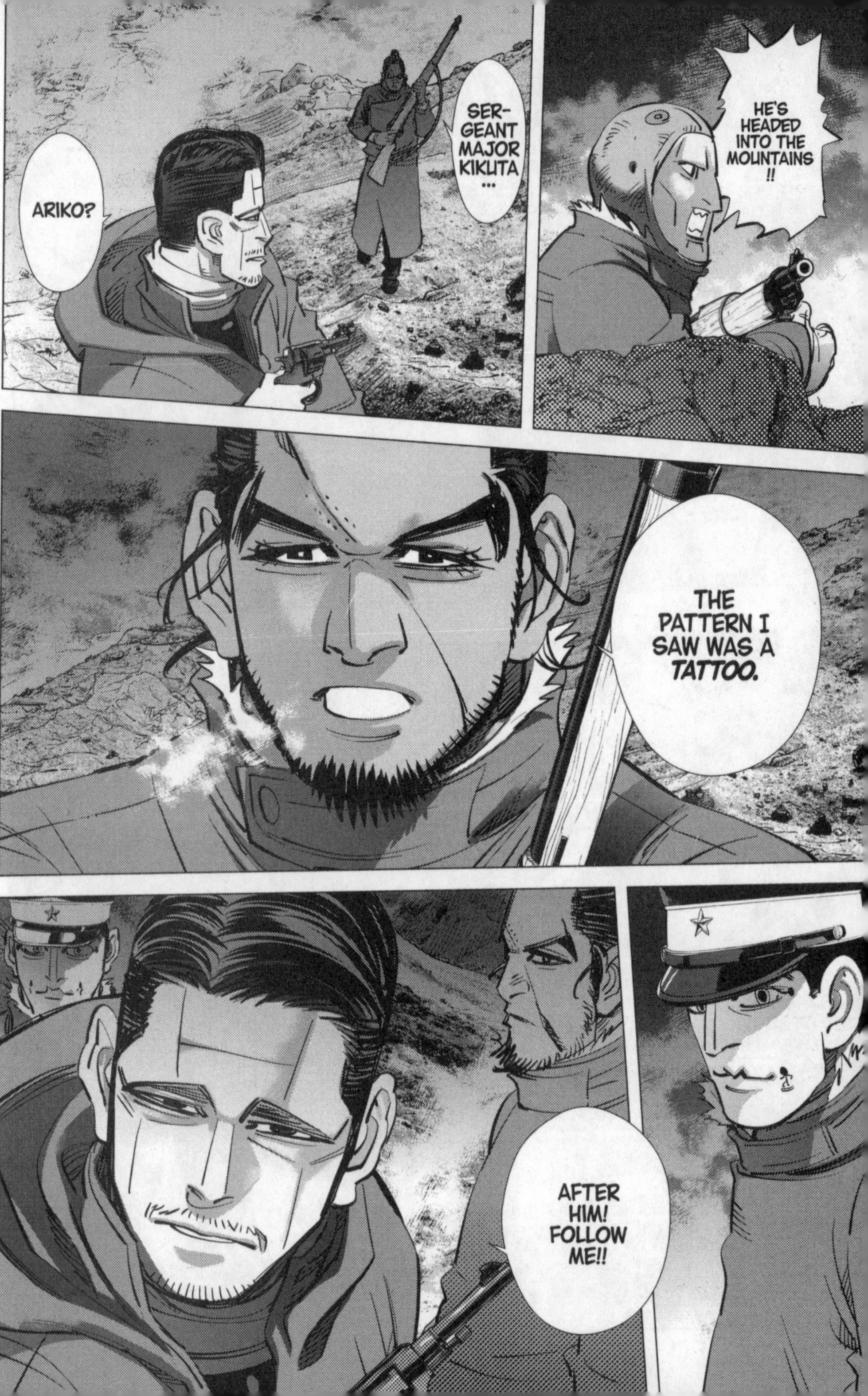
HE'S HEADED INTO THE MOUNTAINS !!
SER-GEANT MAJOR KIKUTA ...
ARIKO?
THE PATTERN I SAW WAS A *TATTOO.*
AFTER HIM! FOLLOW ME!!

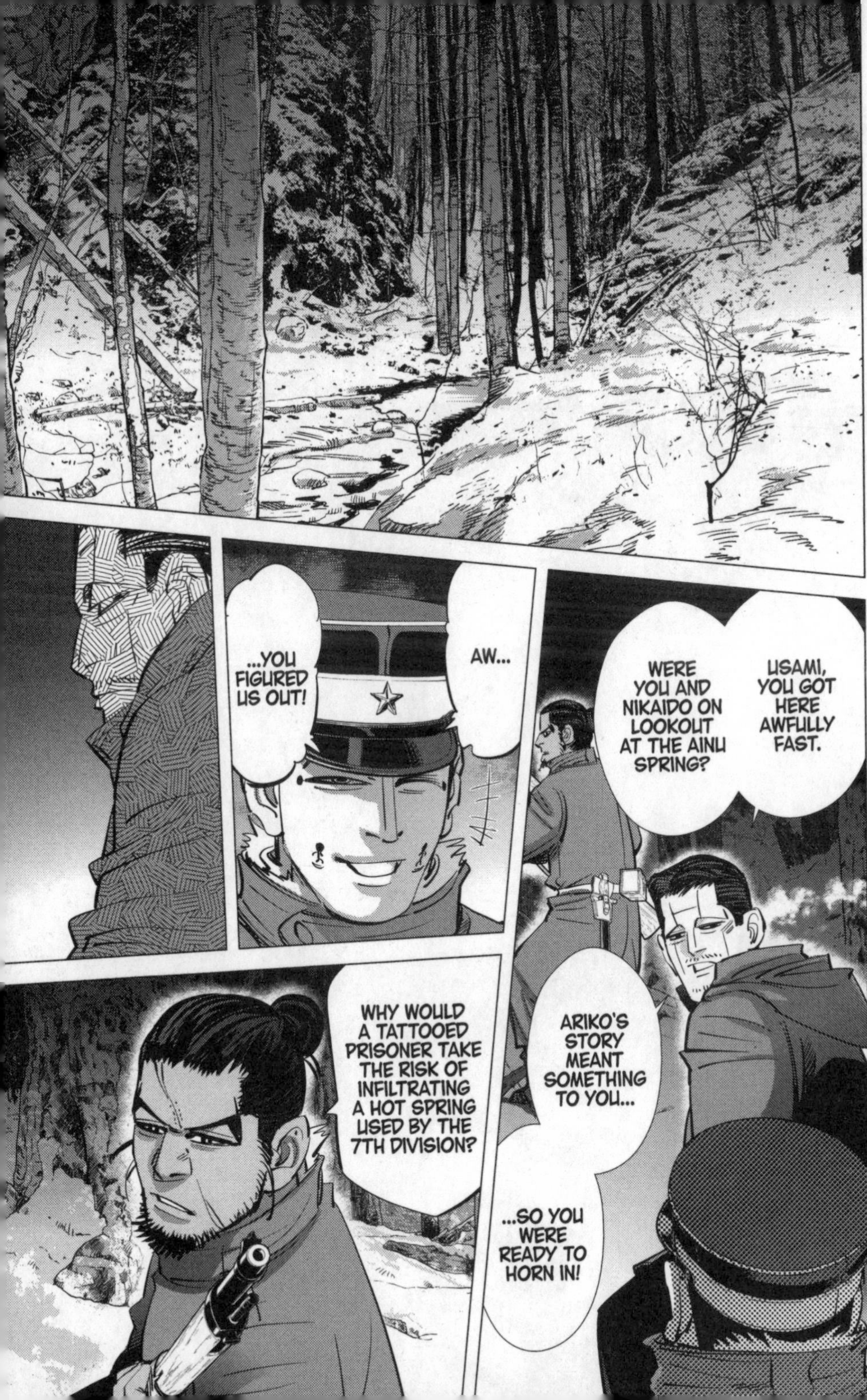
USAMI, YOU GOT HERE AWFULLY FAST.
WERE YOU AND NIKAIDO ON LOOKOUT AT THE AINU SPRING?
ARIKO'S STORY MEANT SOMETHING TO YOU...
...SO YOU WERE READY TO HORN IN!
AW...
...YOU FIGURED US OUT!
WHY WOULD A TATTOOED PRISONER TAKE THE RISK OF INFILTRATING A HOT SPRING USED BY THE 7TH DIVISION?

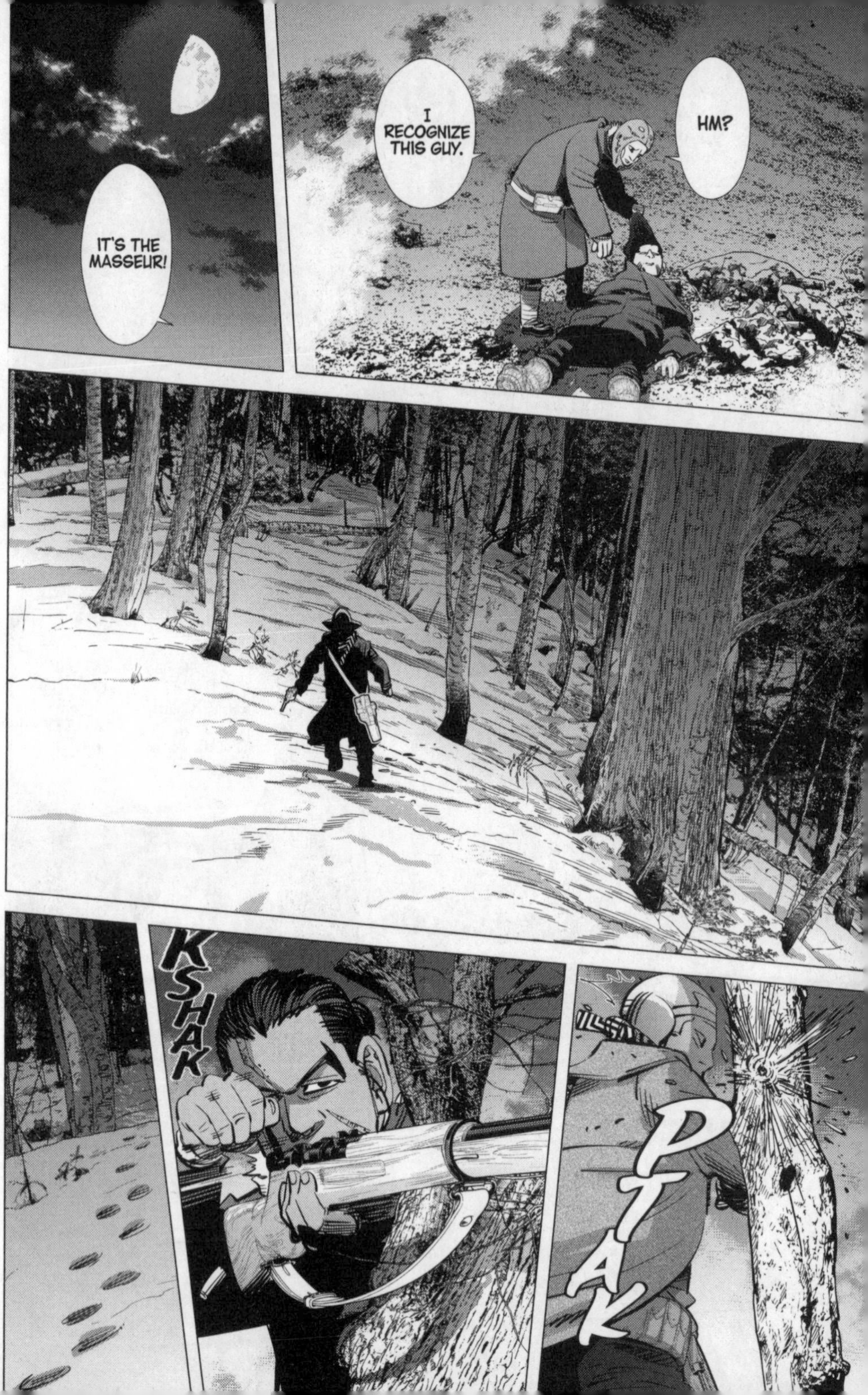
HM?
I RECOGNIZE THIS GUY.
IT'S THE MASSEUR!
PTAK
KSHAK

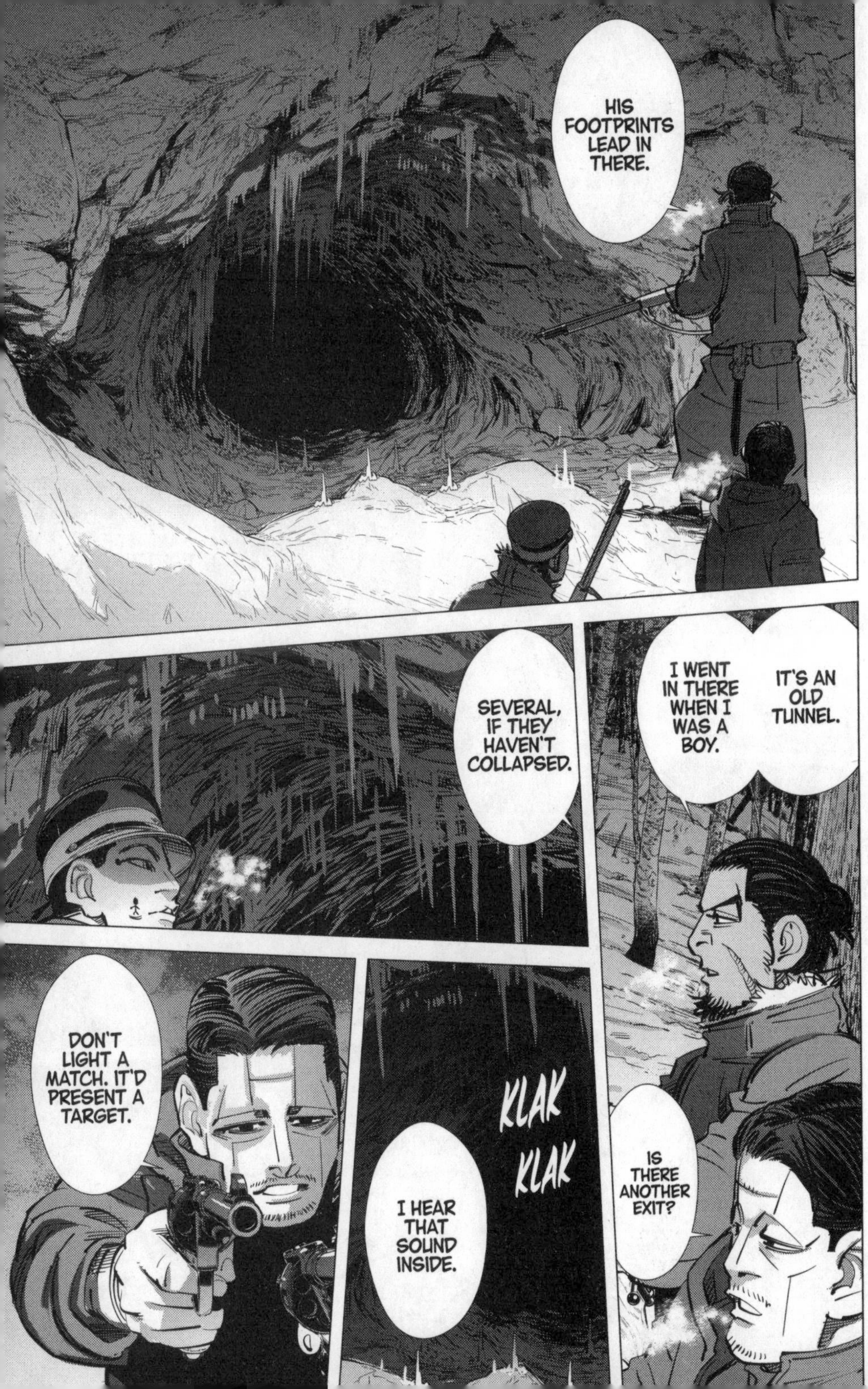
HIS FOOTPRINTS LEAD IN THERE.
IT'S AN OLD TUNNEL.
I WENT IN THERE WHEN I WAS A BOY.
IS THERE ANOTHER EXIT?
SEVERAL, IF THEY HAVEN'T COLLAPSED.
KLAK
KLAK
I HEAR THAT SOUND INSIDE.
DON'T LIGHT A MATCH. IT'D PRESENT A TARGET.

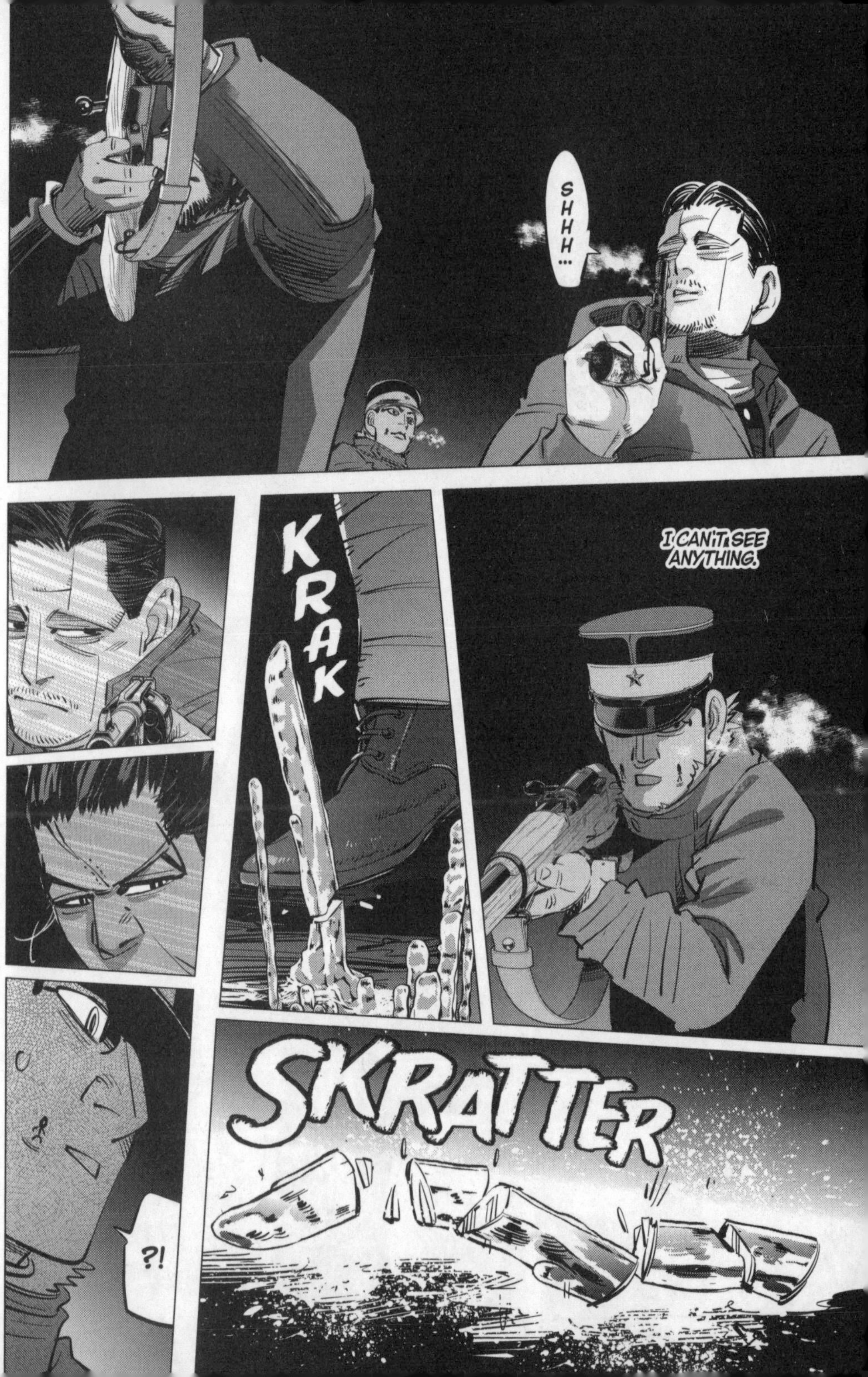
SHHH...
I CAN'T SEE ANYTHING.
KRAK
SKRATTER
?!

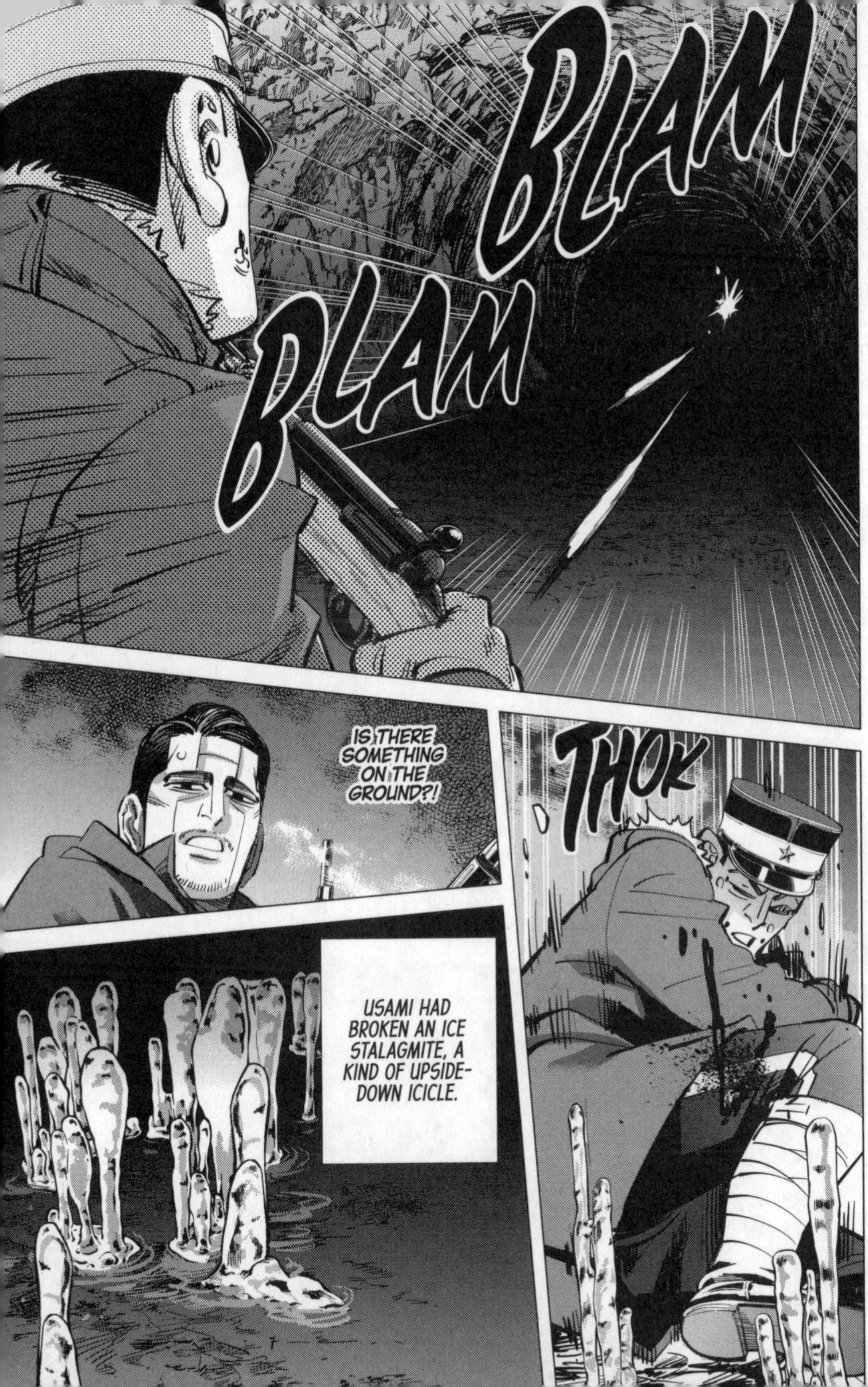
BLAM
BLAM
THOK
IS THERE SOMETHING ON THE GROUND?!
USAMI HAD BROKEN AN ICE STALAGMITE, A KIND OF UPSIDE-DOWN ICICLE.

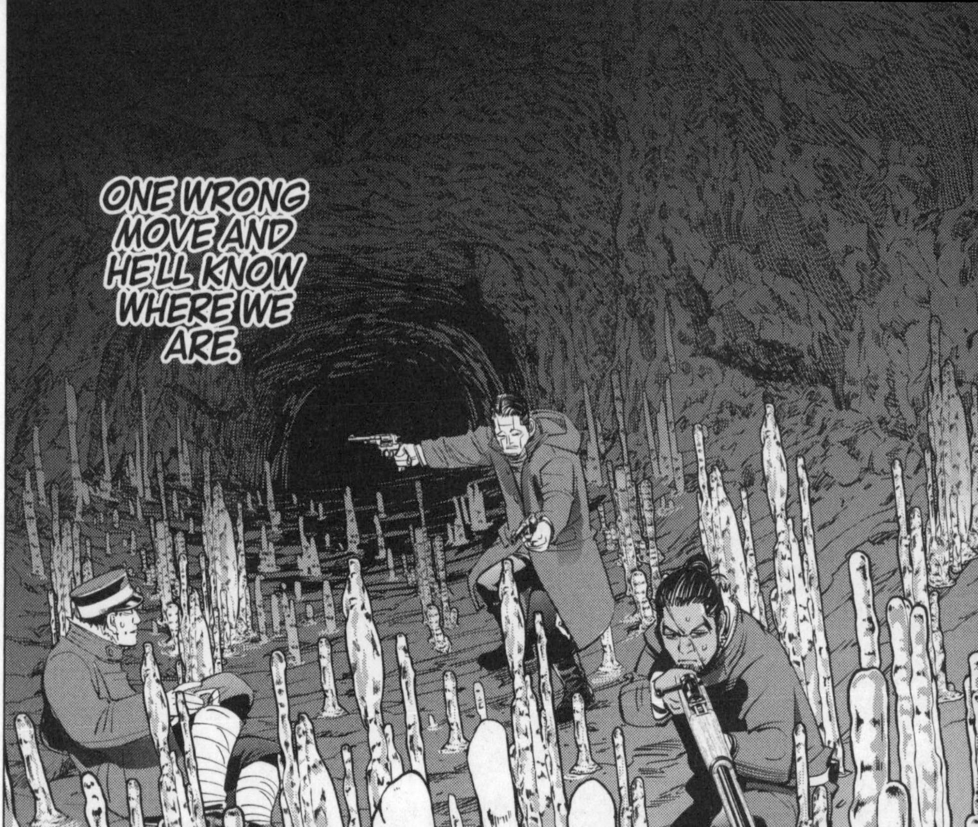
ONE WRONG MOVE AND HE'LL KNOW WHERE WE ARE.
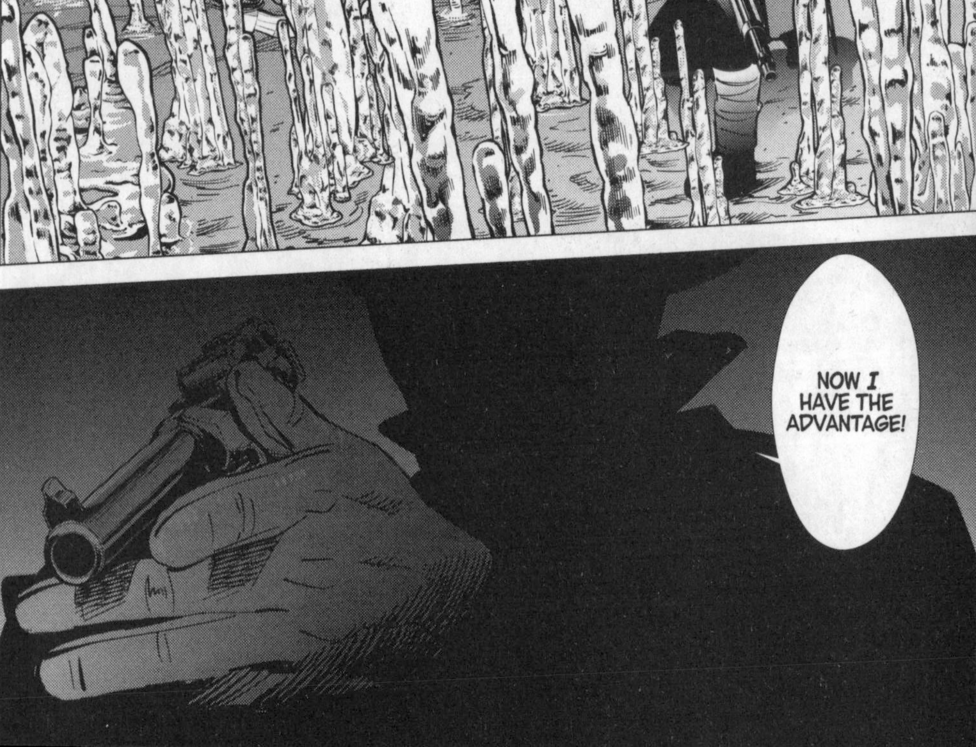
NOW I HAVE THE ADVANTAGE!

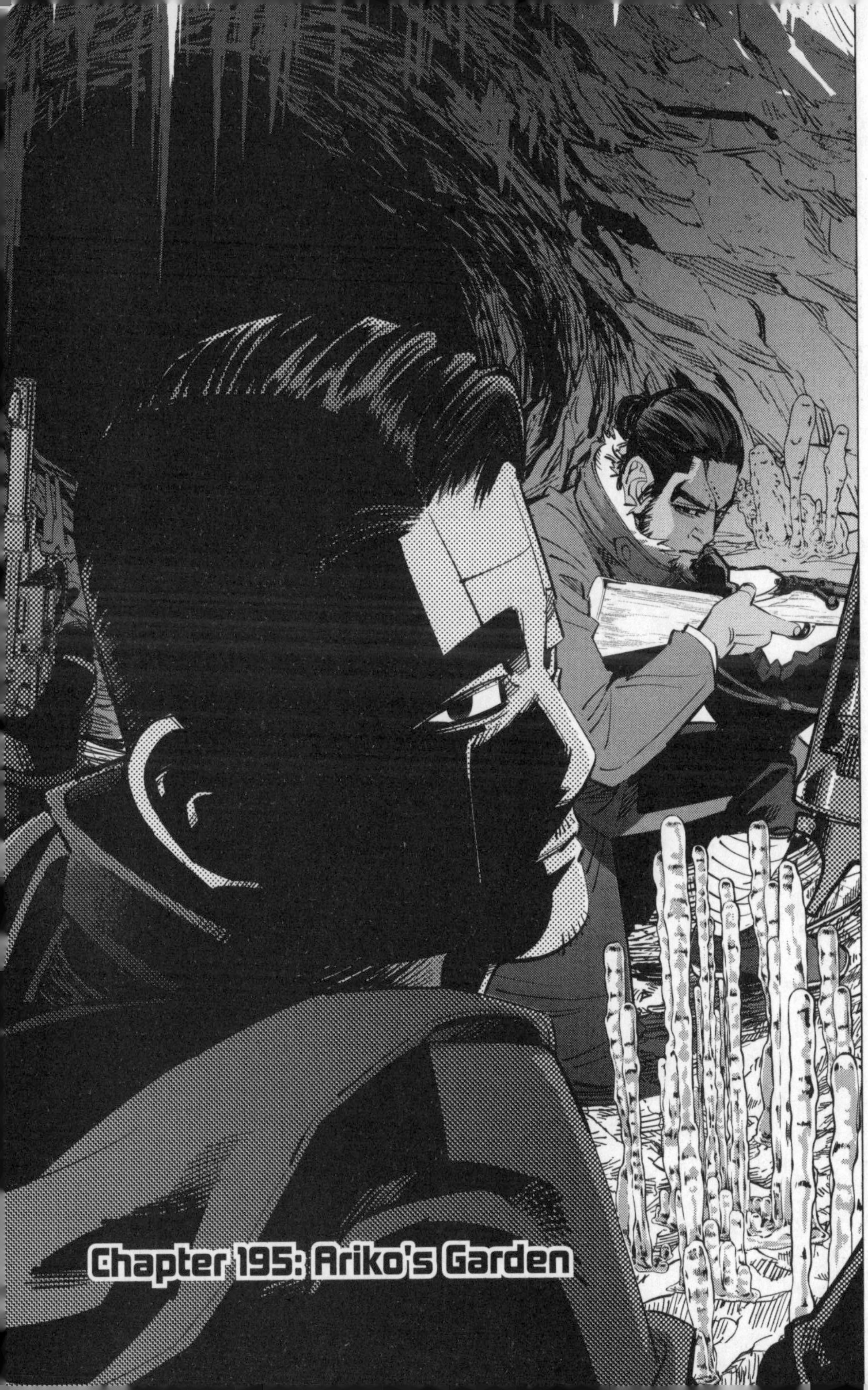
Chapter 195: Ariko's Garden

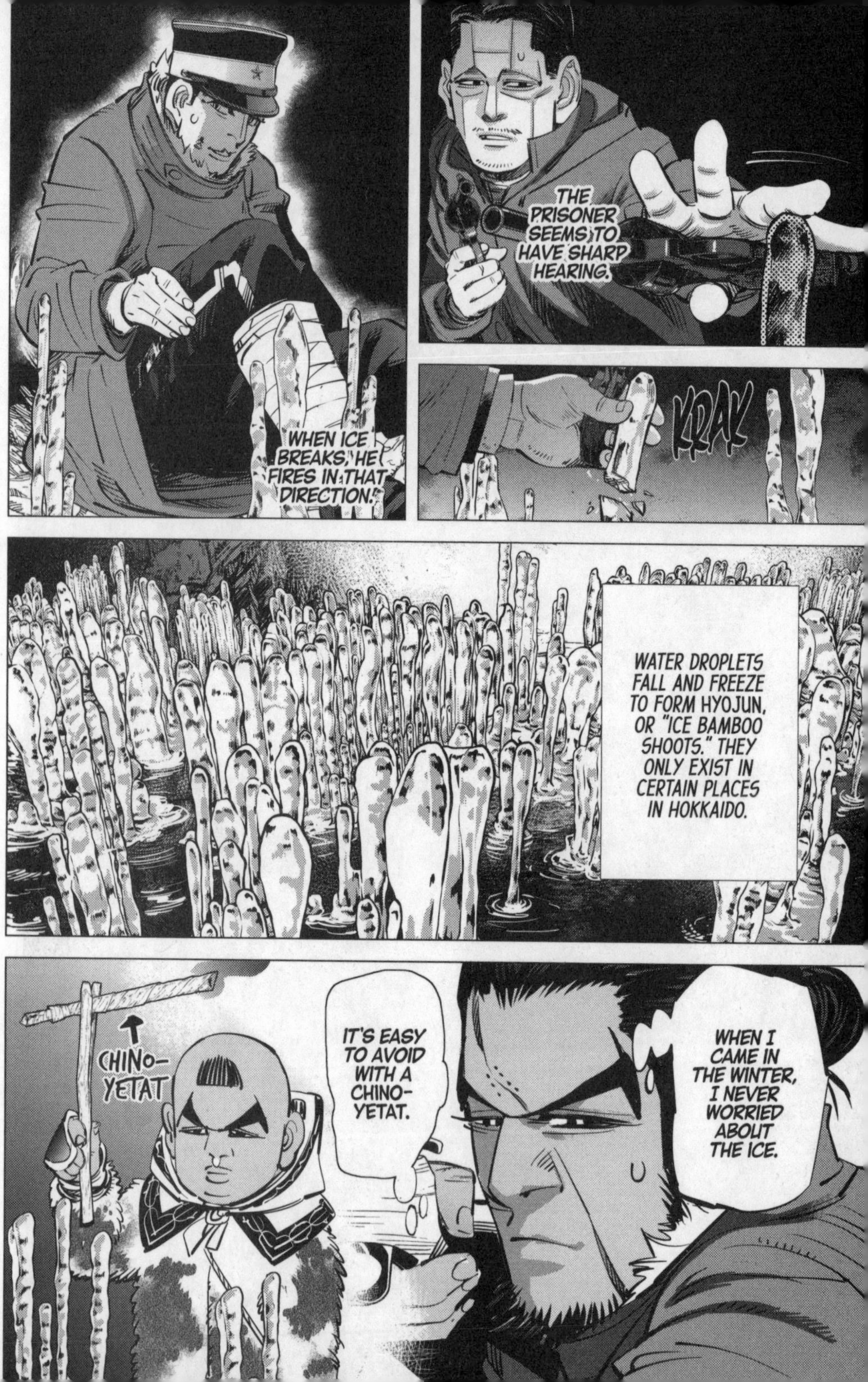
THE PRISONER SEEMS TO HAVE SHARP HEARING.
KRAK
WHEN ICE BREAKS, HE FIRES IN THAT DIRECTION!
WATER DROPLETS FALL AND FREEZE TO FORM HYOJUN, OR "ICE BAMBOO SHOOTS." THEY ONLY EXIST IN CERTAIN PLACES IN HOKKAIDO.
WHEN I CAME IN THE WINTER, I NEVER WORRIED ABOUT THE ICE.
IT'S EASY TO AVOID WITH A CHINO-YETAT.
CHINO-YETAT

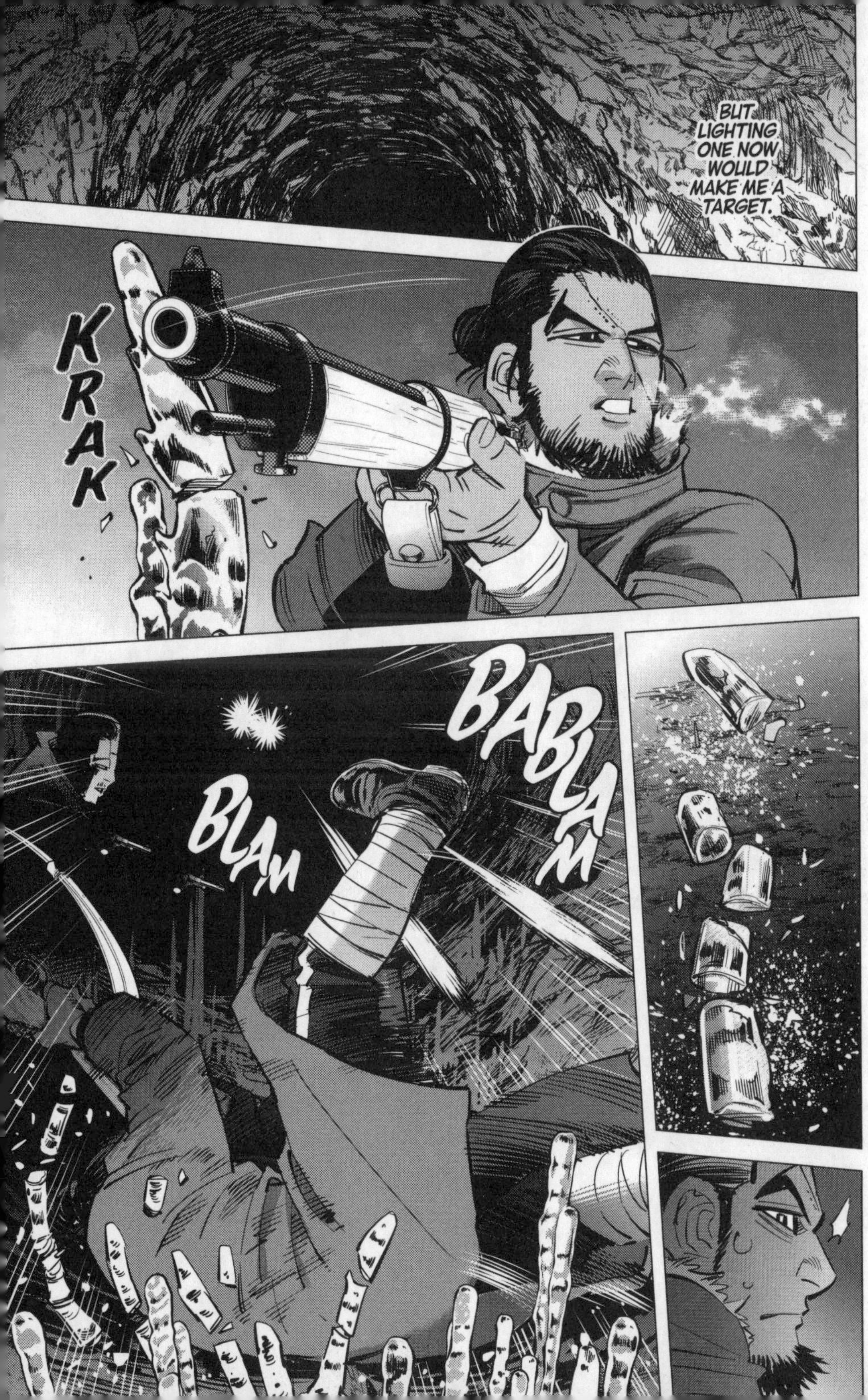
BUT LIGHTING ONE NOW WOULD MAKE ME A TARGET.
KRAK
BABLAM
BLAM

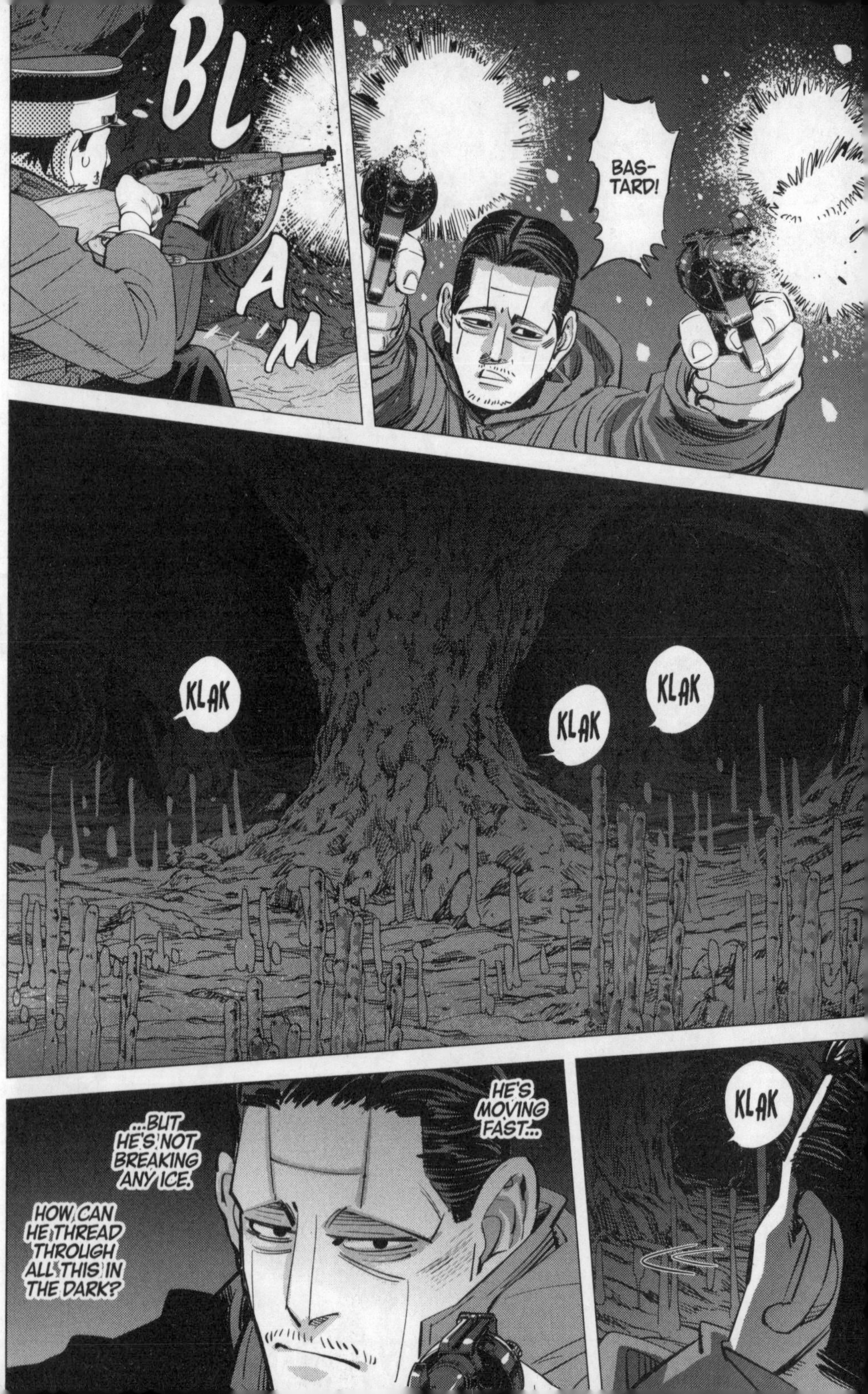
BAS-TARD!
BLAM
KLAK
KLAK
KLAK
KLAK
HE'S MOVING FAST...
...BUT HE'S NOT BREAKING ANY ICE.
HOW CAN HE THREAD THROUGH ALL THIS IN THE DARK?

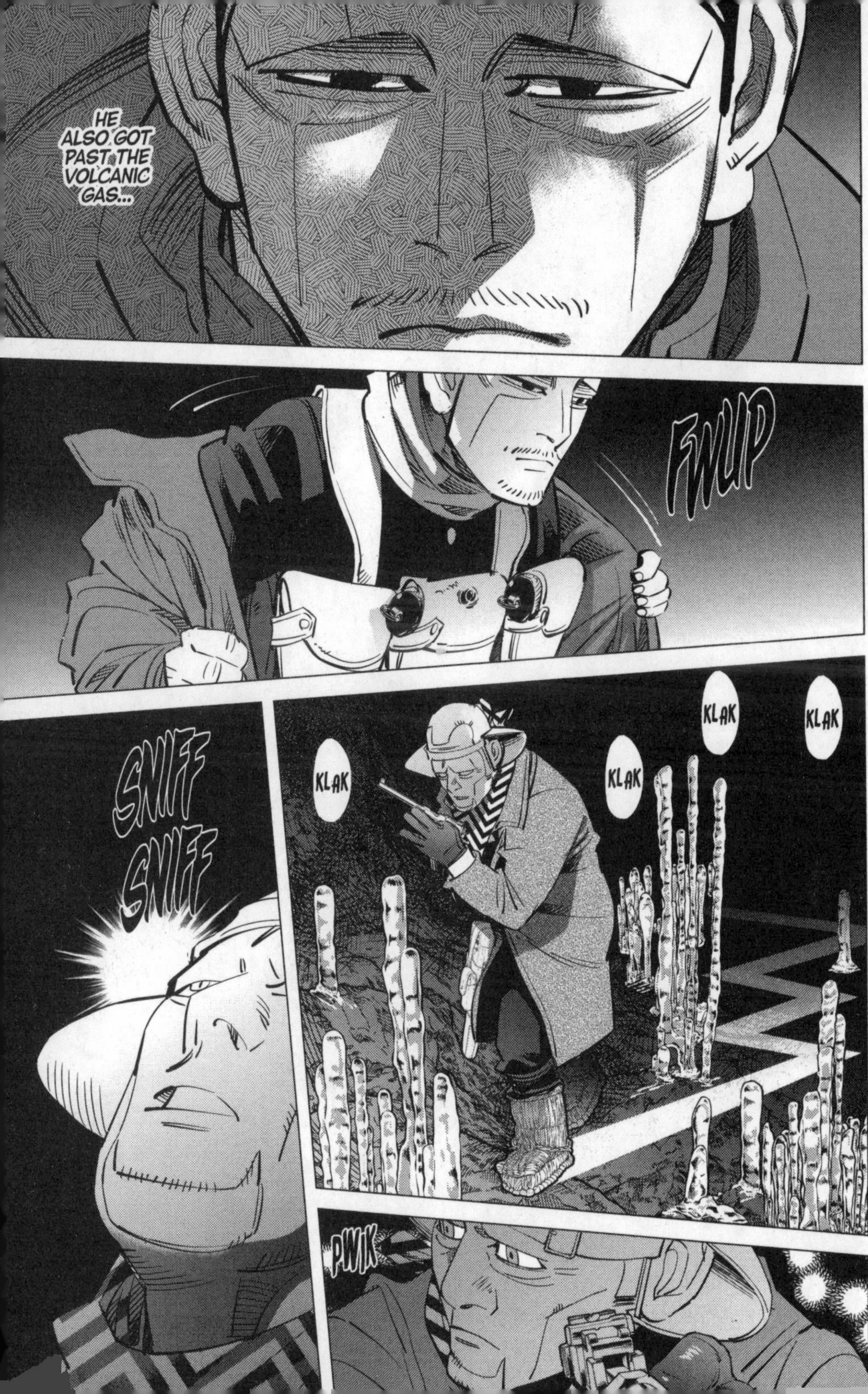
HE ALSO GOT PAST THE VOLCANIC GAS...
FWUP
KLAK
KLAK
KLAK
KLAK
PWIK
SNIFF SNIFF

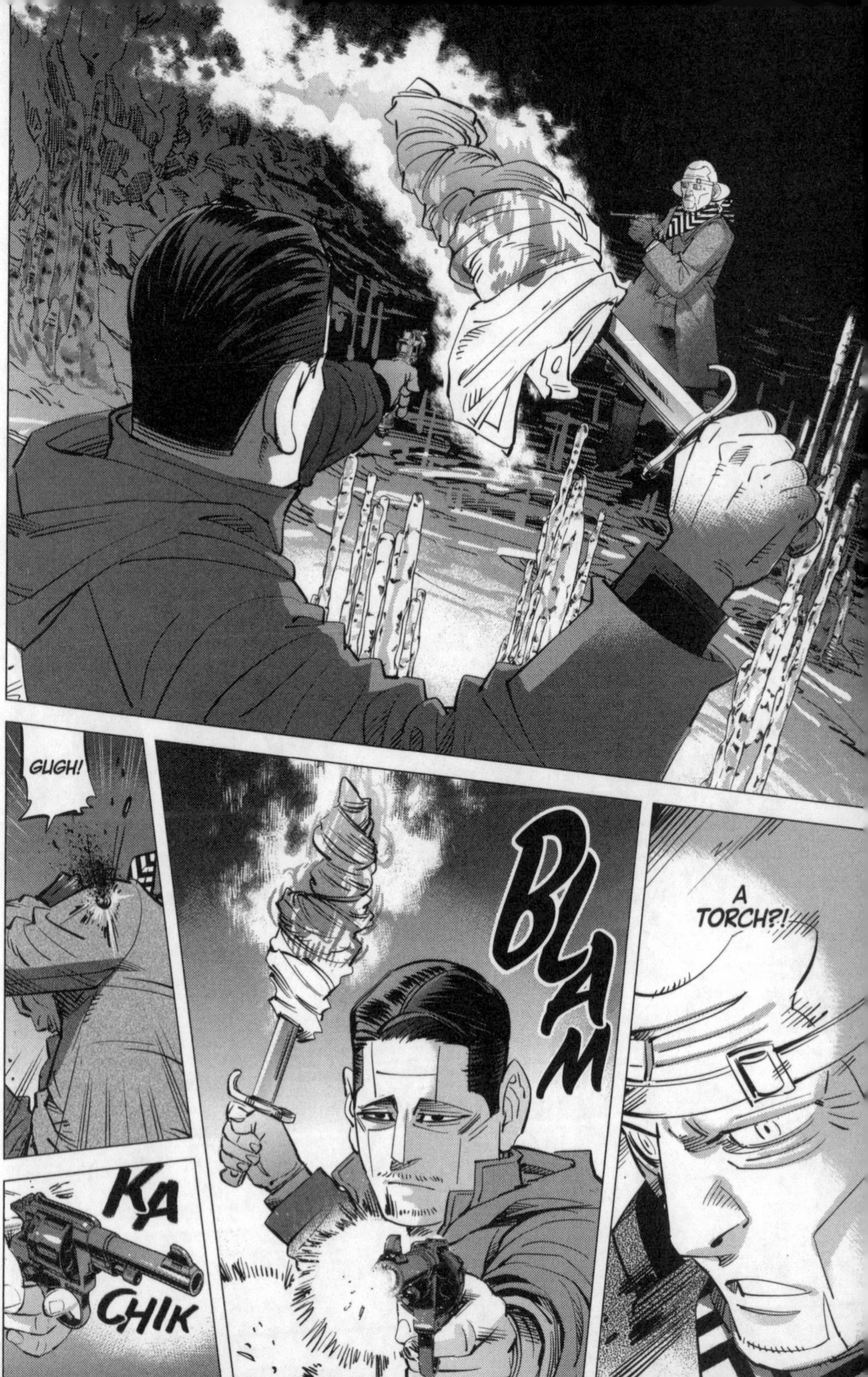
A TORCH?!
BLAM
GUGH!
KA CHIK

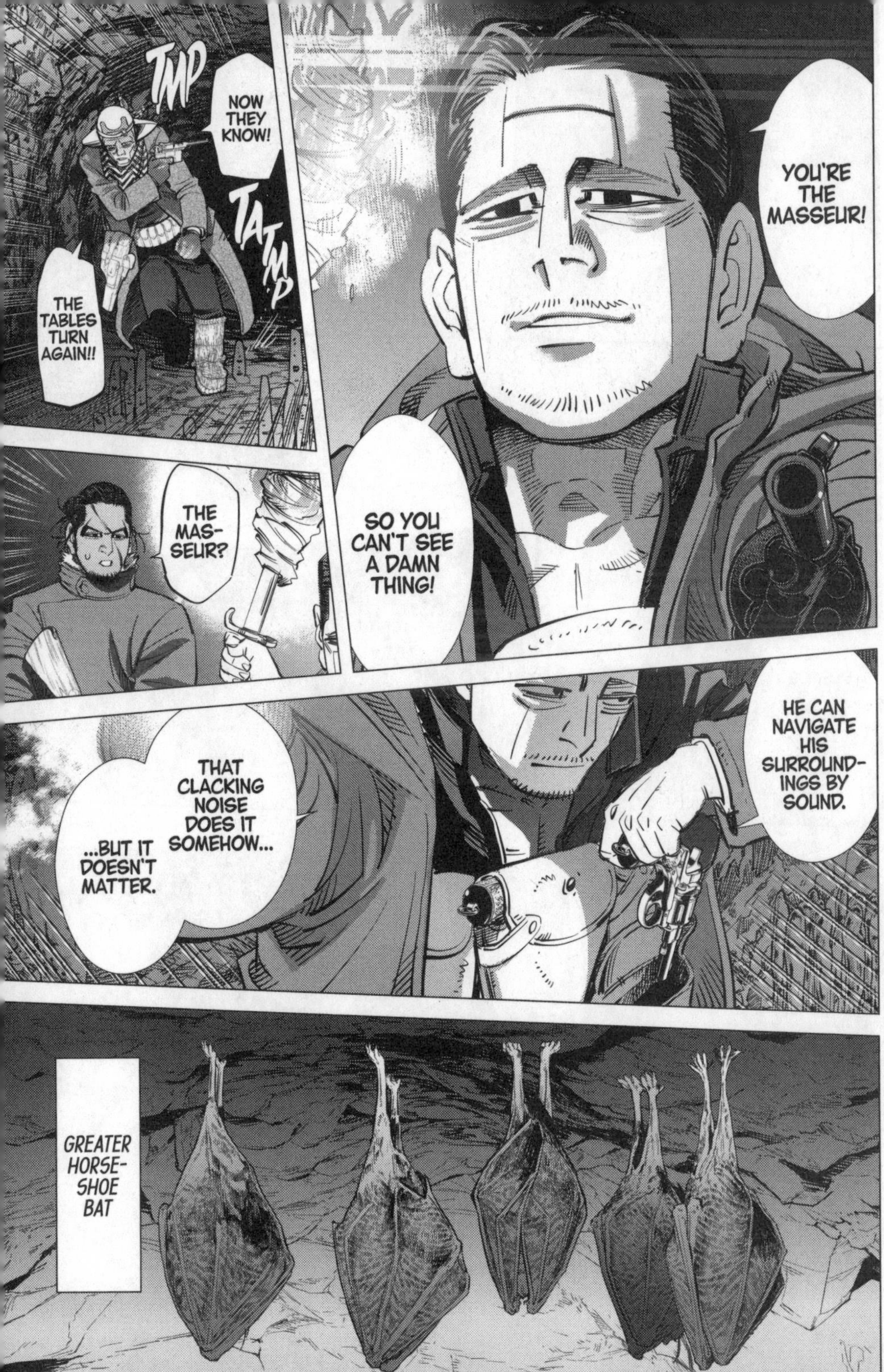
YOU'RE THE MASSEUR!
SO YOU CAN'T SEE A DAMN THING!
TMP
NOW THEY KNOW!
TATMP
THE TABLES TURN AGAIN!!
THE MAS-SEUR?
HE CAN NAVIGATE HIS SURROUND-INGS BY SOUND.
THAT CLACKING NOISE DOES IT SOMEHOW...
...BUT IT DOESN'T MATTER.
GREATER HORSE-SHOE BAT

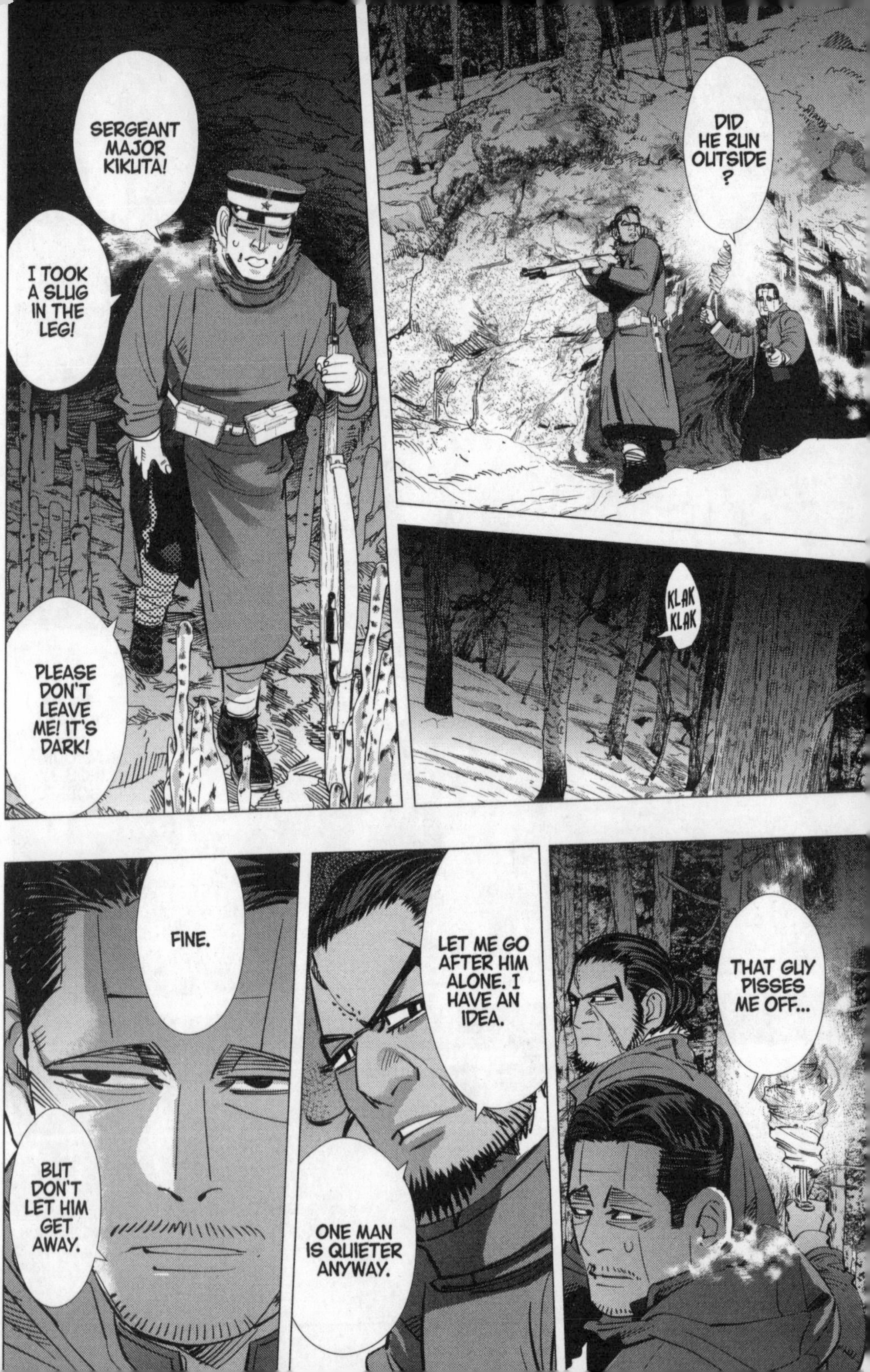
DID HE RUN OUTSIDE?
KLAK KLAK
SERGEANT MAJOR KIKUTA!
I TOOK A SLUG IN THE LEG!
PLEASE DON'T LEAVE ME! IT'S DARK!
THAT GUY PISSES ME OFF...
LET ME GO AFTER HIM ALONE. I HAVE AN IDEA.
ONE MAN IS QUIETER ANYWAY.
FINE.
BUT DON'T LET HIM GET AWAY.

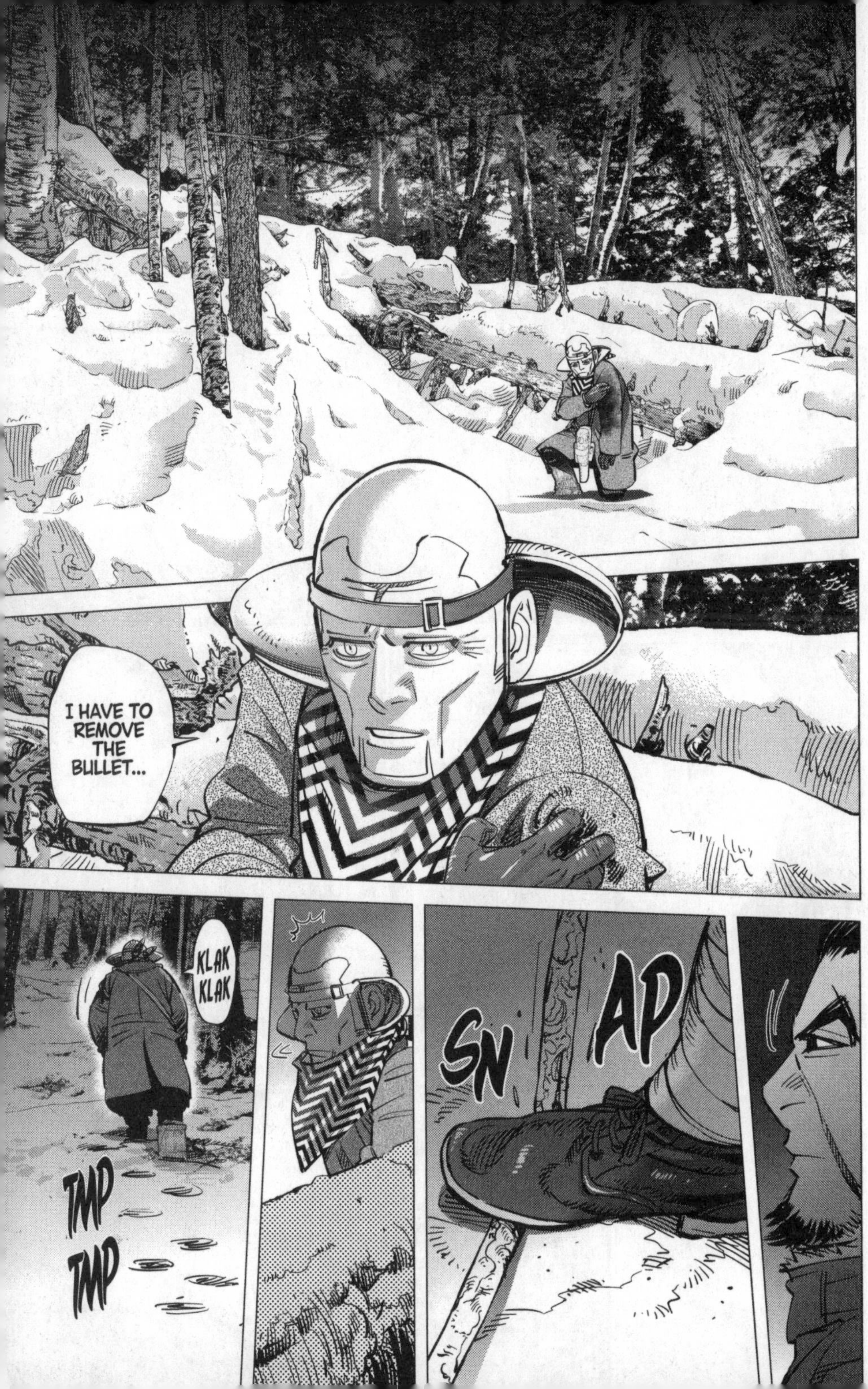
I HAVE TO REMOVE THE BULLET...
SNAP
KLAK KLAK
TMP TMP

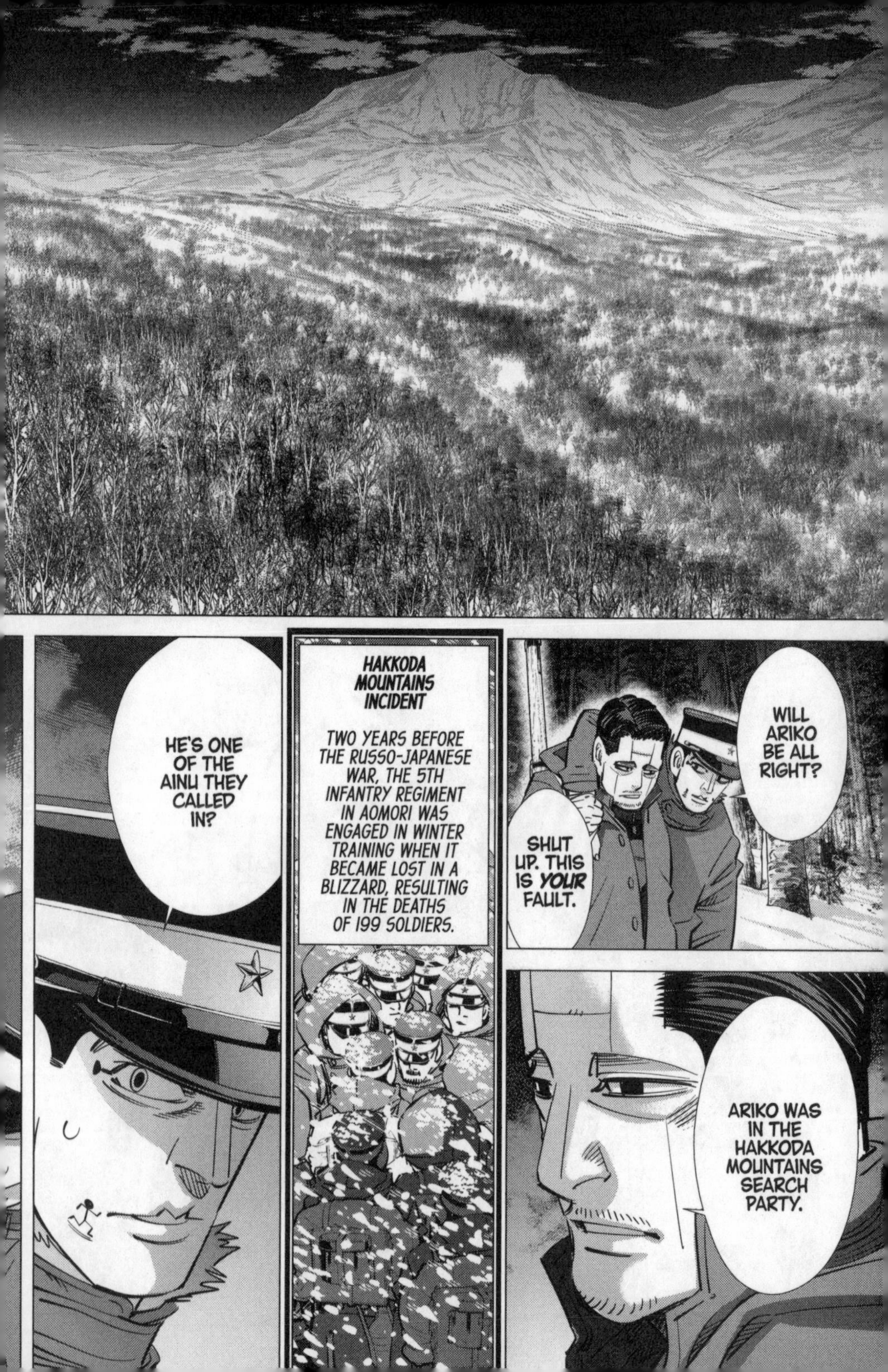
WILL ARIKO BE ALL RIGHT?
SHUT UP. THIS IS *YOUR* FAULT.
ARIKO WAS IN THE HAKKODA MOUNTAINS SEARCH PARTY.
HAKKODA MOUNTAINS INCIDENT
TWO YEARS BEFORE THE RUSSO-JAPANESE WAR, THE 5TH INFANTRY REGIMENT IN AOMORI WAS ENGAGED IN WINTER TRAINING WHEN IT BECAME LOST IN A BLIZZARD, RESULTING IN THE DEATHS OF 199 SOLDIERS.
HE'S ONE OF THE AINU THEY CALLED IN?

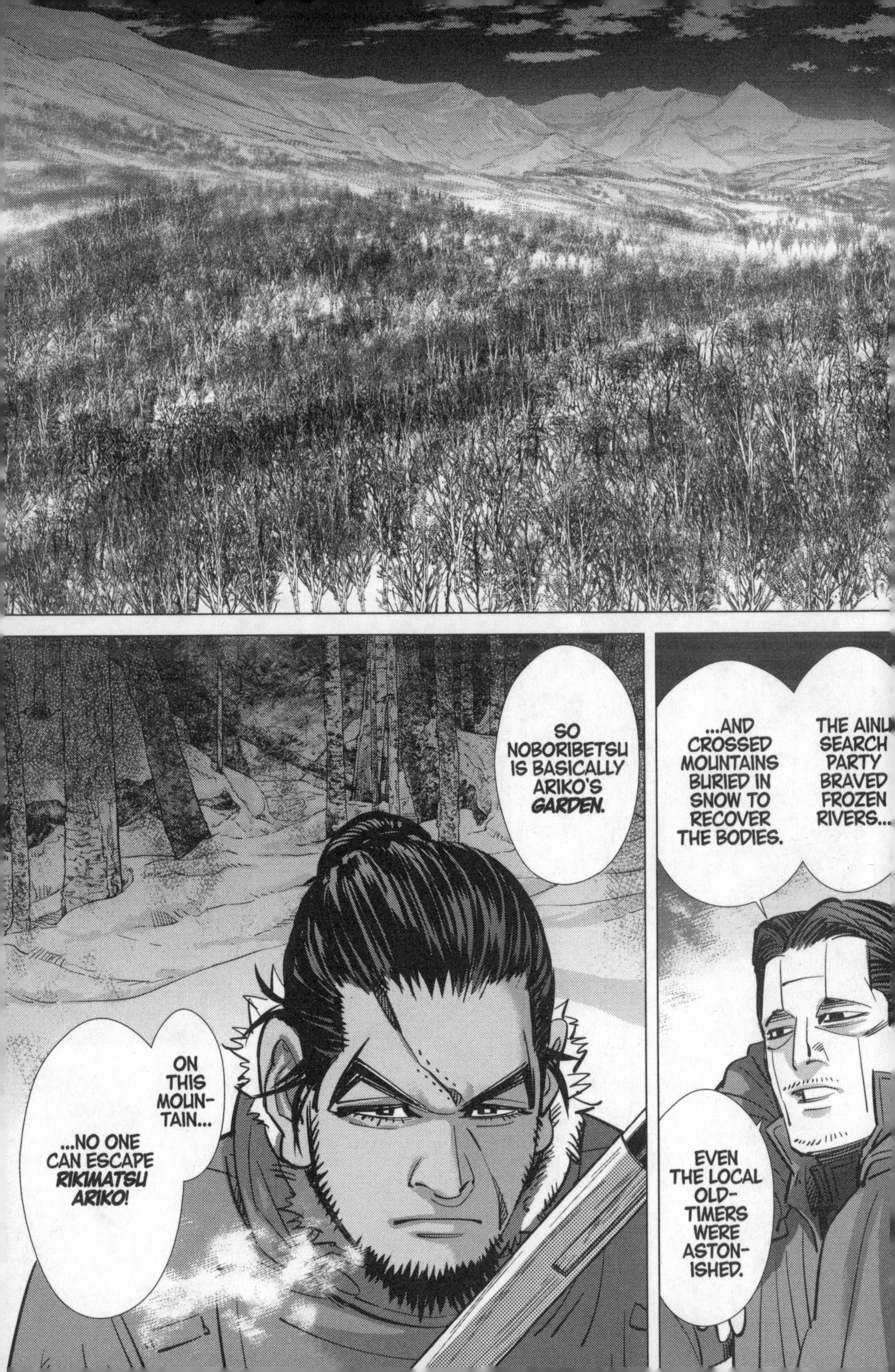
THE AINU SEARCH PARTY BRAVED FROZEN RIVERS...
...AND CROSSED MOUNTAINS BURIED IN SNOW TO RECOVER THE BODIES.
EVEN THE LOCAL OLD-TIMERS WERE ASTON-ISHED.
SO NOBORIBETSU IS BASICALLY ARIKO'S **GARDEN.**
ON THIS MOUN-TAIN...
...NO ONE CAN ESCAPE **RIKIMATSU ARIKO!**

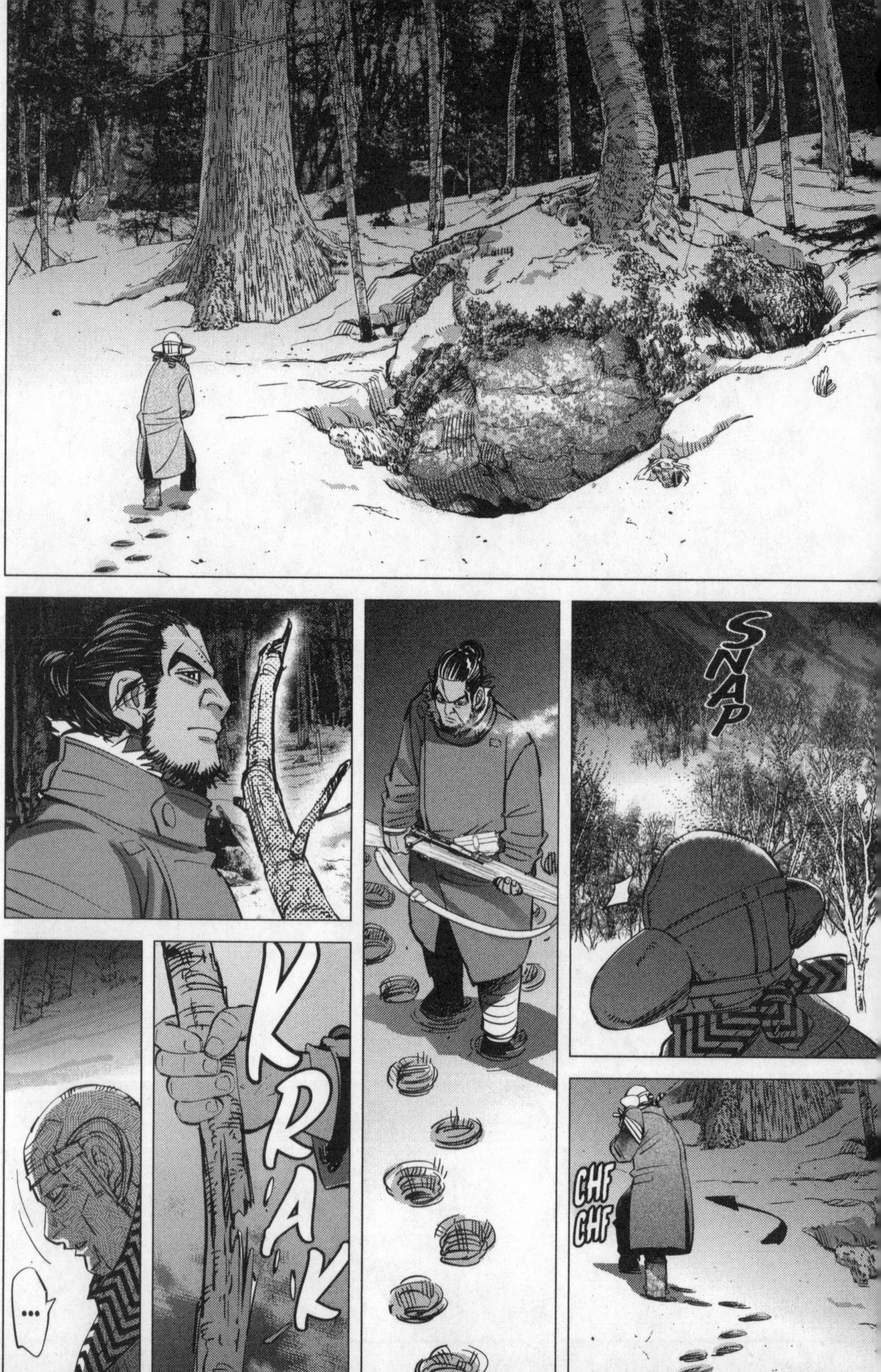
SNAP
CHF CHF
KRAK
...

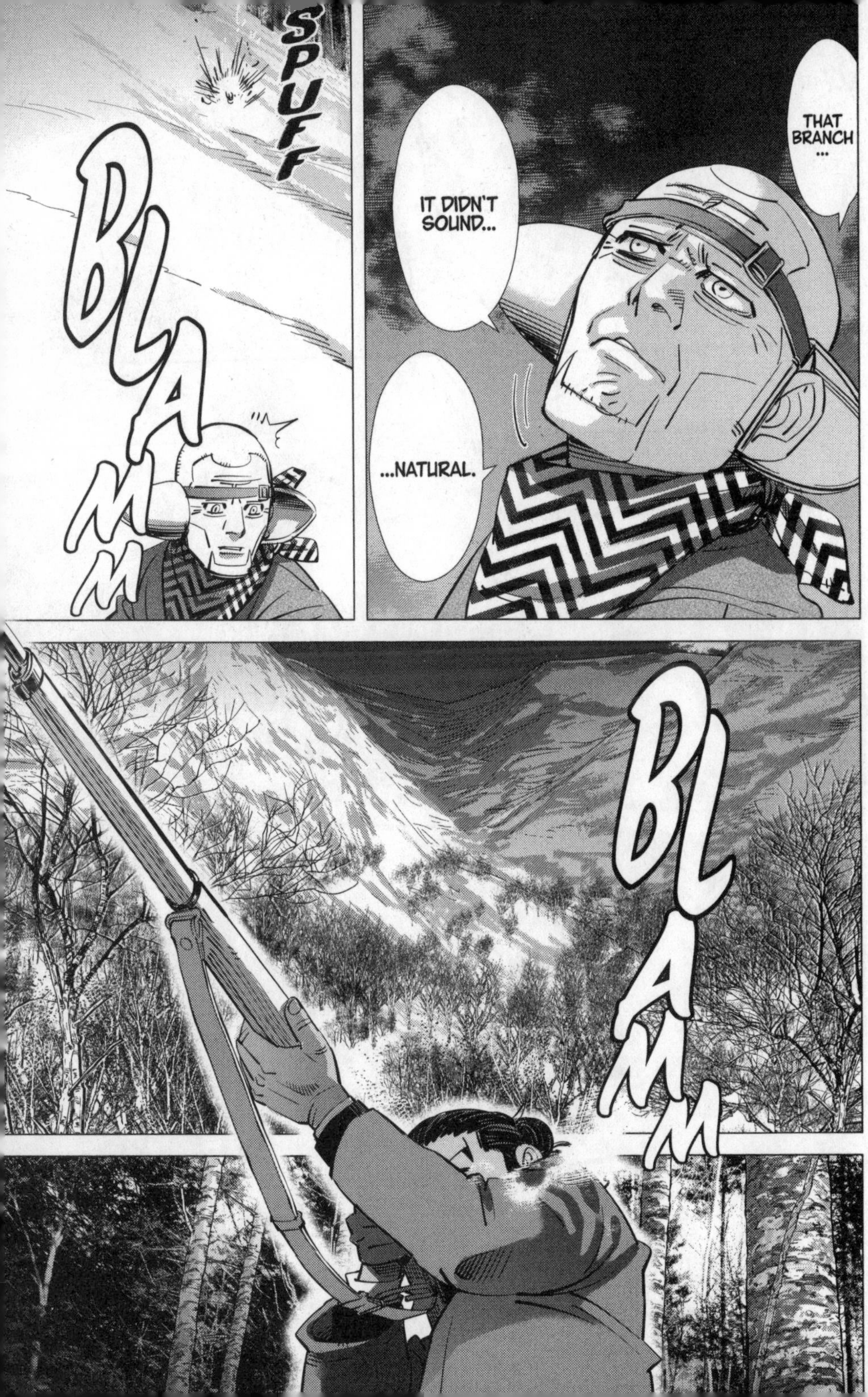
THAT BRANCH...
IT DIDN'T SOUND...
...NATURAL.
SPUFF
BLAMM
BLAMM

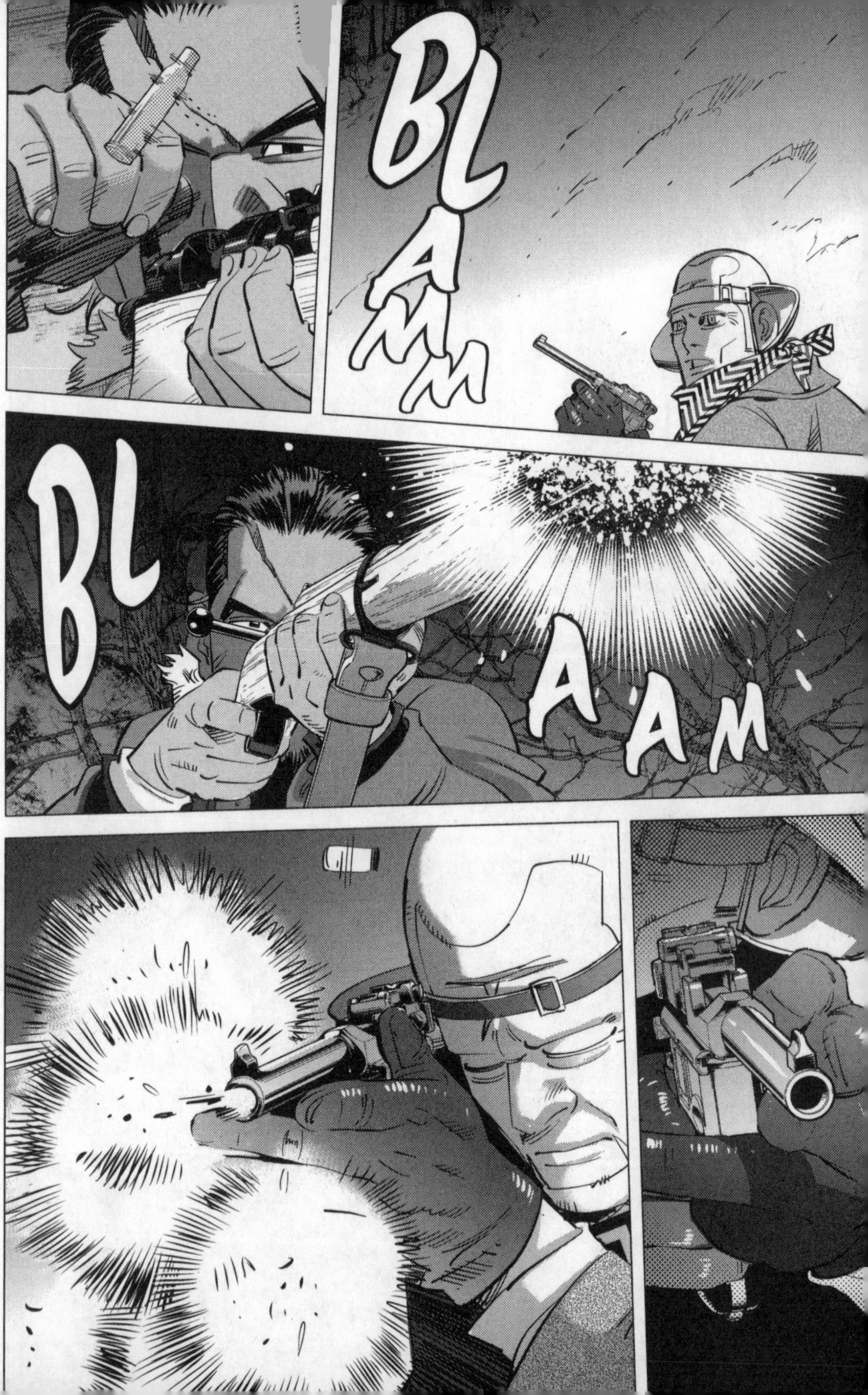
BLAMM
BLAAAM

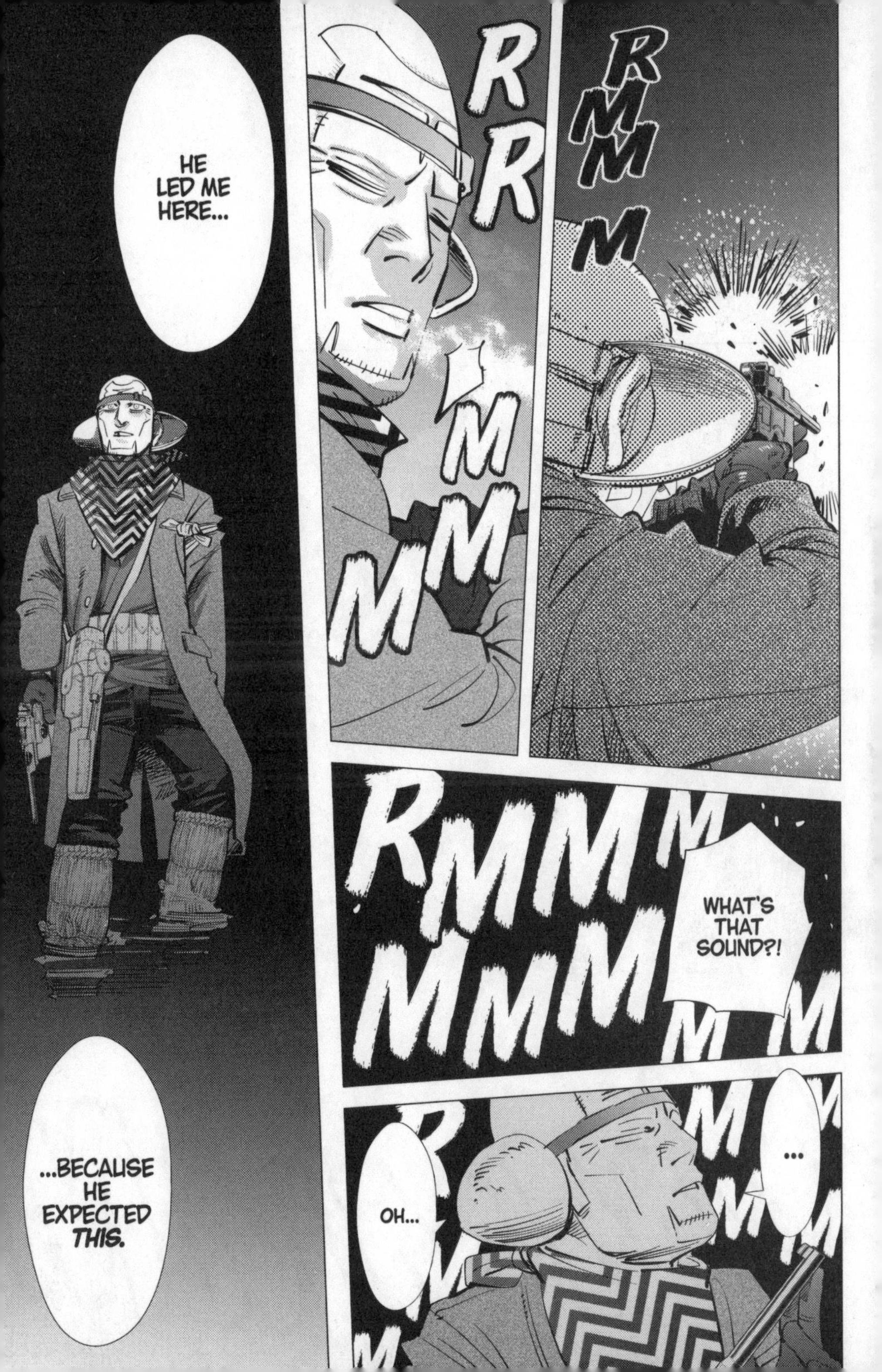
RMMM
RRMMMM
RMMMMMMMMM
WHAT'S THAT SOUND?!
...
OH...
HE LED ME HERE...
...BECAUSE HE EXPECTED THIS.

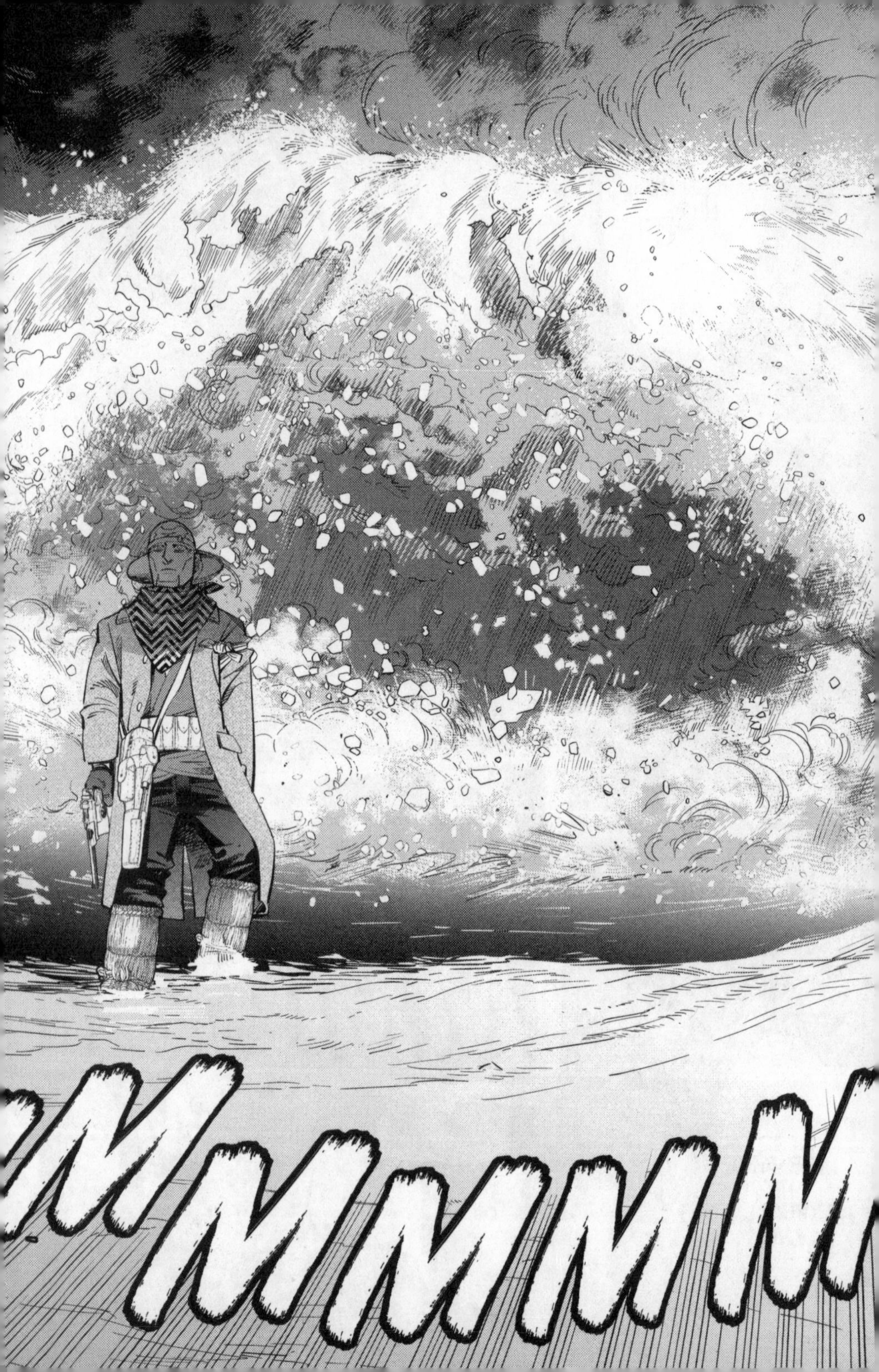
MMMMMM

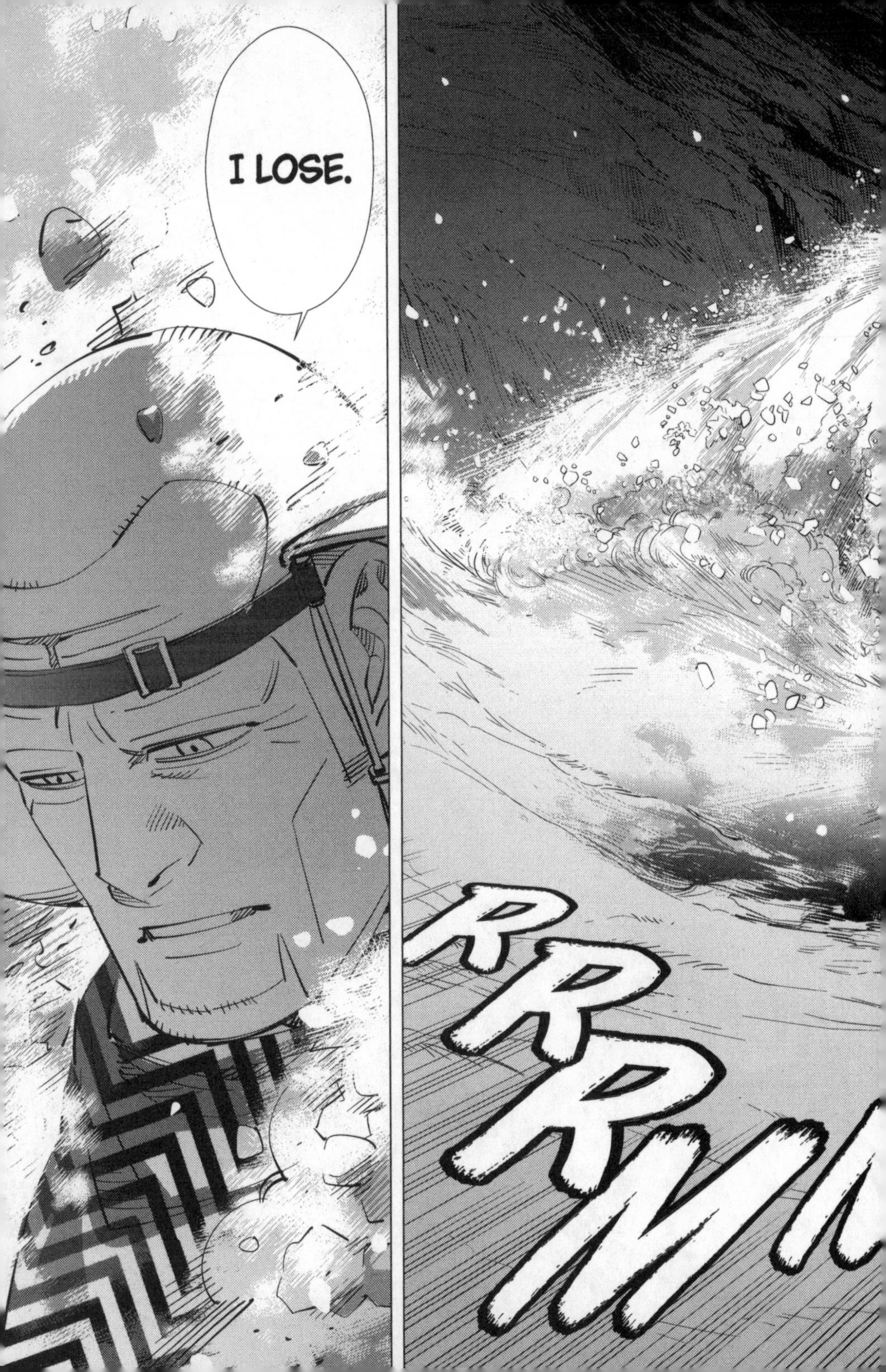
RRRM
I LOSE.

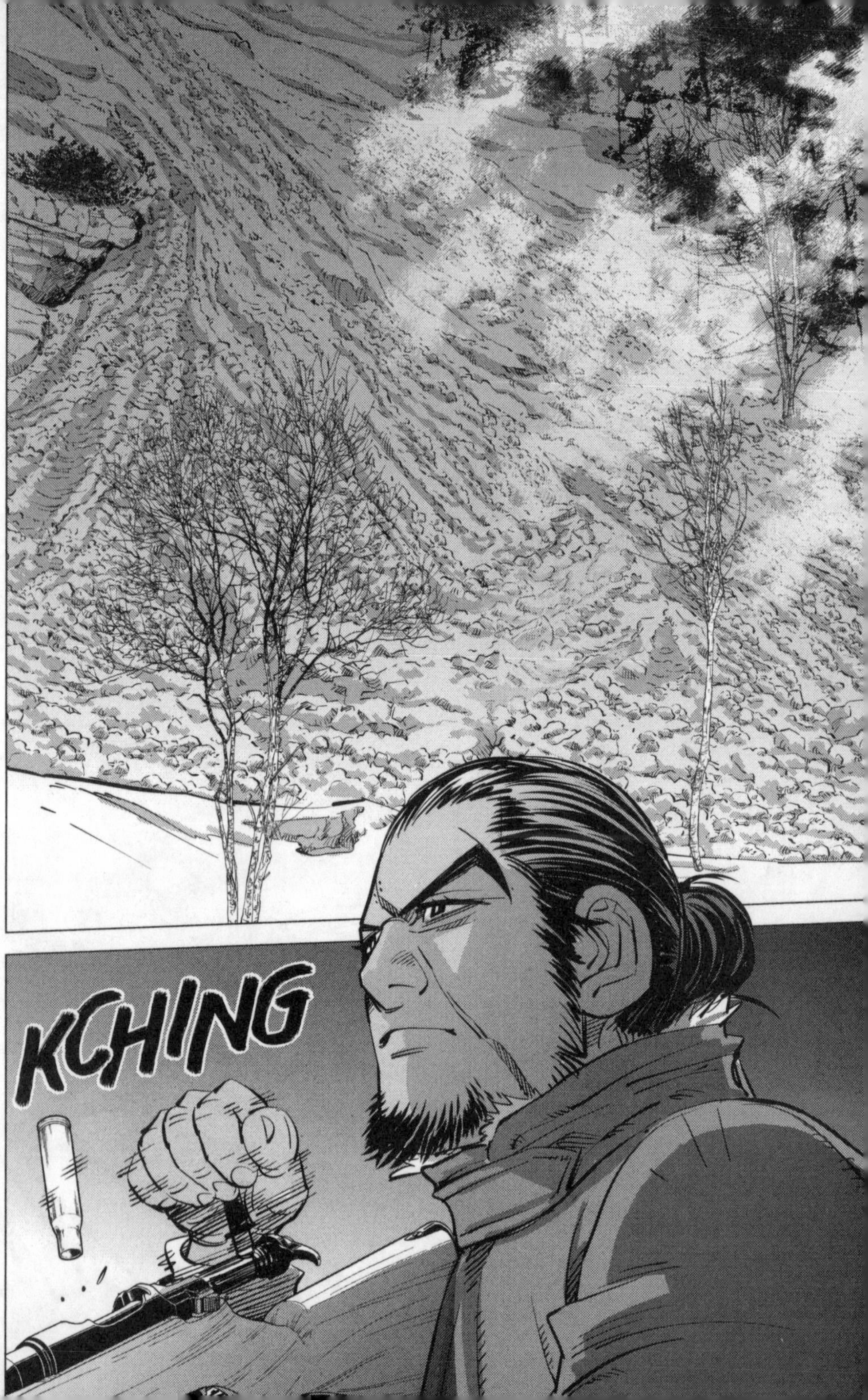
KCHING

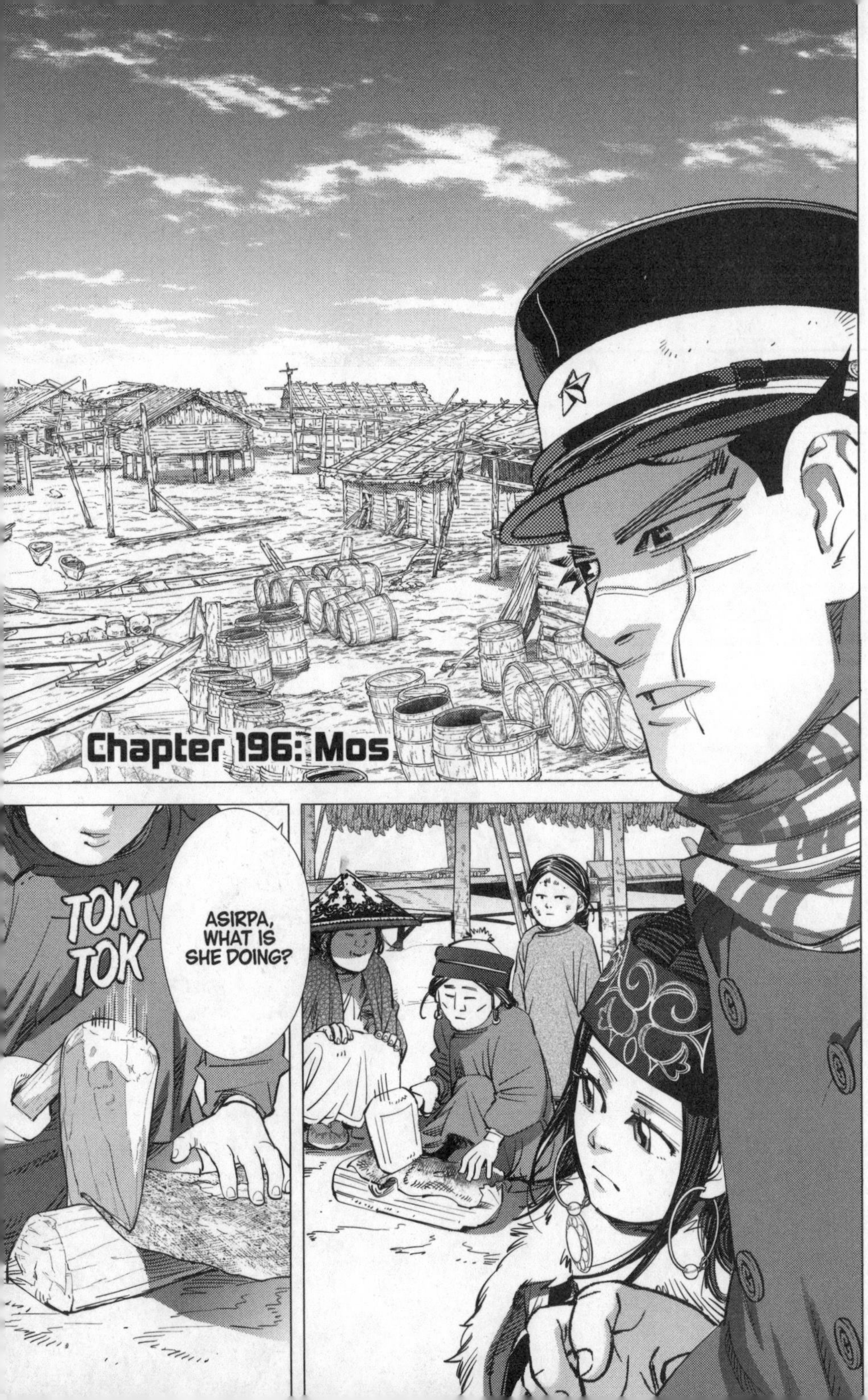
Chapter 196: Mos
ASIRPA, WHAT IS SHE DOING?
TOK TOK

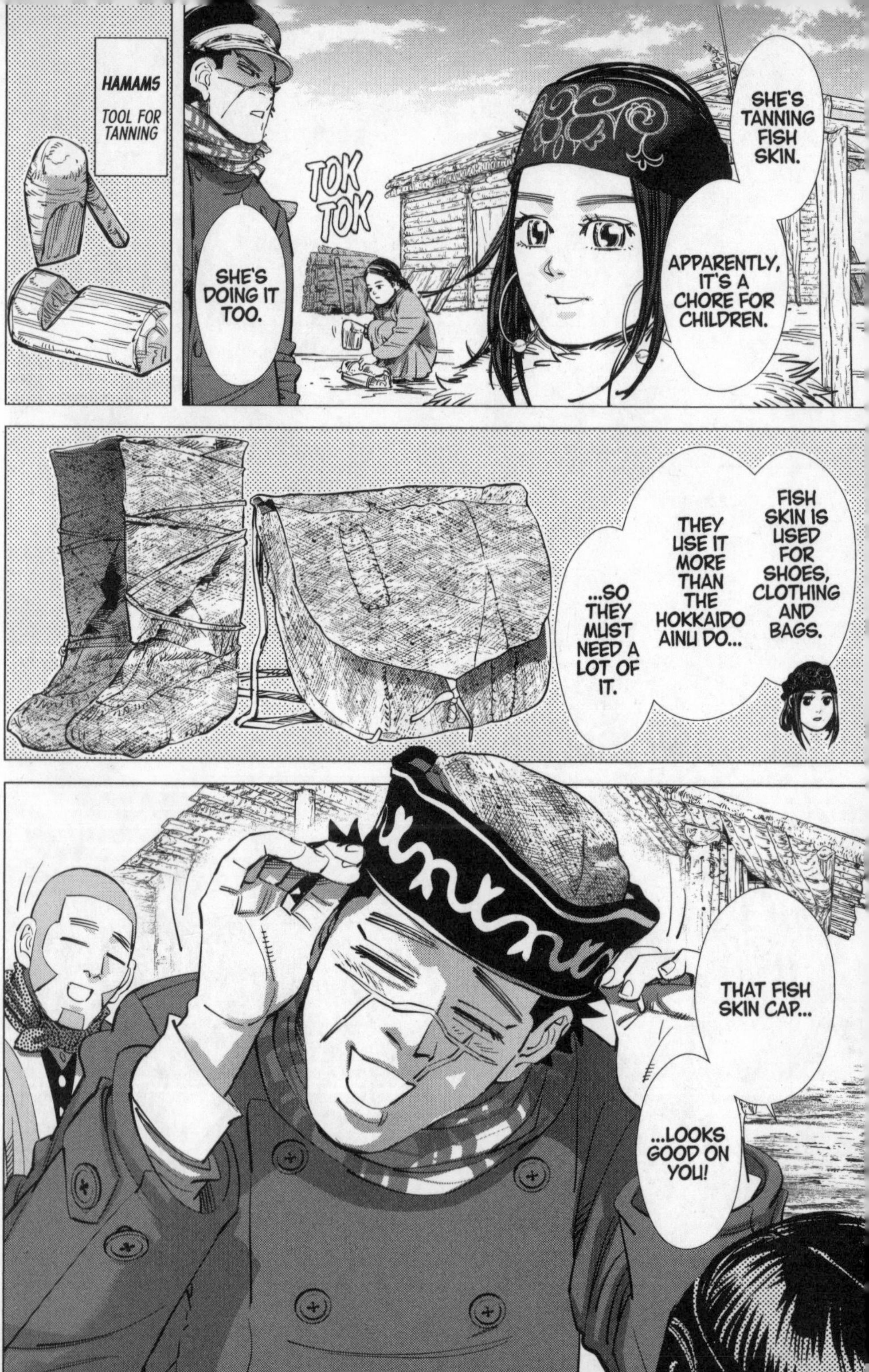
SHE'S TANNING FISH SKIN.
APPARENTLY, IT'S A CHORE FOR CHILDREN.
TOK TOK
SHE'S DOING IT TOO.
HAMAMS
TOOL FOR TANNING
FISH SKIN IS USED FOR SHOES, CLOTHING AND BAGS.
THEY USE IT MORE THAN THE HOKKAIDO AINU DO...
...SO THEY MUST NEED A LOT OF IT.
THAT FISH SKIN CAP...
...LOOKS GOOD ON YOU!

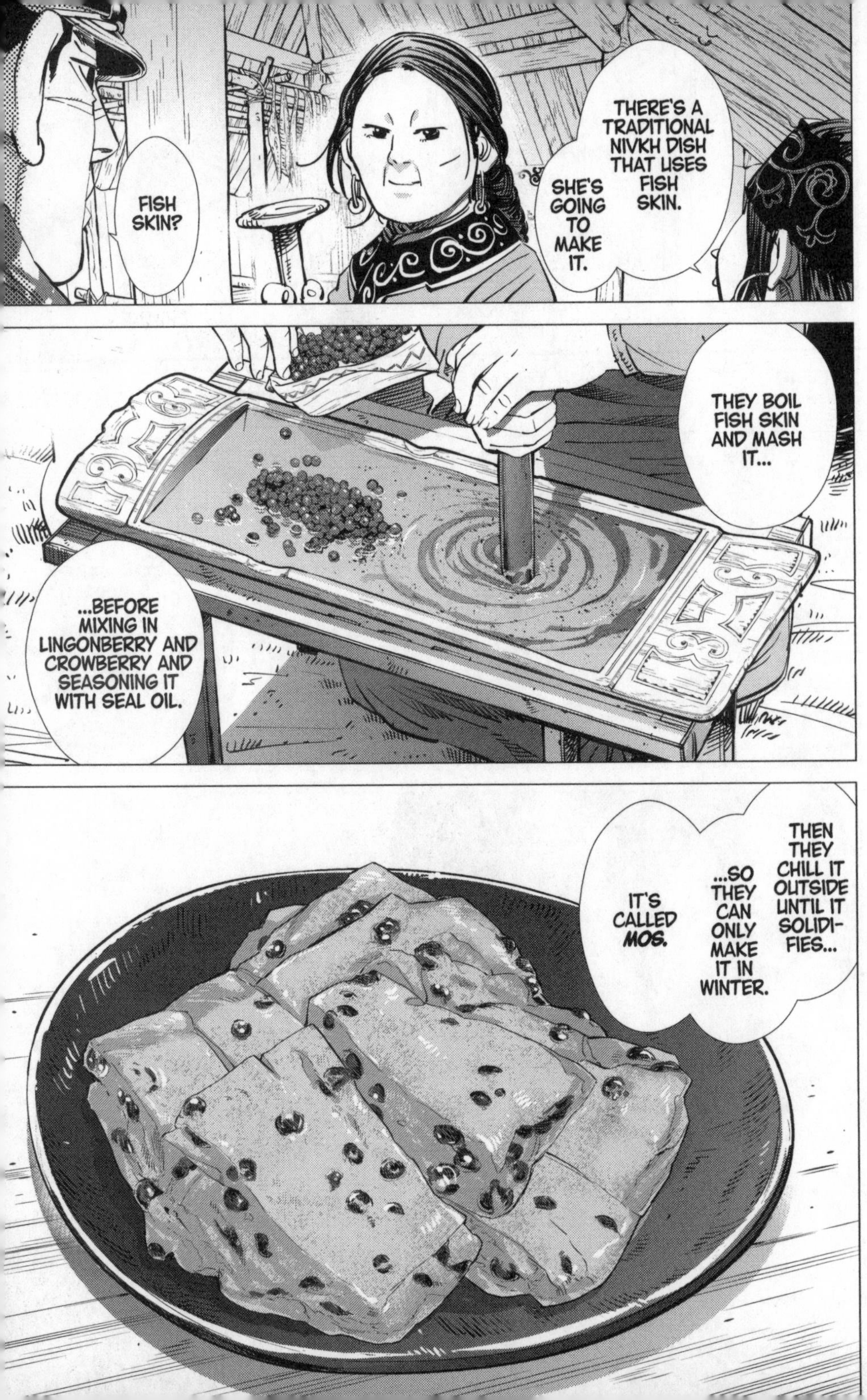
THERE'S A TRADITIONAL NIVKH DISH THAT USES FISH SKIN.
SHE'S GOING TO MAKE IT.
FISH SKIN?
THEY BOIL FISH SKIN AND MASH IT...
...BEFORE MIXING IN LINGONBERRY AND CROWBERRY AND SEASONING IT WITH SEAL OIL.
THEN THEY CHILL IT OUTSIDE UNTIL IT SOLIDI-FIES...
...SO THEY CAN ONLY MAKE IT IN WINTER.
IT'S CALLED *MOS.*

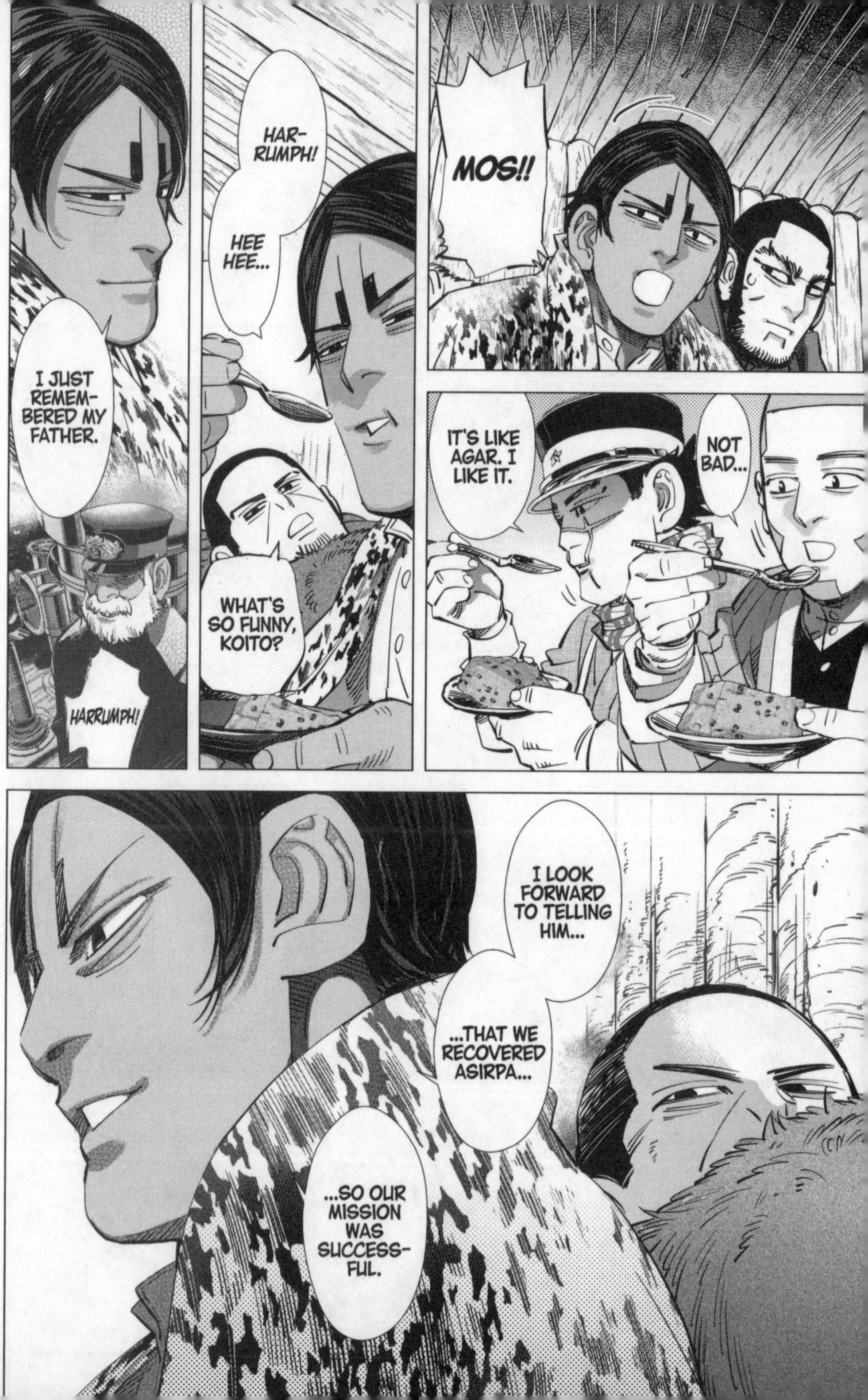
MOS!!
NOT BAD...
IT'S LIKE AGAR. I LIKE IT.
HAR-RUMPH!
HEE HEE...
WHAT'S SO FUNNY, KOITO?
I JUST REMEM-BERED MY FATHER.
HARRUMPH!
I LOOK FORWARD TO TELLING HIM...
...THAT WE RECOVERED ASIRPA...
...SO OUR MISSION WAS SUCCESS-FUL.

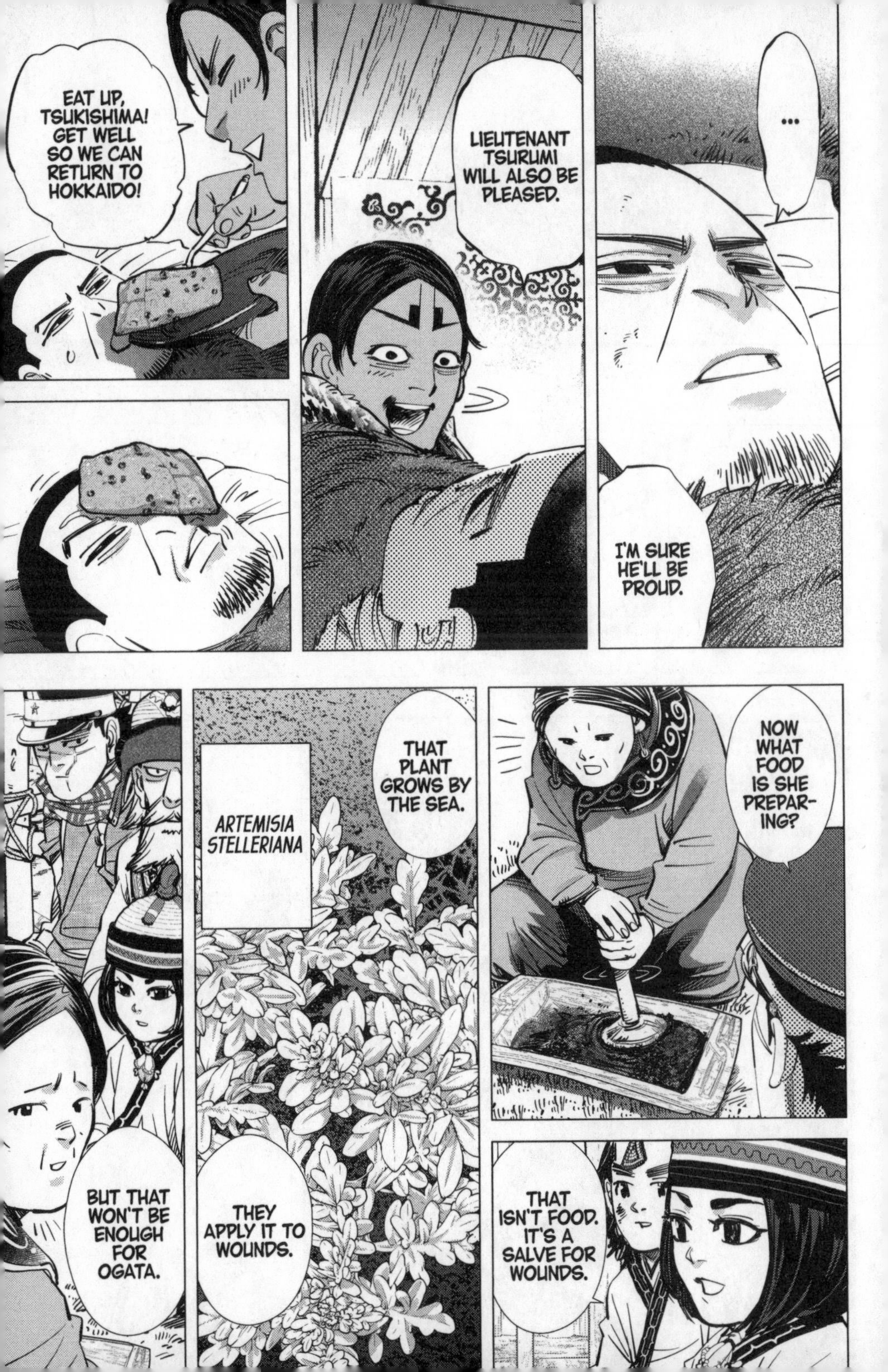
...
I'M SURE HE'LL BE PROUD.
LIEUTENANT TSURUMI WILL ALSO BE PLEASED.
EAT UP, TSUKISHIMA! GET WELL SO WE CAN RETURN TO HOKKAIDO!
NOW WHAT FOOD IS SHE PREPARING?
THAT ISN'T FOOD. IT'S A SALVE FOR WOUNDS.
THAT PLANT GROWS BY THE SEA.
ARTEMISIA STELLERIANA
THEY APPLY IT TO WOUNDS.
BUT THAT WON'T BE ENOUGH FOR OGATA.

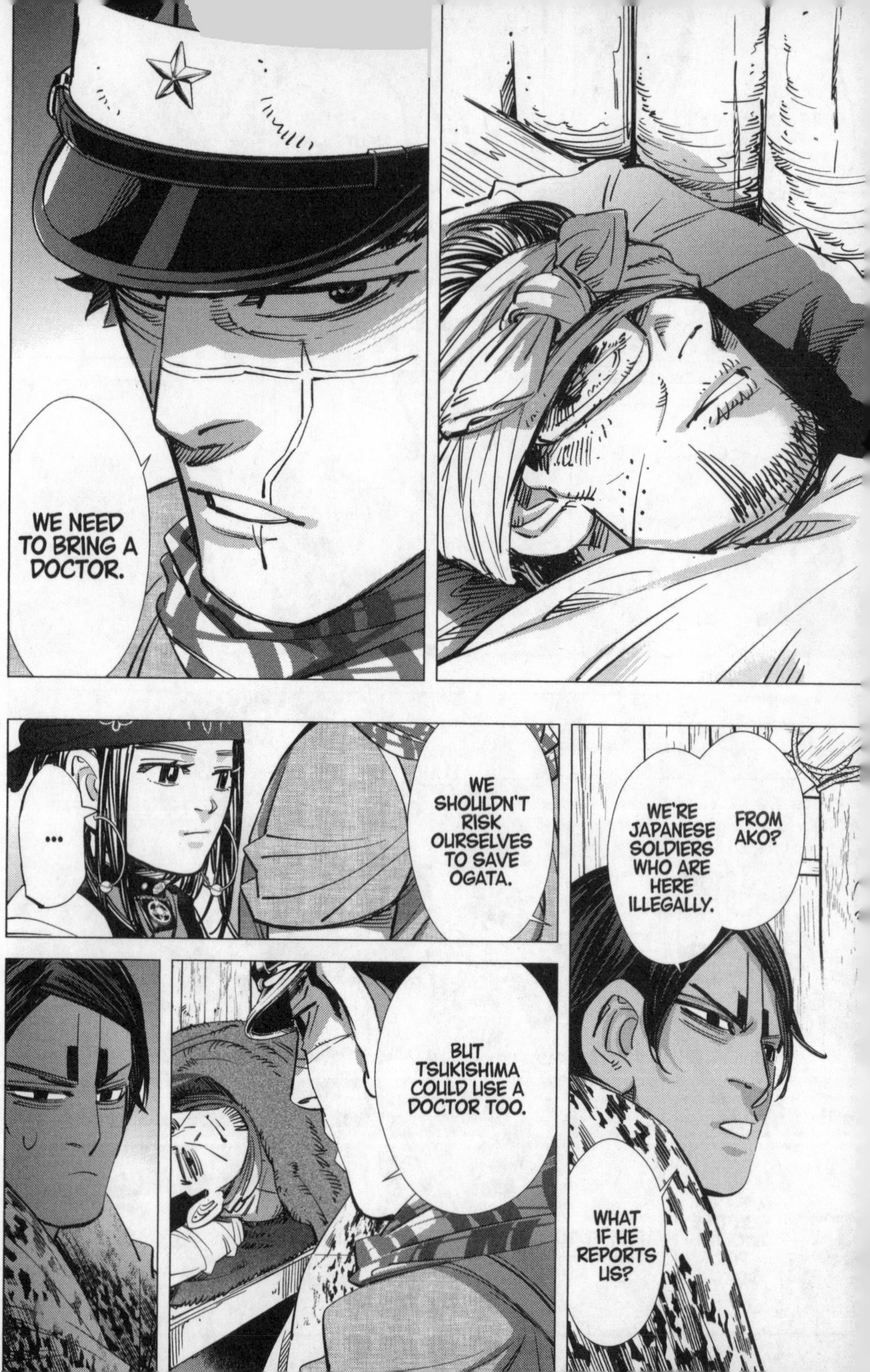
WE NEED TO BRING A DOCTOR.
FROM AKO?
WE'RE JAPANESE SOLDIERS WHO ARE HERE ILLEGALLY.
WHAT IF HE REPORTS US?
WE SHOULDN'T RISK OURSELVES TO SAVE OGATA.
...
BUT TSUKISHIMA COULD USE A DOCTOR TOO.

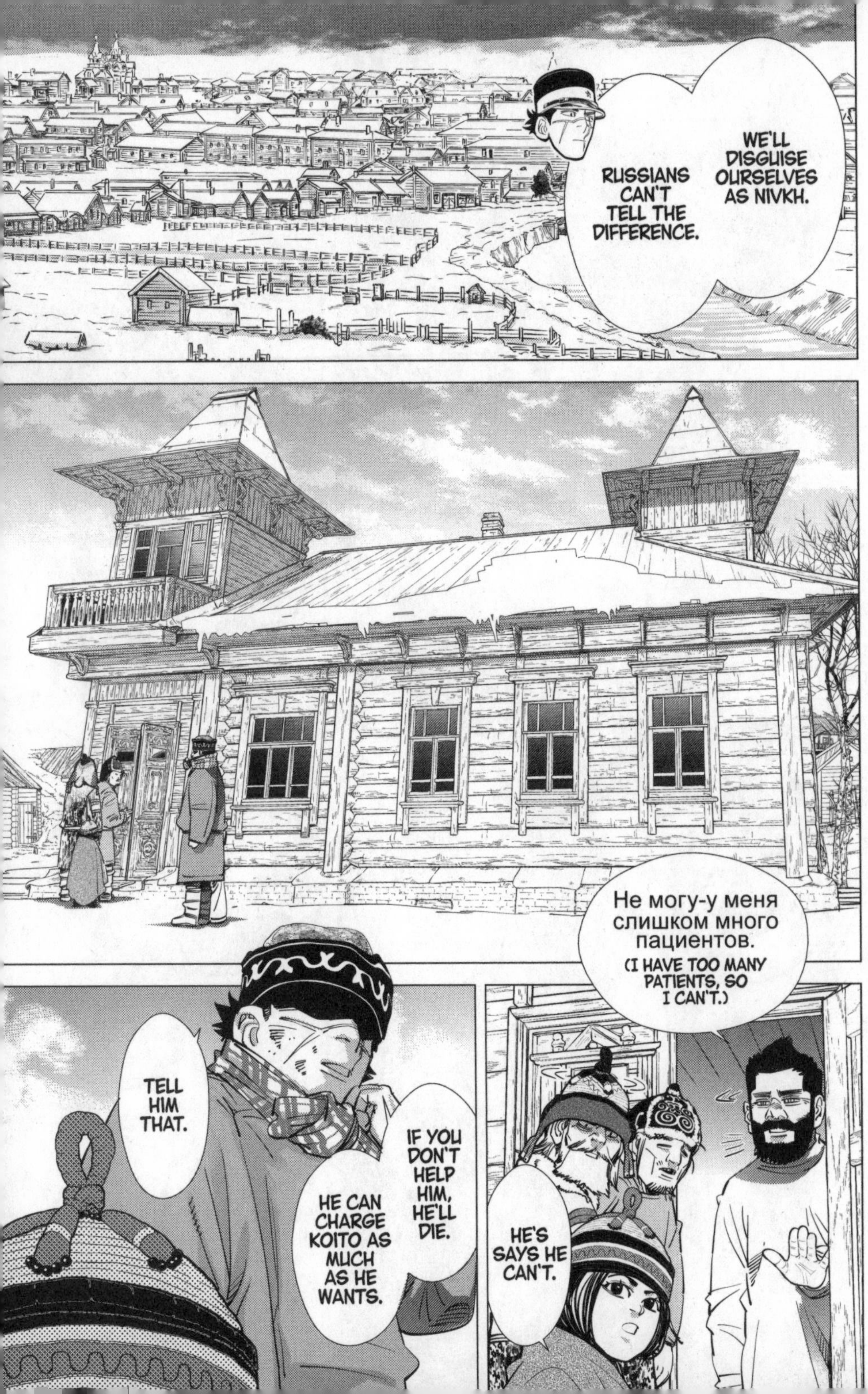
WE'LL DISGUISE OURSELVES AS NIVKH.
RUSSIANS CAN'T TELL THE DIFFERENCE.
Не могу-у меня слишком много пациентов.
(I HAVE TOO MANY PATIENTS, SO I CAN'T.)
HE'S SAYS HE CAN'T.
IF YOU DON'T HELP HIM, HE'LL DIE.
HE CAN CHARGE KOITO AS MUCH AS HE WANTS.
TELL HIM THAT.

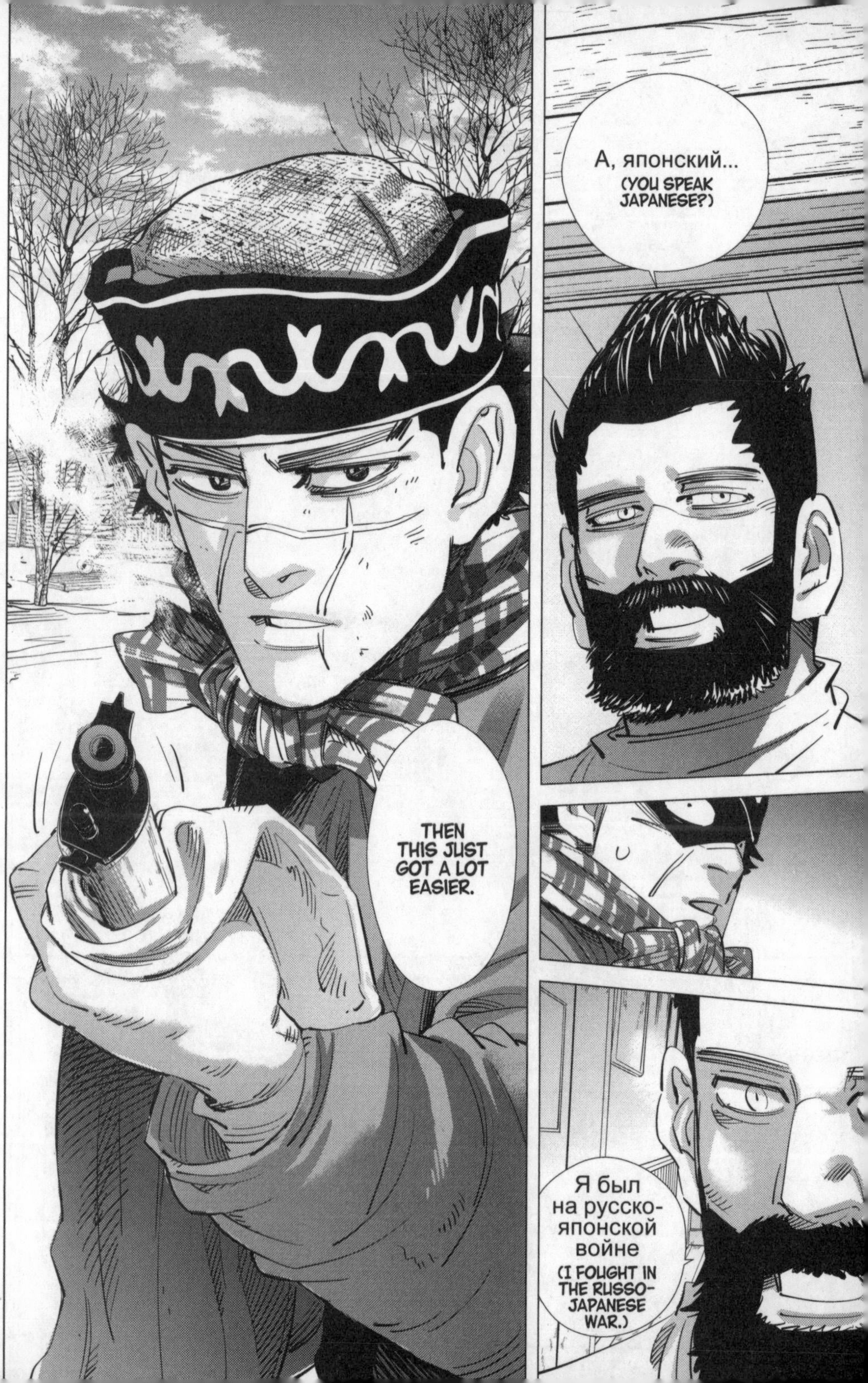
А, японский...
(YOU SPEAK JAPANESE?)
Я был на русско-японской войне
(I FOUGHT IN THE RUSSO-JAPANESE WAR.)
THEN THIS JUST GOT A LOT EASIER.

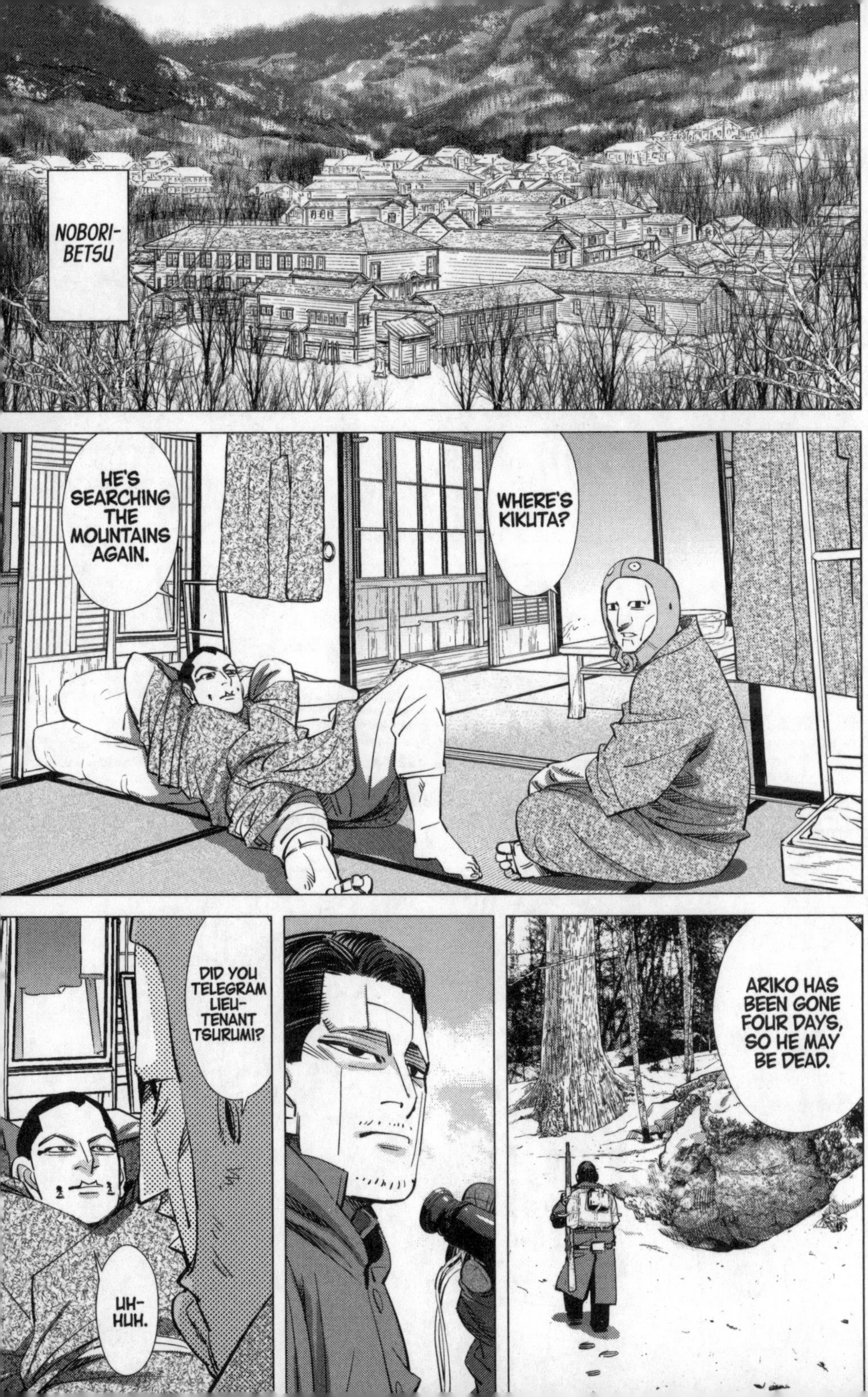
NOBORI-BETSU
WHERE'S KIKUTA?
HE'S SEARCHING THE MOUNTAINS AGAIN.
ARIKO HAS BEEN GONE FOUR DAYS, SO HE MAY BE DEAD.
DID YOU TELEGRAM LIEU-TENANT TSURUMI?
UH-HUH.

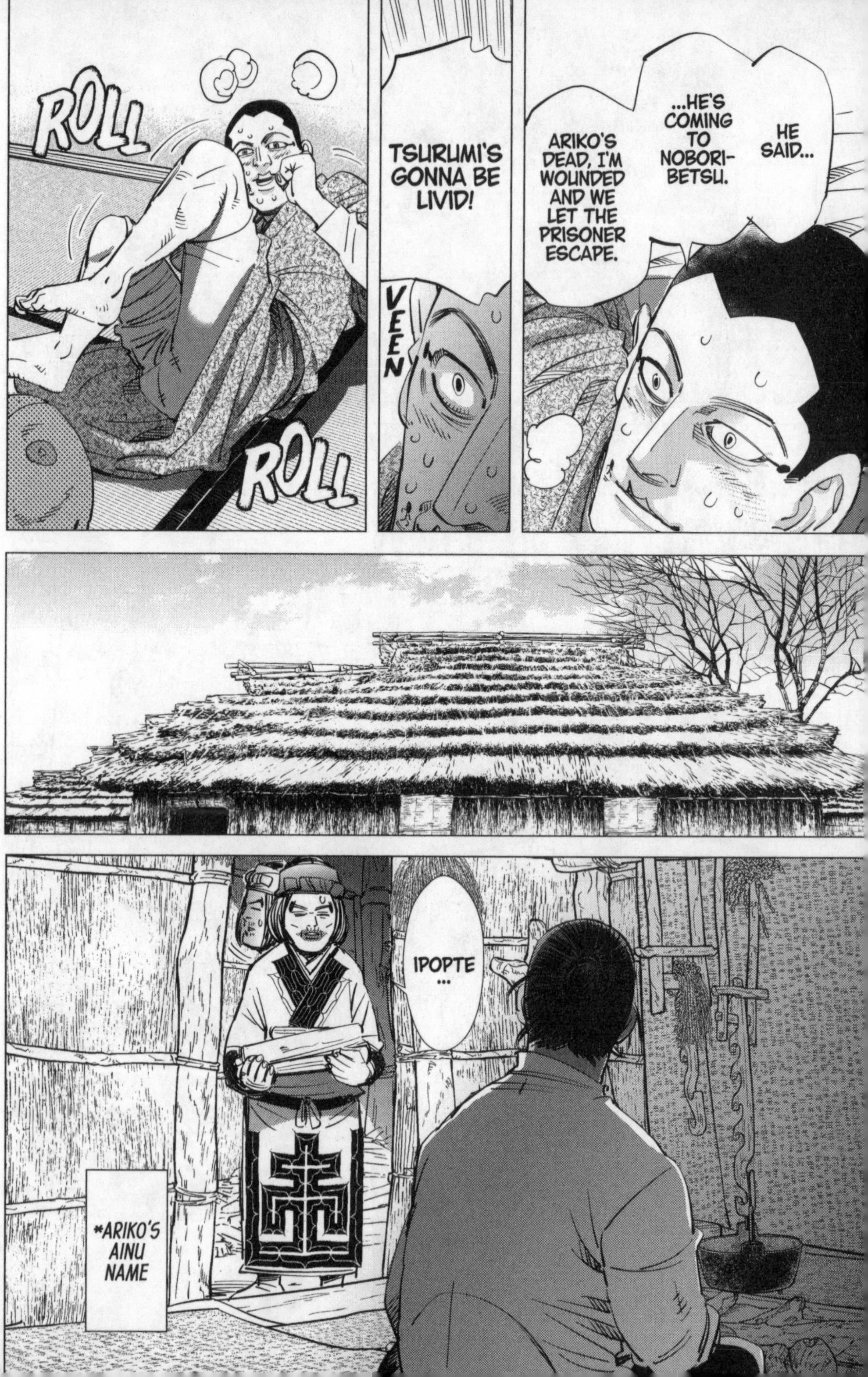
HE SAID...
...HE'S COMING TO NOBORI-BETSU.
ARIKO'S DEAD, I'M WOUNDED AND WE LET THE PRISONER ESCAPE.
TSURUMI'S GONNA BE LIVID!
VEEN
ROLL
ROLL
IPOPTE ...
*ARIKO'S AINU NAME

ARIKO...

...YOU SHOULD'VE TOLD US YOU WERE ALIVE.

I WAS WAITING FOR YOU.

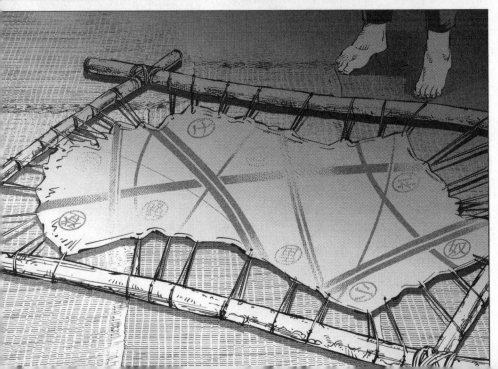

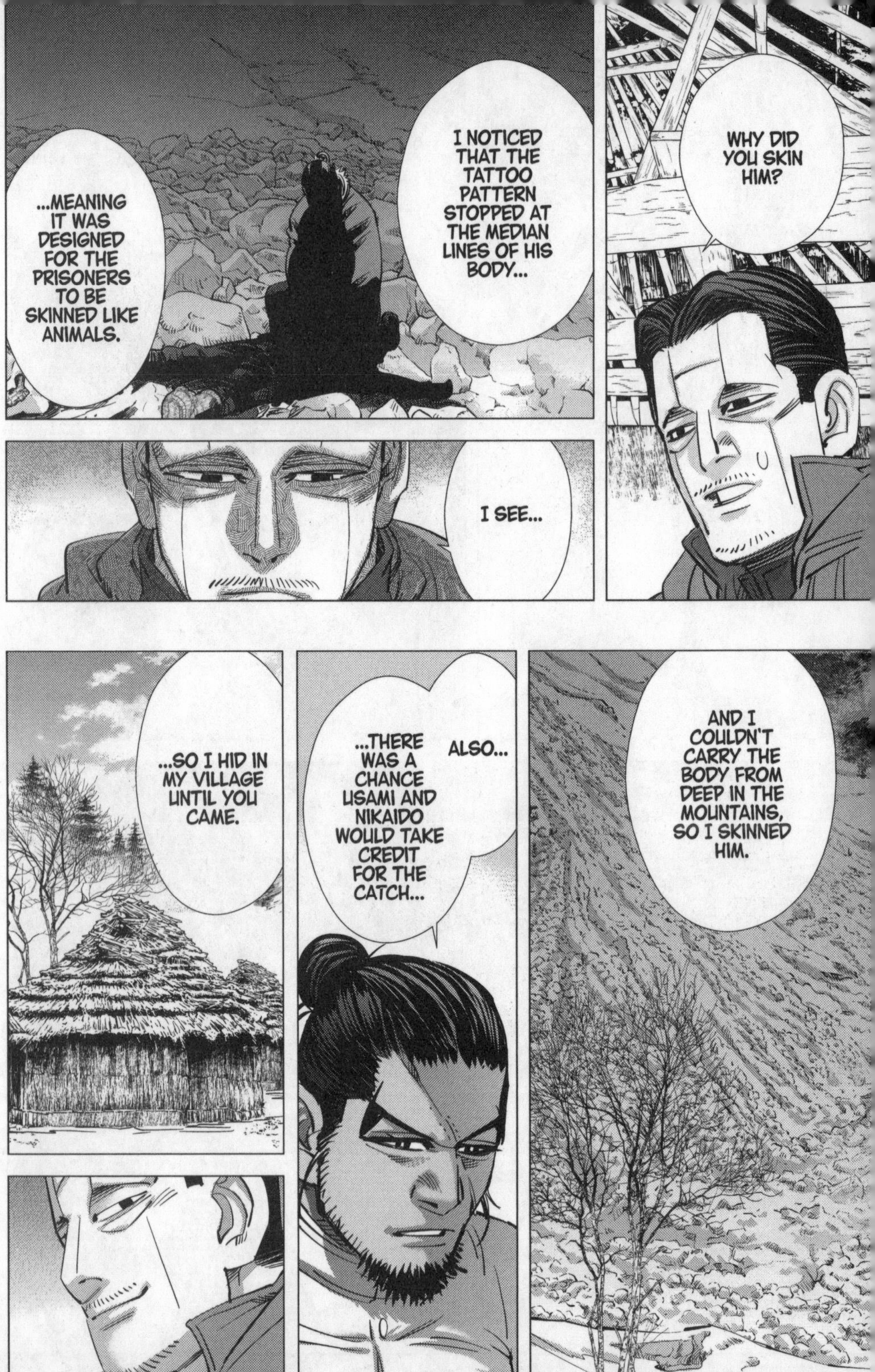
WHY DID YOU SKIN HIM?
I NOTICED THAT THE TATTOO PATTERN STOPPED AT THE MEDIAN LINES OF HIS BODY...
...MEANING IT WAS DESIGNED FOR THE PRISONERS TO BE SKINNED LIKE ANIMALS.
I SEE...
AND I COULDN'T CARRY THE BODY FROM DEEP IN THE MOUNTAINS, SO I SKINNED HIM.
ALSO...
...THERE WAS A CHANCE USAMI AND NIKAIDO WOULD TAKE CREDIT FOR THE CATCH...
...SO I HID IN MY VILLAGE UNTIL YOU CAME.

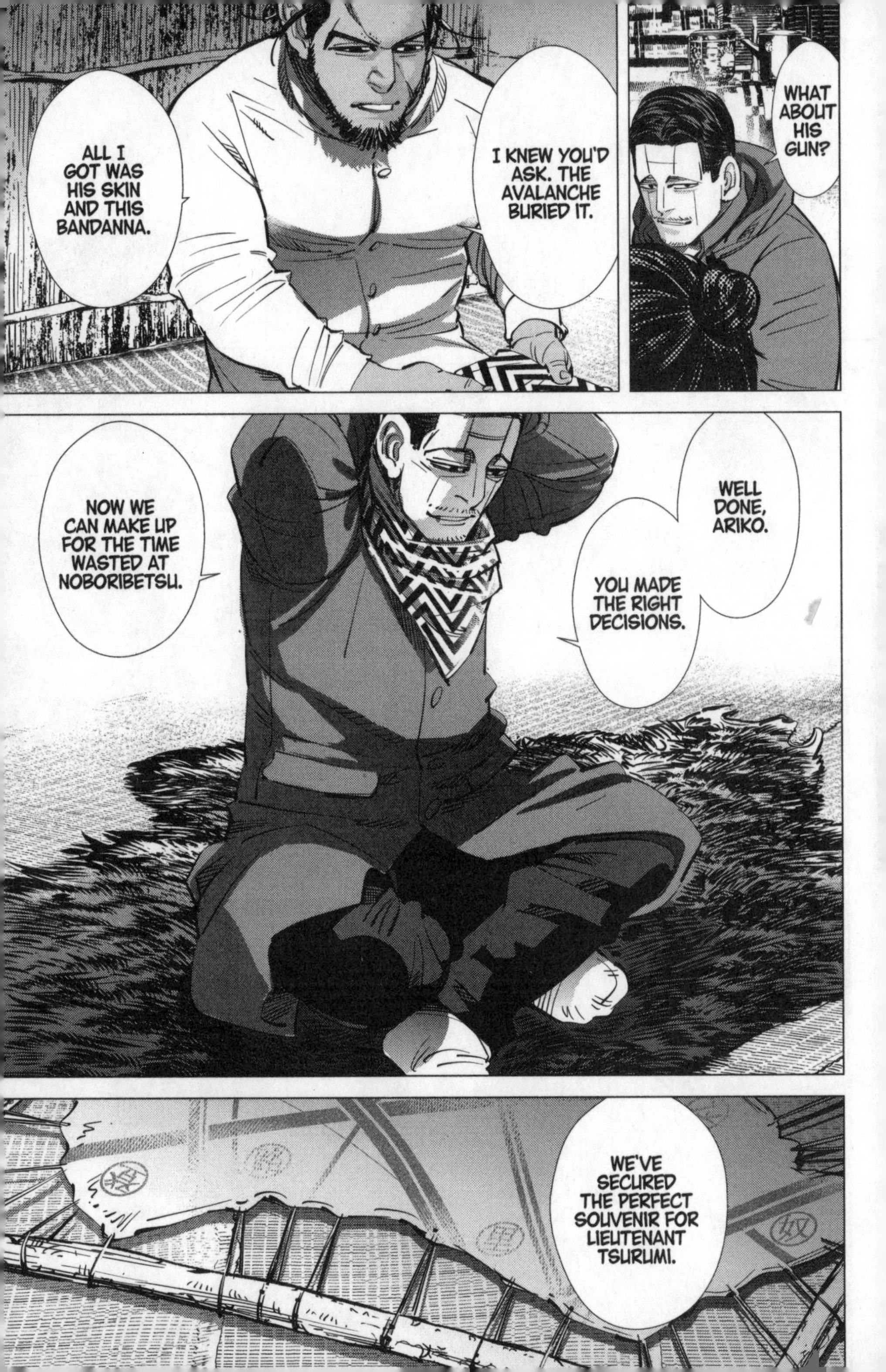
WHAT ABOUT HIS GUN?
I KNEW YOU'D ASK. THE AVALANCHE BURIED IT.
ALL I GOT WAS HIS SKIN AND THIS BANDANNA.
WELL DONE, ARIKO.
YOU MADE THE RIGHT DECISIONS.
NOW WE CAN MAKE UP FOR THE TIME WASTED AT NOBORIBETSU.
WE'VE SECURED THE PERFECT SOUVENIR FOR LIEUTENANT TSURUMI.

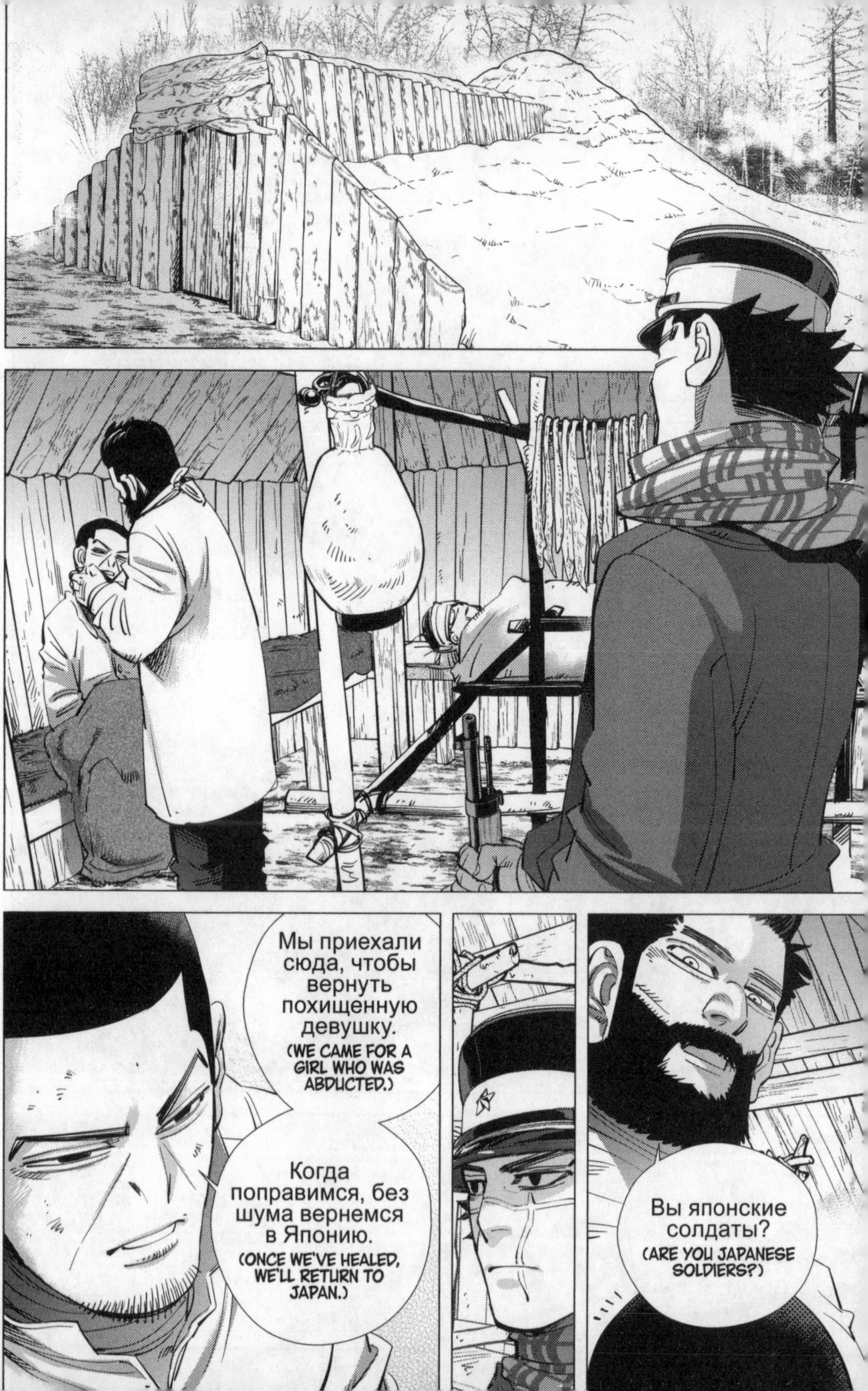
Вы японские солдаты?
(ARE YOU JAPANESE SOLDIERS?)
Мы приехали сюда, чтобы вернуть похищенную девушку.
(WE CAME FOR A GIRL WHO WAS ABDUCTED.)
Когда поправимся, без шума вернемся в Японию.
(ONCE WE'VE HEALED, WE'LL RETURN TO JAPAN.)

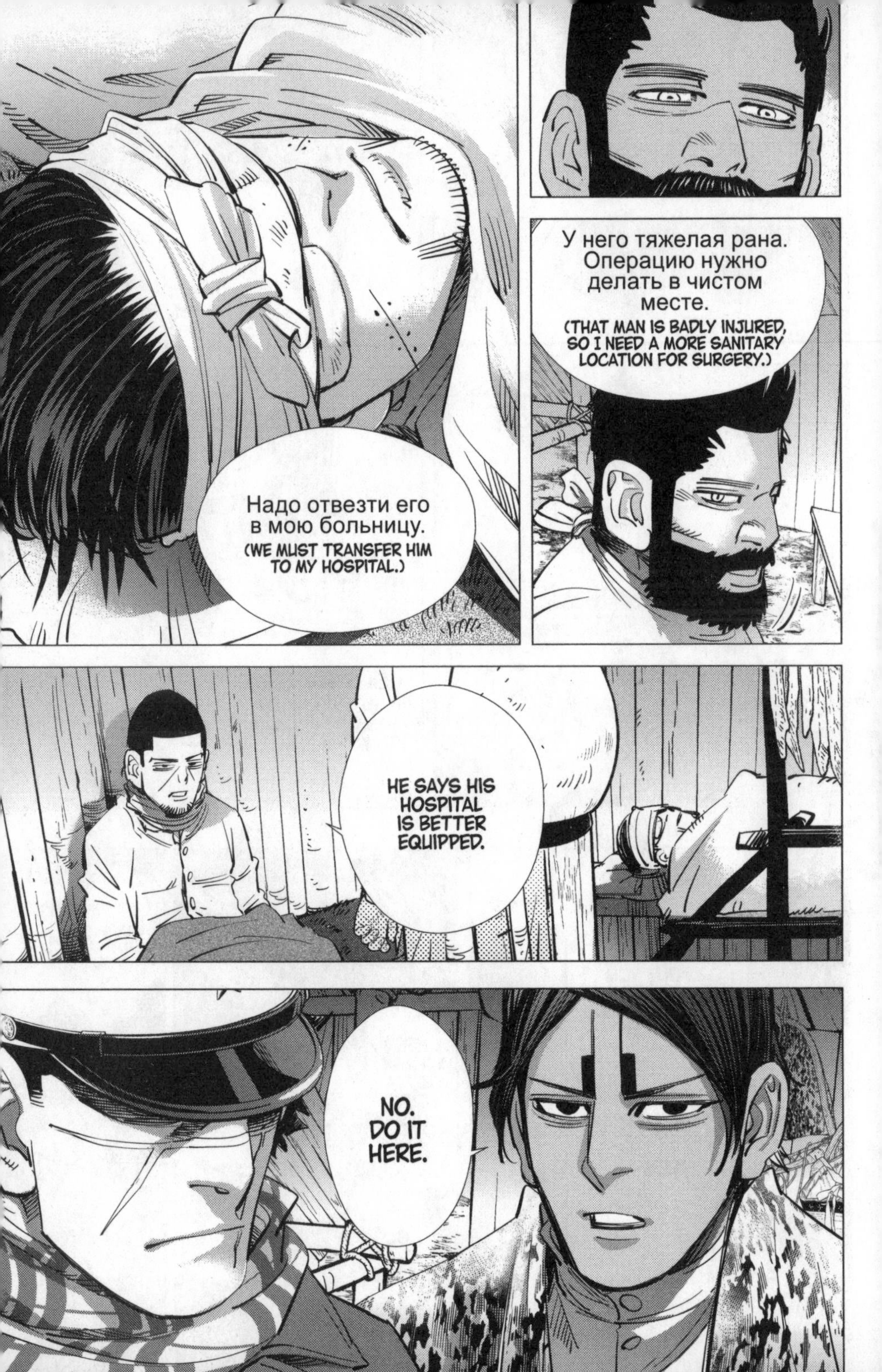
У него тяжелая рана. Операцию нужно делать в чистом месте.
(THAT MAN IS BADLY INJURED, SO I NEED A MORE SANITARY LOCATION FOR SURGERY.)
Надо отвезти его в мою больницу.
(WE MUST TRANSFER HIM TO MY HOSPITAL.)
HE SAYS HIS HOSPITAL IS BETTER EQUIPPED.
NO. DO IT HERE.

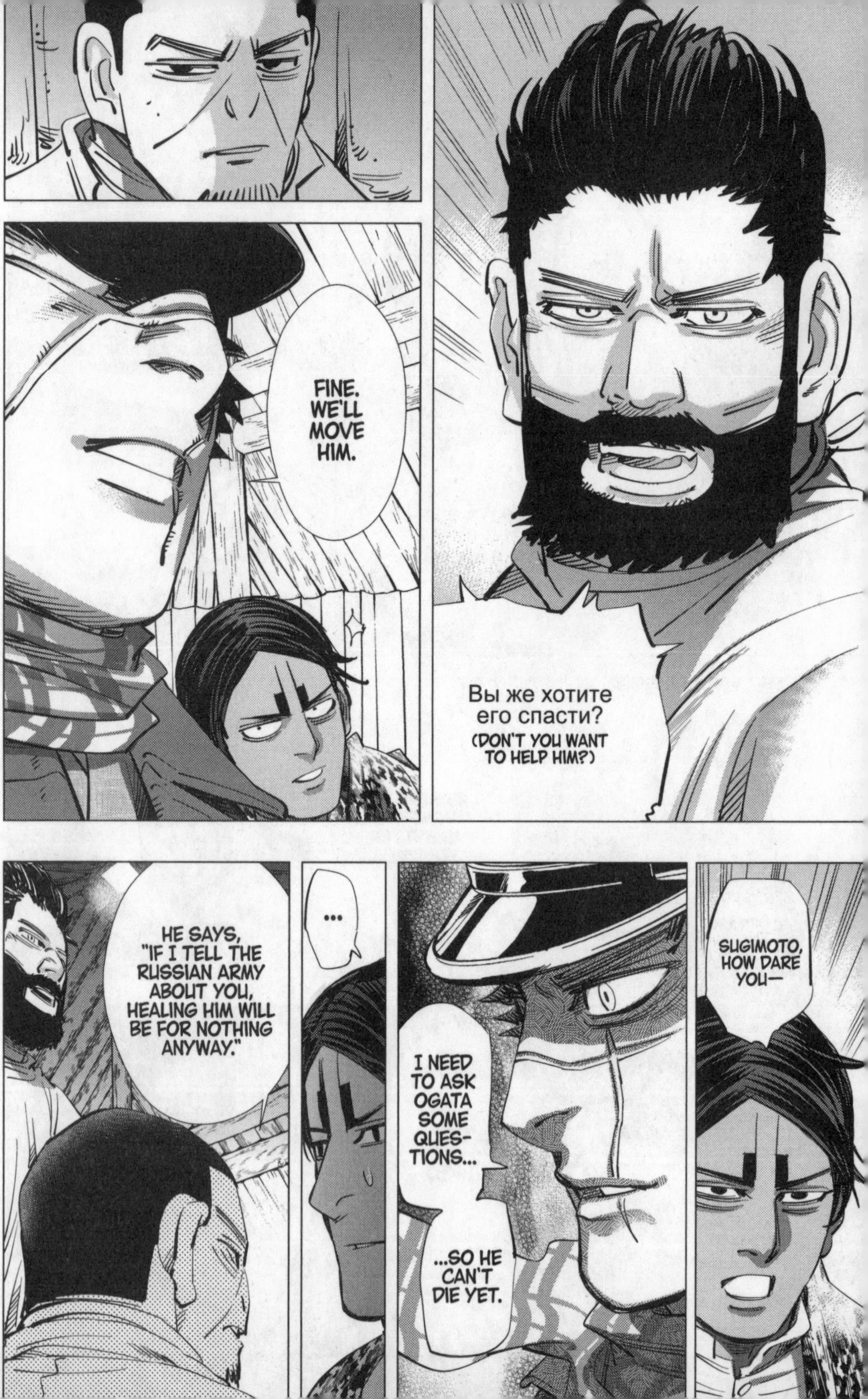
Вы же хотите его спасти?
(DON'T YOU WANT TO HELP HIM?)
FINE. WE'LL MOVE HIM.
SUGIMOTO, HOW DARE YOU—
I NEED TO ASK OGATA SOME QUES-TIONS...
...SO HE CAN'T DIE YET.
...
HE SAYS, "IF I TELL THE RUSSIAN ARMY ABOUT YOU, HEALING HIM WILL BE FOR NOTHING ANYWAY."

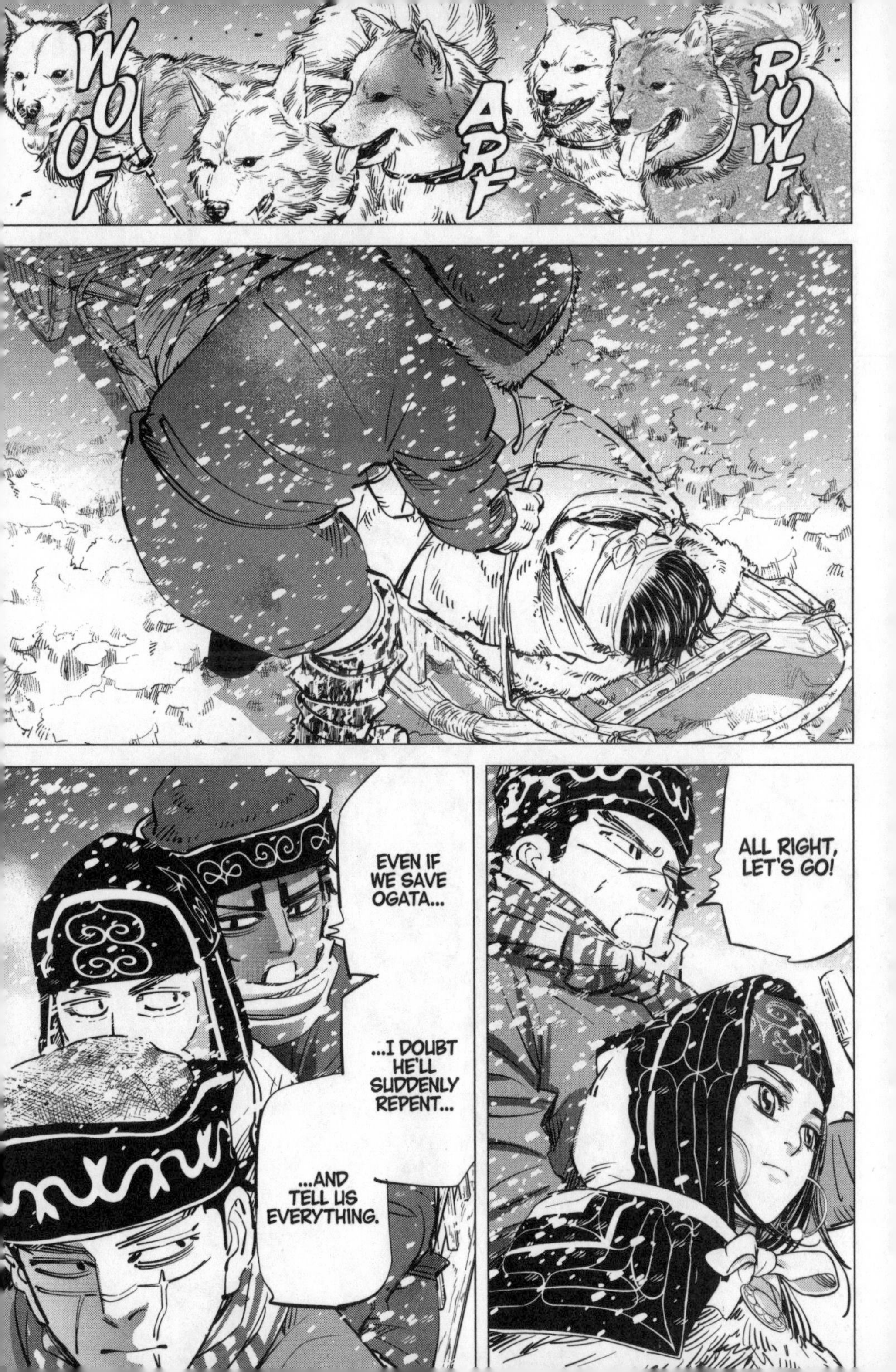
ROWF
ARF
WOOF
ALL RIGHT, LET'S GO!
EVEN IF WE SAVE OGATA...
...I DOUBT HE'LL SUDDENLY REPENT...
...AND TELL US EVERYTHING.

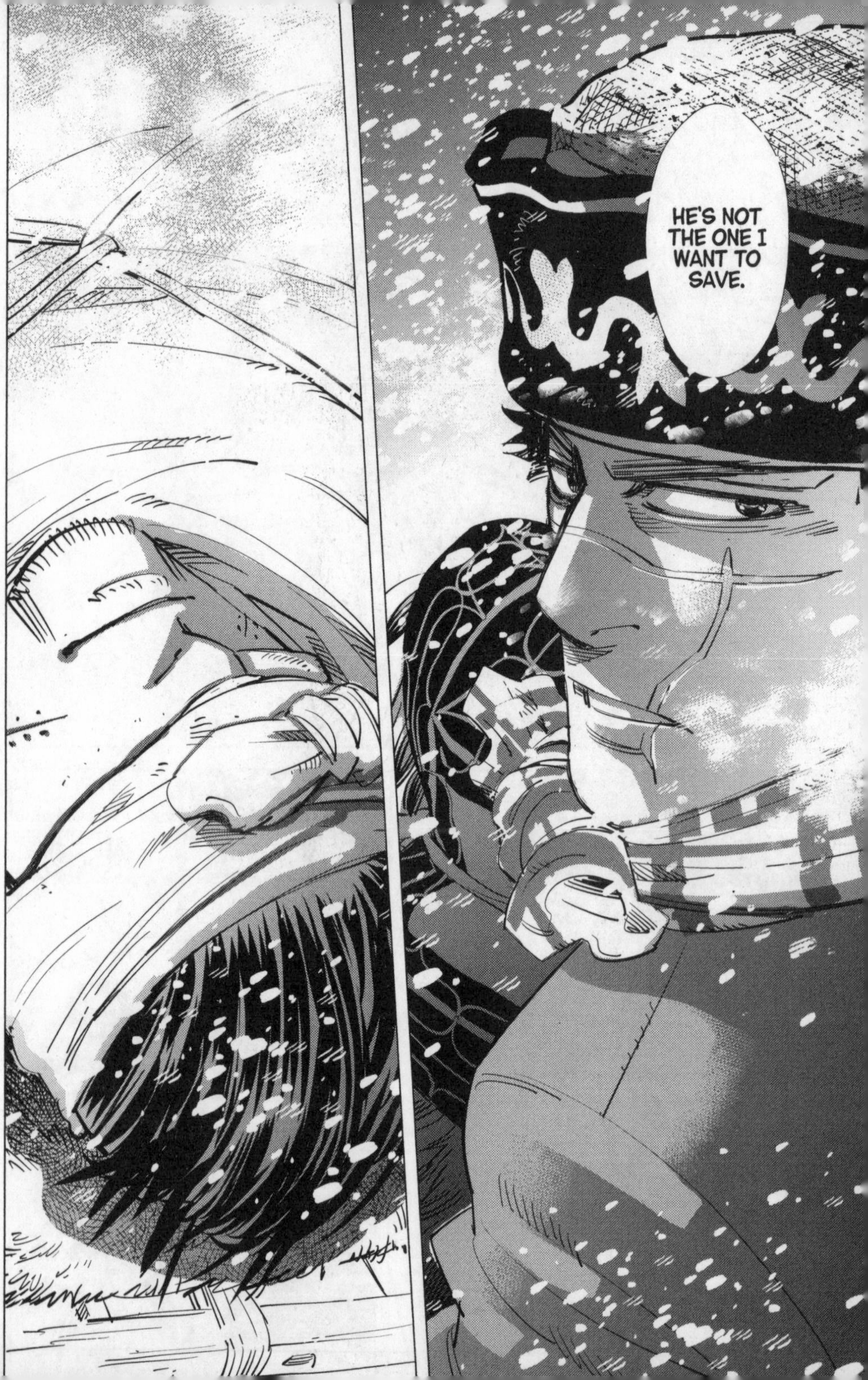
HE'S NOT THE ONE I WANT TO SAVE.

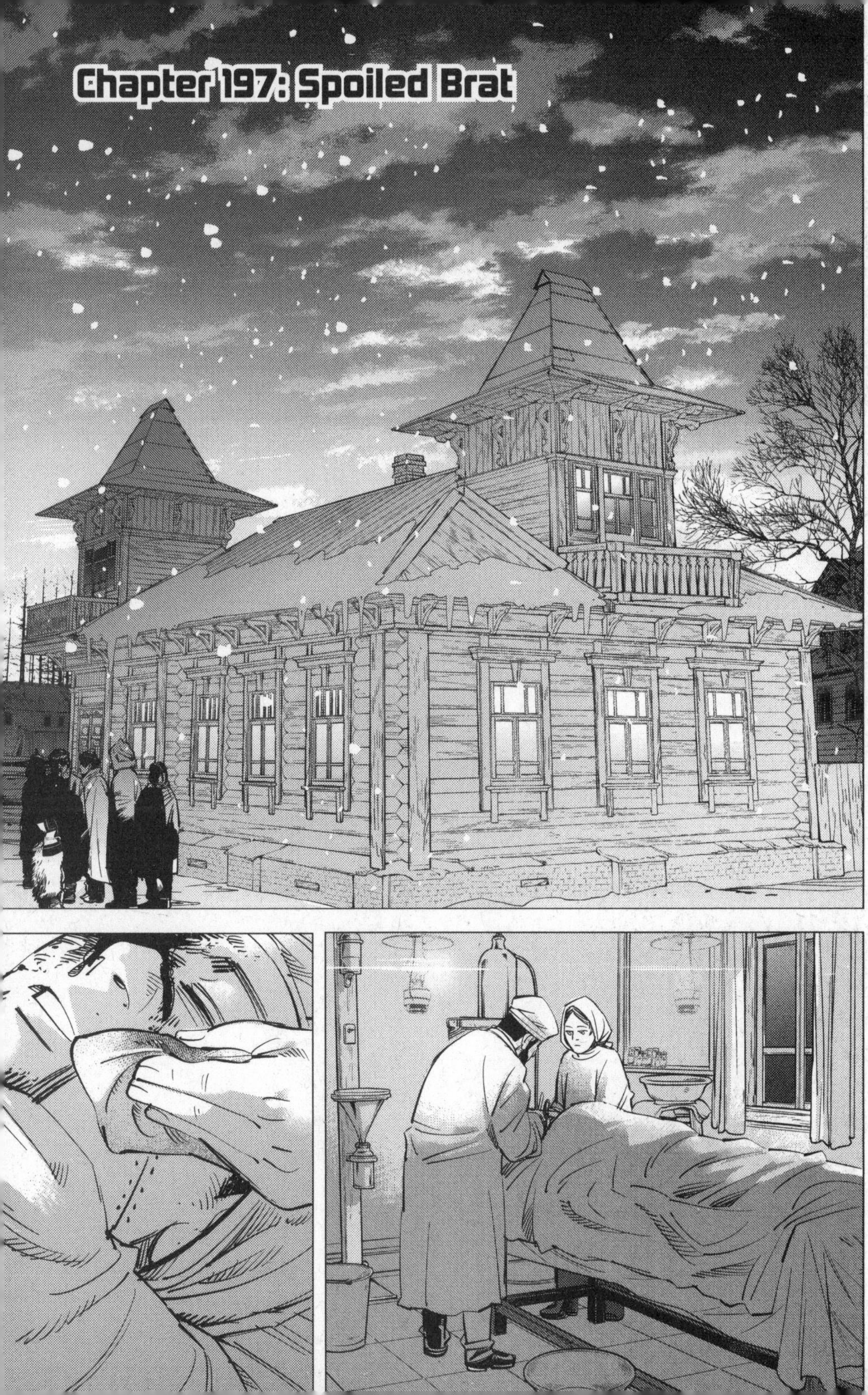
Chapter 197: Spoiled Brat

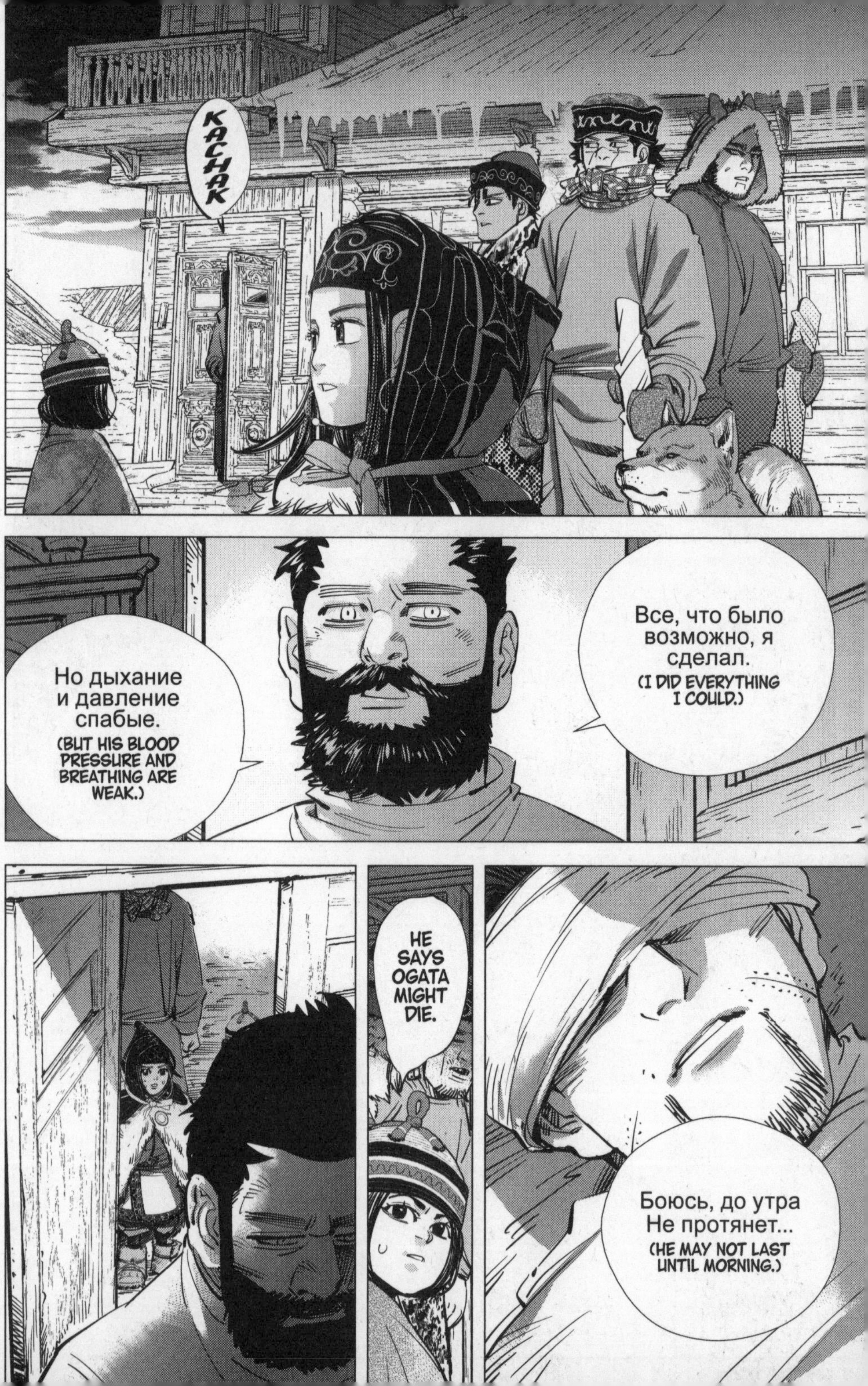
KACHAK
Все, что было возможно, я сделал.
(I DID EVERYTHING I COULD.)
Но дыхание и давление спабые.
(BUT HIS BLOOD PRESSURE AND BREATHING ARE WEAK.)
Боюсь, до утра Не протянет...
(HE MAY NOT LAST UNTIL MORNING.)
HE SAYS OGATA MIGHT DIE.

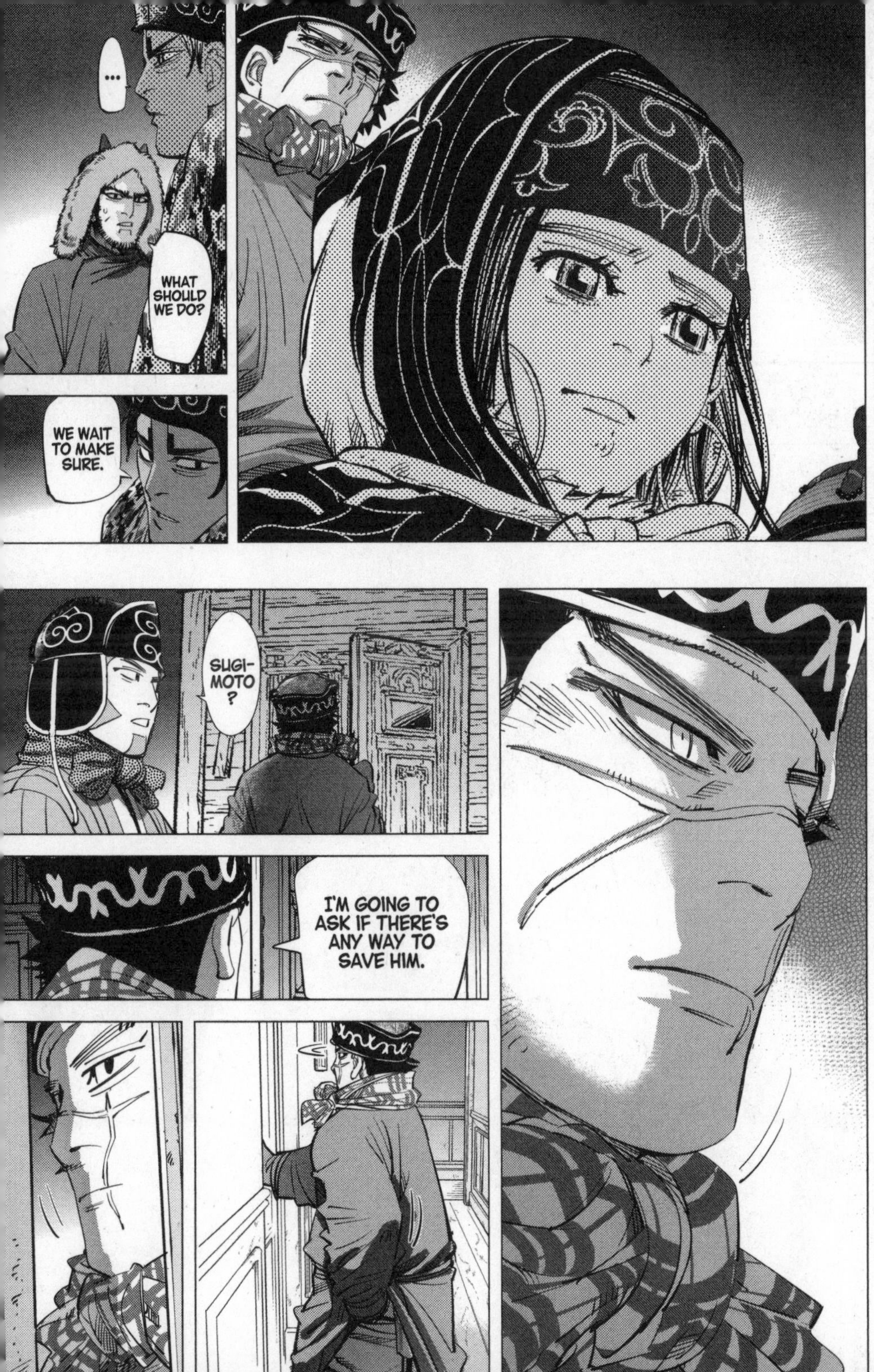
...
WHAT SHOULD WE DO?
WE WAIT TO MAKE SURE.
SUGI-MOTO?
I'M GOING TO ASK IF THERE'S ANY WAY TO SAVE HIM.

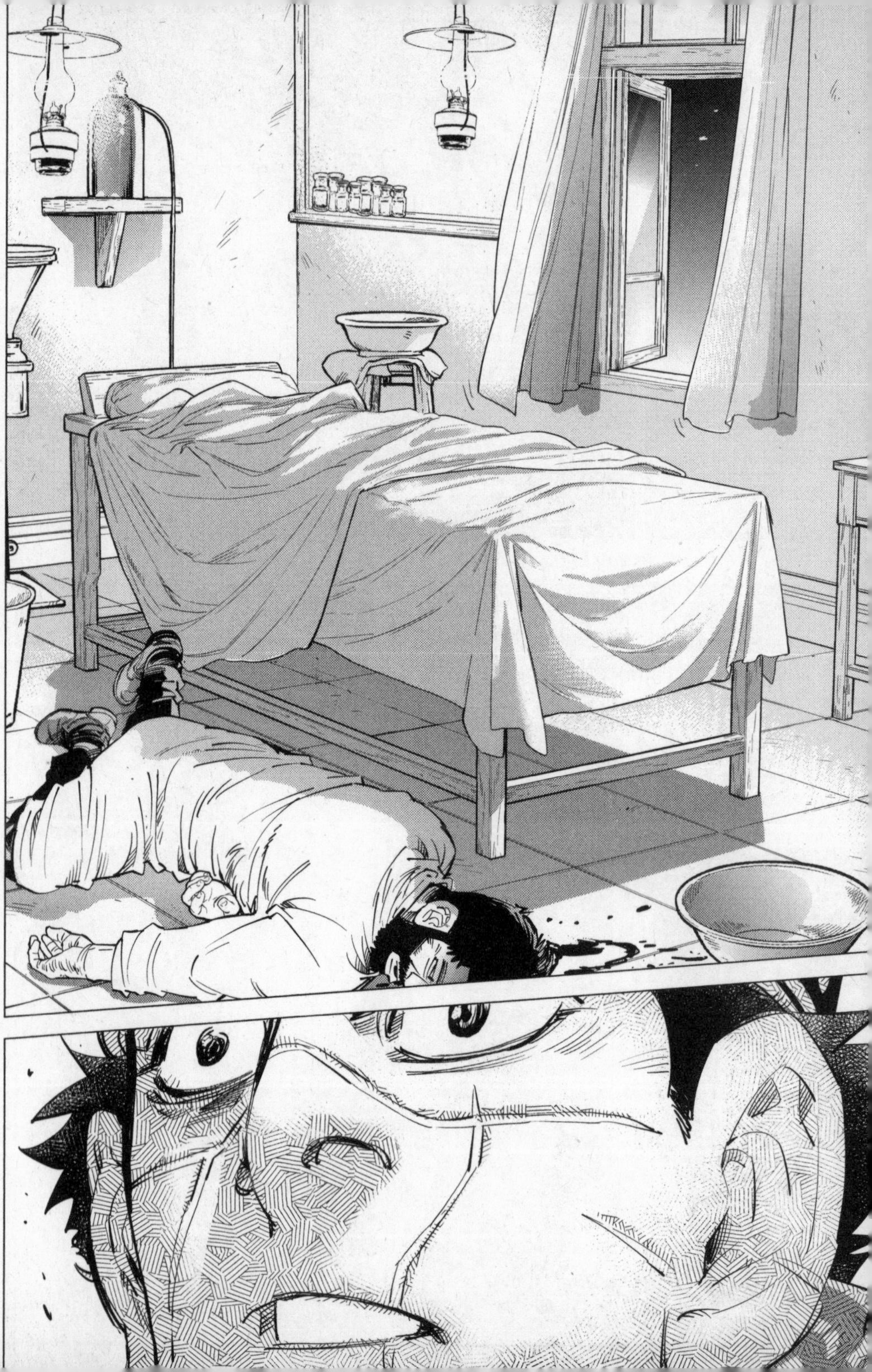

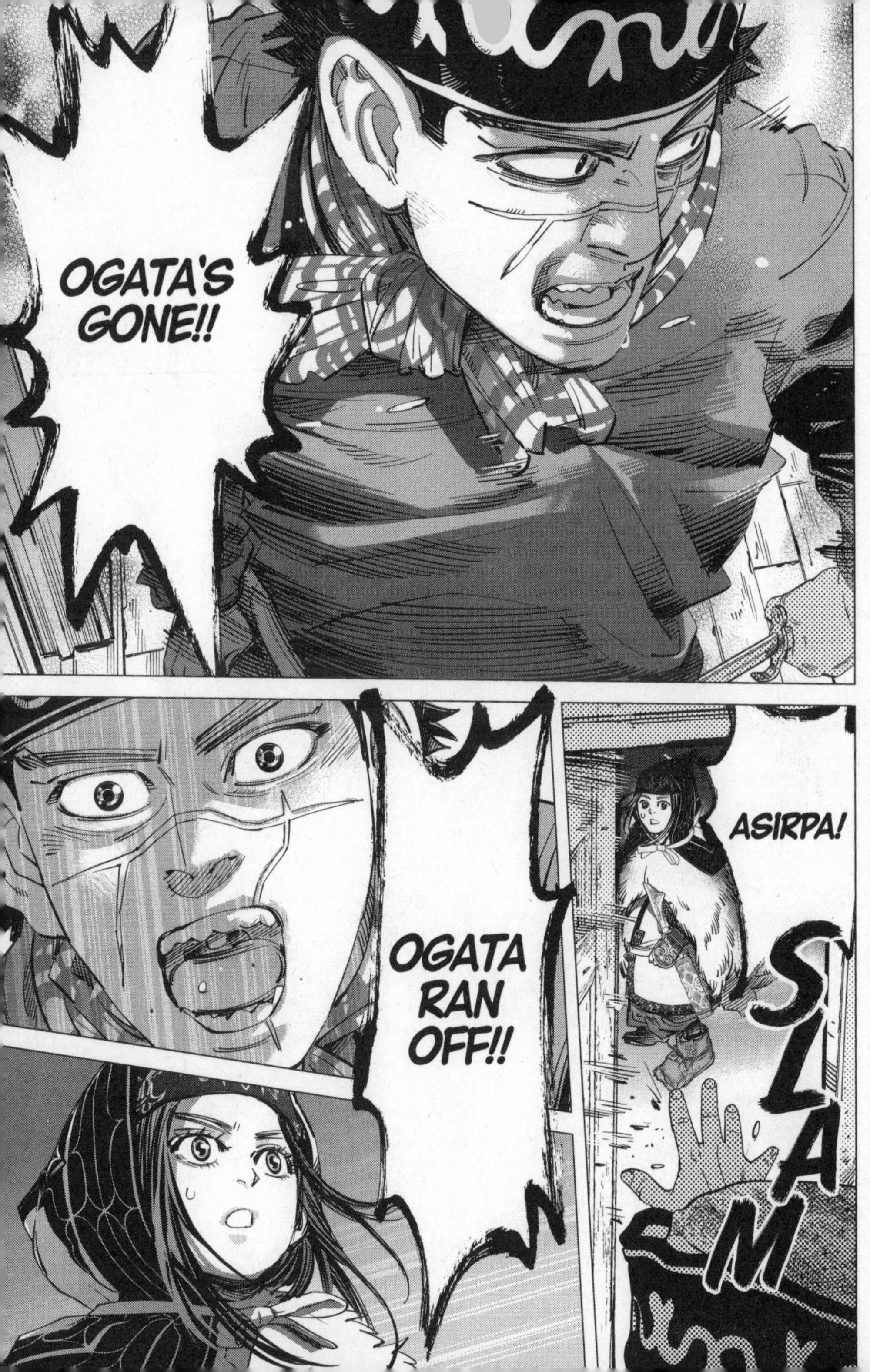
OGATA'S GONE!!
ASIRPA!
SLAM
OGATA RAN OFF!!

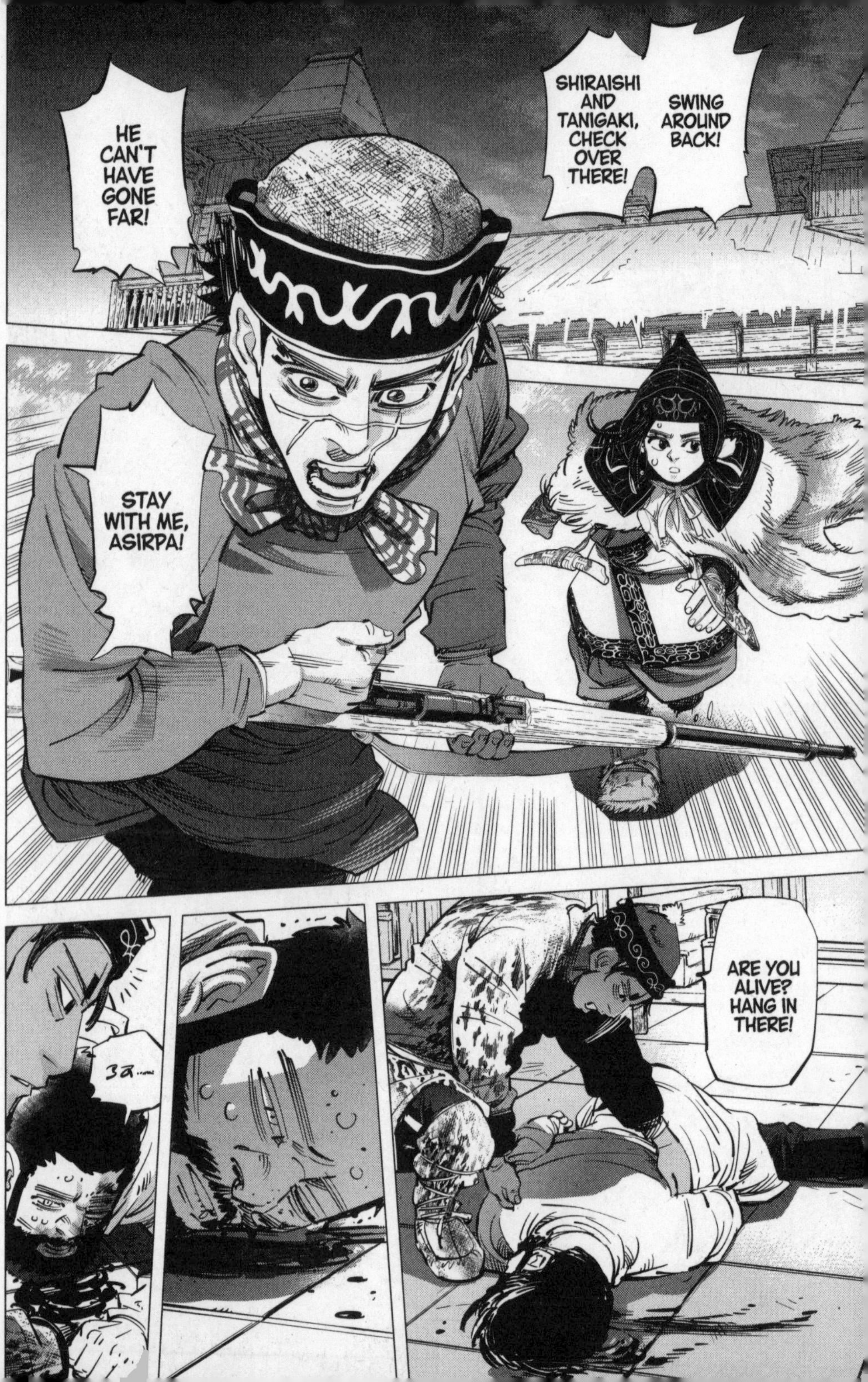
SWING AROUND BACK!
SHIRAISHI AND TANIGAKI, CHECK OVER THERE!
HE CAN'T HAVE GONE FAR!
STAY WITH ME, ASIRPA!
ARE YOU ALIVE? HANG IN THERE!

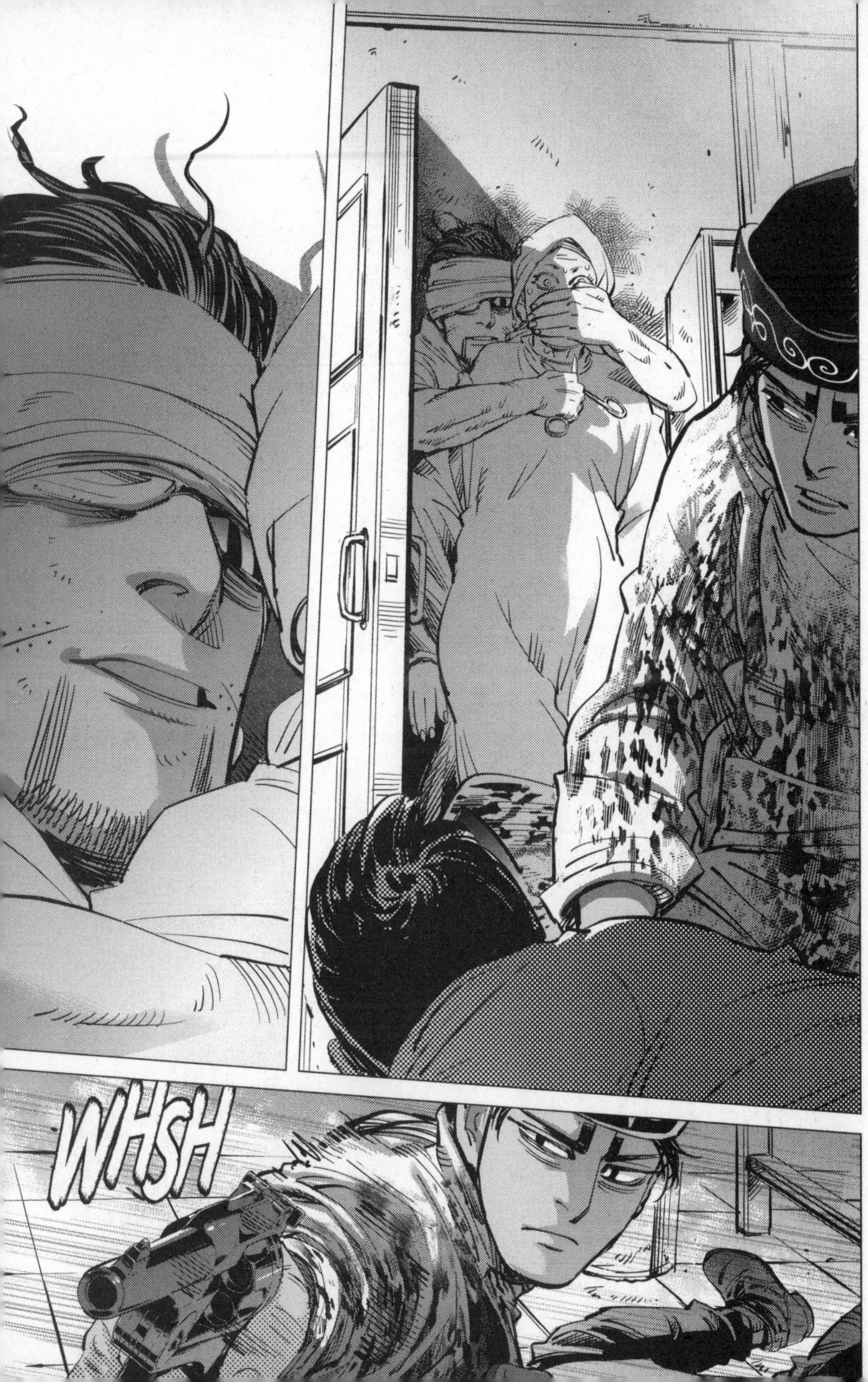
WHSH

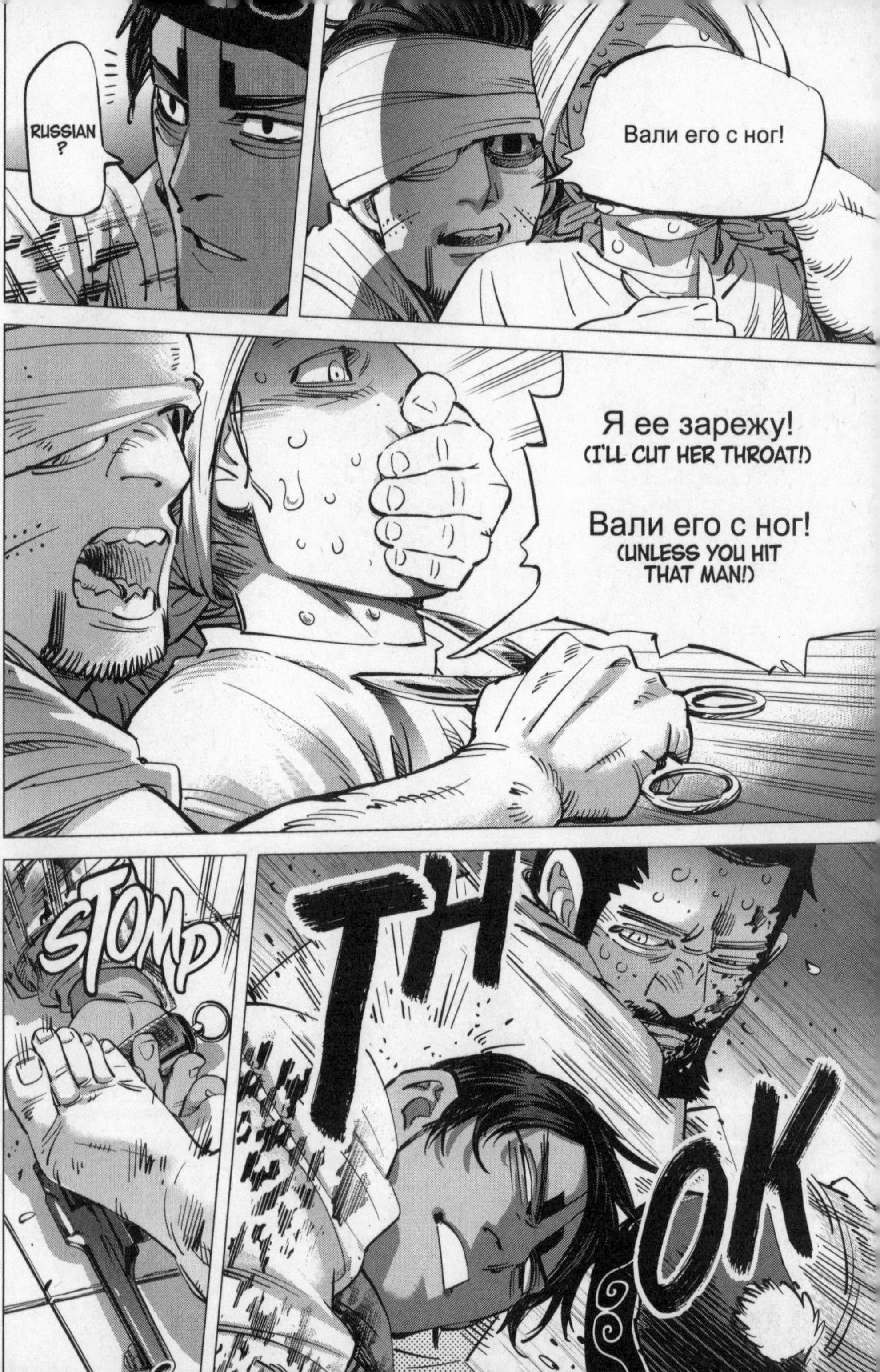
Вали его с ног!
RUSSIAN ?
Я ее зарежу!
(I'LL CUT HER THROAT!)
Вали его с ног!
(UNLESS YOU HIT THAT MAN!)
THOK
STOMP

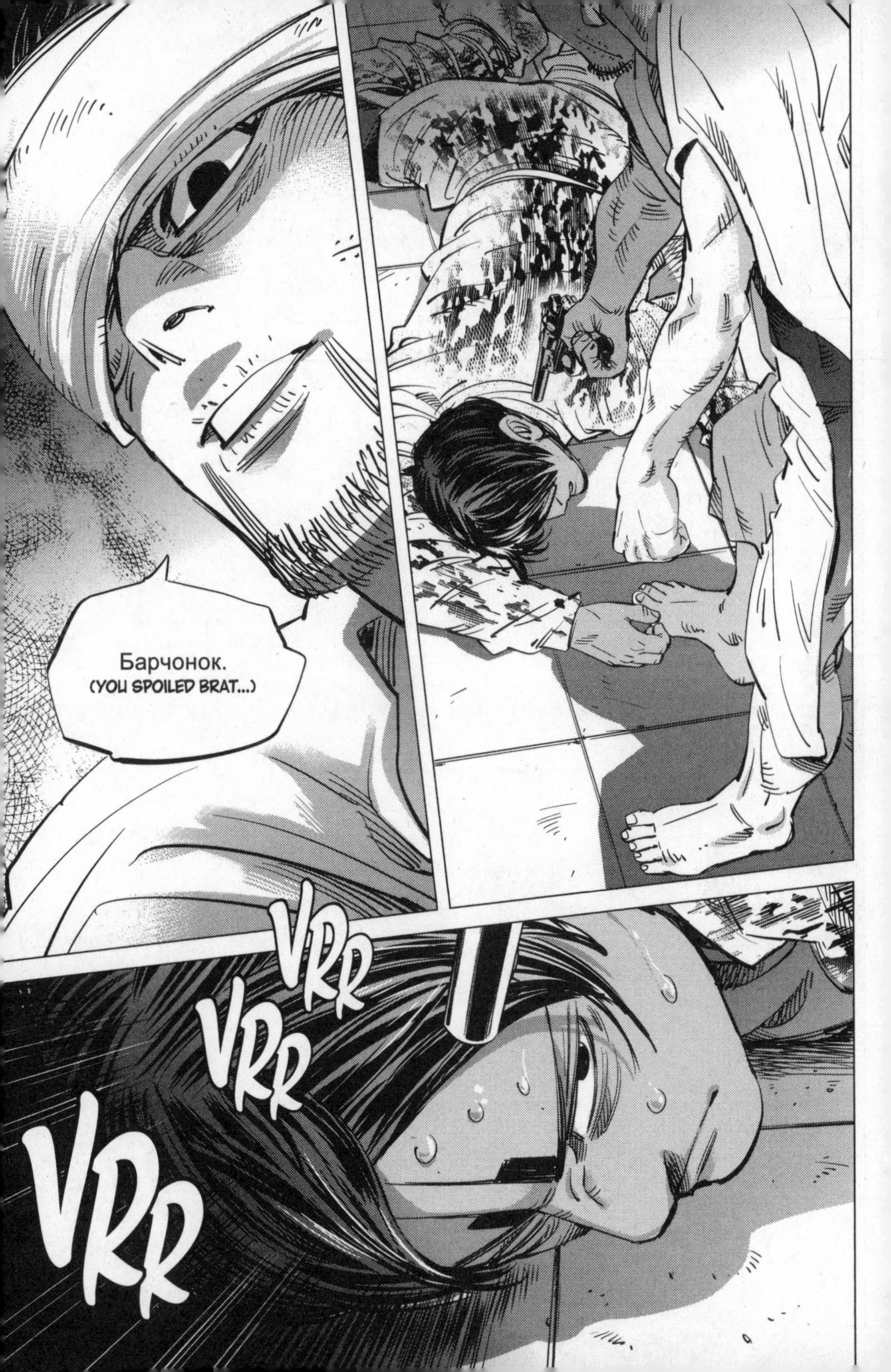
Барчонок.
(YOU SPOILED BRAT...)
VRR
VRR
VRR

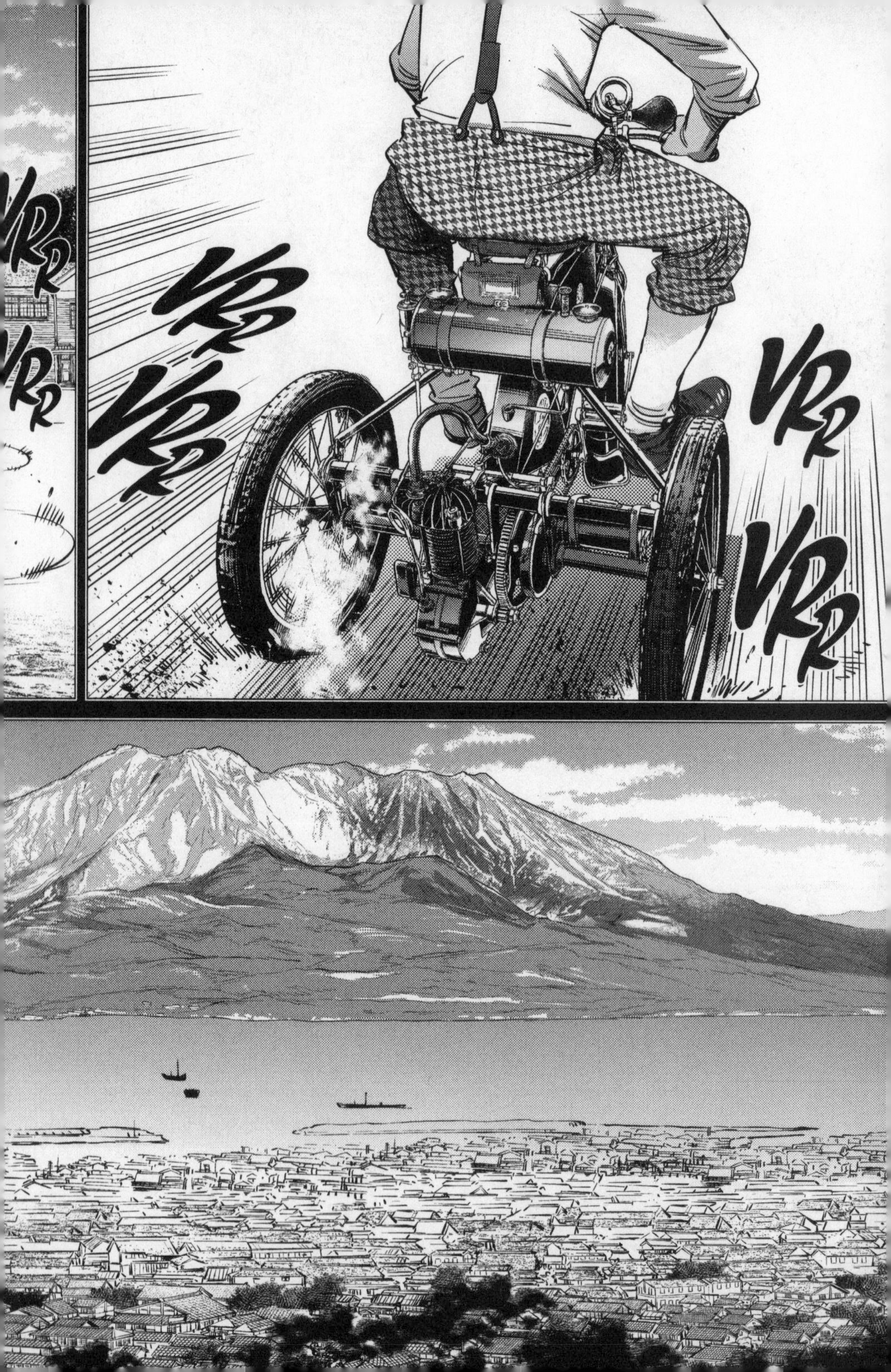
VRR
VRR
VRR
VRR
VRR
VRR

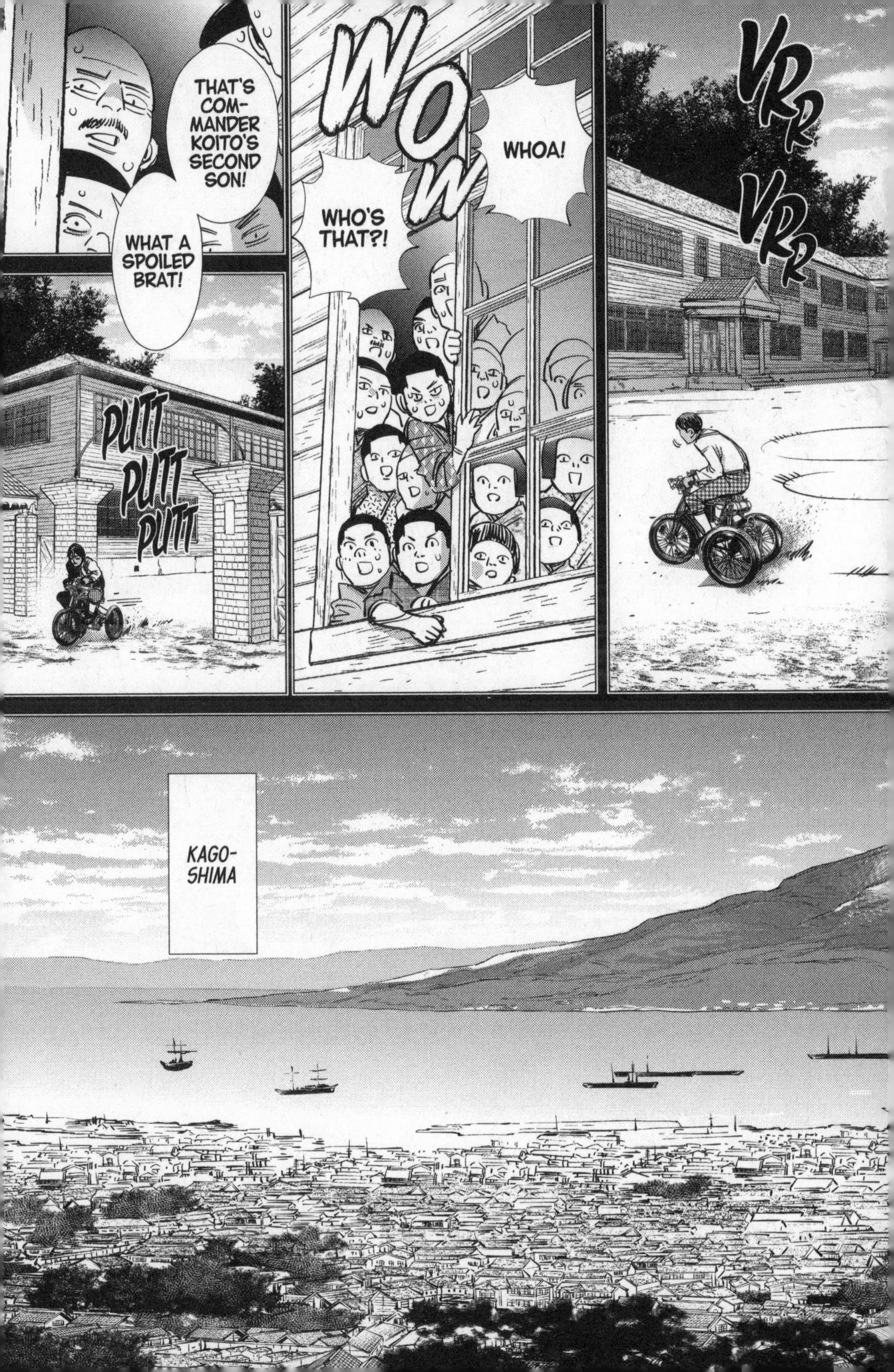
VRR VRR
WOW
WHOA!
WHO'S THAT?!
THAT'S COM-MANDER KOITO'S SECOND SON!
WHAT A SPOILED BRAT!
PUTT PUTT PUTT
KAGO-SHIMA

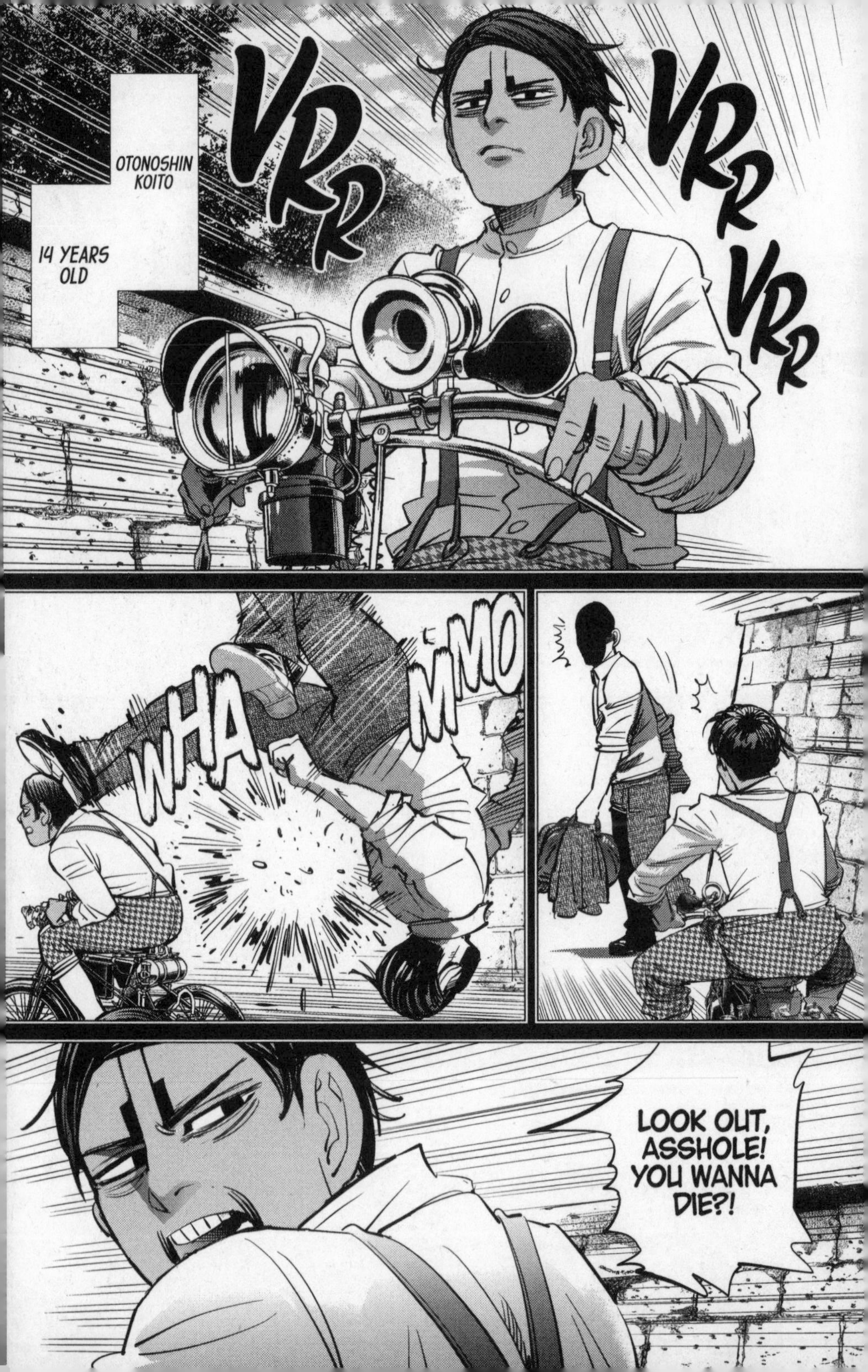
VRR VRR
VRR
OTONOSHIN KOITO
14 YEARS OLD
WHAMMO
LOOK OUT, ASSHOLE! YOU WANNA DIE?!

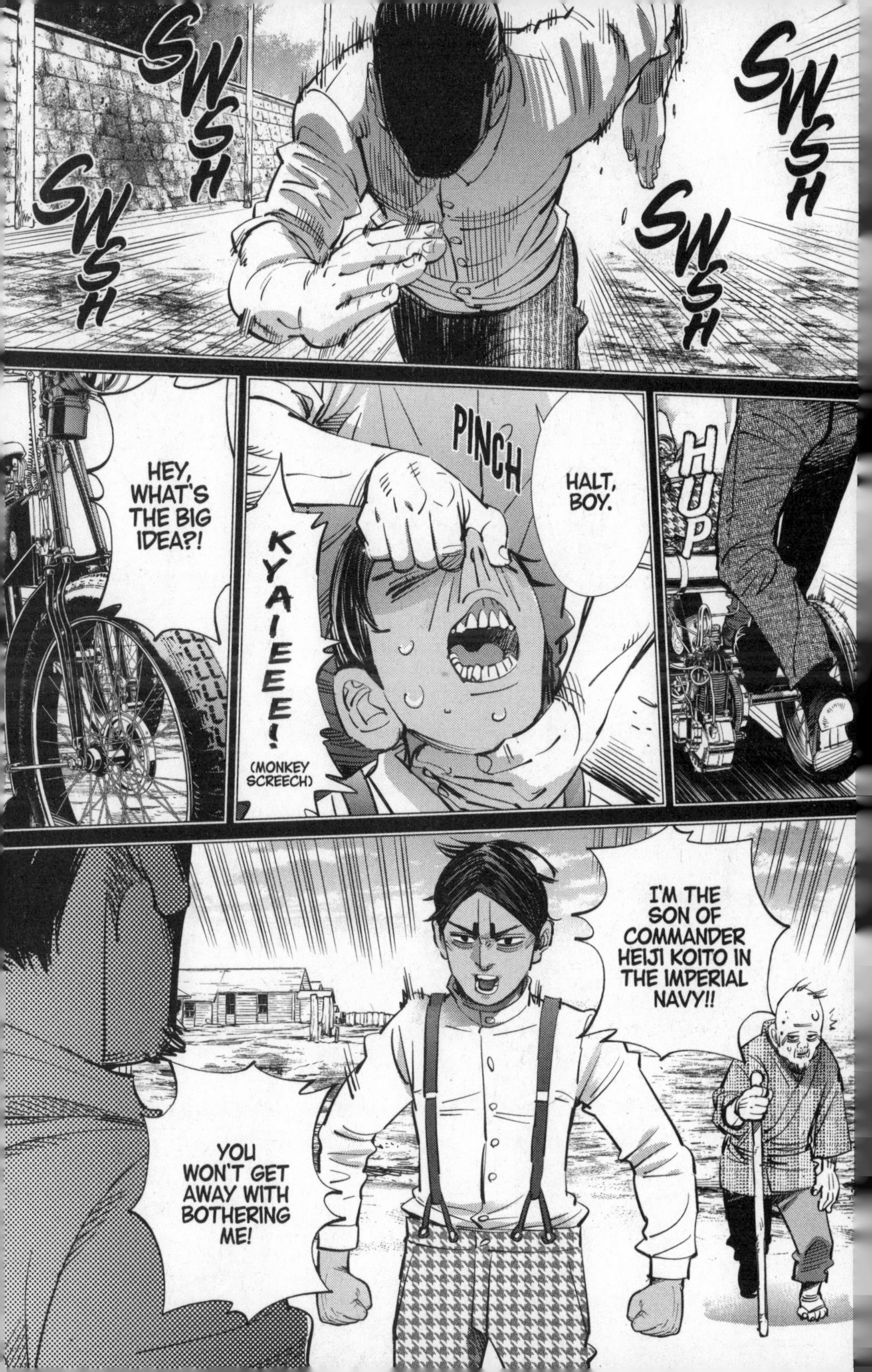
SWSH
SWSH
SWSH
SWSH
HUP
PINCH
HALT, BOY.
KYAIEEE!
(MONKEY SCREECH)
HEY, WHAT'S THE BIG IDEA?!
I'M THE SON OF COMMANDER HEIJI KOITO IN THE IMPERIAL NAVY!!
YOU WON'T GET AWAY WITH BOTHERING ME!

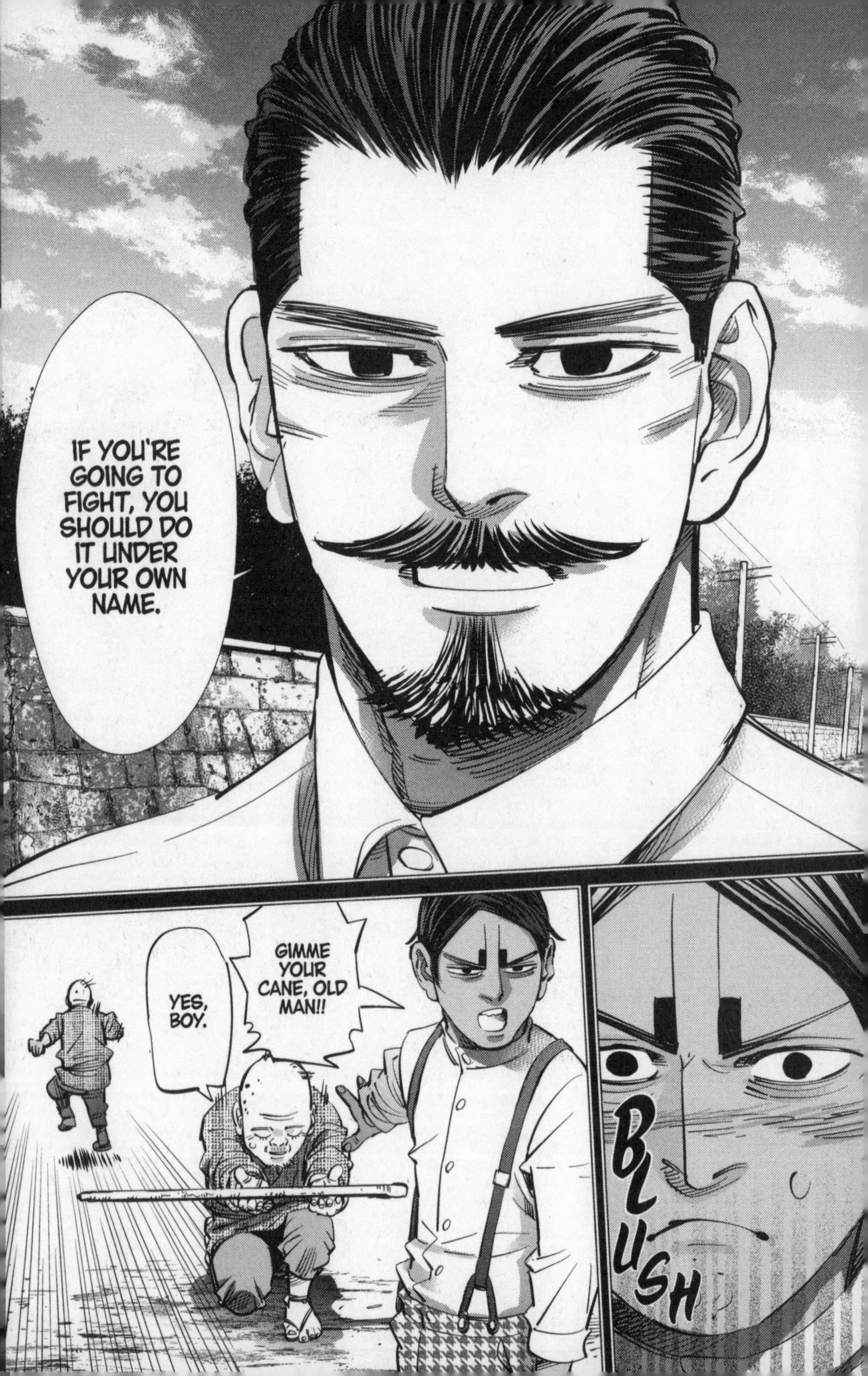
IF YOU'RE GOING TO FIGHT, YOU SHOULD DO IT UNDER YOUR OWN NAME.
BLUSH
GIMME YOUR CANE, OLD MAN!!
YES, BOY.

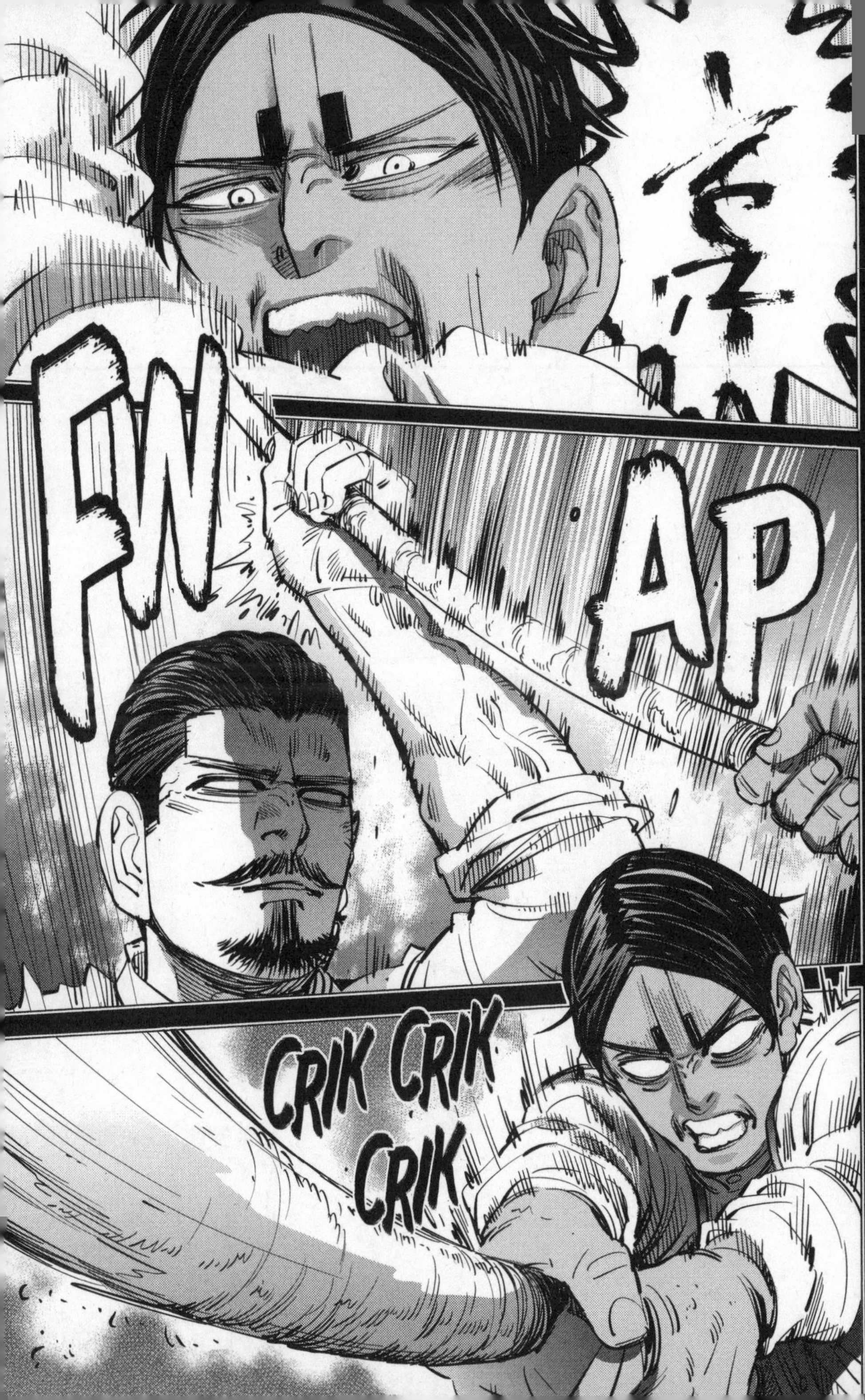
FWAP
CRIK CRIK
CRIK

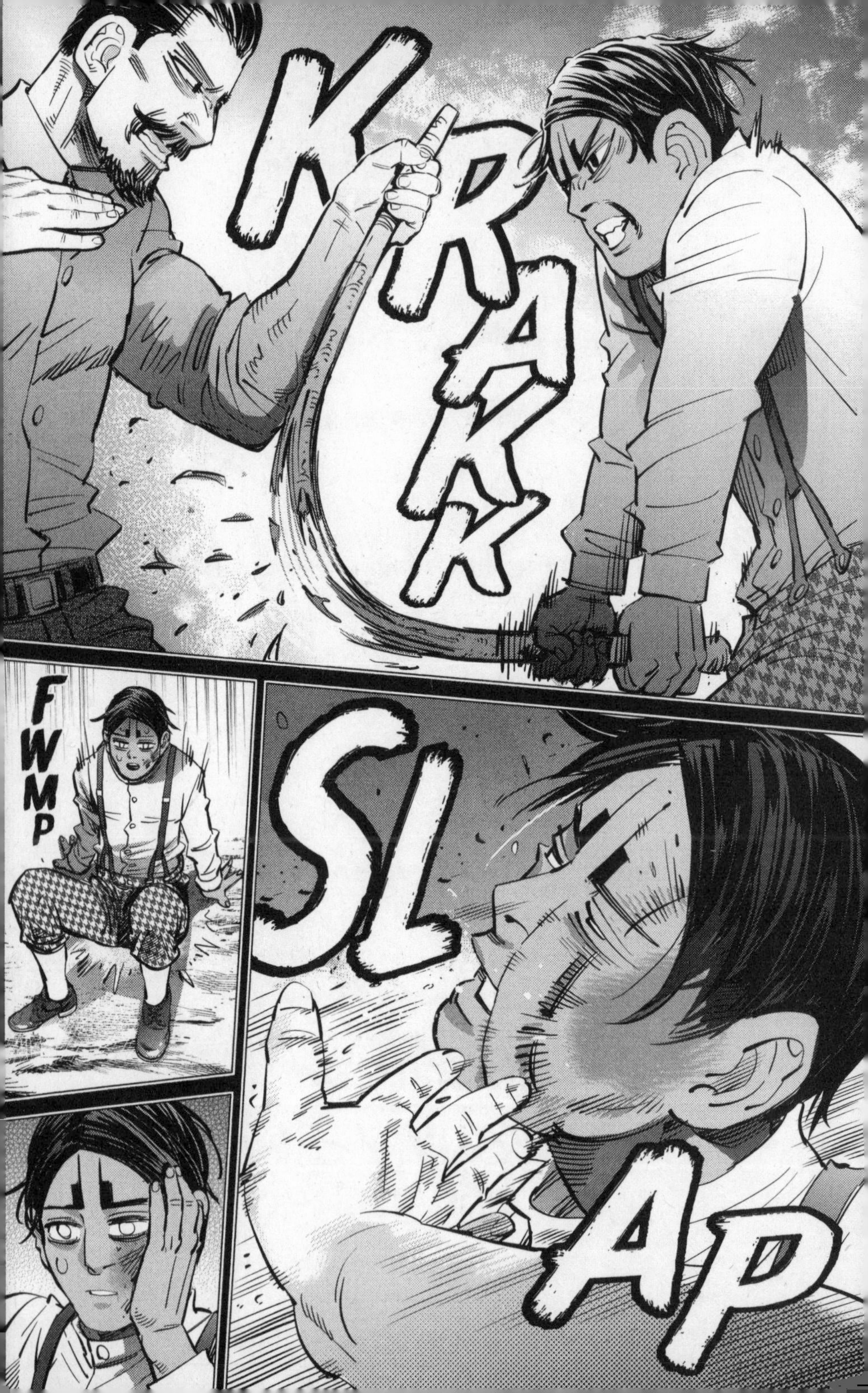
KRAKK
SLAP
FWMP

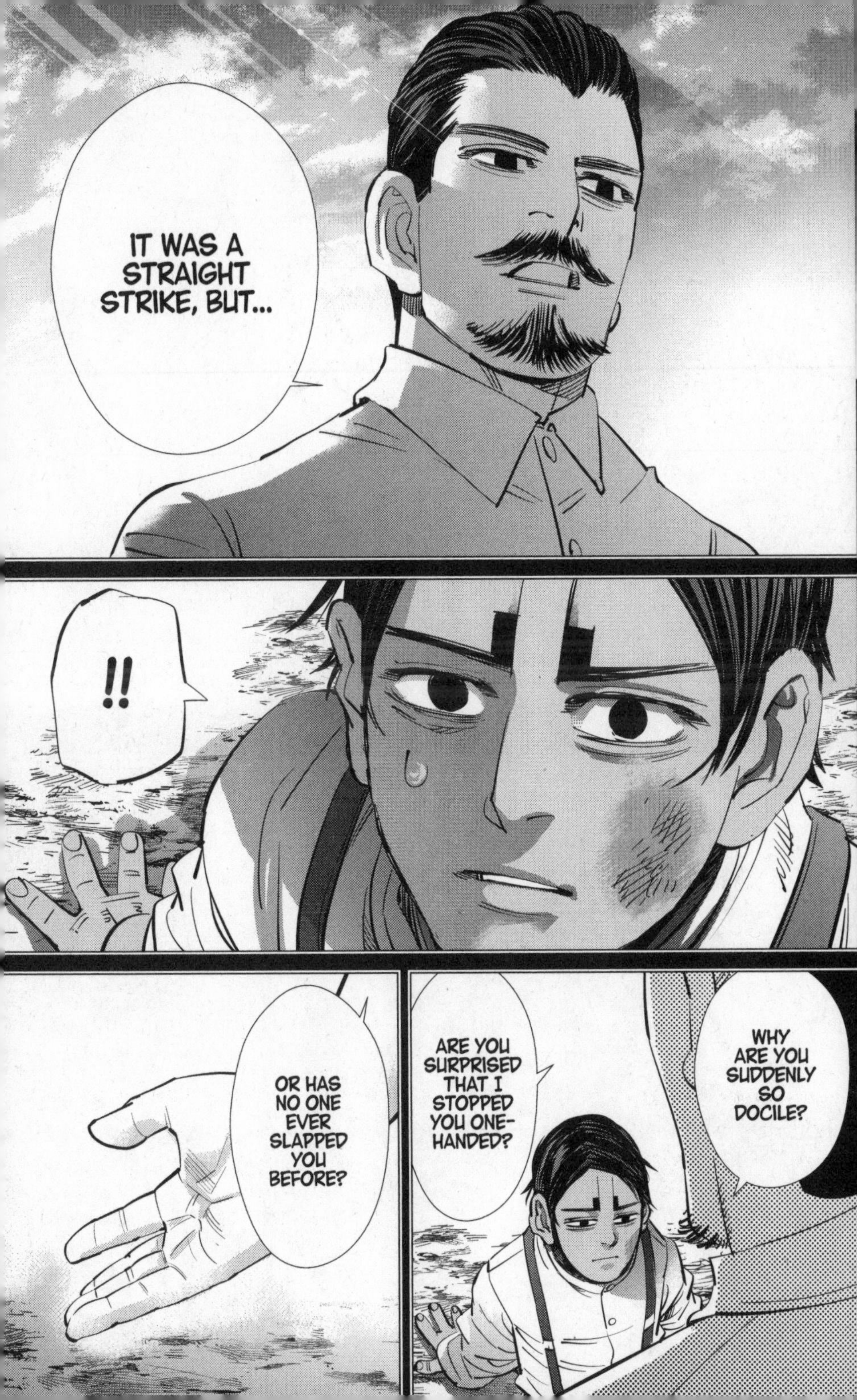
IT WAS A STRAIGHT STRIKE, BUT...
!!
WHY ARE YOU SUDDENLY SO DOCILE?
ARE YOU SURPRISED THAT I STOPPED YOU ONE-HANDED?
OR HAS NO ONE EVER SLAPPED YOU BEFORE?

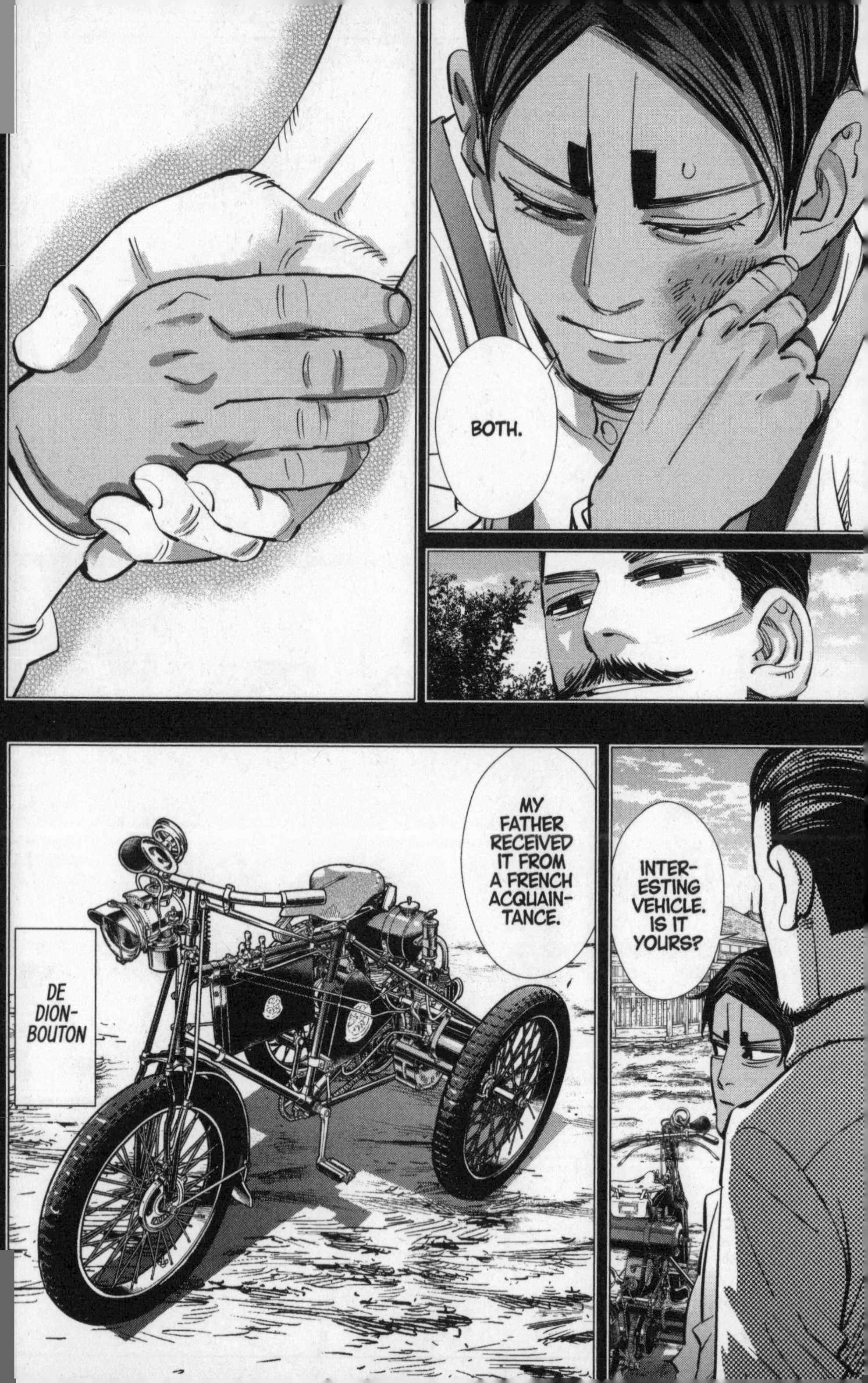
BOTH.
INTER-ESTING VEHICLE. IS IT YOURS?
MY FATHER RECEIVED IT FROM A FRENCH ACQUAIN-TANCE.
DE DION-BOUTON

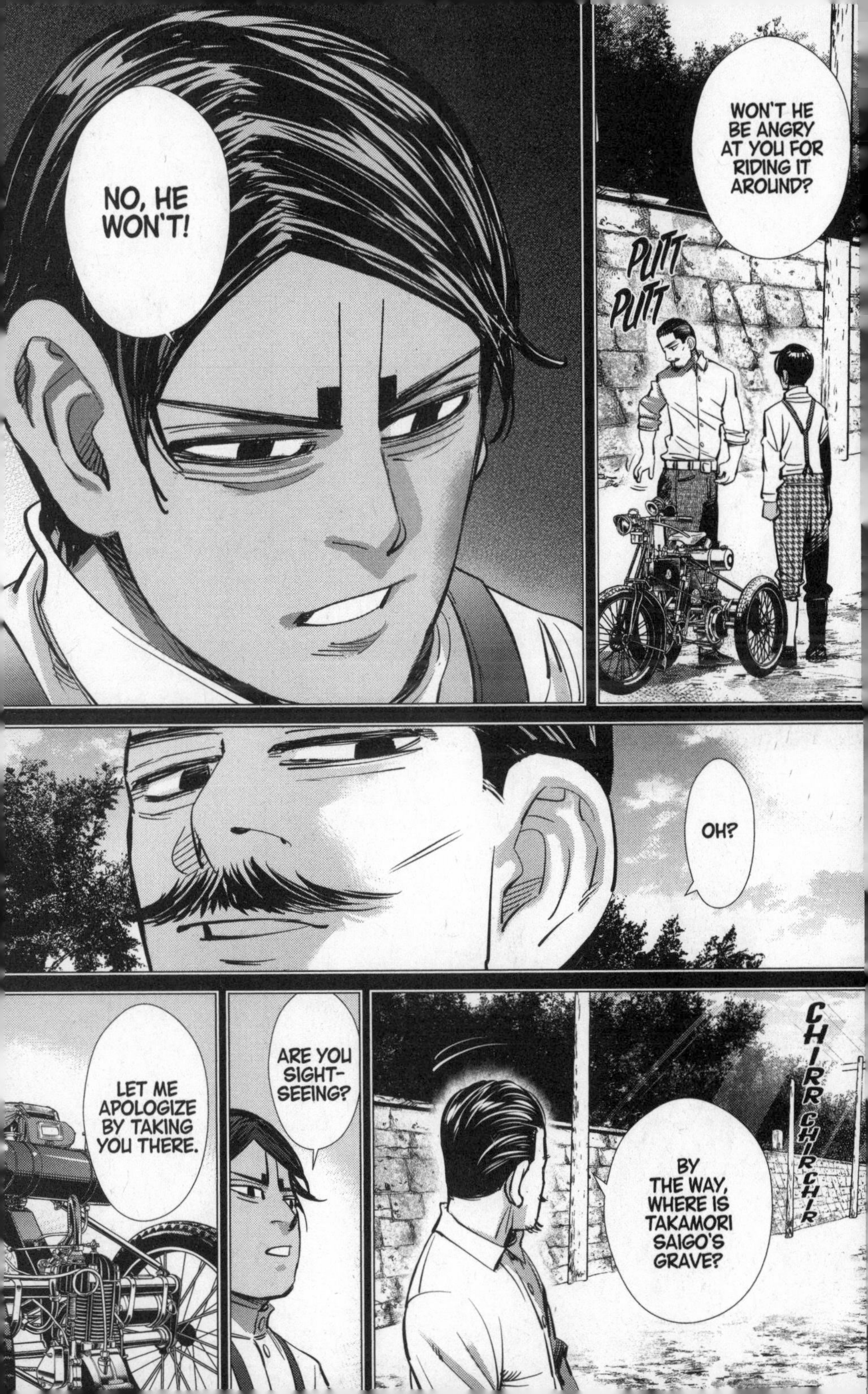
WON'T HE BE ANGRY AT YOU FOR RIDING IT AROUND?
PUTT PUTT
NO, HE WON'T!
OH?
CHIRR CHIRR CHIR
BY THE WAY, WHERE IS TAKAMORI SAIGO'S GRAVE?
ARE YOU SIGHT-SEEING?
LET ME APOLOGIZE BY TAKING YOU THERE.

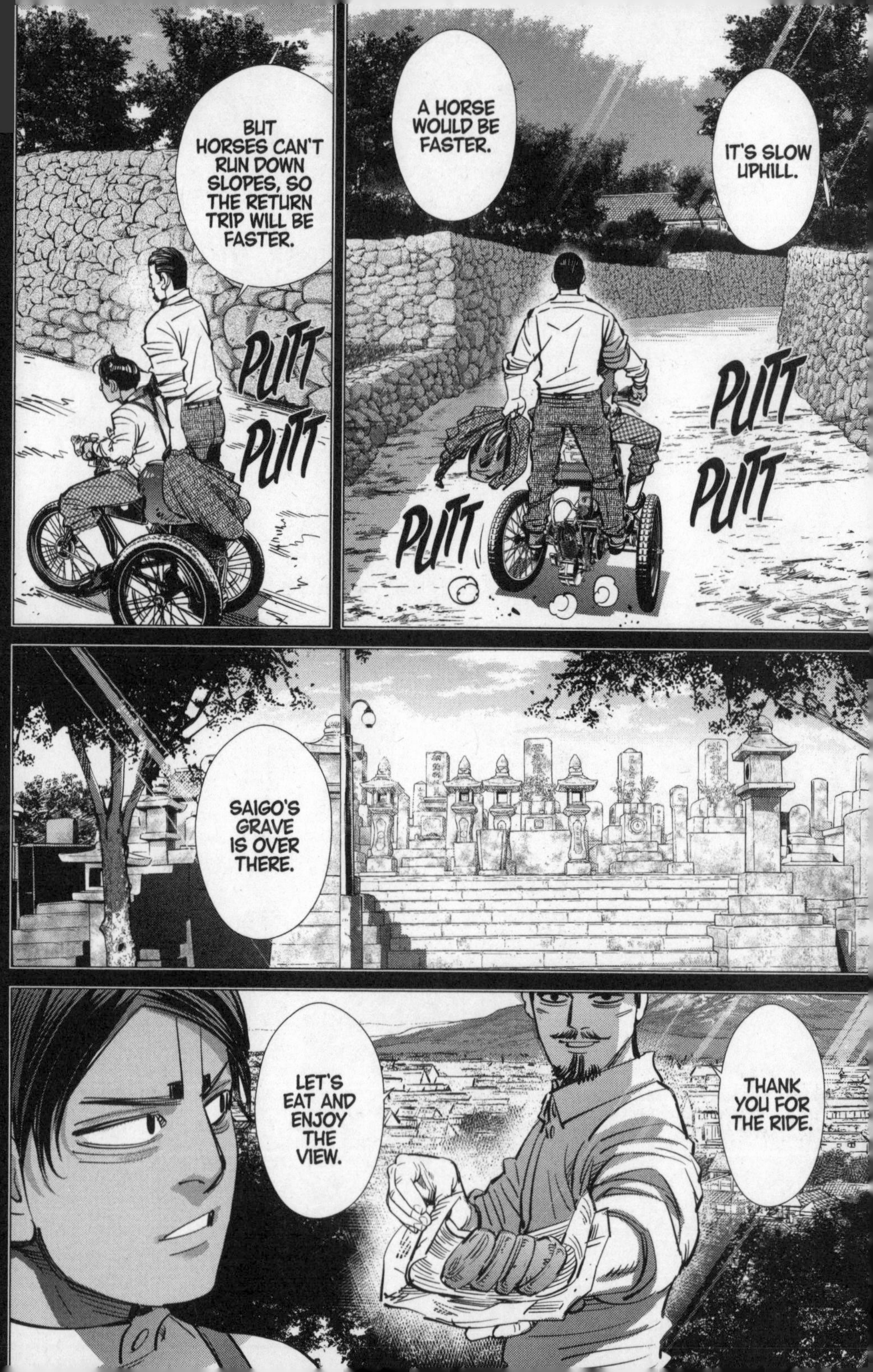

IT'S SLOW UPHILL.
A HORSE WOULD BE FASTER.
PUTT PUTT
PUTT
BUT HORSES CAN'T RUN DOWN SLOPES, SO THE RETURN TRIP WILL BE FASTER.
PUTT PUTT
SAIGO'S GRAVE IS OVER THERE.
THANK YOU FOR THE RIDE.
LET'S EAT AND ENJOY THE VIEW.

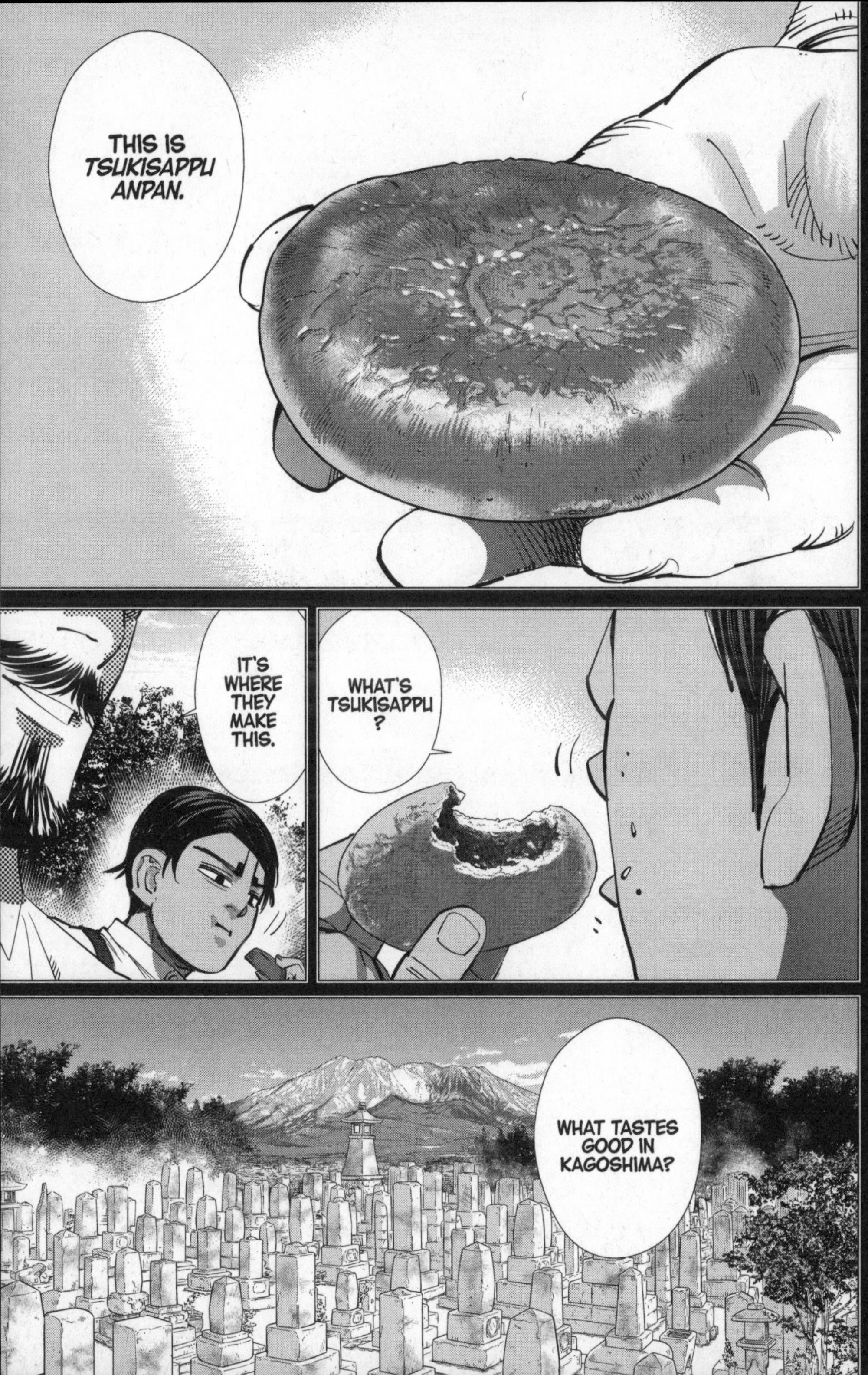
THIS IS TSUKISAPPU ANPAN.
WHAT'S TSUKISAPPU?
IT'S WHERE THEY MAKE THIS.
WHAT TASTES GOOD IN KAGOSHIMA?

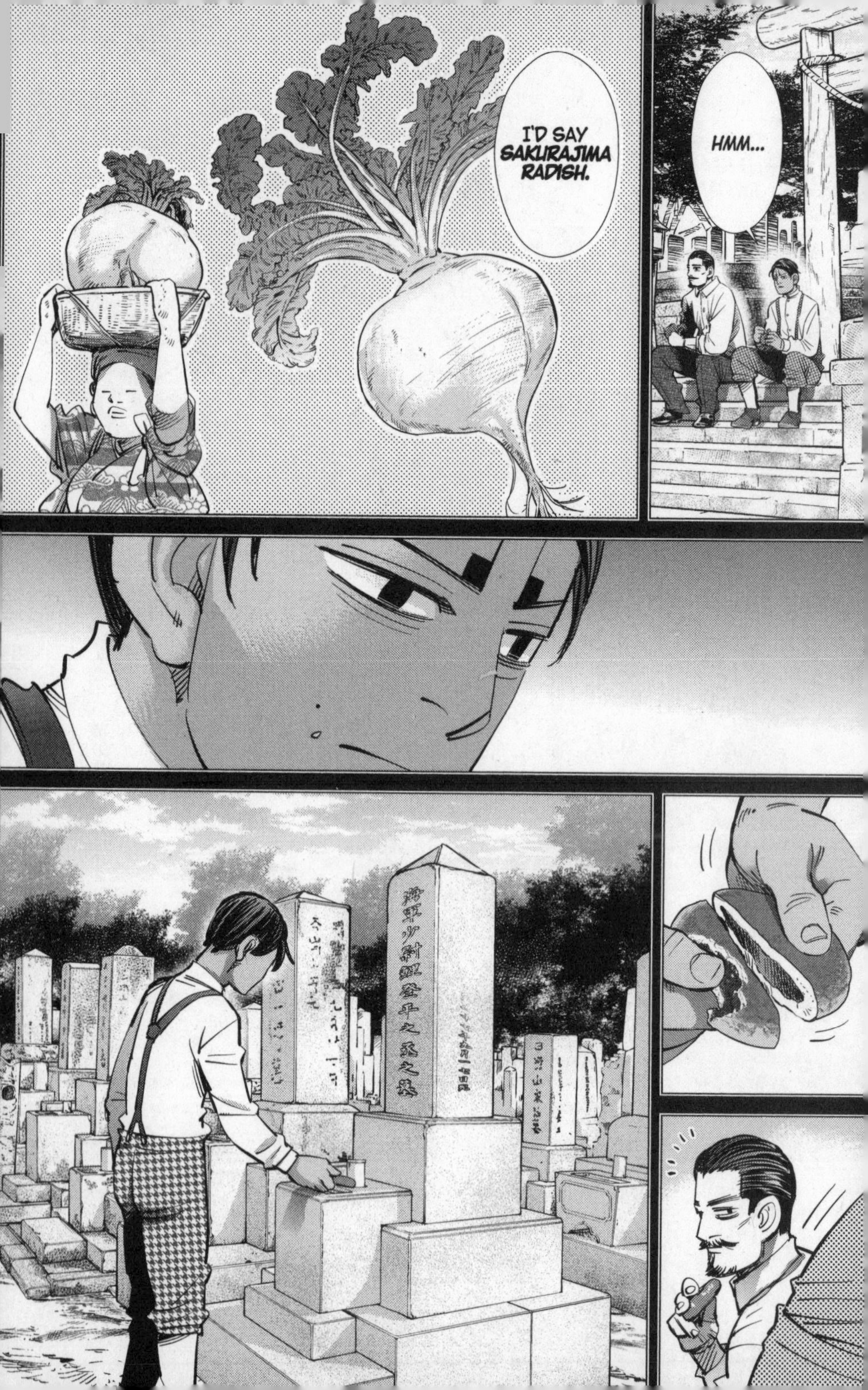
HMM...
I'D SAY SAKURAJIMA RADISH.

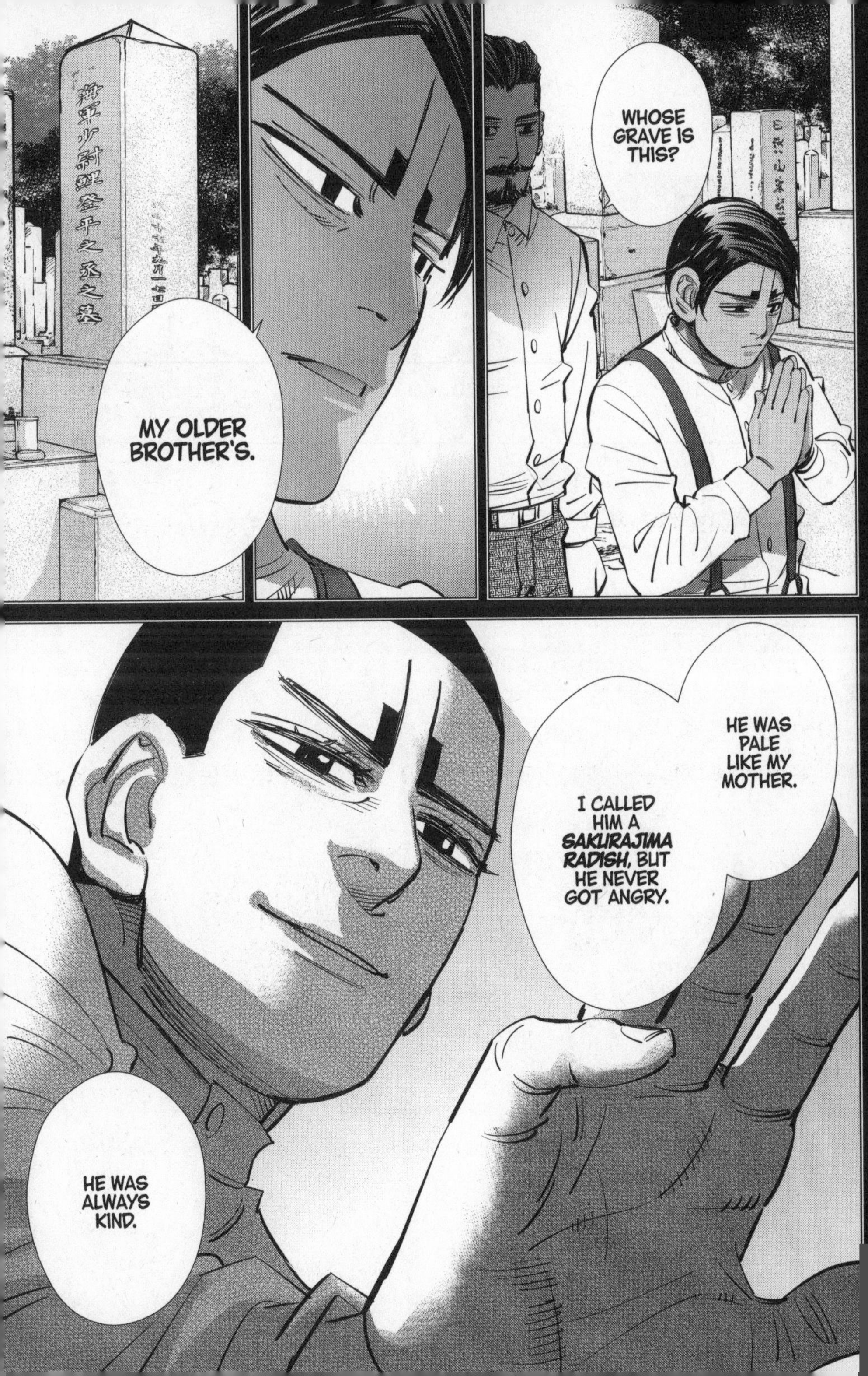
WHOSE GRAVE IS THIS?
MY OLDER BROTHER'S.
HE WAS PALE LIKE MY MOTHER.
I CALLED HIM A SAKURAJIMA RADISH, BUT HE NEVER GOT ANGRY.
HE WAS ALWAYS KIND.

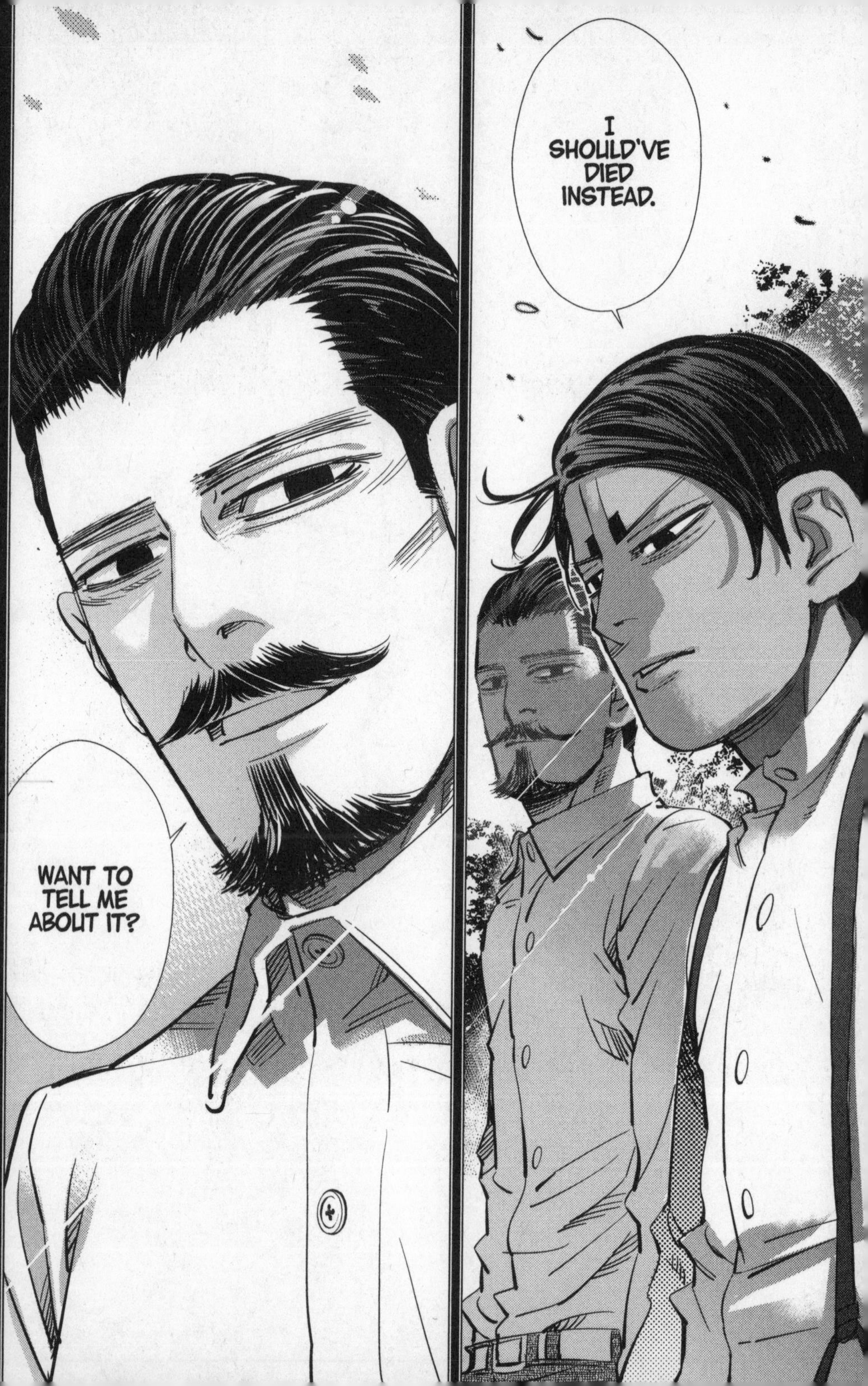
I SHOULD'VE DIED INSTEAD.
WANT TO TELL ME ABOUT IT?

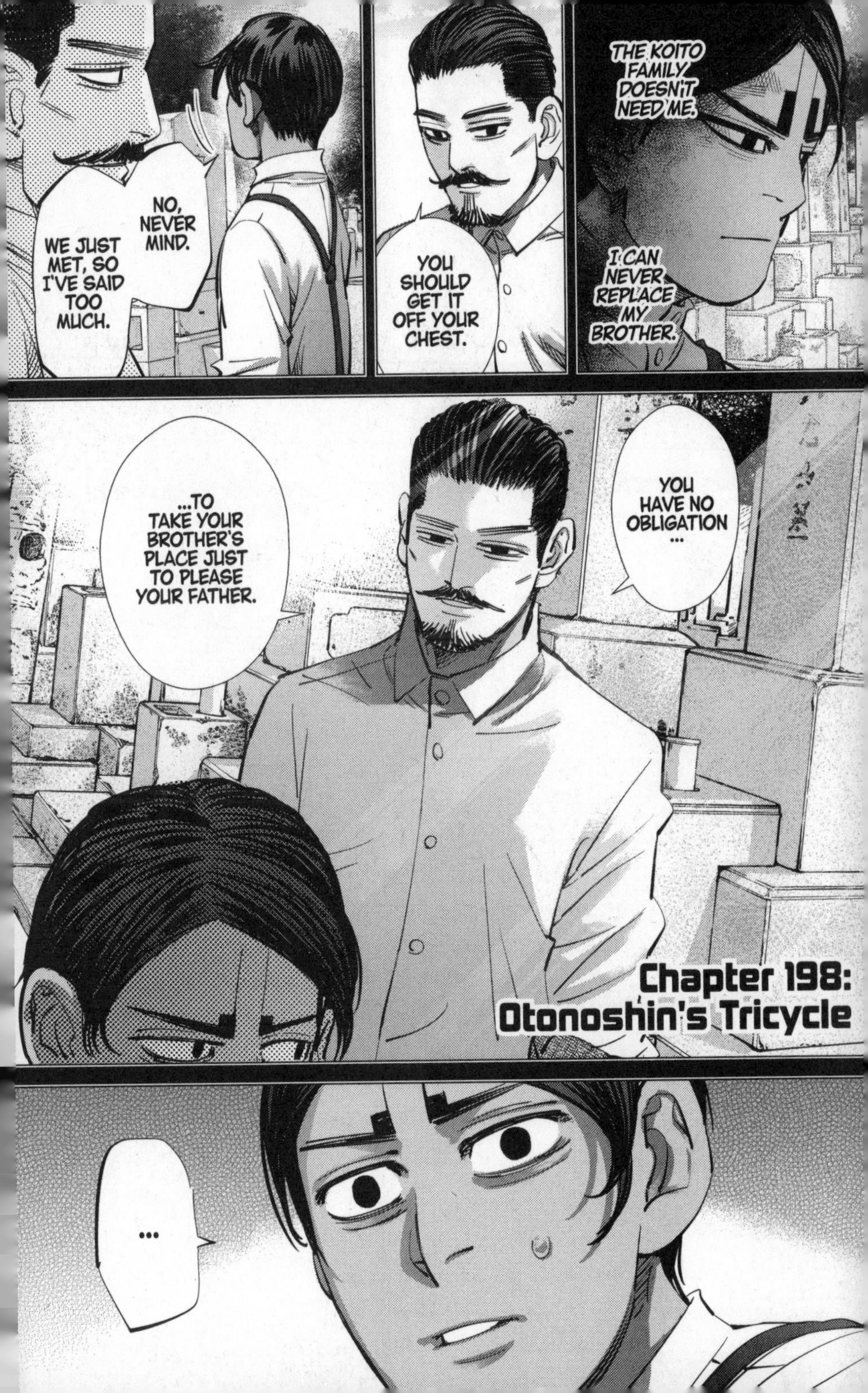
THE KOITO FAMILY DOESN'T NEED ME.
I CAN NEVER REPLACE MY BROTHER.
YOU SHOULD GET IT OFF YOUR CHEST.
NO, NEVER MIND.
WE JUST MET, SO I'VE SAID TOO MUCH.
YOU HAVE NO OBLIGATION...
...TO TAKE YOUR BROTHER'S PLACE JUST TO PLEASE YOUR FATHER.
Chapter 198: Otonoshin's Tricycle
...

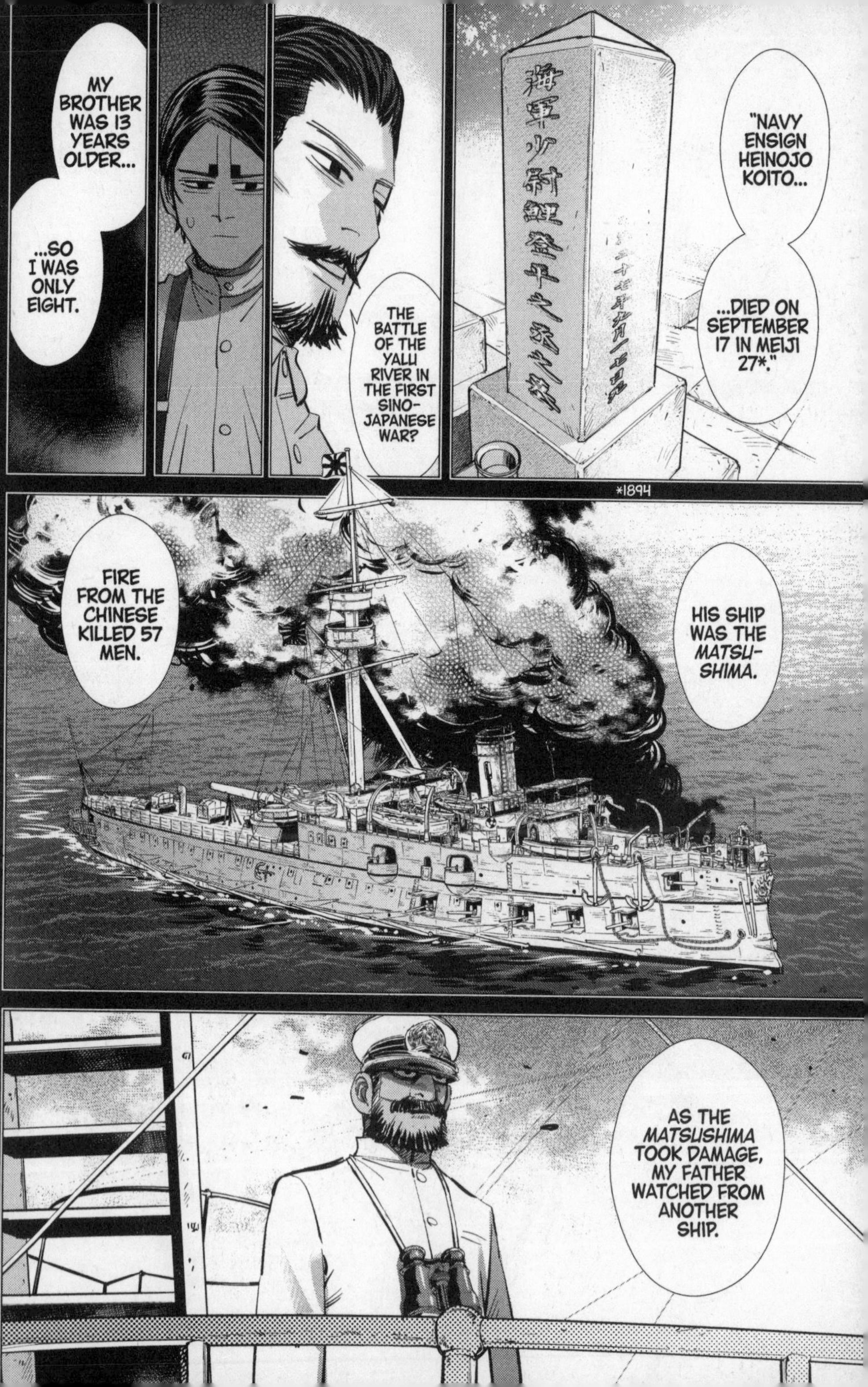
"NAVY ENSIGN HEINOJO KOITO...
...DIED ON SEPTEMBER 17 IN MEIJI 27*."
*1894
THE BATTLE OF THE YALU RIVER IN THE FIRST SINO-JAPANESE WAR?
MY BROTHER WAS 13 YEARS OLDER...
...SO I WAS ONLY EIGHT.
HIS SHIP WAS THE *MATSUSHIMA*.
FIRE FROM THE CHINESE KILLED 57 MEN.
AS THE *MATSUSHIMA* TOOK DAMAGE, MY FATHER WATCHED FROM ANOTHER SHIP.

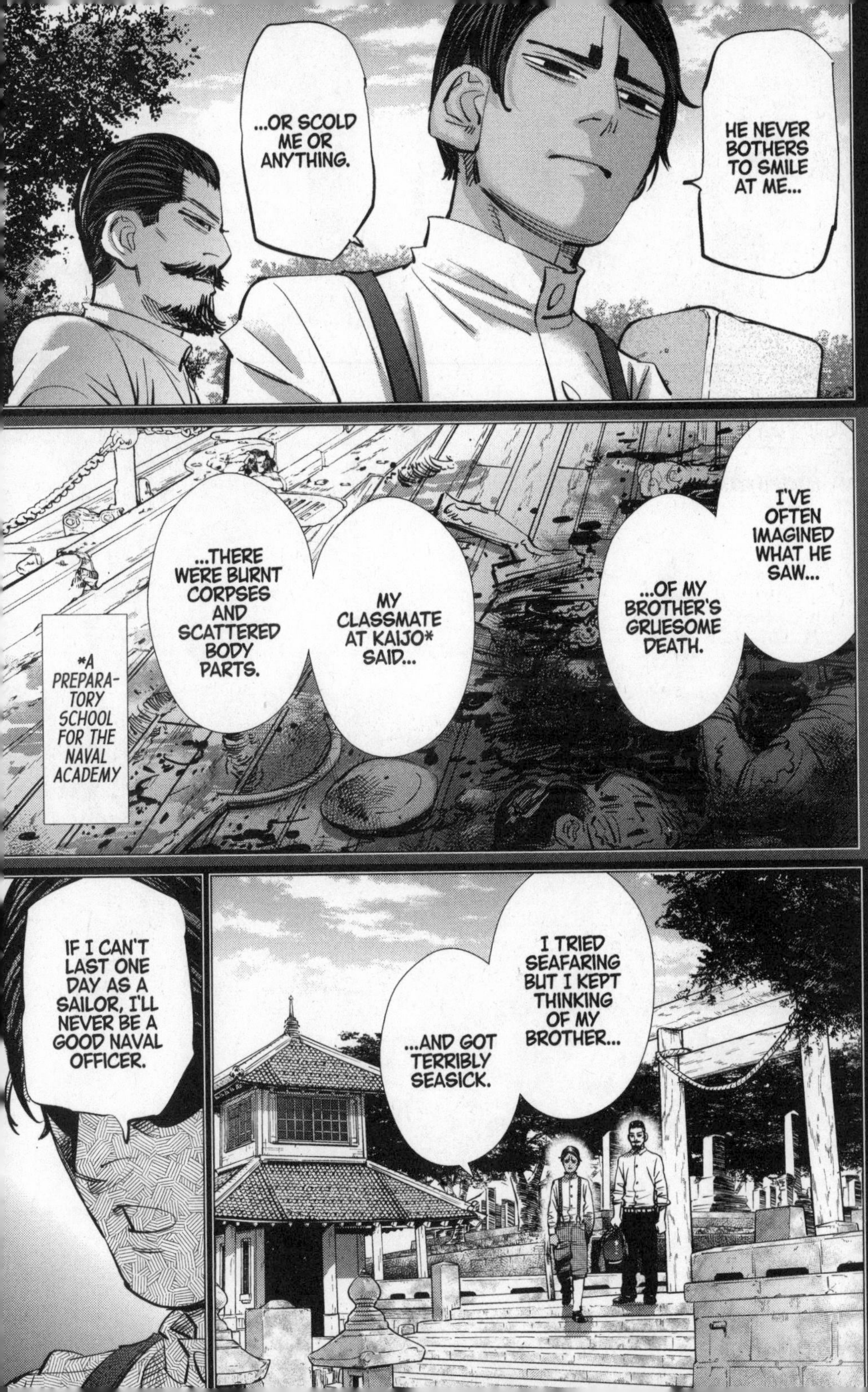
HE NEVER BOTHERS TO SMILE AT ME...
...OR SCOLD ME OR ANYTHING.
I'VE OFTEN IMAGINED WHAT HE SAW...
...OF MY BROTHER'S GRUESOME DEATH.
MY CLASSMATE AT KAIJO* SAID...
...THERE WERE BURNT CORPSES AND SCATTERED BODY PARTS.
*A PREPARATORY SCHOOL FOR THE NAVAL ACADEMY
I TRIED SEAFARING BUT I KEPT THINKING OF MY BROTHER...
...AND GOT TERRIBLY SEASICK.
IF I CAN'T LAST ONE DAY AS A SAILOR, I'LL NEVER BE A GOOD NAVAL OFFICER.

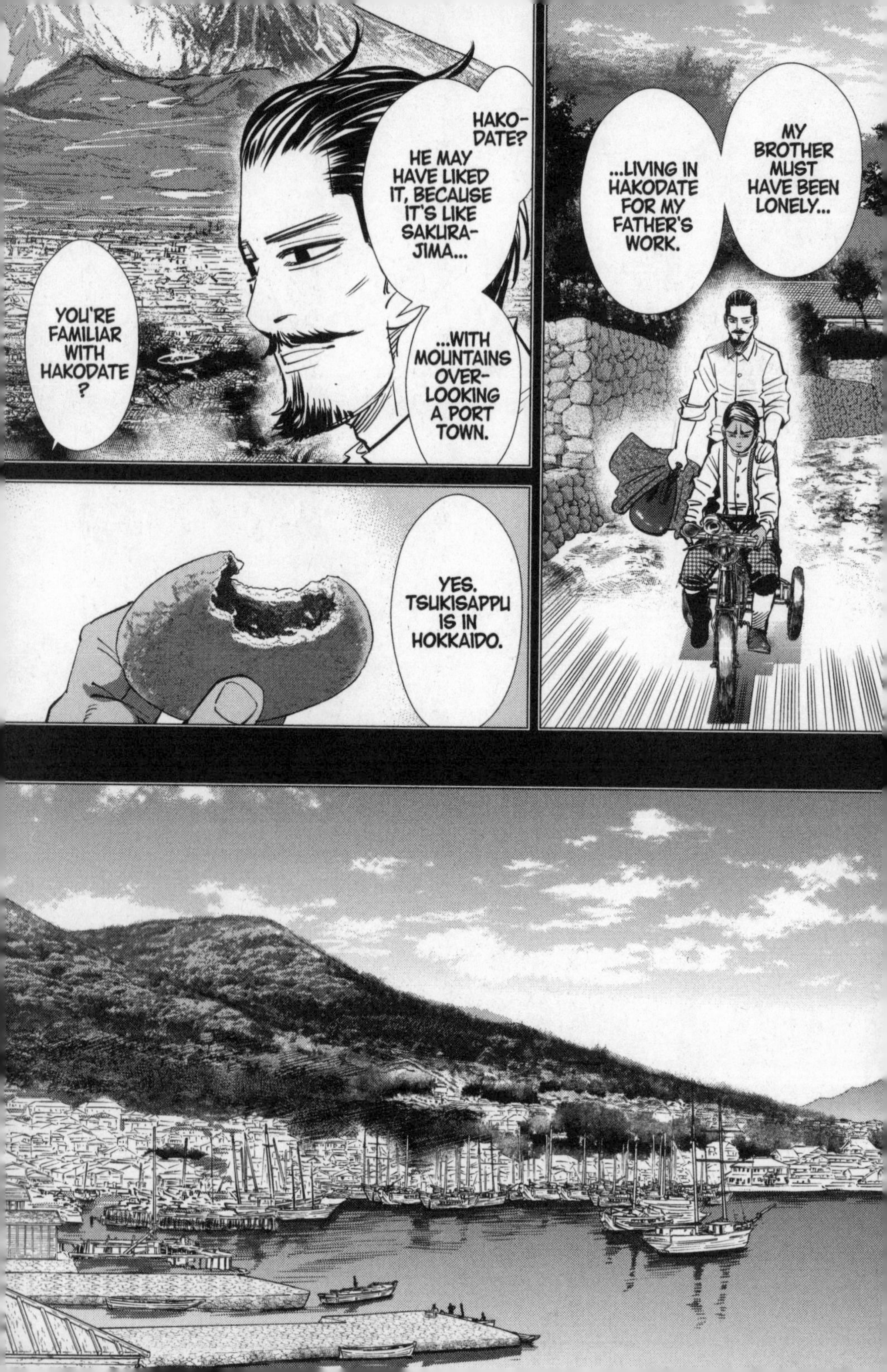
MY BROTHER MUST HAVE BEEN LONELY...
...LIVING IN HAKODATE FOR MY FATHER'S WORK.
HAKO-DATE?
HE MAY HAVE LIKED IT, BECAUSE IT'S LIKE SAKURA-JIMA...
...WITH MOUNTAINS OVER-LOOKING A PORT TOWN.
YOU'RE FAMILIAR WITH HAKODATE?
YES. TSUKISAPPU IS IN HOKKAIDO.

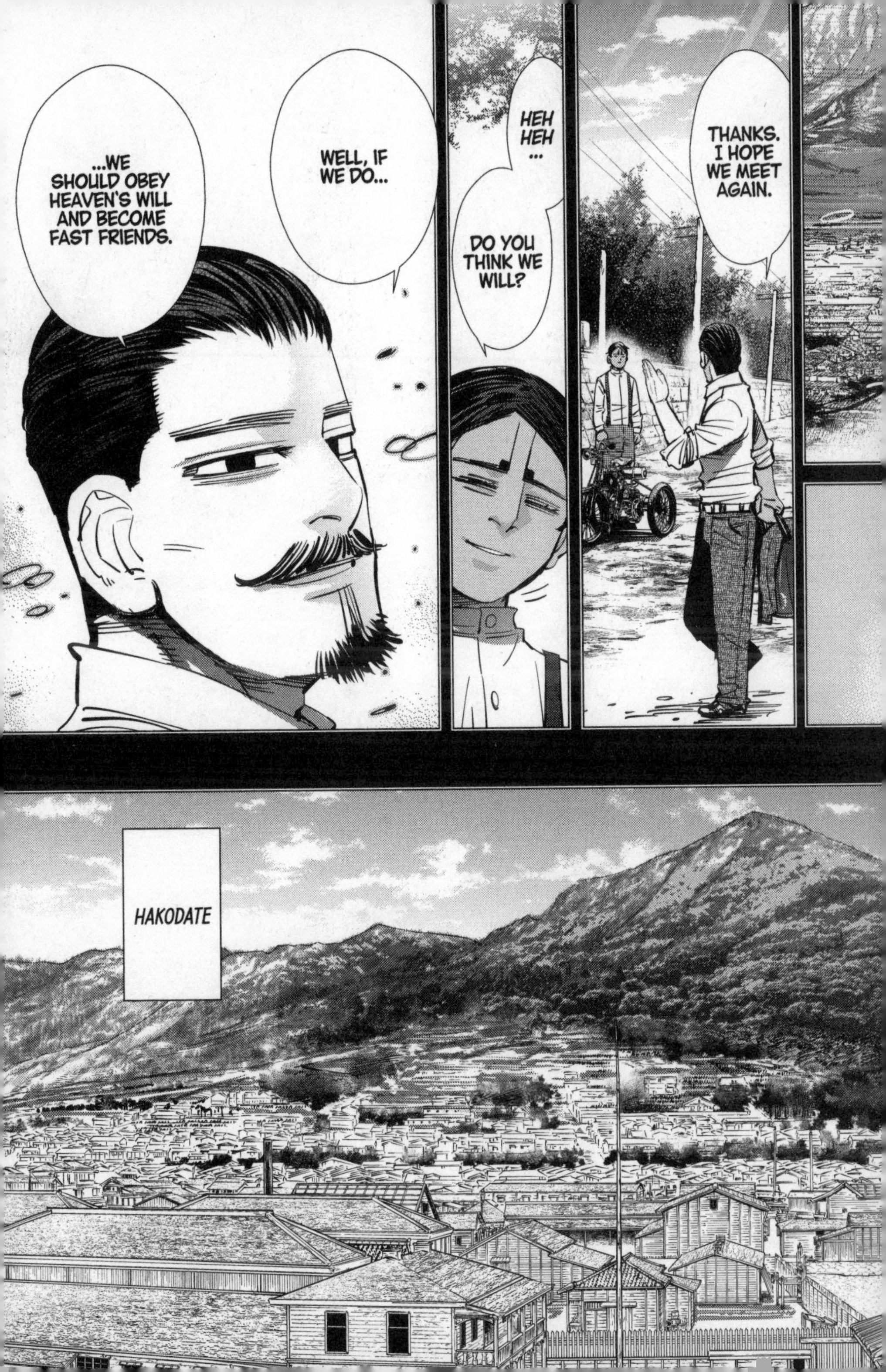
THANKS. I HOPE WE MEET AGAIN.
HEH HEH ...
DO YOU THINK WE WILL?
WELL, IF WE DO...
...WE SHOULD OBEY HEAVEN'S WILL AND BECOME FAST FRIENDS.
HAKODATE

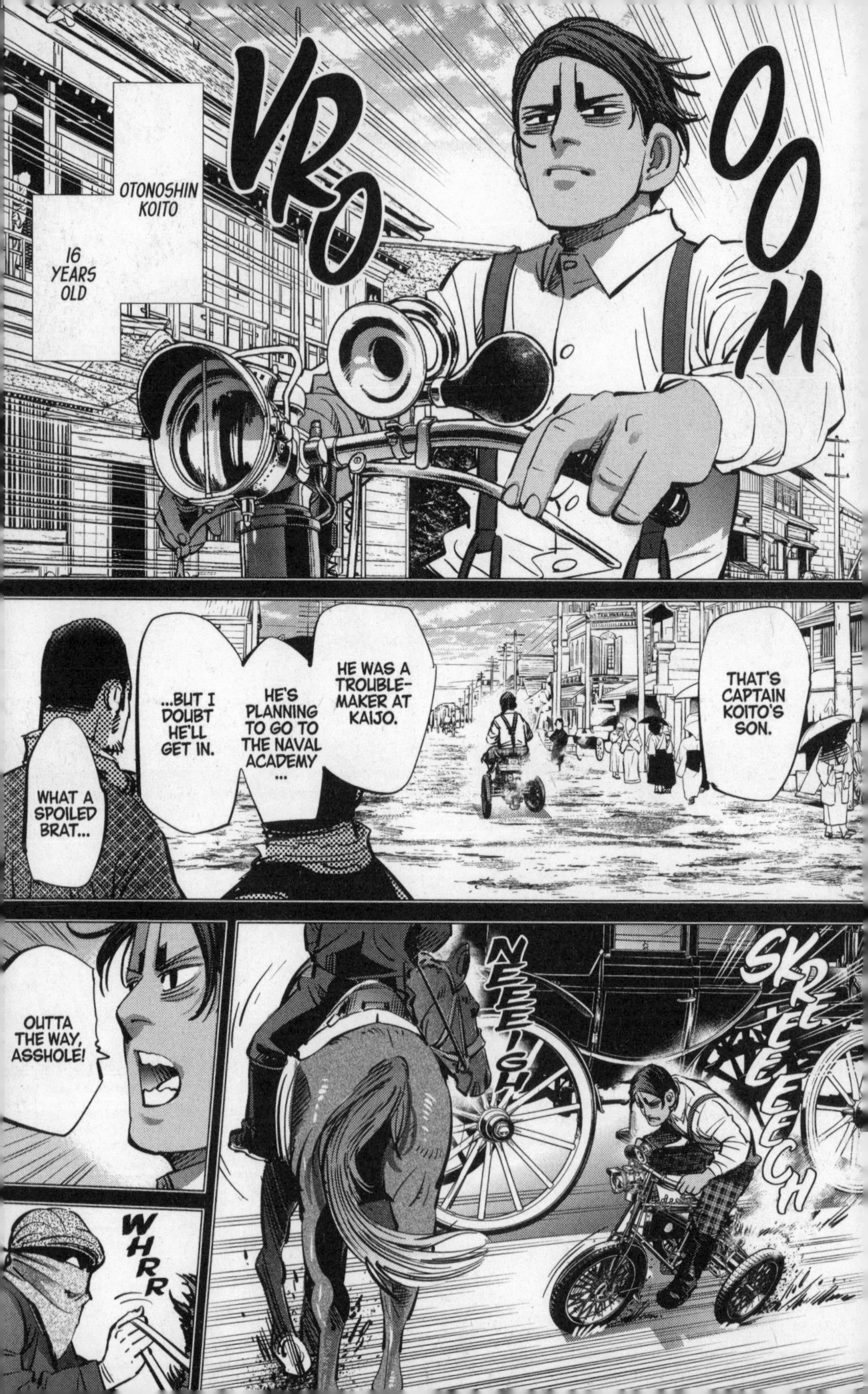
VROOOM
OTONOSHIN KOITO
16 YEARS OLD
THAT'S CAPTAIN KOITO'S SON.
HE WAS A TROUBLE-MAKER AT KAIJO.
HE'S PLANNING TO GO TO THE NAVAL ACADEMY...
...BUT I DOUBT HE'LL GET IN.
WHAT A SPOILED BRAT...
SKREEEEECH
NEEEIGH
OUTTA THE WAY, ASSHOLE!
WHRR

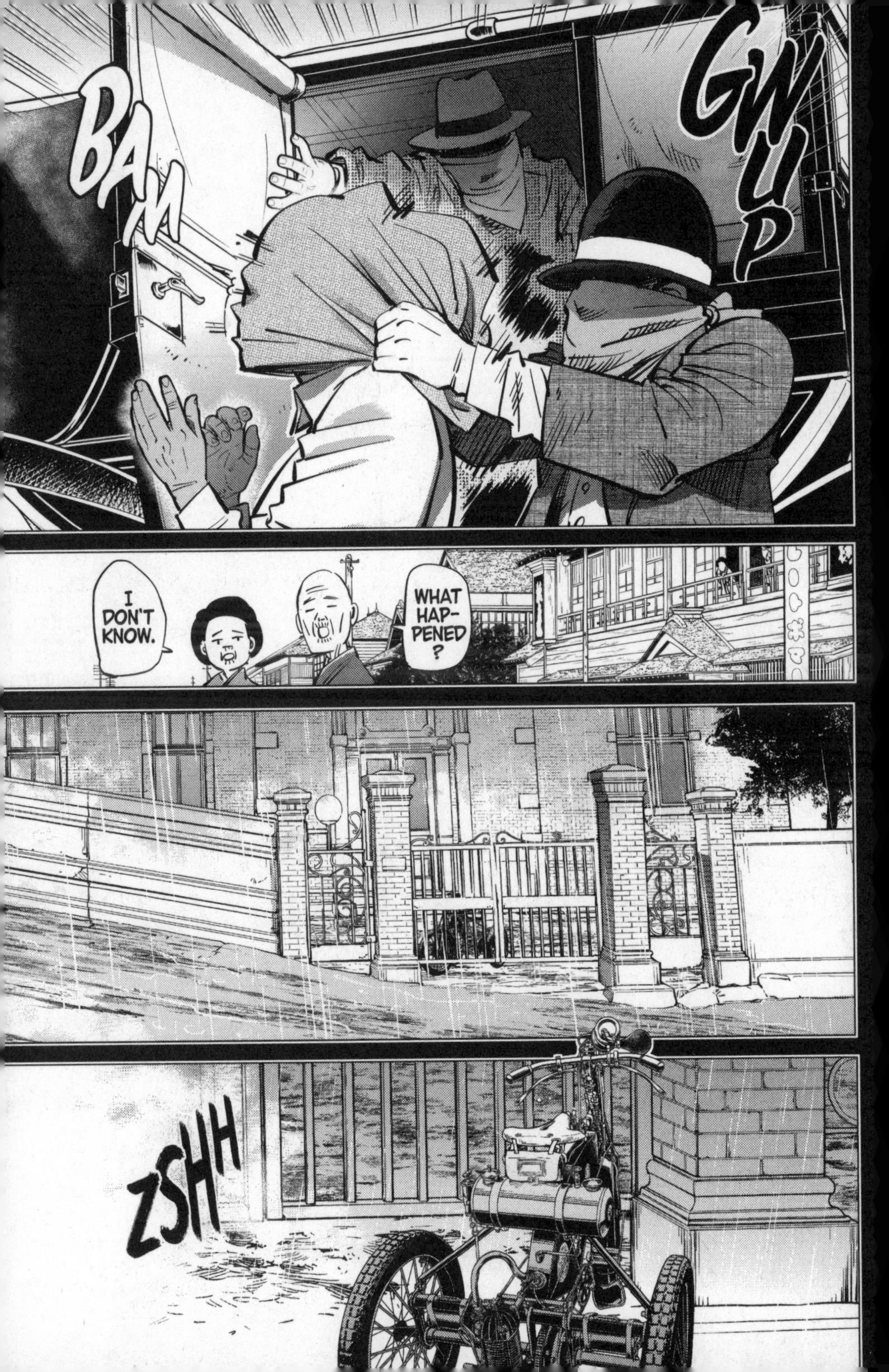
GWUP
BAM
WHAT HAP-PENED?
I DON'T KNOW.
ZSHH

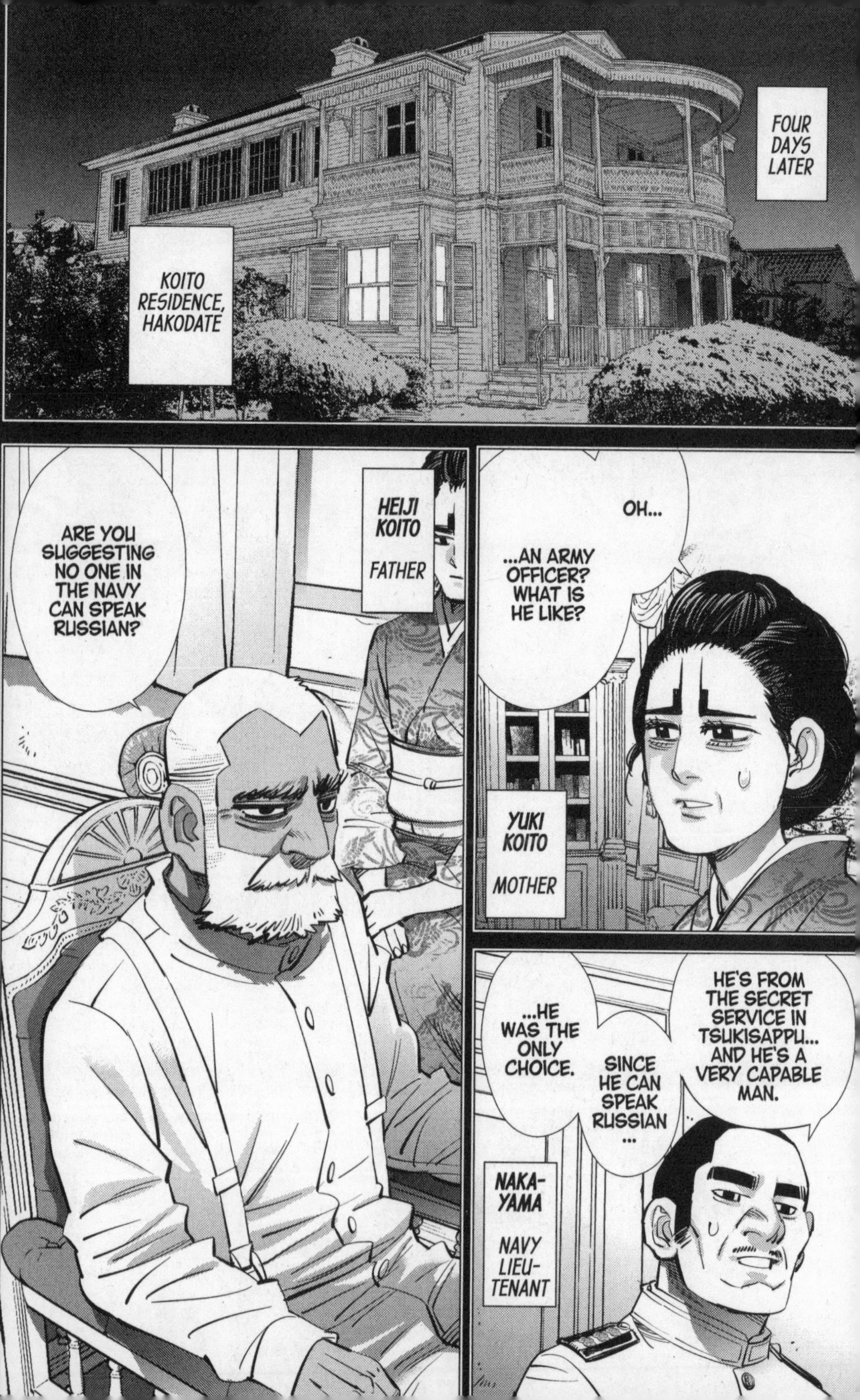
FOUR DAYS LATER
KOITO RESIDENCE, HAKODATE
OH...
...AN ARMY OFFICER? WHAT IS HE LIKE?
YUKI KOITO
MOTHER
HE'S FROM THE SECRET SERVICE IN TSUKISAPPU... AND HE'S A VERY CAPABLE MAN.
SINCE HE CAN SPEAK RUSSIAN ...
...HE WAS THE ONLY CHOICE.
NAKA-YAMA
NAVY LIEU-TENANT
HEIJI KOITO
FATHER
ARE YOU SUGGESTING NO ONE IN THE NAVY CAN SPEAK RUSSIAN?

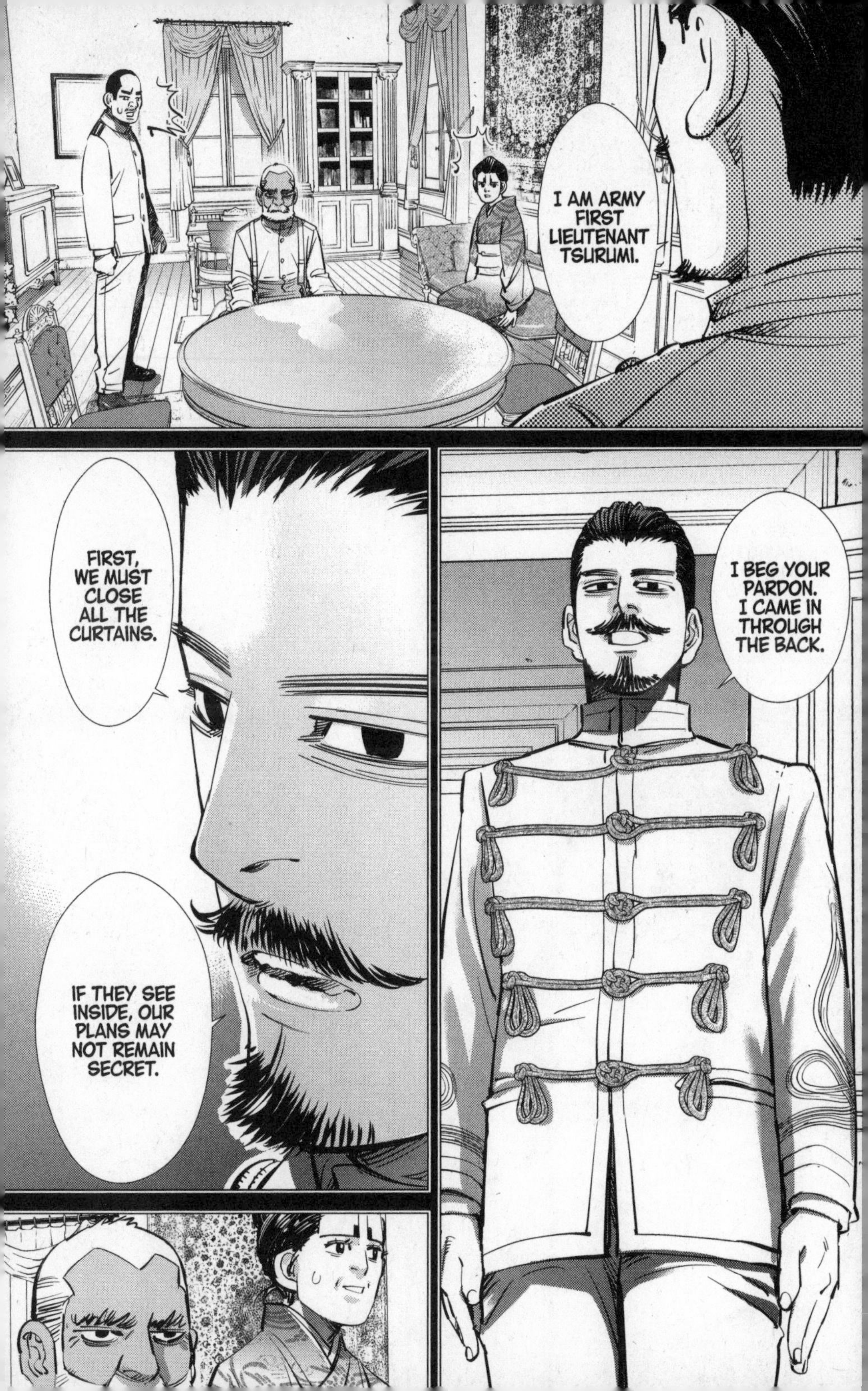
I AM ARMY FIRST LIEUTENANT TSURUMI.
I BEG YOUR PARDON. I CAME IN THROUGH THE BACK.
FIRST, WE MUST CLOSE ALL THE CURTAINS.
IF THEY SEE INSIDE, OUR PLANS MAY NOT REMAIN SECRET.

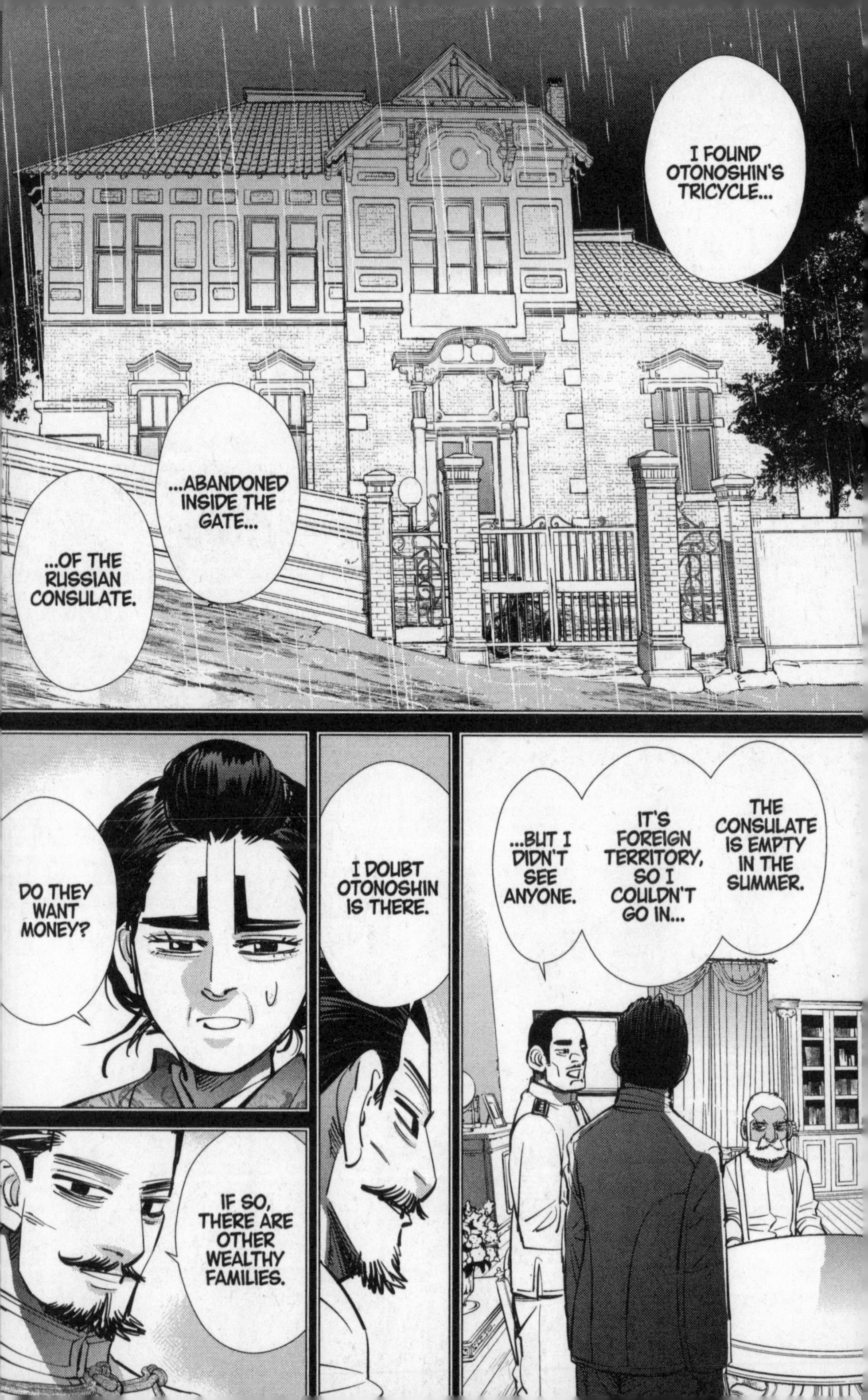
I FOUND OTONOSHIN'S TRICYCLE...
...ABANDONED INSIDE THE GATE...
...OF THE RUSSIAN CONSULATE.
THE CONSULATE IS EMPTY IN THE SUMMER.
IT'S FOREIGN TERRITORY, SO I COULDN'T GO IN...
...BUT I DIDN'T SEE ANYONE.
I DOUBT OTONOSHIN IS THERE.
DO THEY WANT MONEY?
IF SO, THERE ARE OTHER WEALTHY FAMILIES.

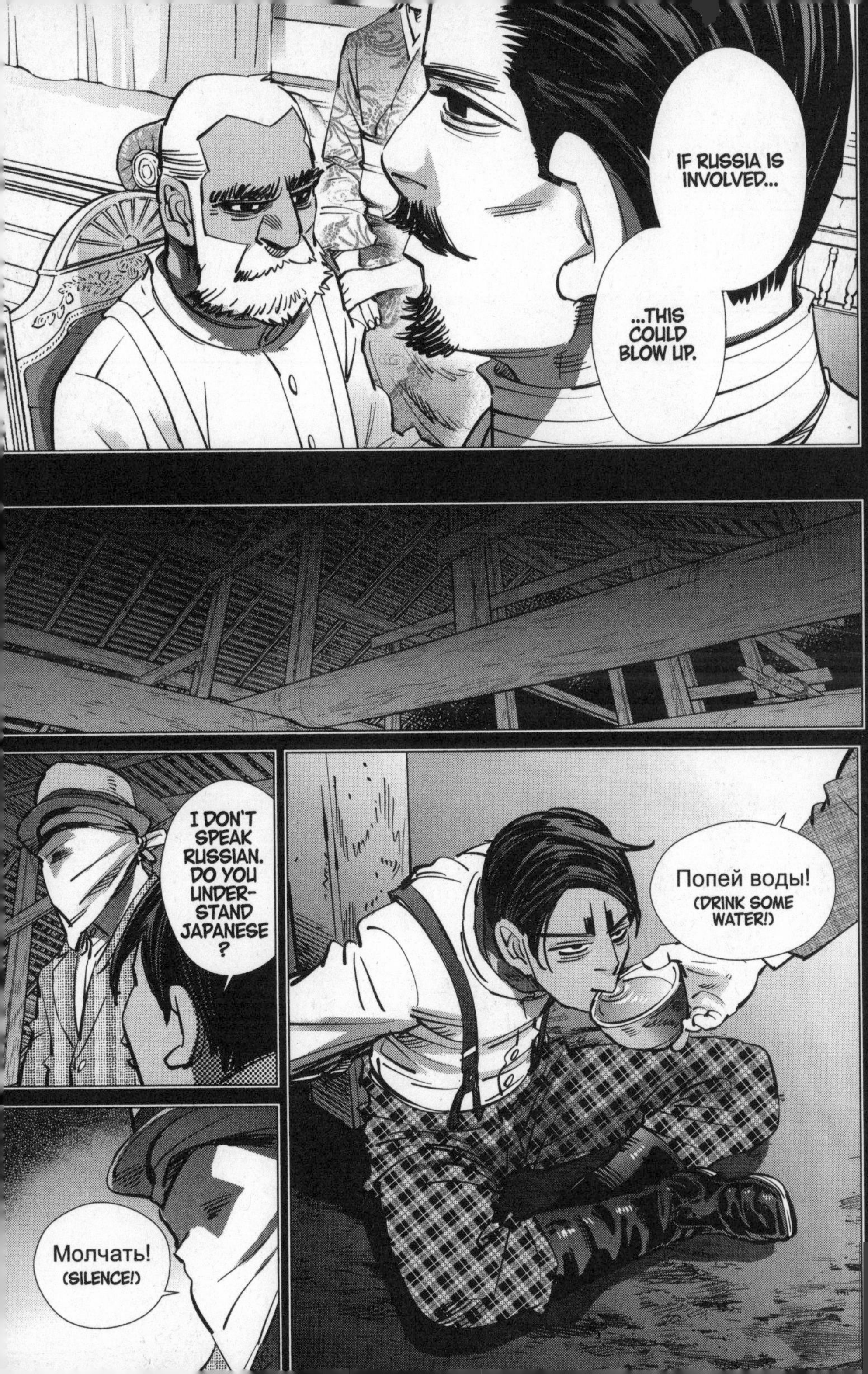
IF RUSSIA IS INVOLVED...
...THIS COULD BLOW UP.
Попей воды!
(DRINK SOME WATER!)
I DON'T SPEAK RUSSIAN. DO YOU UNDERSTAND JAPANESE?
Молчать!
(SILENCE!)

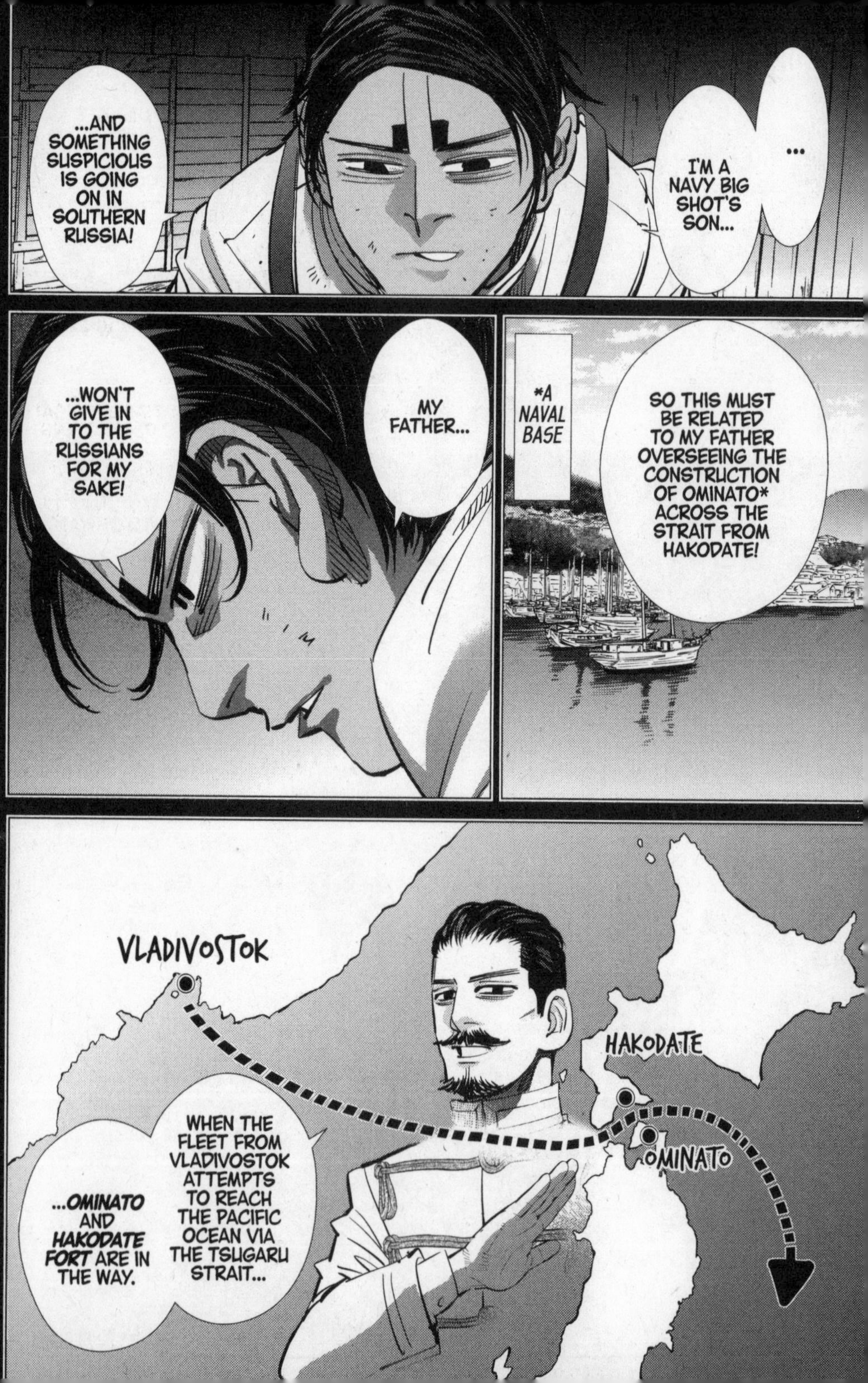
...
I'M A NAVY BIG SHOT'S SON...
...AND SOMETHING SUSPICIOUS IS GOING ON IN SOUTHERN RUSSIA!
SO THIS MUST BE RELATED TO MY FATHER OVERSEEING THE CONSTRUCTION OF OMINATO* ACROSS THE STRAIT FROM HAKODATE!
*A NAVAL BASE
MY FATHER...
...WON'T GIVE IN TO THE RUSSIANS FOR MY SAKE!
VLADIVOSTOK
HAKODATE
OMINATO
WHEN THE FLEET FROM VLADIVOSTOK ATTEMPTS TO REACH THE PACIFIC OCEAN VIA THE TSUGARU STRAIT...
...*OMINATO* AND *HAKODATE FORT* ARE IN THE WAY.

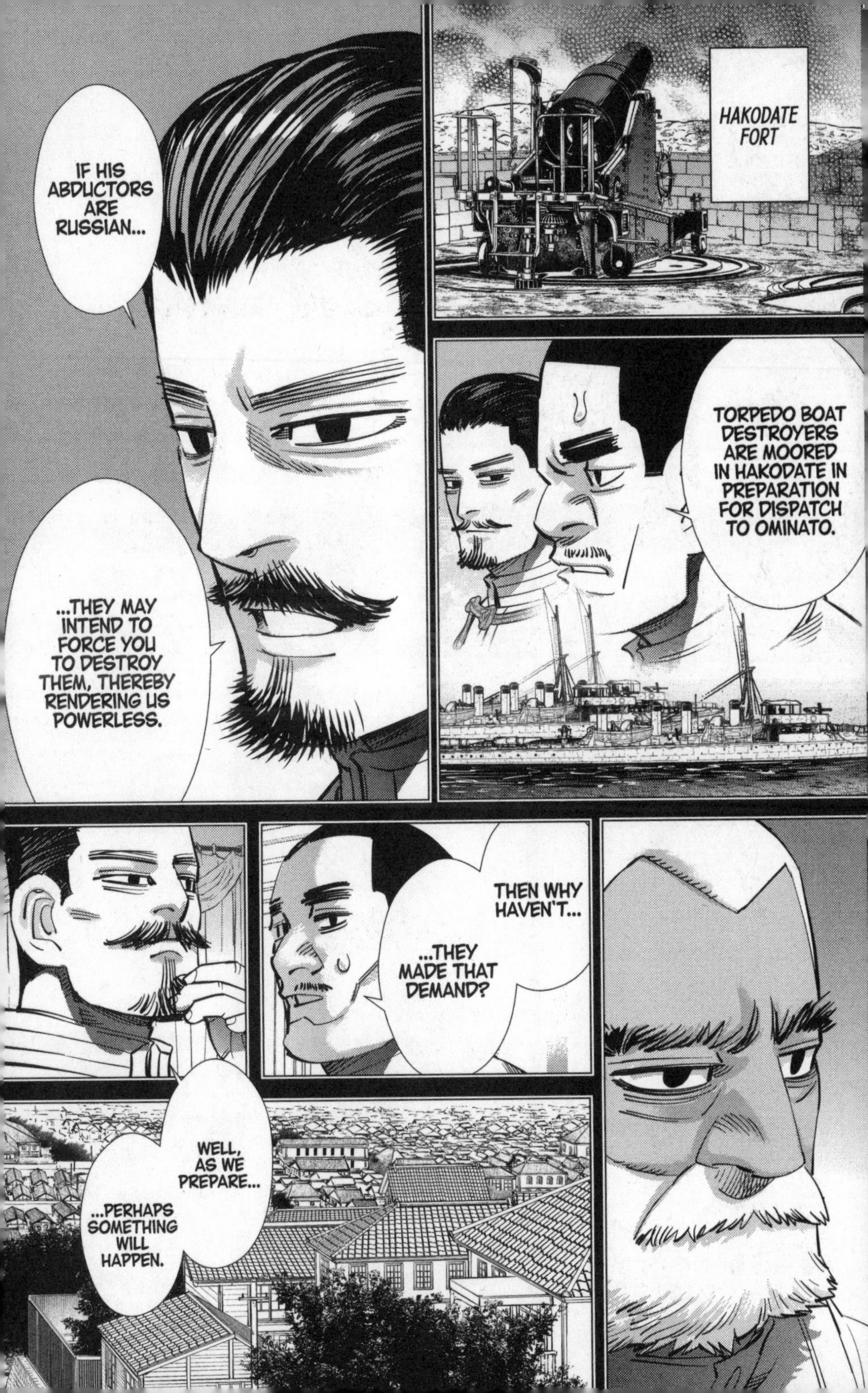
HAKODATE FORT
TORPEDO BOAT DESTROYERS ARE MOORED IN HAKODATE IN PREPARATION FOR DISPATCH TO OMINATO.
IF HIS ABDUCTORS ARE RUSSIAN...
...THEY MAY INTEND TO FORCE YOU TO DESTROY THEM, THEREBY RENDERING US POWERLESS.
THEN WHY HAVEN'T...
...THEY MADE THAT DEMAND?
WELL, AS WE PREPARE...
...PERHAPS SOMETHING WILL HAPPEN.

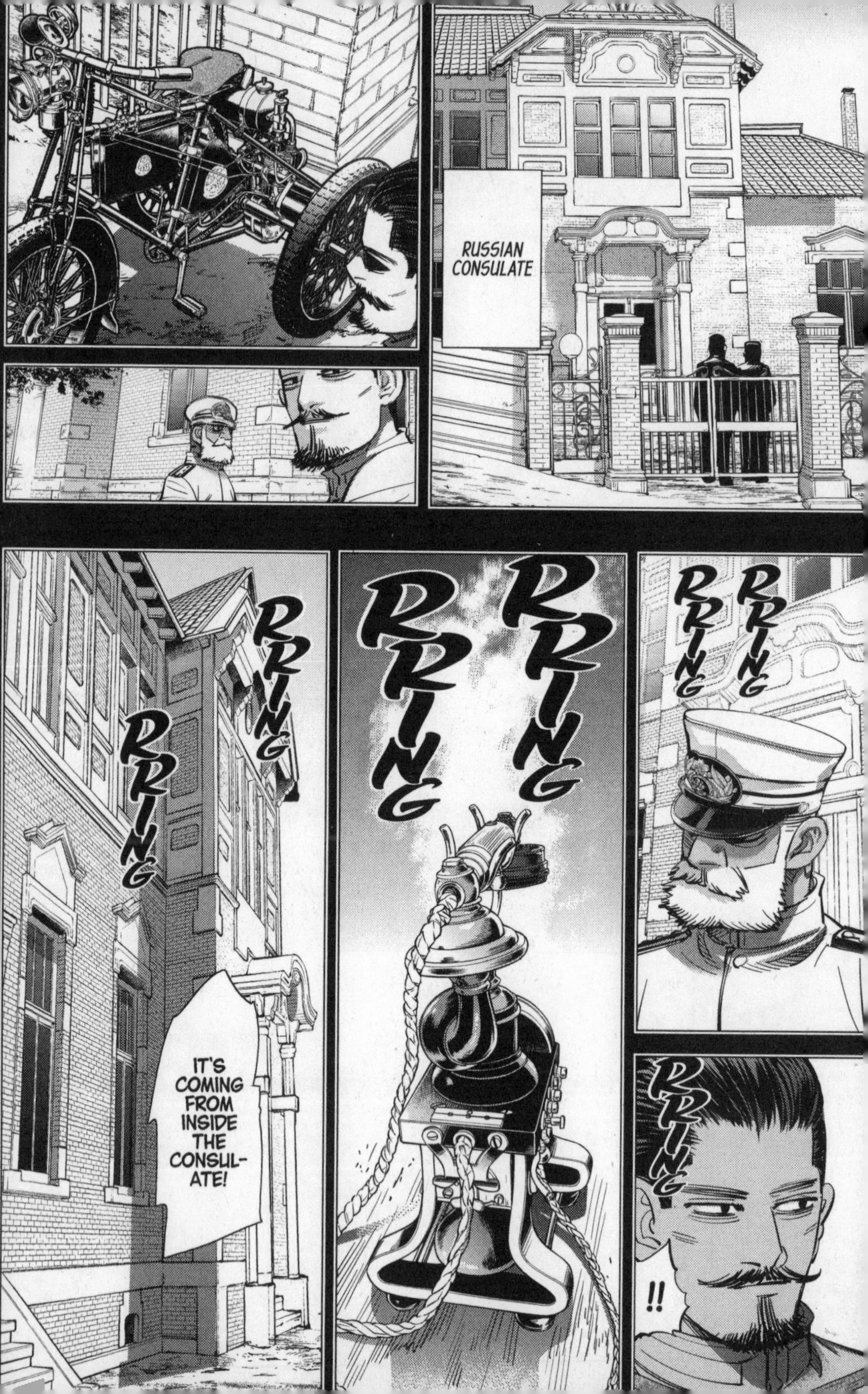
RUSSIAN CONSULATE
RRING RRING
RRING
!!
RRING RRING
RRING RRING
IT'S COMING FROM INSIDE THE CONSUL-ATE!

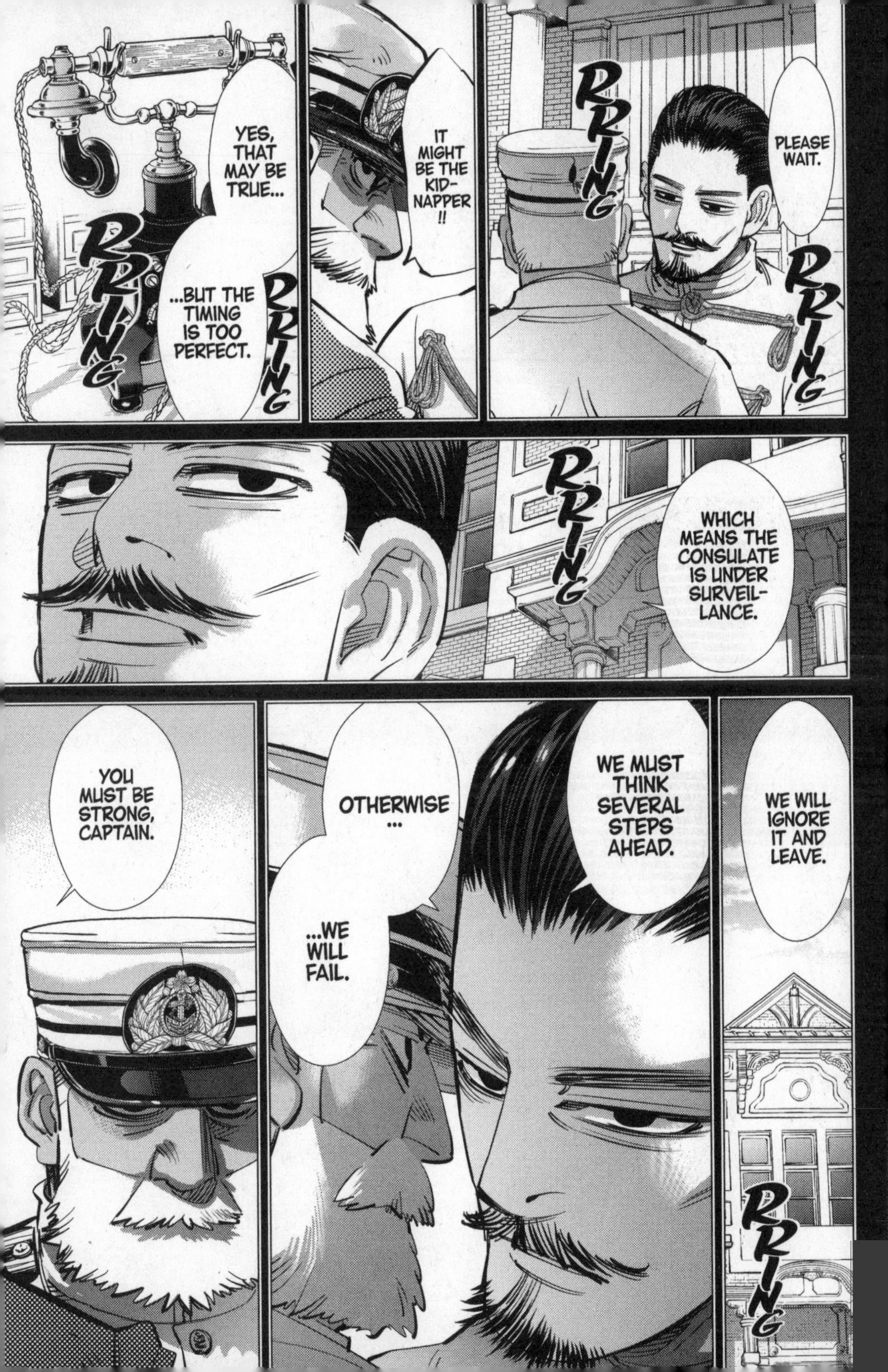
RRING
PLEASE WAIT.
RRING
IT MIGHT BE THE KID-NAPPER!!
YES, THAT MAY BE TRUE...
RRING
...BUT THE TIMING IS TOO PERFECT.
RRING
RRING
WHICH MEANS THE CONSULATE IS UNDER SURVEIL-LANCE.
WE WILL IGNORE IT AND LEAVE.
RRING
WE MUST THINK SEVERAL STEPS AHEAD.
OTHERWISE...
...WE WILL FAIL.
YOU MUST BE STRONG, CAPTAIN.

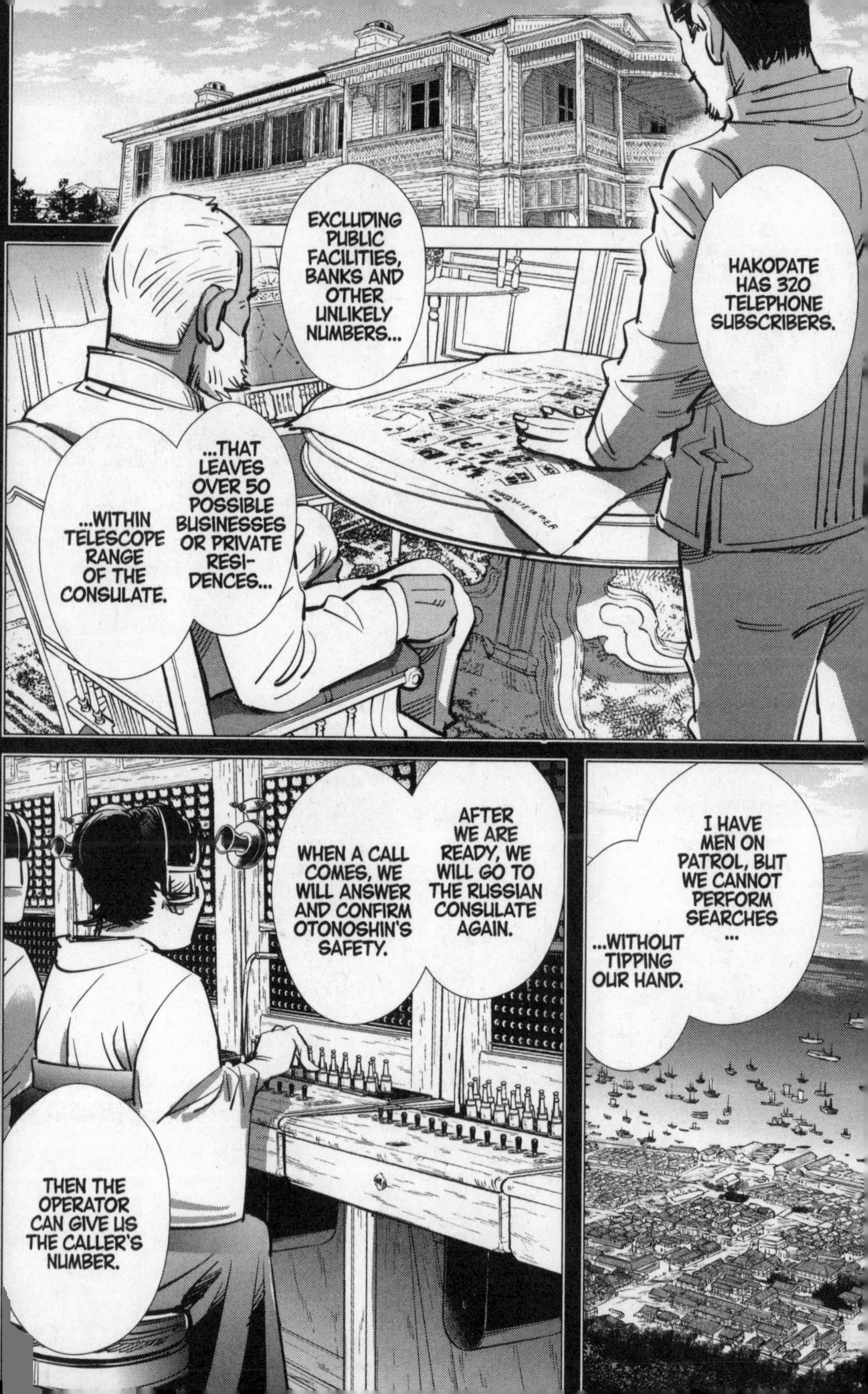
HAKODATE HAS 320 TELEPHONE SUBSCRIBERS.
EXCLUDING PUBLIC FACILITIES, BANKS AND OTHER UNLIKELY NUMBERS...
...THAT LEAVES OVER 50 POSSIBLE BUSINESSES OR PRIVATE RESI-DENCES...
...WITHIN TELESCOPE RANGE OF THE CONSULATE.
I HAVE MEN ON PATROL, BUT WE CANNOT PERFORM SEARCHES...
...WITHOUT TIPPING OUR HAND.
AFTER WE ARE READY, WE WILL GO TO THE RUSSIAN CONSULATE AGAIN.
WHEN A CALL COMES, WE WILL ANSWER AND CONFIRM OTONOSHIN'S SAFETY.
THEN THE OPERATOR CAN GIVE US THE CALLER'S NUMBER.

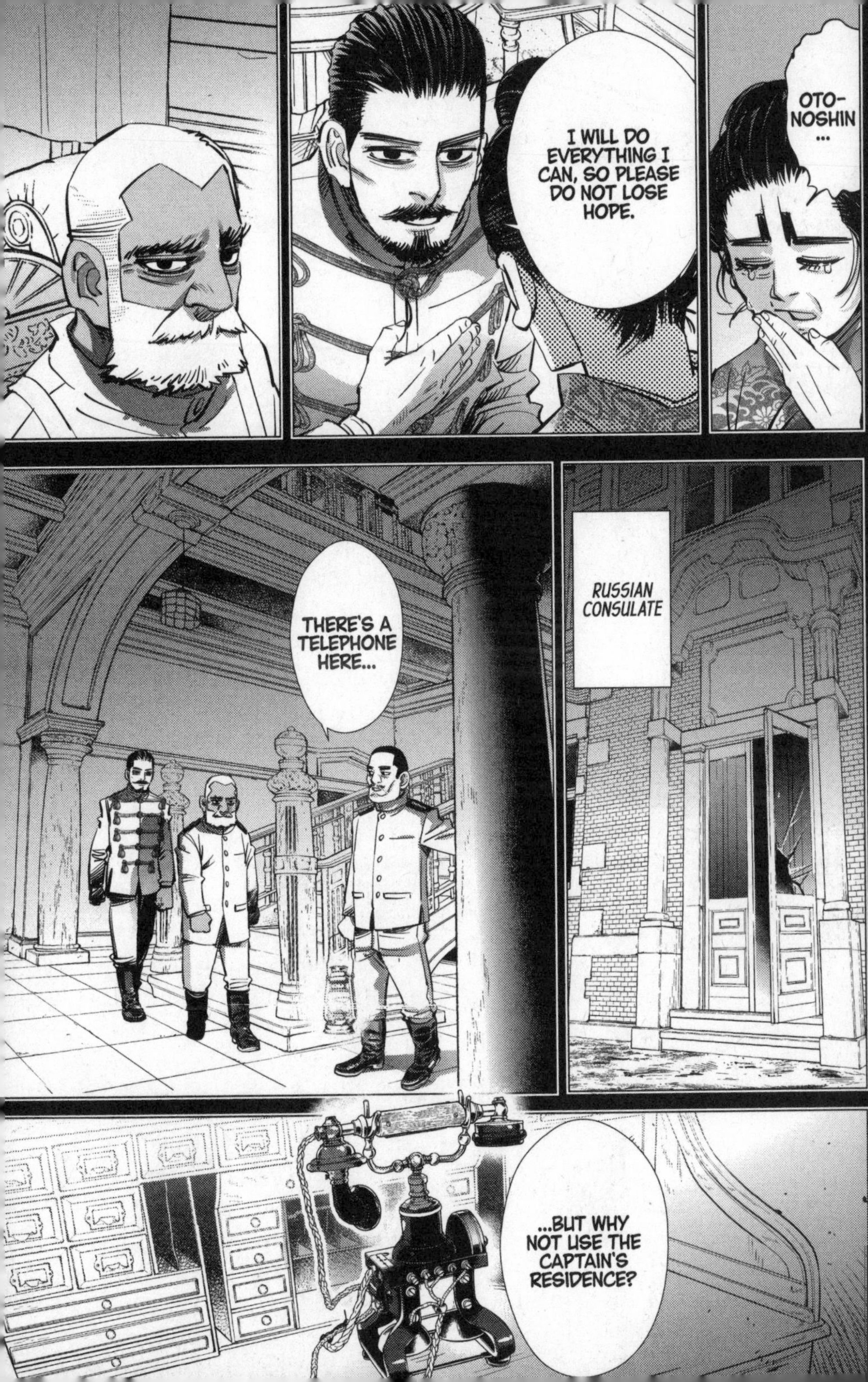
OTO-NOSHIN...
I WILL DO EVERYTHING I CAN, SO PLEASE DO NOT LOSE HOPE.
RUSSIAN CONSULATE
THERE'S A TELEPHONE HERE...
...BUT WHY NOT USE THE CAPTAIN'S RESIDENCE?

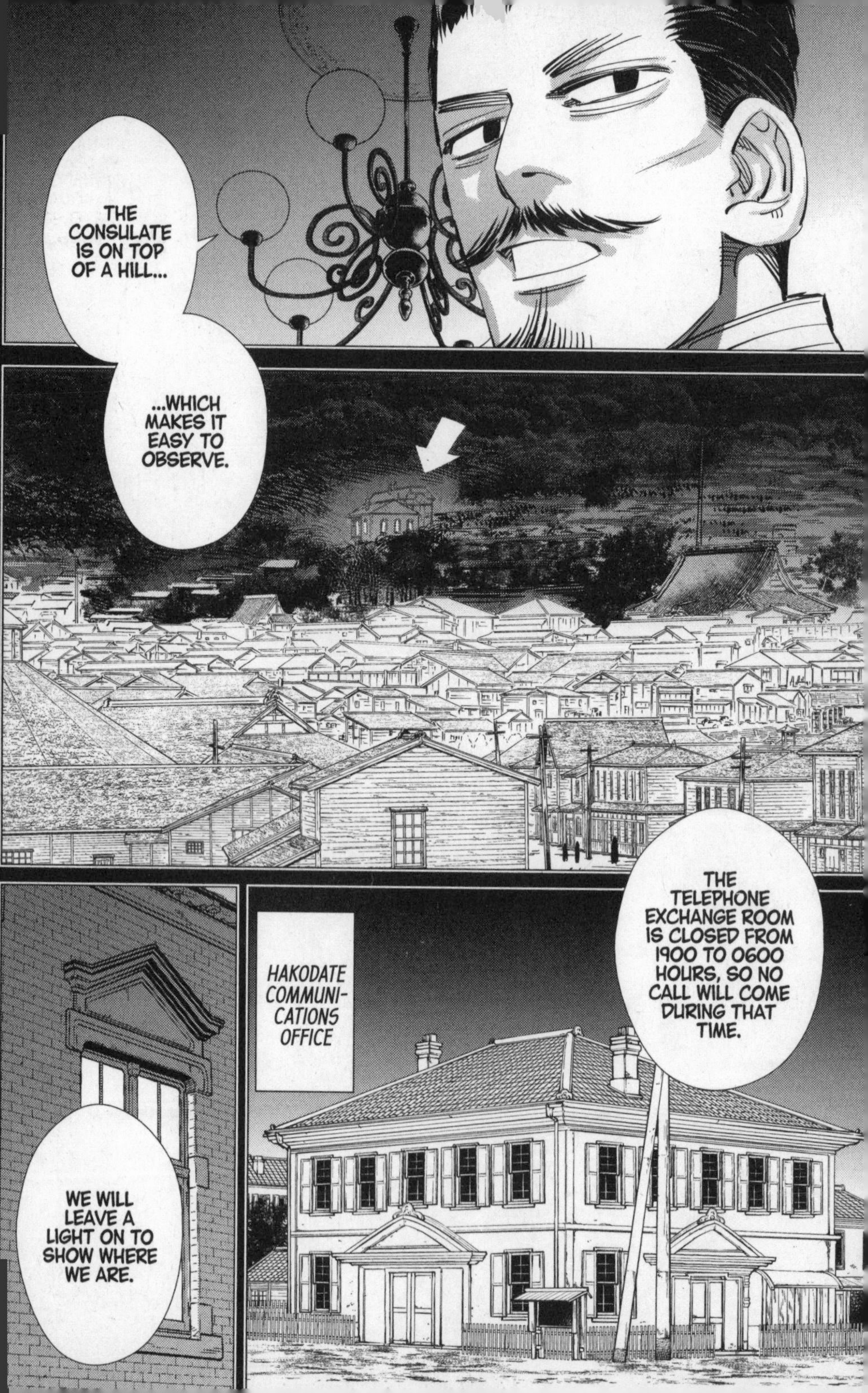
THE CONSULATE IS ON TOP OF A HILL...
...WHICH MAKES IT EASY TO OBSERVE.
THE TELEPHONE EXCHANGE ROOM IS CLOSED FROM 1900 TO 0600 HOURS, SO NO CALL WILL COME DURING THAT TIME.
HAKODATE COMMUNICATIONS OFFICE
WE WILL LEAVE A LIGHT ON TO SHOW WHERE WE ARE.

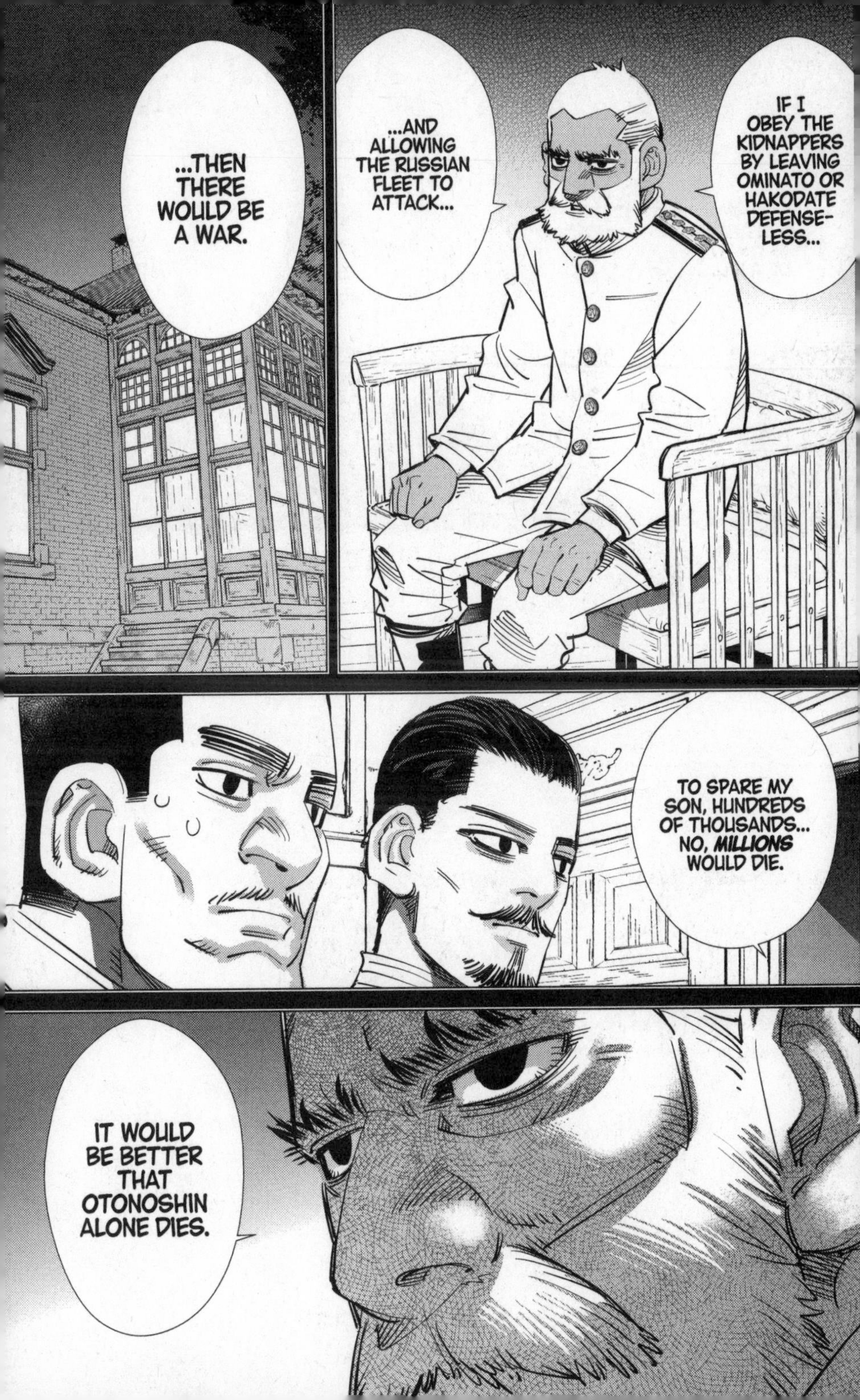
IF I OBEY THE KIDNAPPERS BY LEAVING OMINATO OR HAKODATE DEFENSE-LESS...
...AND ALLOWING THE RUSSIAN FLEET TO ATTACK...
...THEN THERE WOULD BE A WAR.
TO SPARE MY SON, HUNDREDS OF THOUSANDS... NO, *MILLIONS* WOULD DIE.
IT WOULD BE BETTER THAT OTONOSHIN ALONE DIES.

Ешь!
(EAT!)

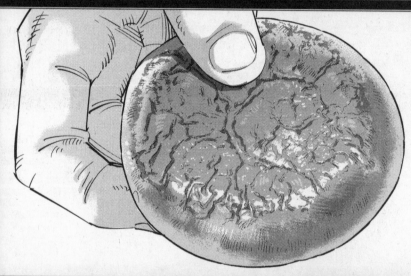

HM?
THIS IS...

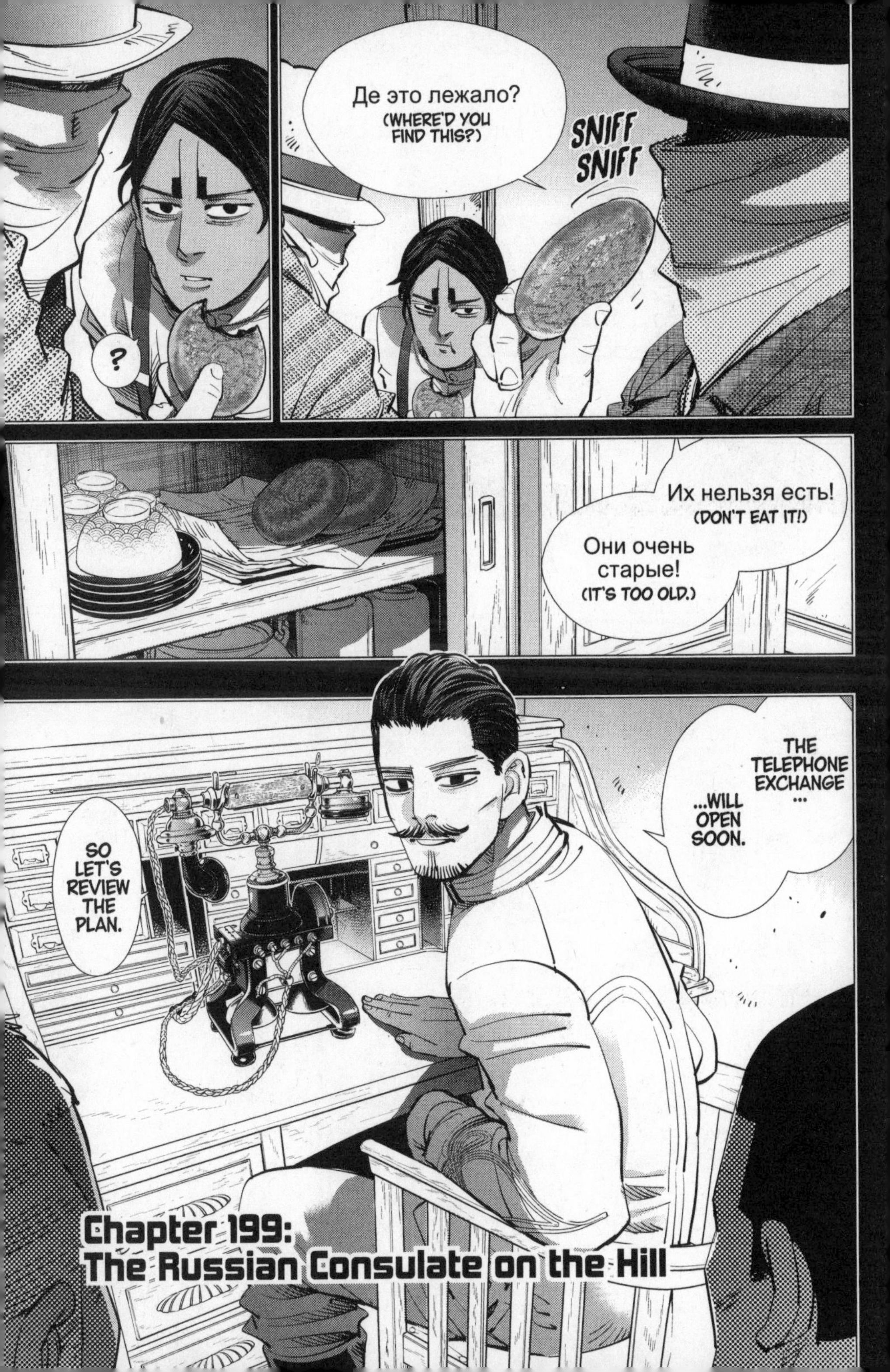
Де это лежало?
(WHERE'D YOU FIND THIS?)
SNIFF SNIFF
?
Их нельзя есть!
(DON'T EAT IT!)
Они очень старые!
(IT'S TOO OLD.)
THE TELEPHONE EXCHANGE...
...WILL OPEN SOON.
SO LET'S REVIEW THE PLAN.
Chapter 199:
The Russian Consulate on the Hill

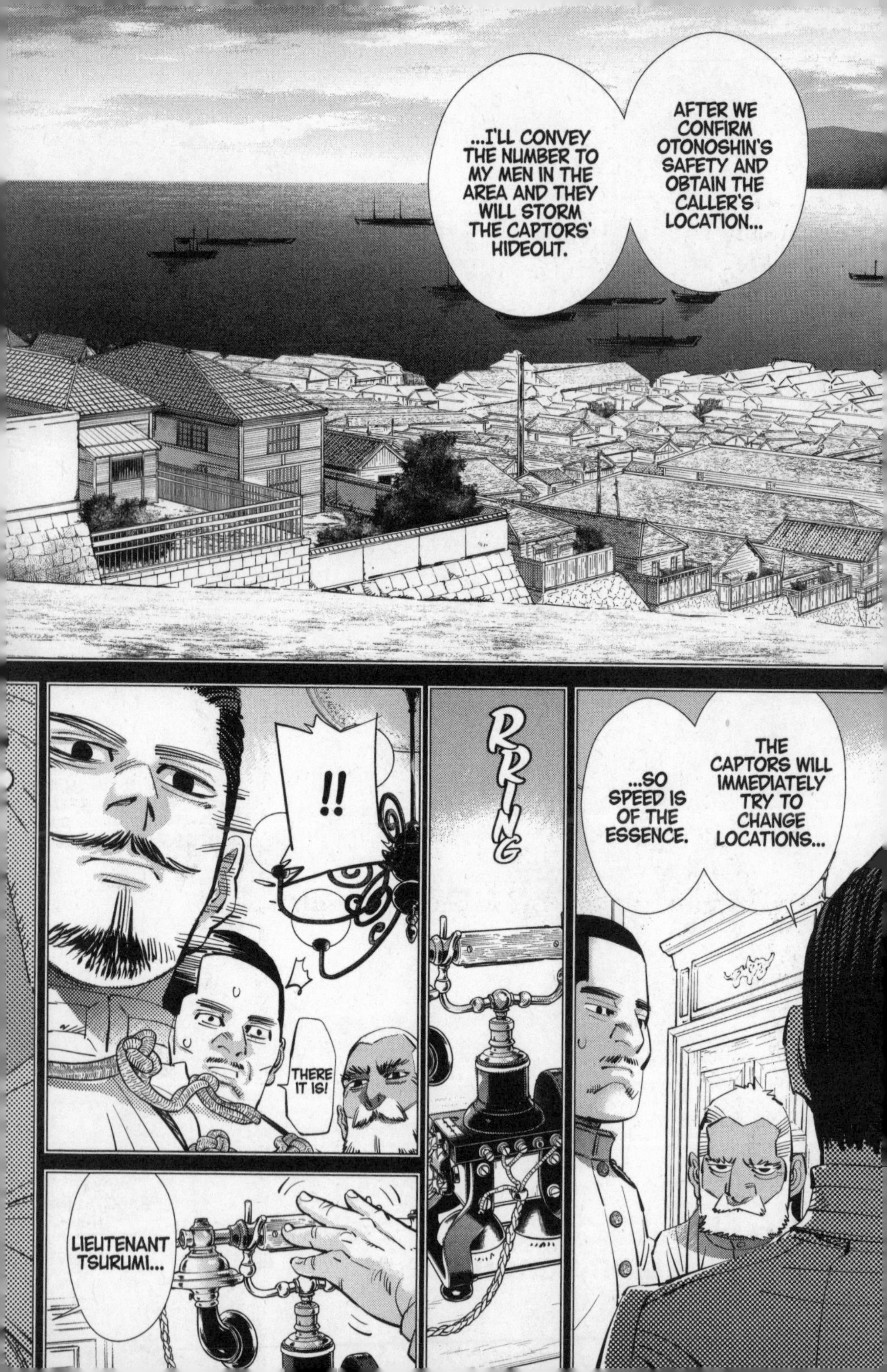
AFTER WE CONFIRM OTONOSHIN'S SAFETY AND OBTAIN THE CALLER'S LOCATION...
...I'LL CONVEY THE NUMBER TO MY MEN IN THE AREA AND THEY WILL STORM THE CAPTORS' HIDEOUT.
THE CAPTORS WILL IMMEDIATELY TRY TO CHANGE LOCATIONS...
...SO SPEED IS OF THE ESSENCE.
RRING
!!
THERE IT IS!
LIEUTENANT TSURUMI...

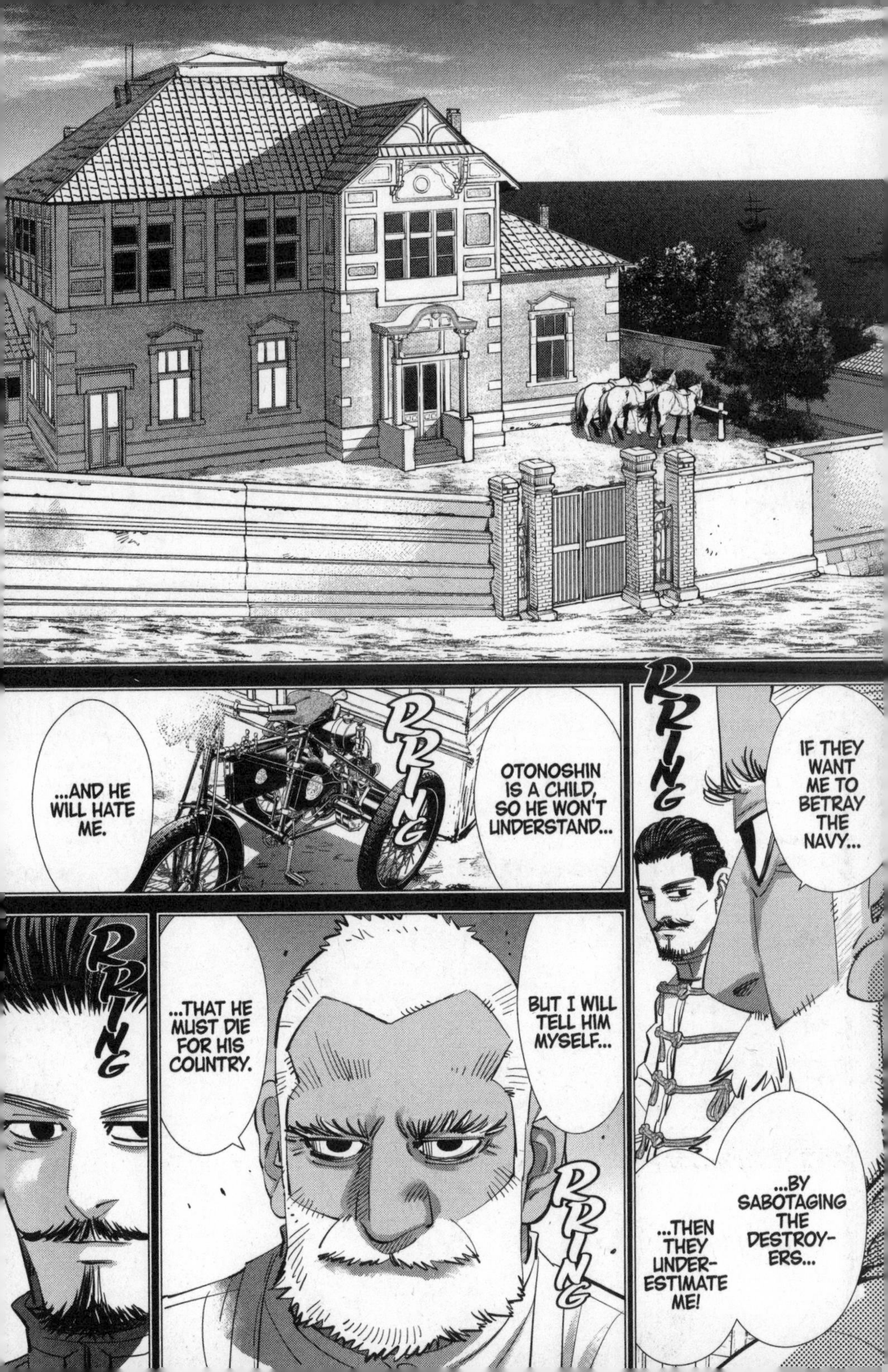
RRING
IF THEY WANT ME TO BETRAY THE NAVY...
...BY SABOTAGING THE DESTROYERS...
...THEN THEY UNDERESTIMATE ME!
RRING
OTONOSHIN IS A CHILD, SO HE WON'T UNDERSTAND...
...AND HE WILL HATE ME.
RRING
BUT I WILL TELL HIM MYSELF...
...THAT HE MUST DIE FOR HIS COUNTRY.
RRING

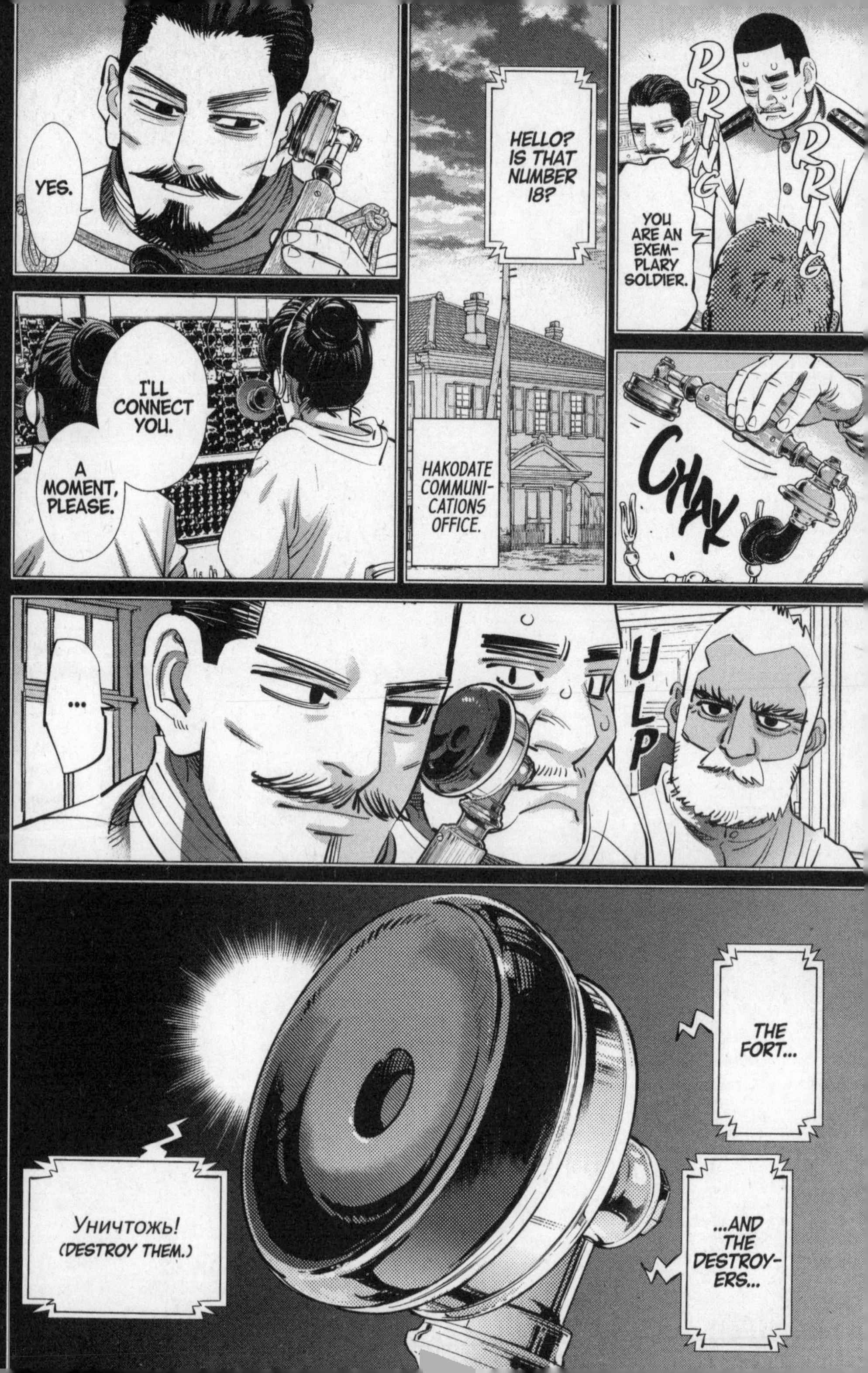
RRING
RRING
YOU ARE AN EXEMPLARY SOLDIER.
CHAK
HELLO? IS THAT NUMBER 18?
HAKODATE COMMUNICATIONS OFFICE.
YES.
I'LL CONNECT YOU.
A MOMENT, PLEASE.
ULP
...
THE FORT...
...AND THE DESTROYERS...
Уничтожь!
(DESTROY THEM.)

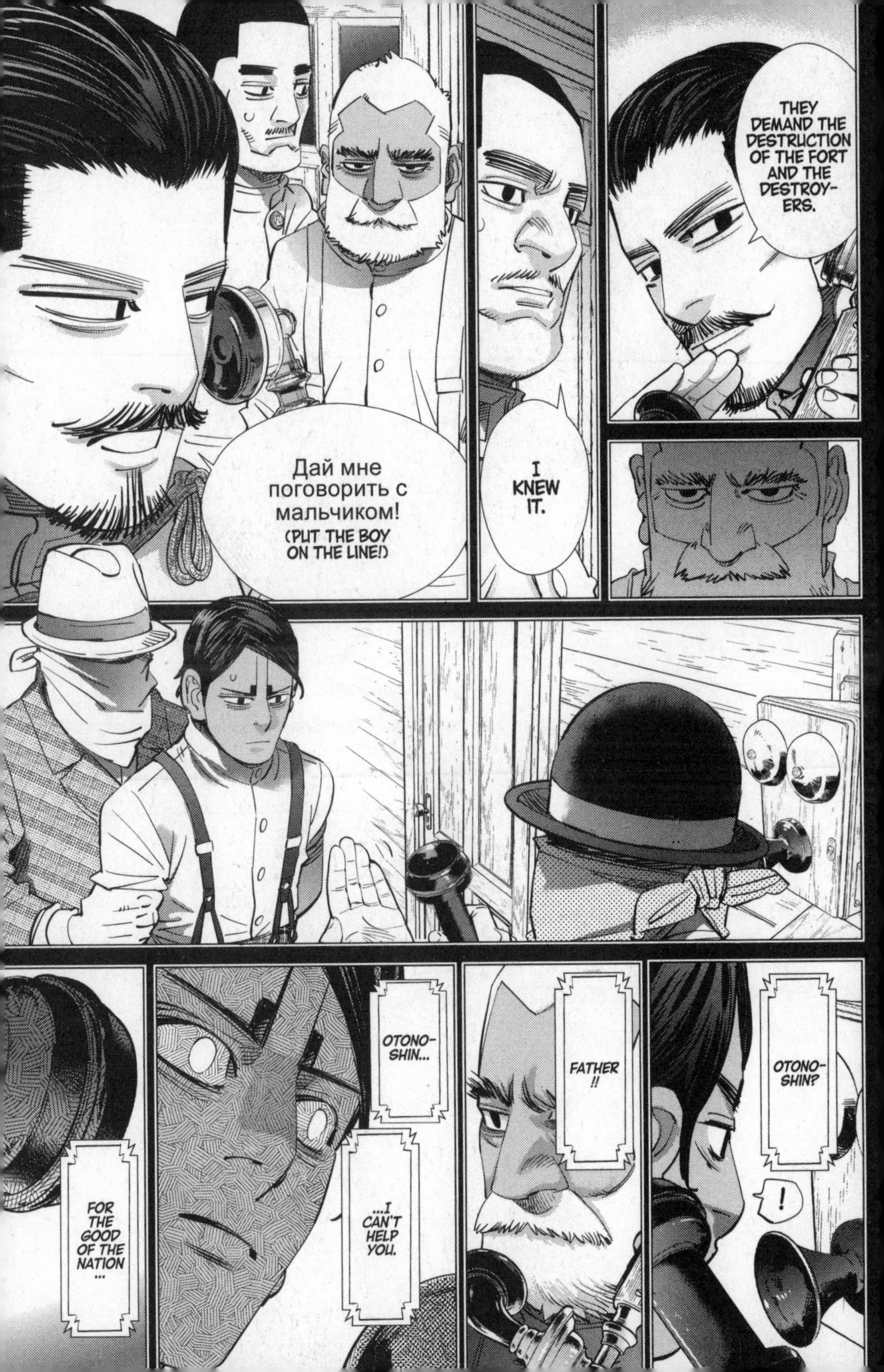
THEY DEMAND THE DESTRUCTION OF THE FORT AND THE DESTROYERS.
I KNEW IT.
Дай мне поговорить с мальчиком!
(PUT THE BOY ON THE LINE!)
OTONO-SHIN?
!
FATHER!!
OTONO-SHIN...
...I CAN'T HELP YOU.
FOR THE GOOD OF THE NATION...

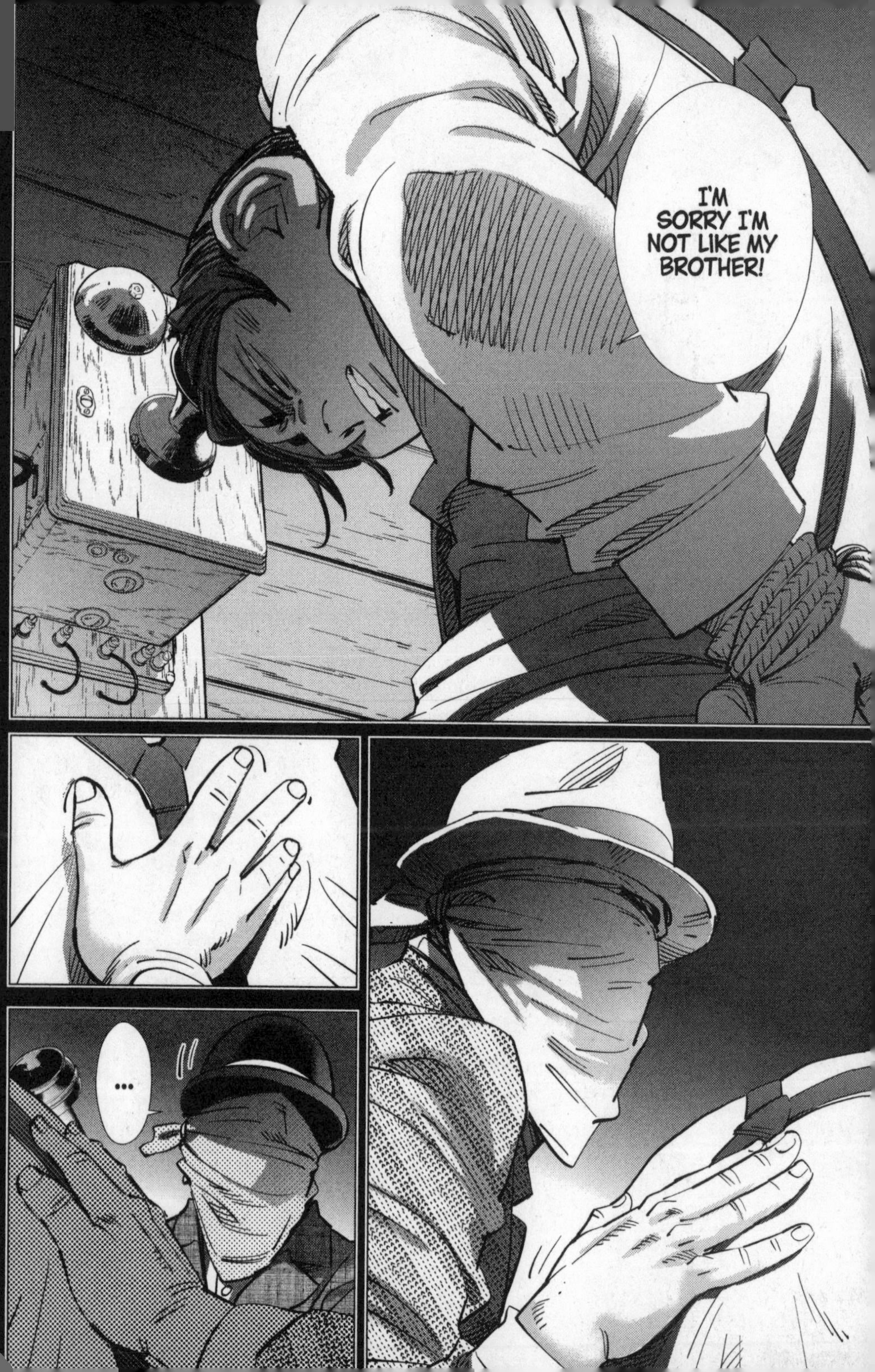
I'M SORRY I'M NOT LIKE MY BROTHER!
...

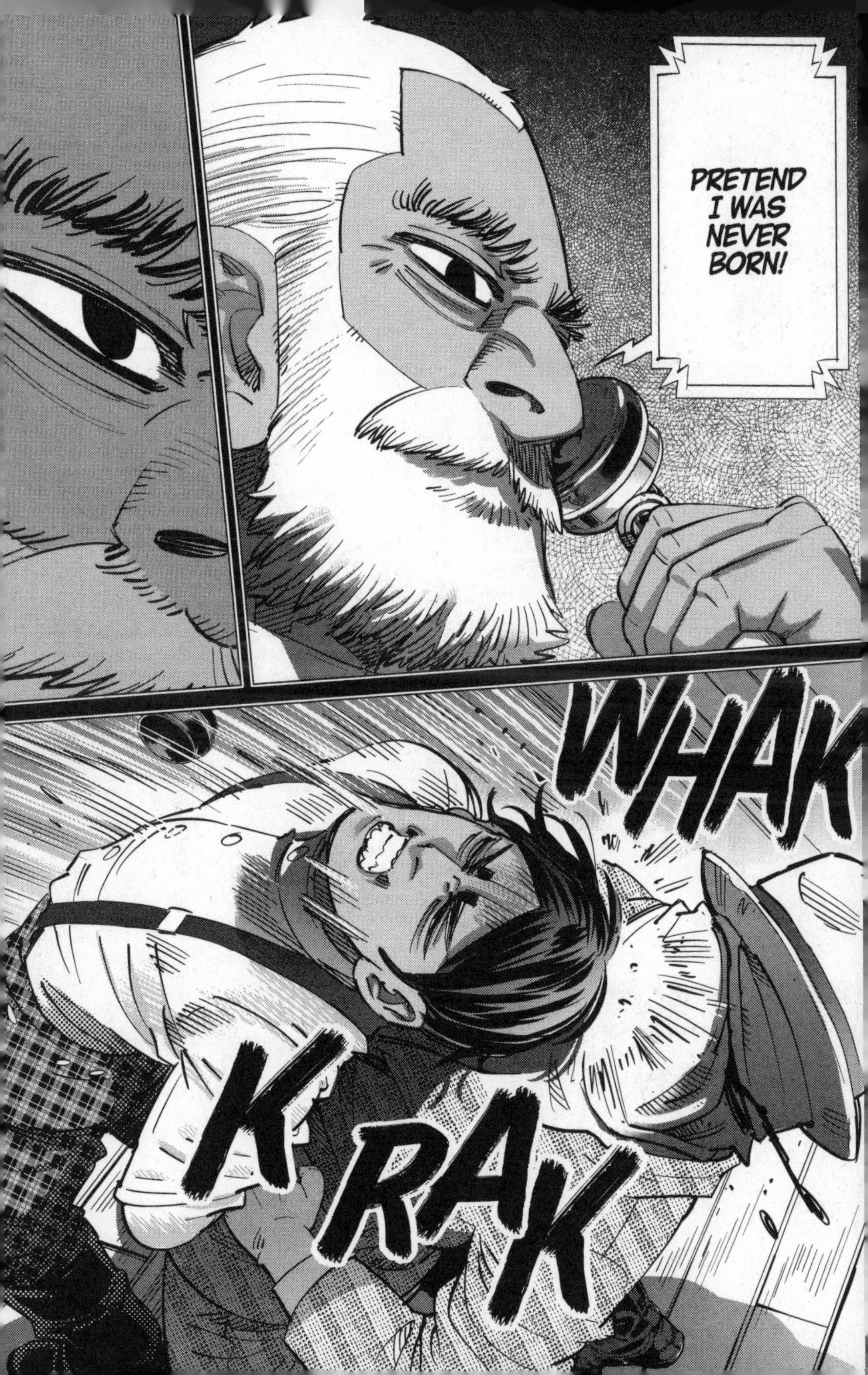
PRETEND I WAS NEVER BORN!
WHAK
K-RAK

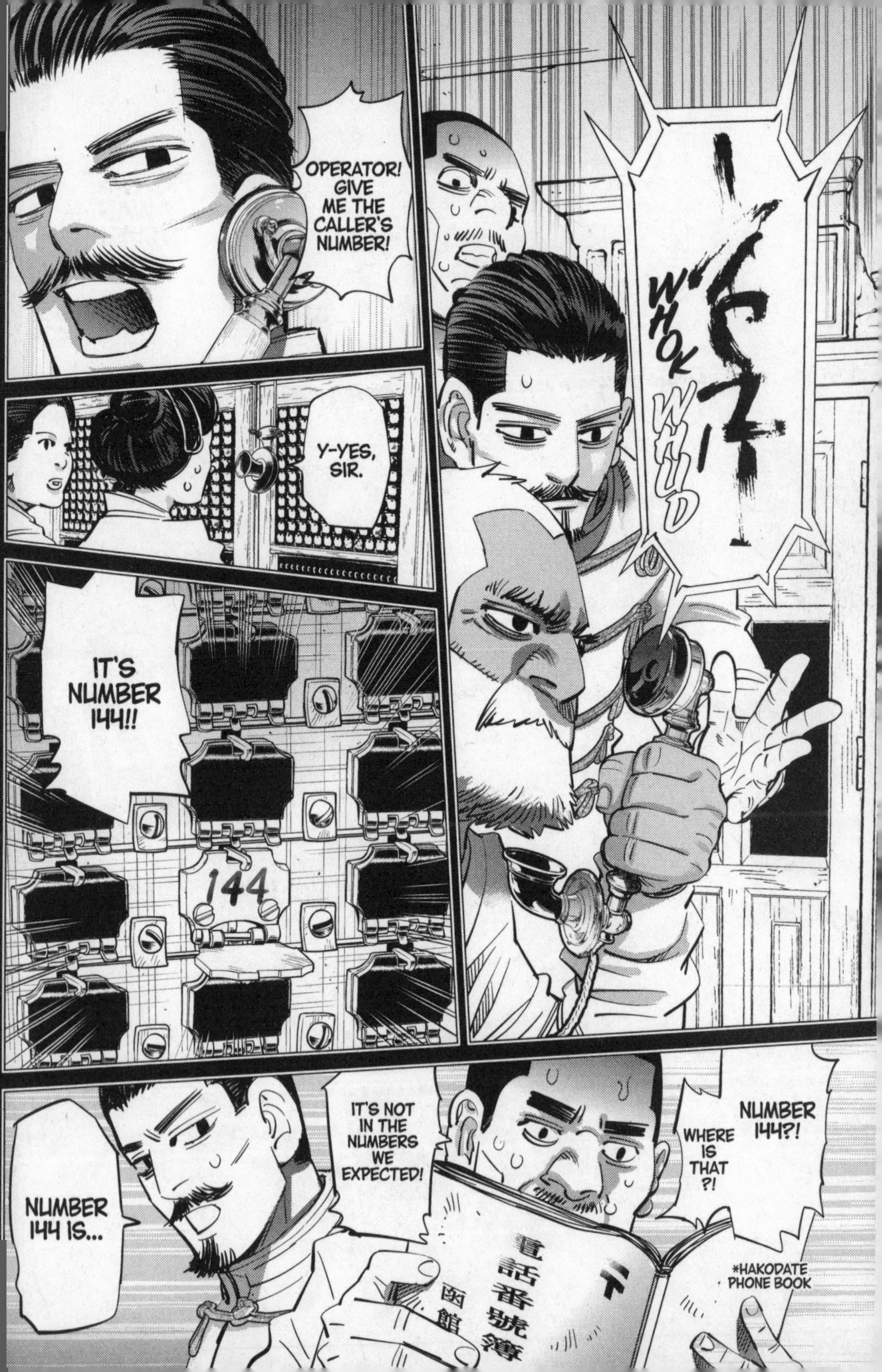
WHOK
WHUD
OPERATOR! GIVE ME THE CALLER'S NUMBER!
Y-YES, SIR.
IT'S NUMBER 144!!
144
NUMBER 144?!
WHERE IS THAT ?!
IT'S NOT IN THE NUMBERS WE EXPECTED!
NUMBER 144 IS...
電話番號簿
函館
*HAKODATE PHONE BOOK

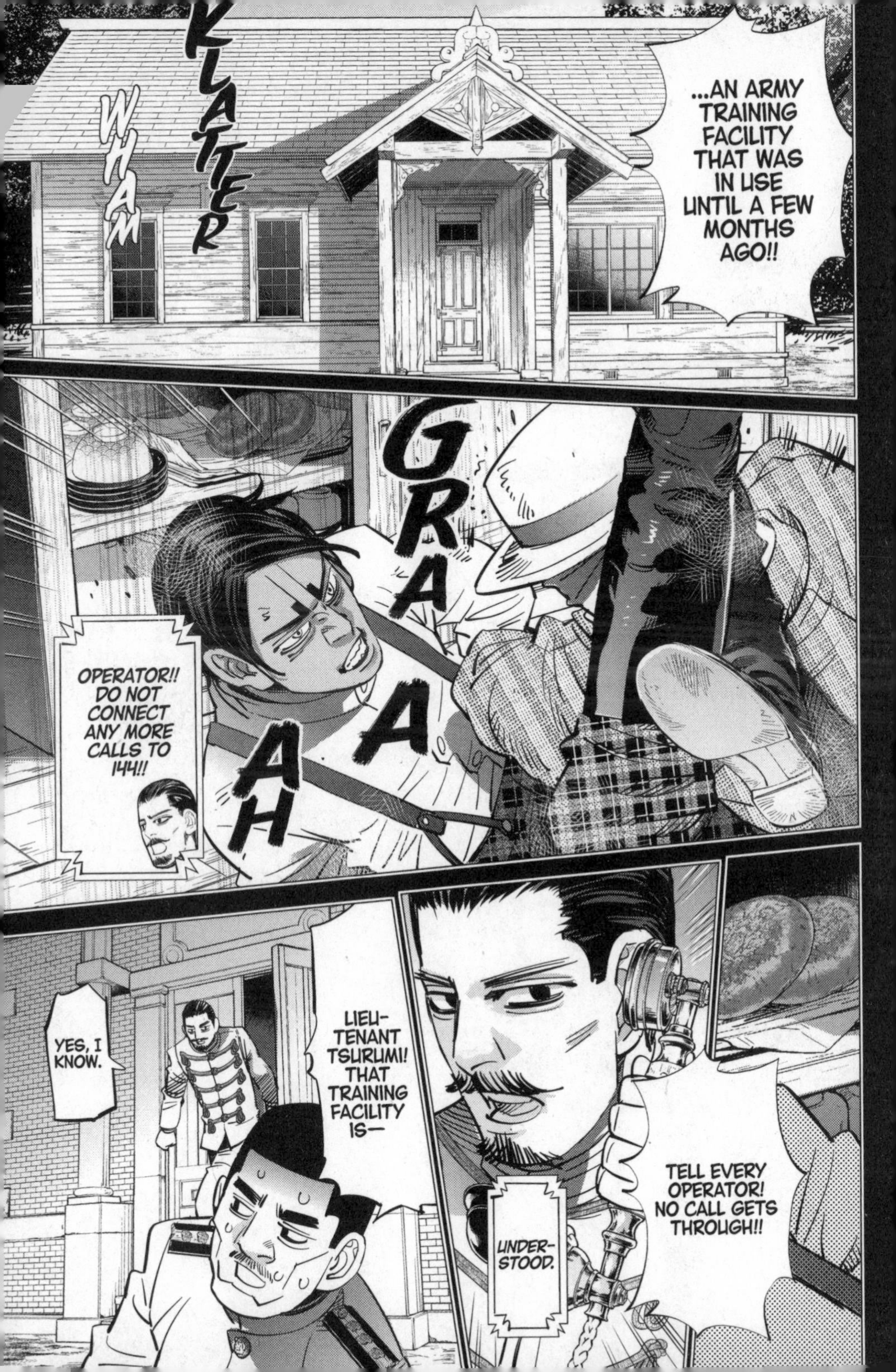
...AN ARMY TRAINING FACILITY THAT WAS IN USE UNTIL A FEW MONTHS AGO!!
KLATTER
WHAM
GRAAAH
OPERATOR!! DO NOT CONNECT ANY MORE CALLS TO 144!!
TELL EVERY OPERATOR! NO CALL GETS THROUGH!!
UNDERSTOOD.
LIEUTENANT TSURUMI! THAT TRAINING FACILITY IS—
YES, I KNOW.

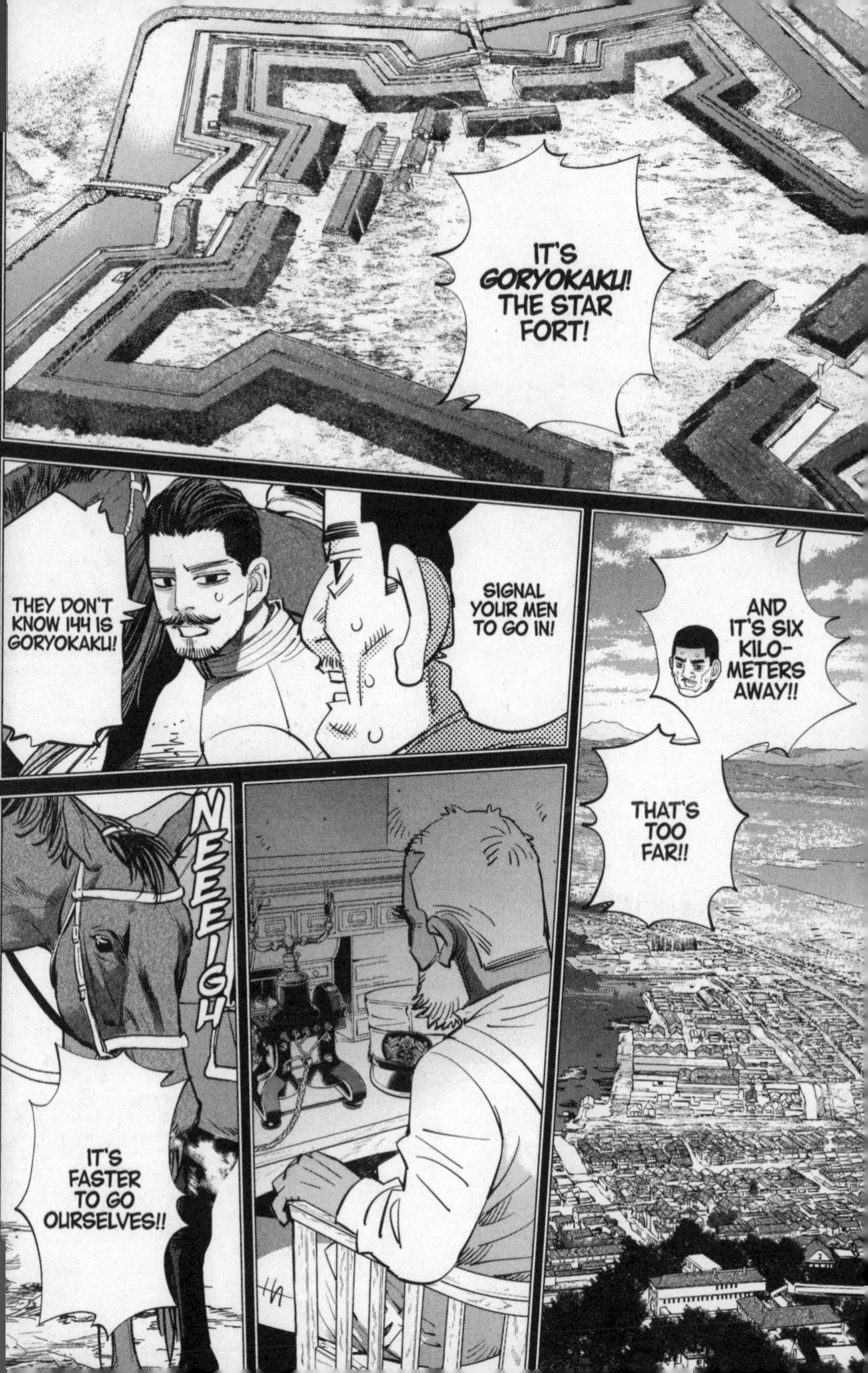
IT'S GORYOKAKU! THE STAR FORT!
AND IT'S SIX KILO-METERS AWAY!!
THAT'S TOO FAR!!
SIGNAL YOUR MEN TO GO IN!
THEY DON'T KNOW 144 IS GORYOKAKU!
NEEEIGH
IT'S FASTER TO GO OURSELVES!!

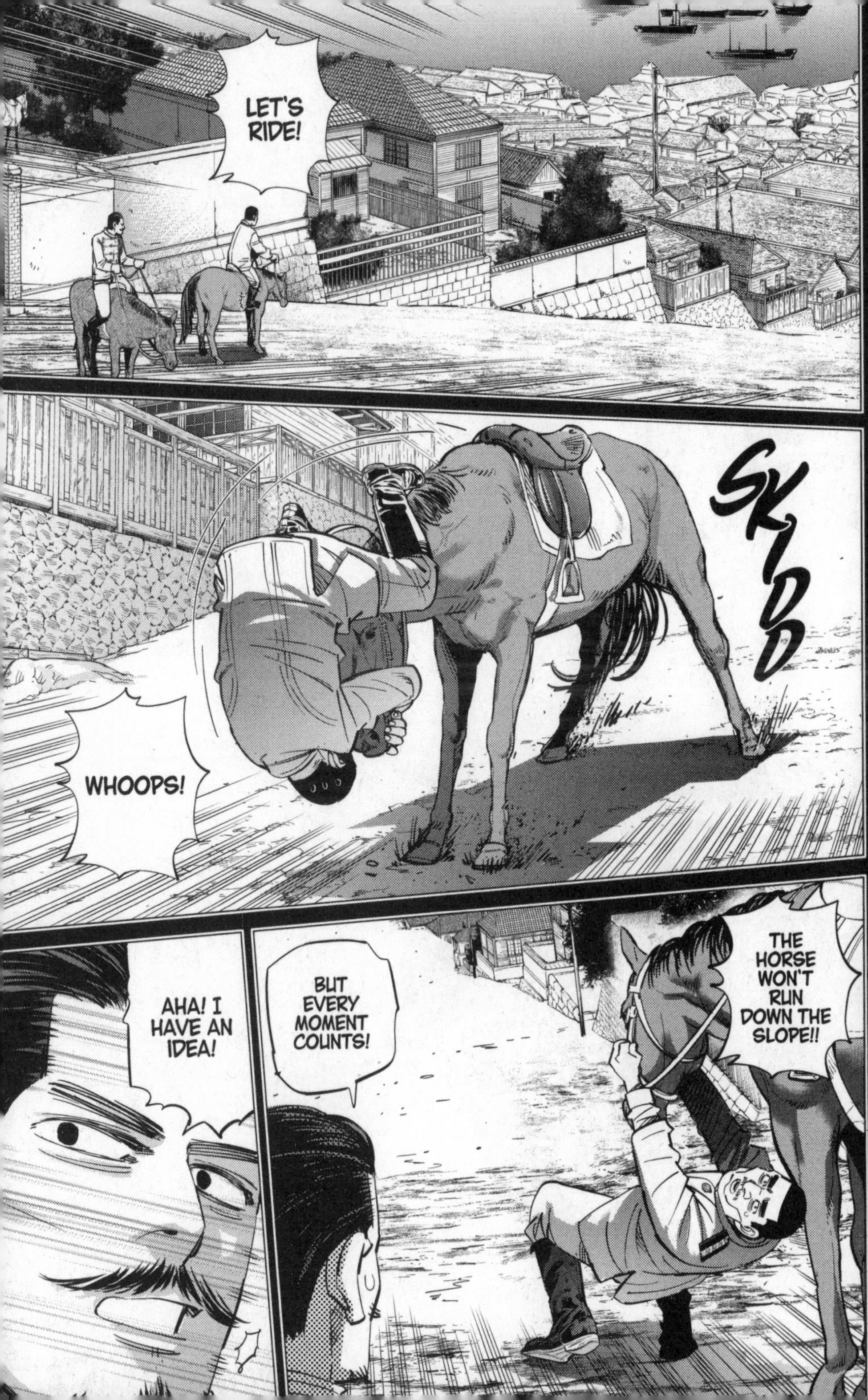
LET'S RIDE!
SKIDD
WHOOPS!
THE HORSE WON'T RUN DOWN THE SLOPE!!
BUT EVERY MOMENT COUNTS!
AHA! I HAVE AN IDEA!

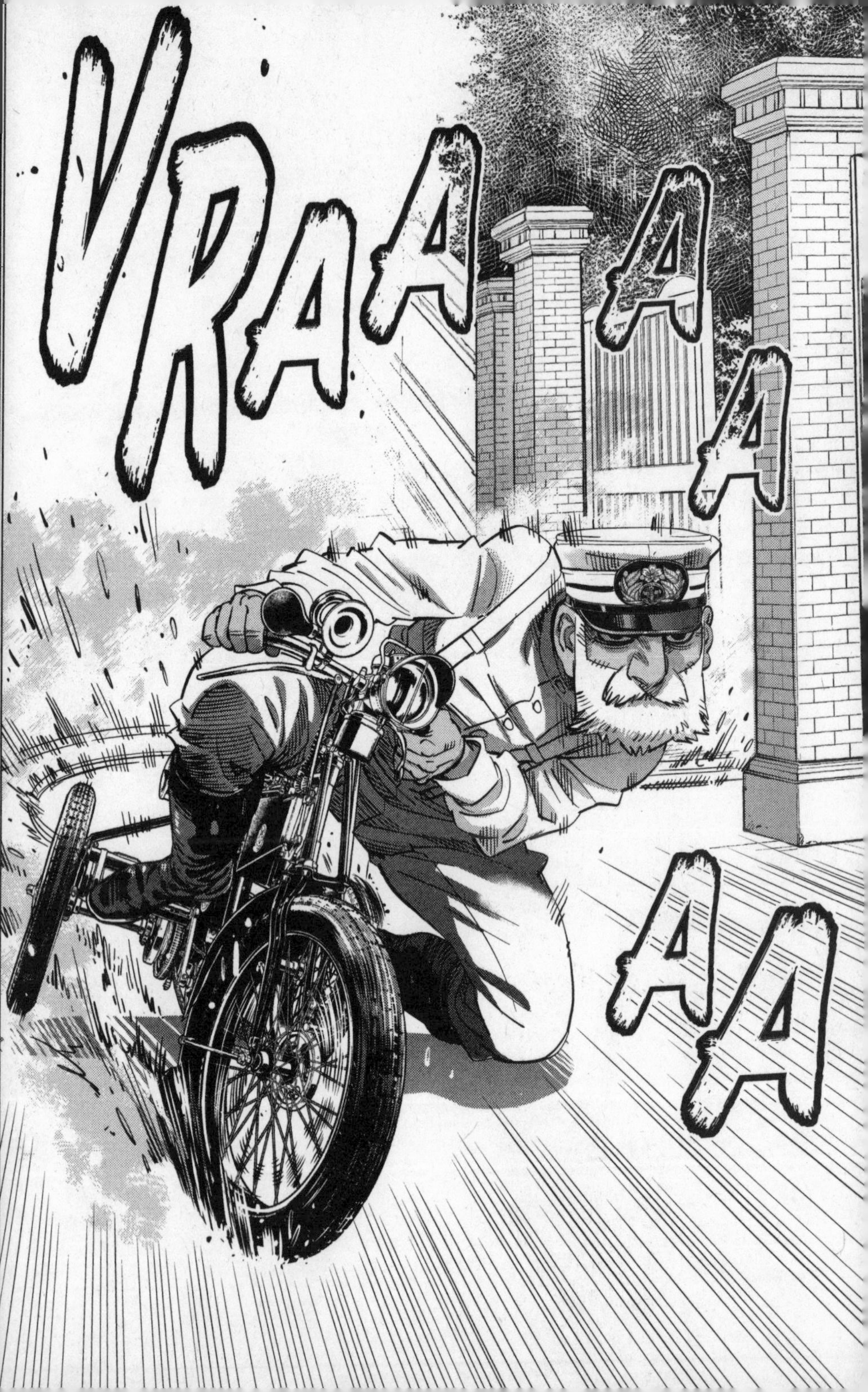
VRAAAAAAA

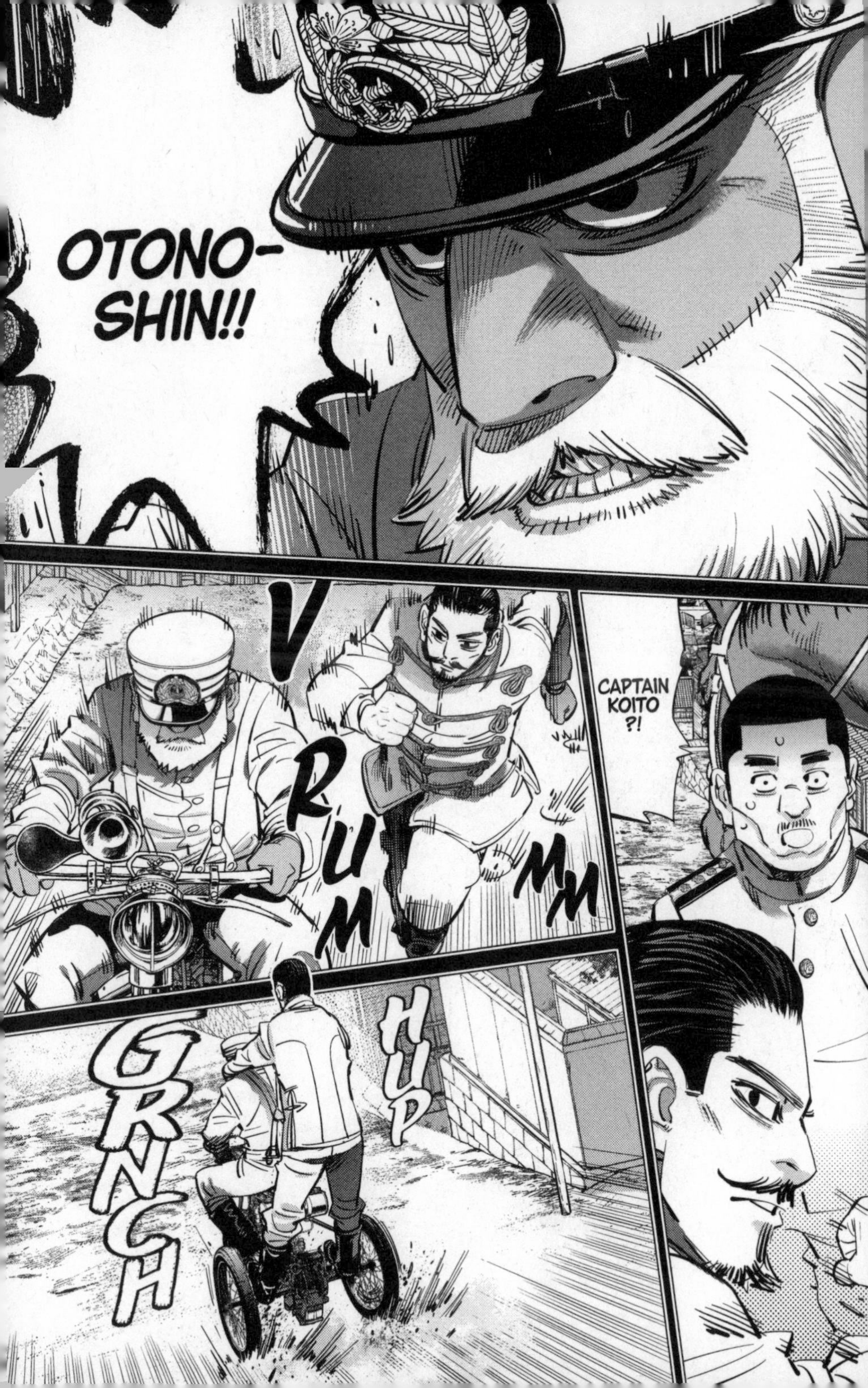
OTONO-SHIN!!
CAPTAIN KOITO ?!
VRUMMM
HUP
GRNCH

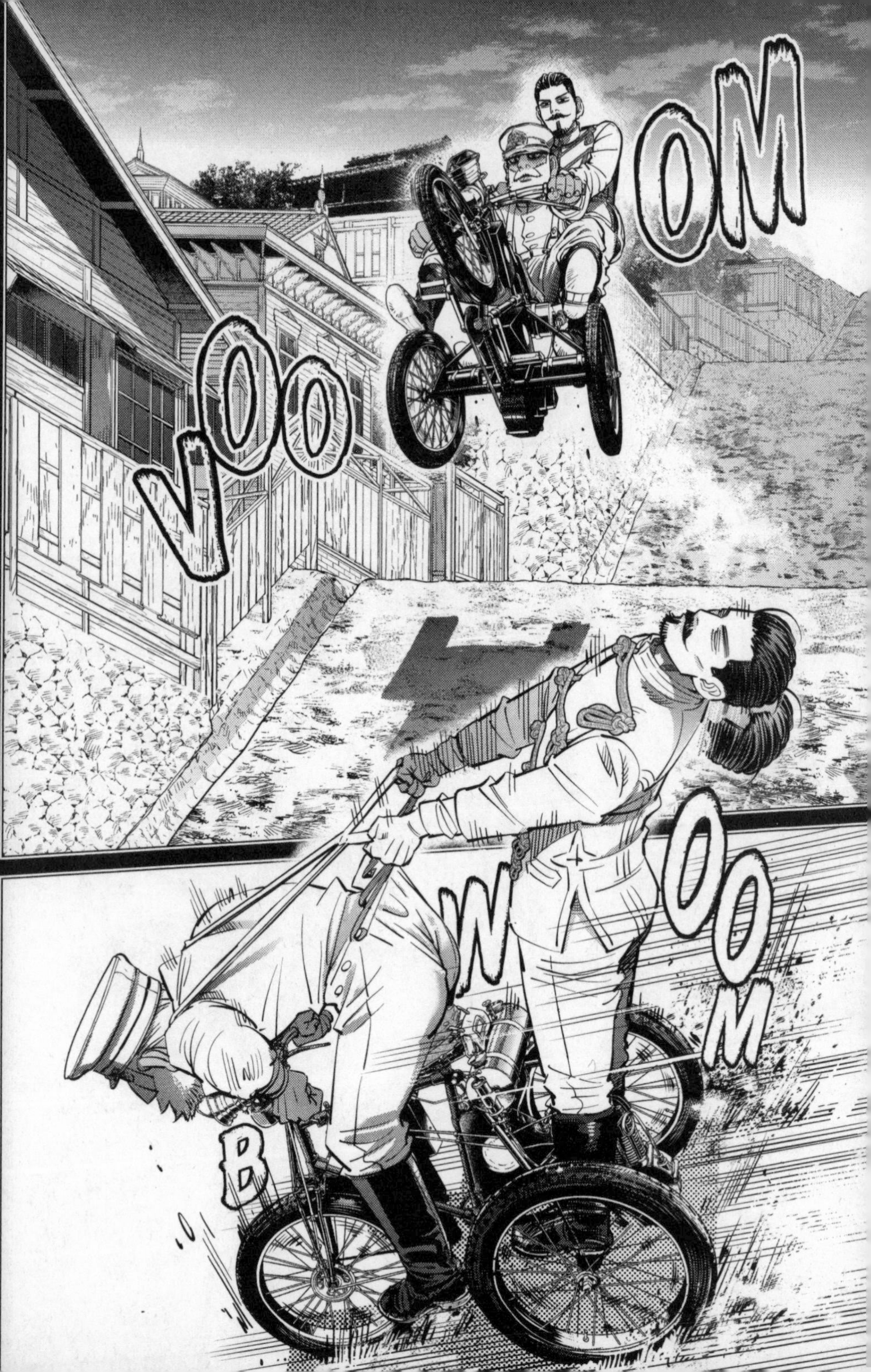
VOOOOM
BWOOOM

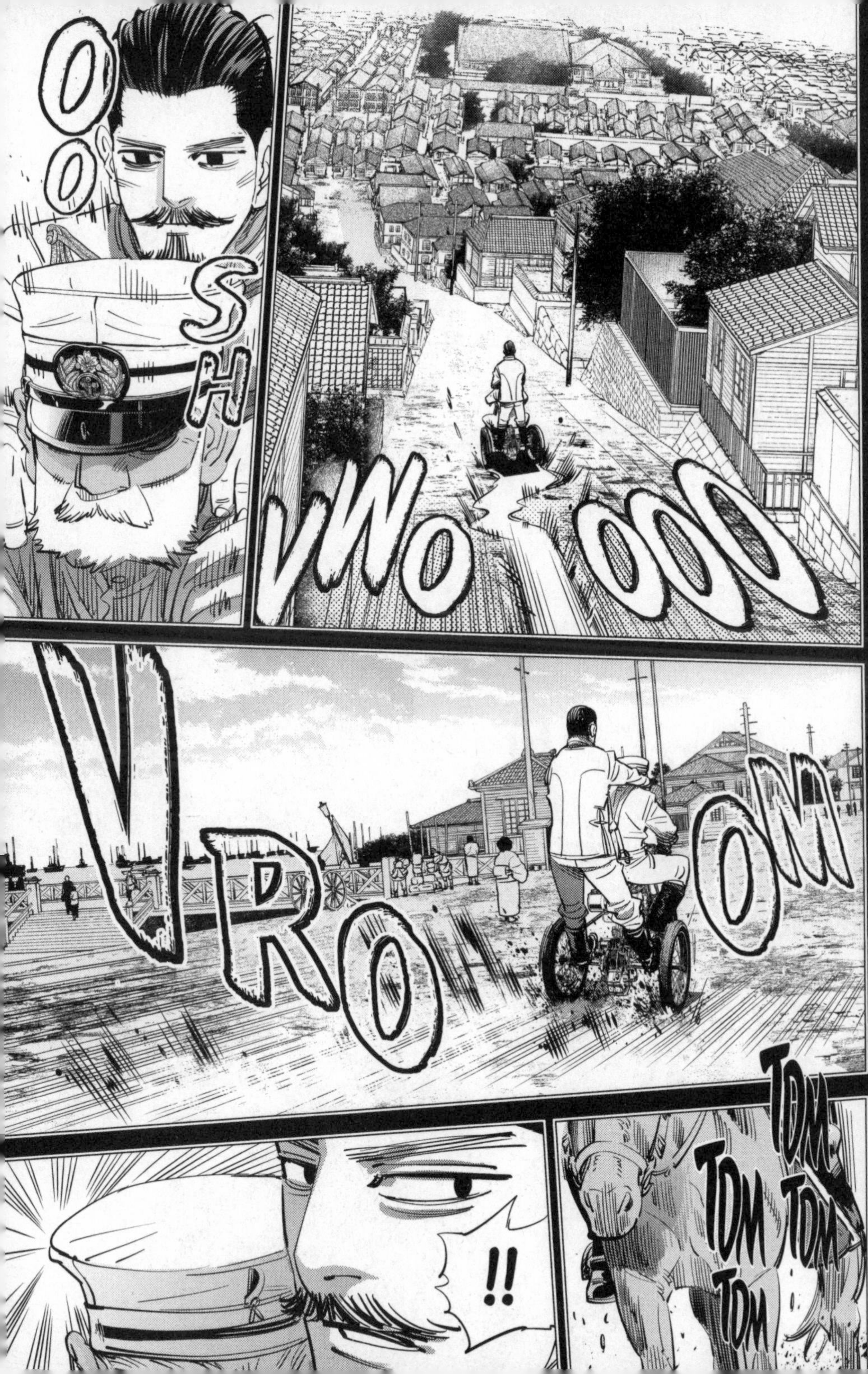

VWOOOO
OOOSH
VROOOM
TOM TOM TOM TOM TOM TOM
!!

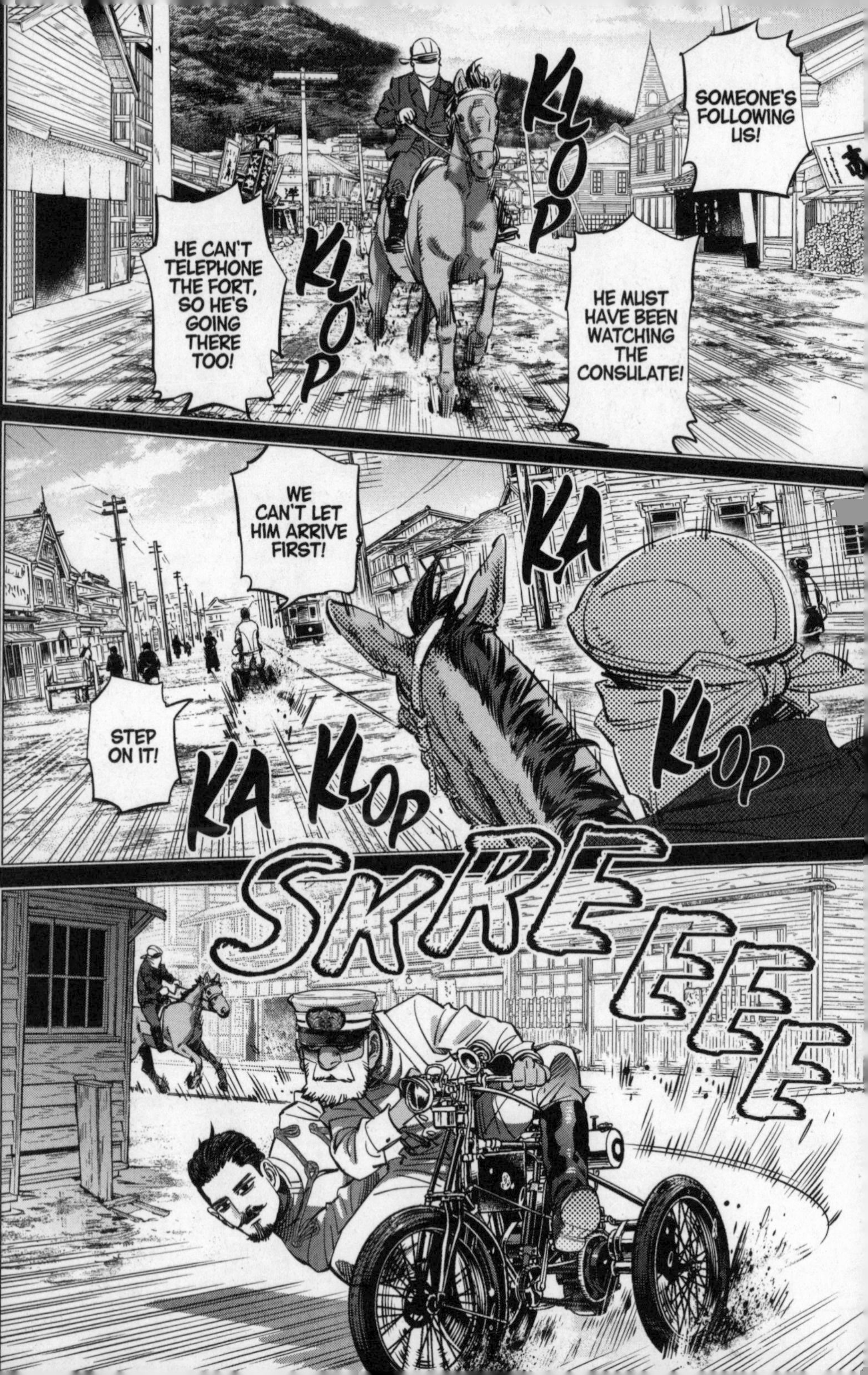
SOMEONE'S FOLLOWING US!
KLOP
HE MUST HAVE BEEN WATCHING THE CONSULATE!
KLOP
HE CAN'T TELEPHONE THE FORT, SO HE'S GOING THERE TOO!
KA
KLOP
WE CAN'T LET HIM ARRIVE FIRST!
KA KLOP
STEP ON IT!
SKREEEEE

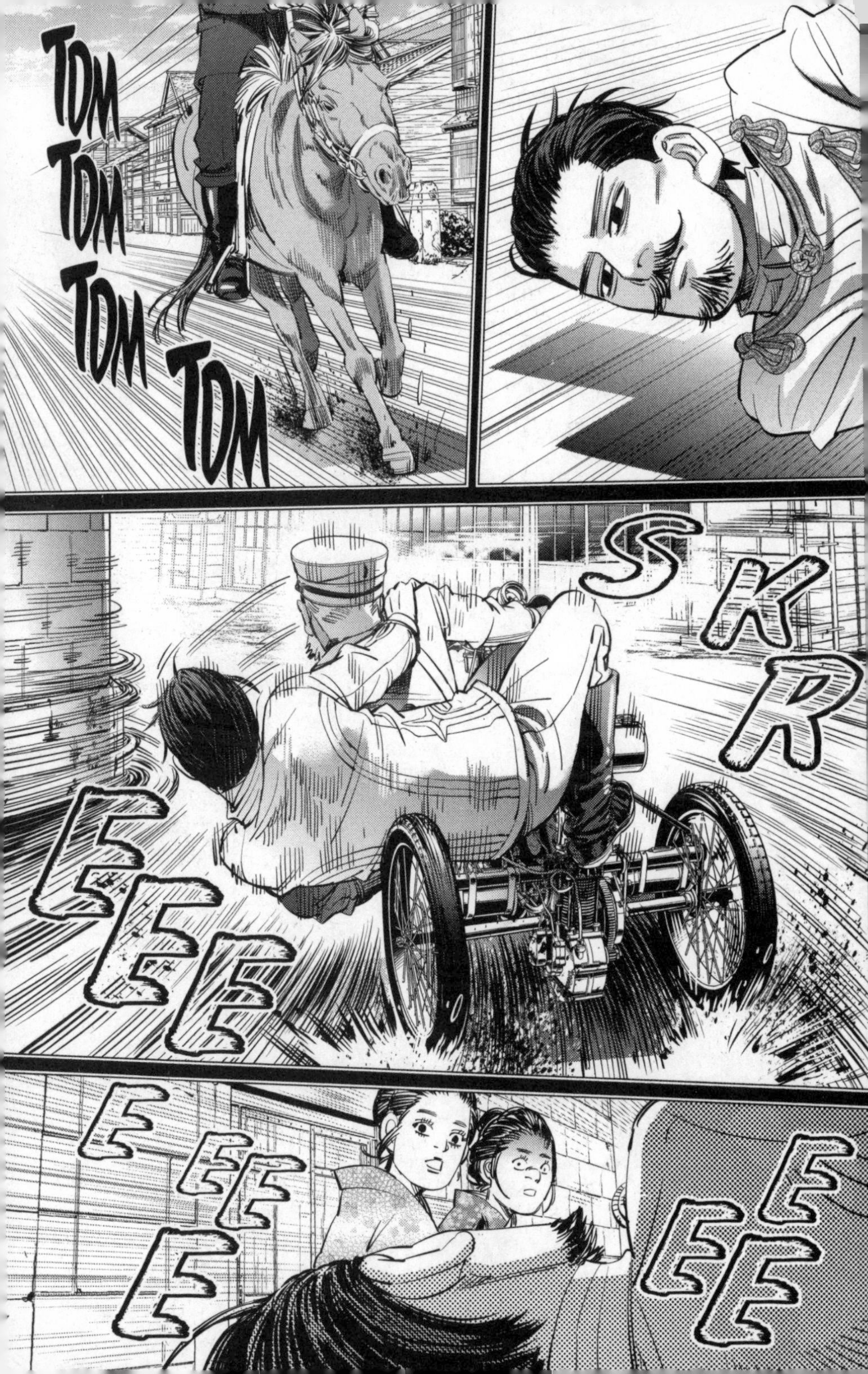
TOM
TOM
TOM
TOM
TOM
SKR
EEEE
EEEEEE
EEEEE

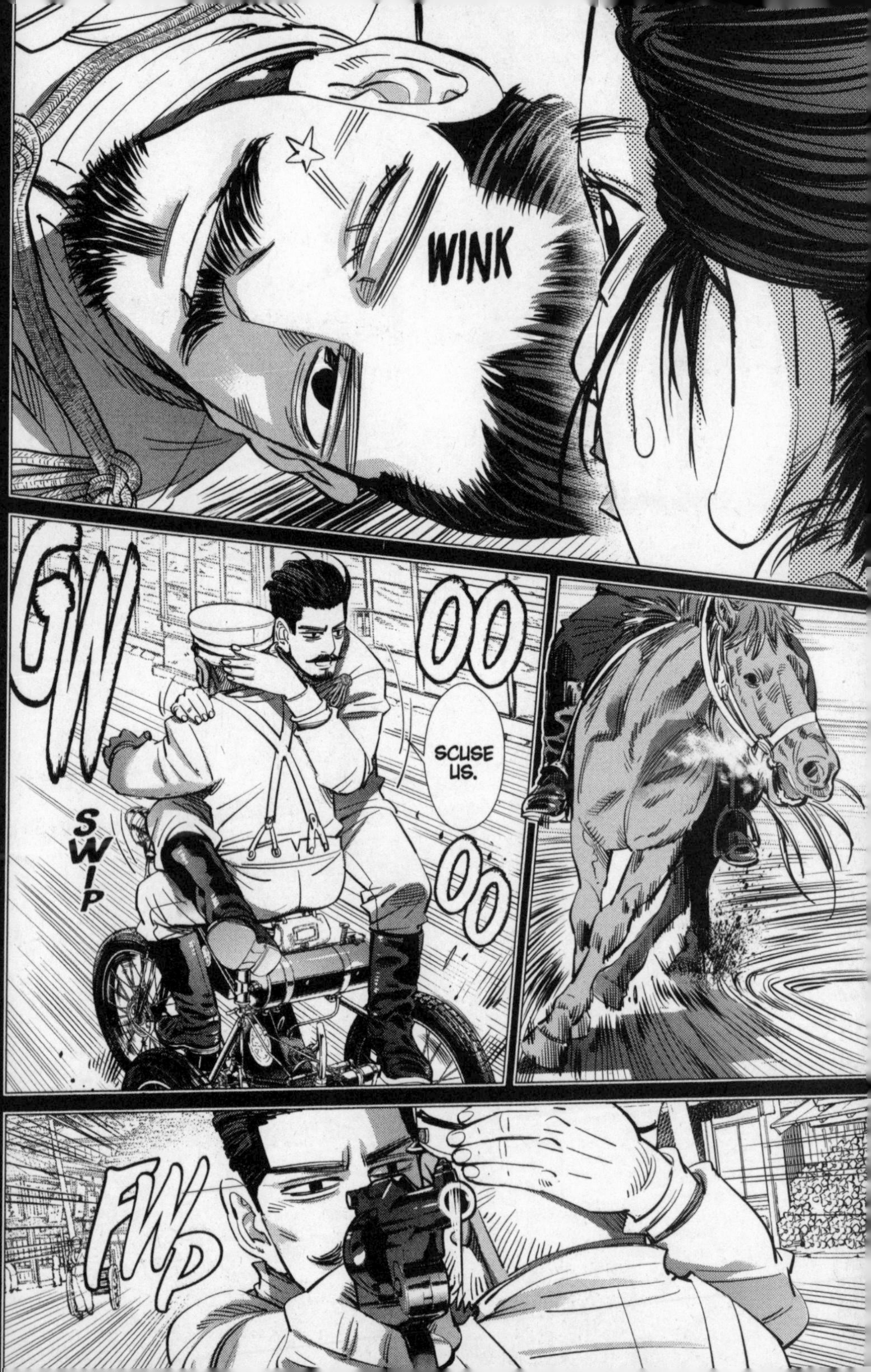
WINK
GOOOO
SCUSE US.
SWIP
FWP

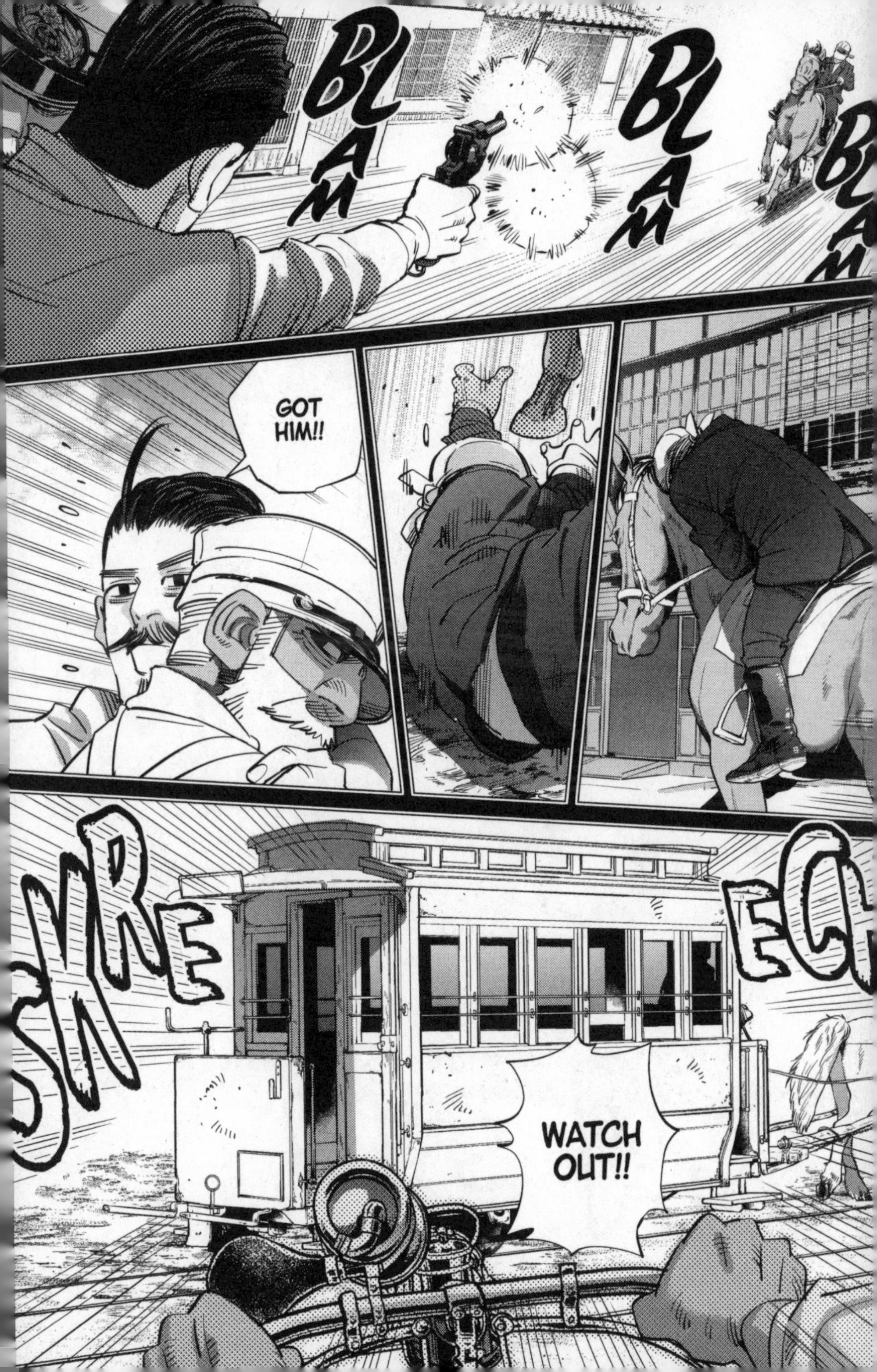
BLAM
BLAM
BLAM
GOT HIM!!
SKRE
ECH
WATCH OUT!!

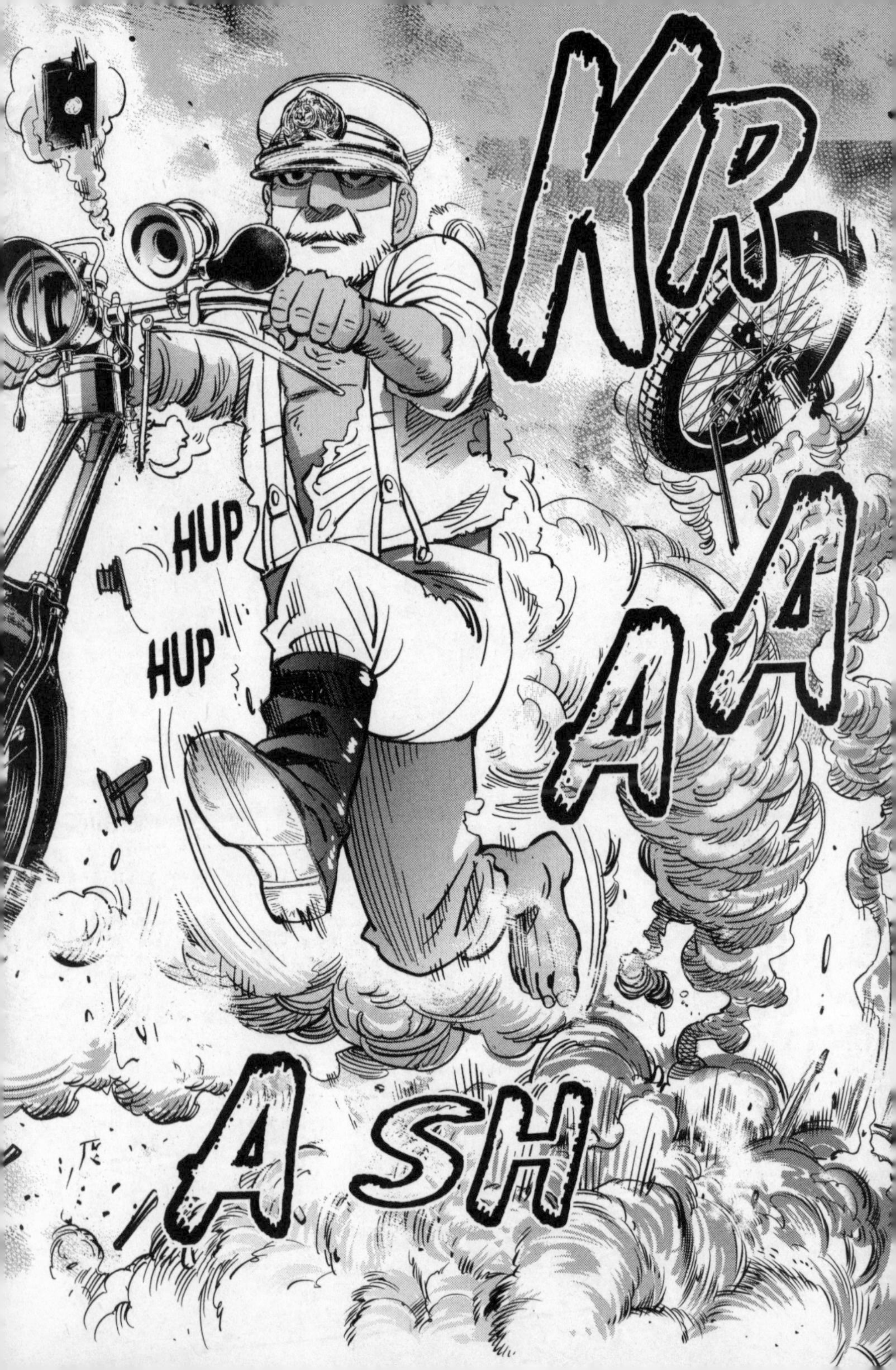
KRAA
ASH
HUP
HUP

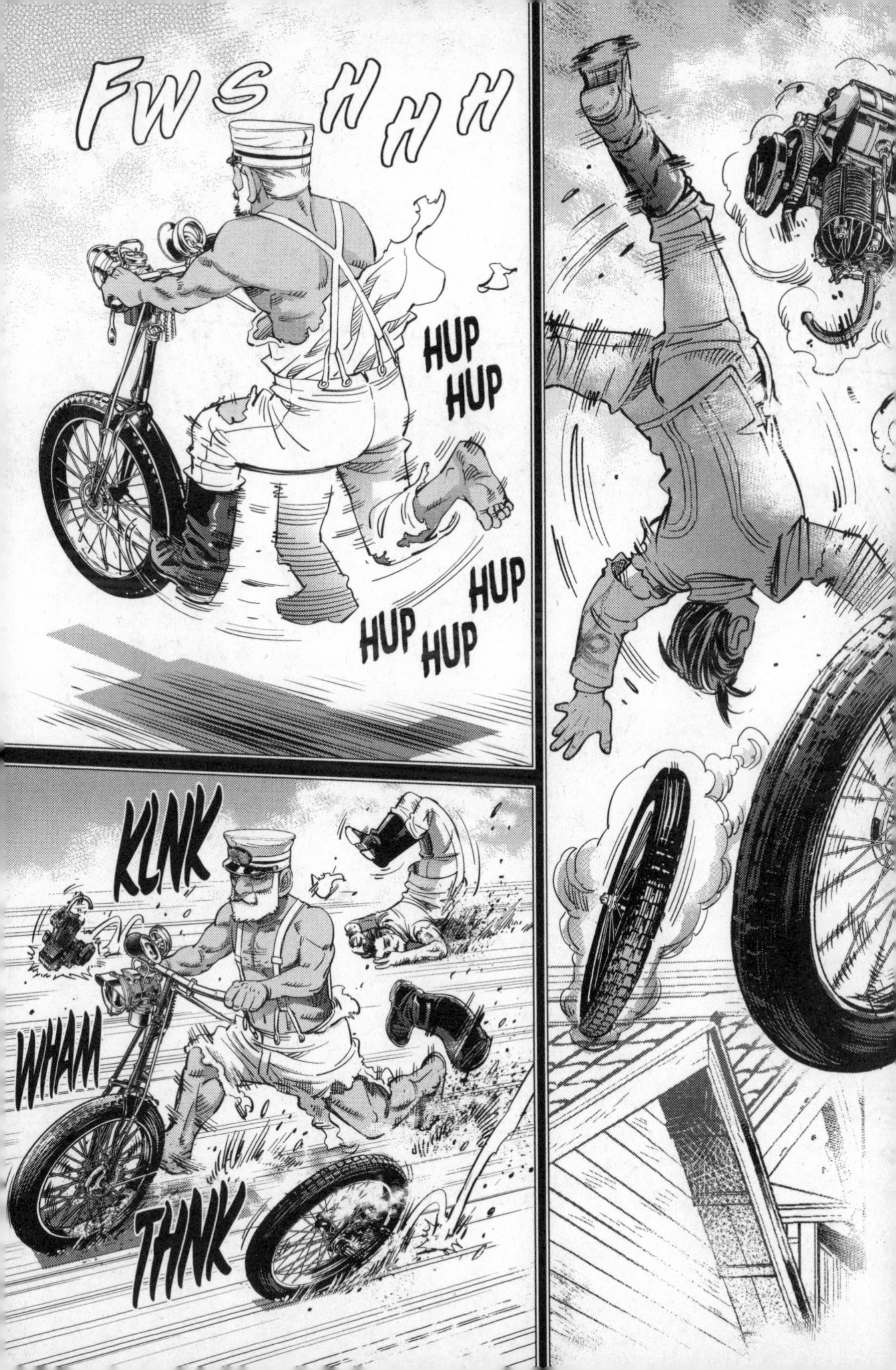
FWSHHHH
HUP HUP
HUP HUP HUP HUP
KLNK
WHAM
THNK

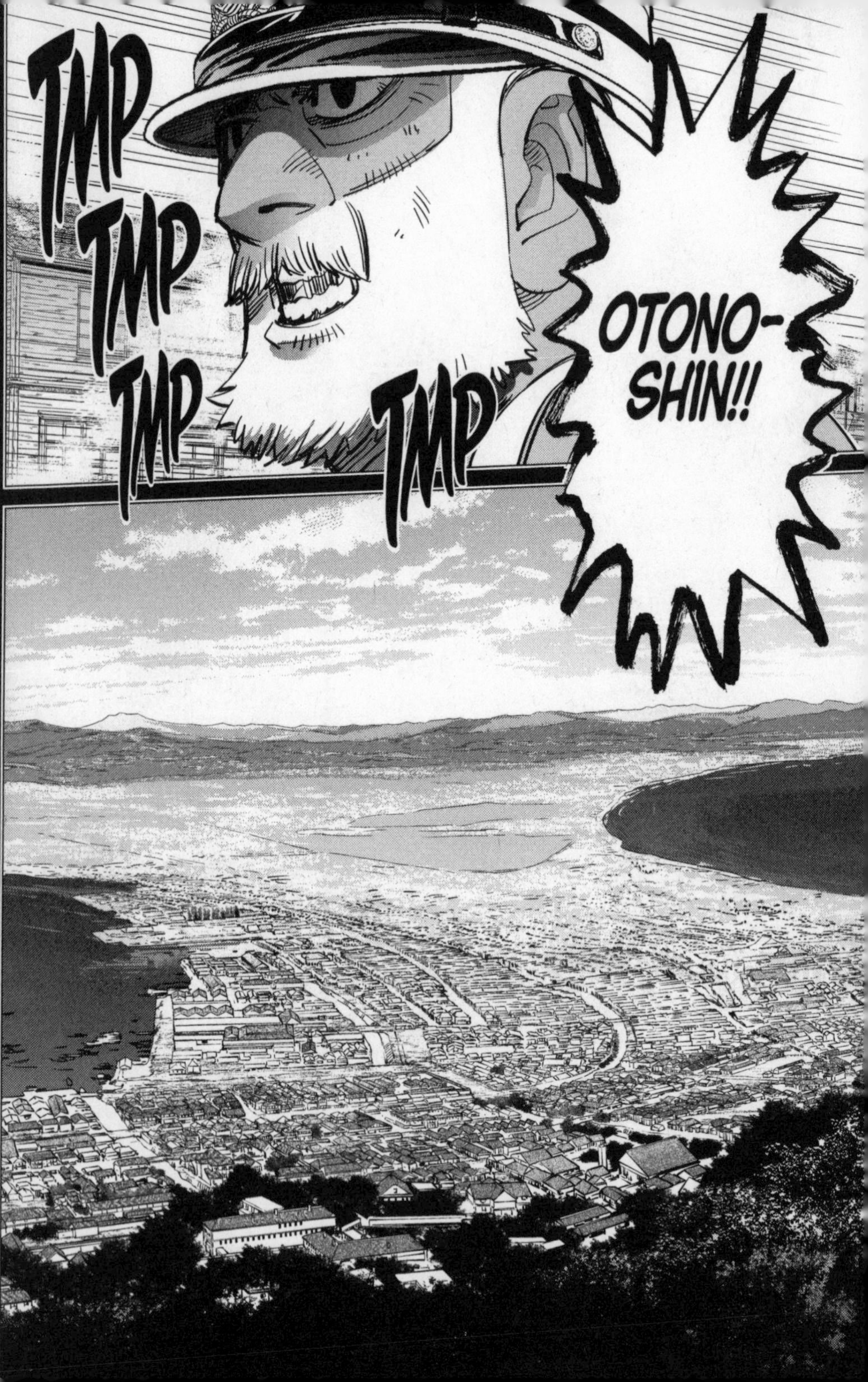
OTONO-SHIN!!
TMP TMP TMP
TMP

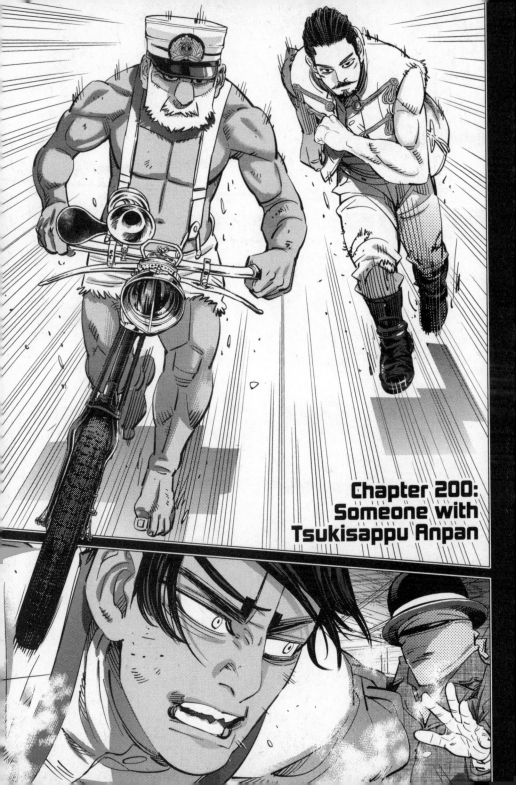

Chapter 200:
Someone with
Tsukisappu Anpan

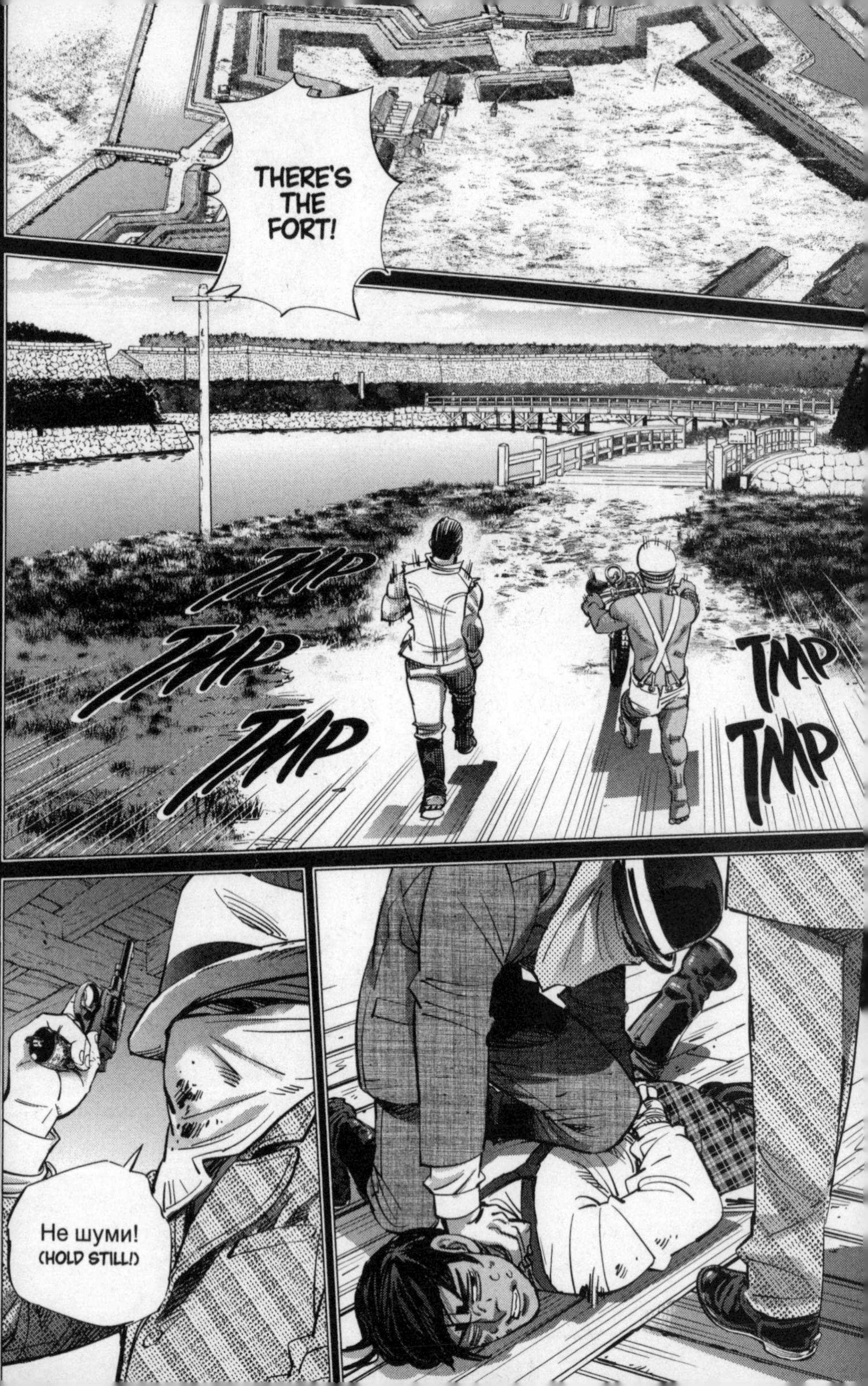
THERE'S THE FORT!
TMP TMP
TMP TMP TMP
Не шуми!
(HOLD STILL!)

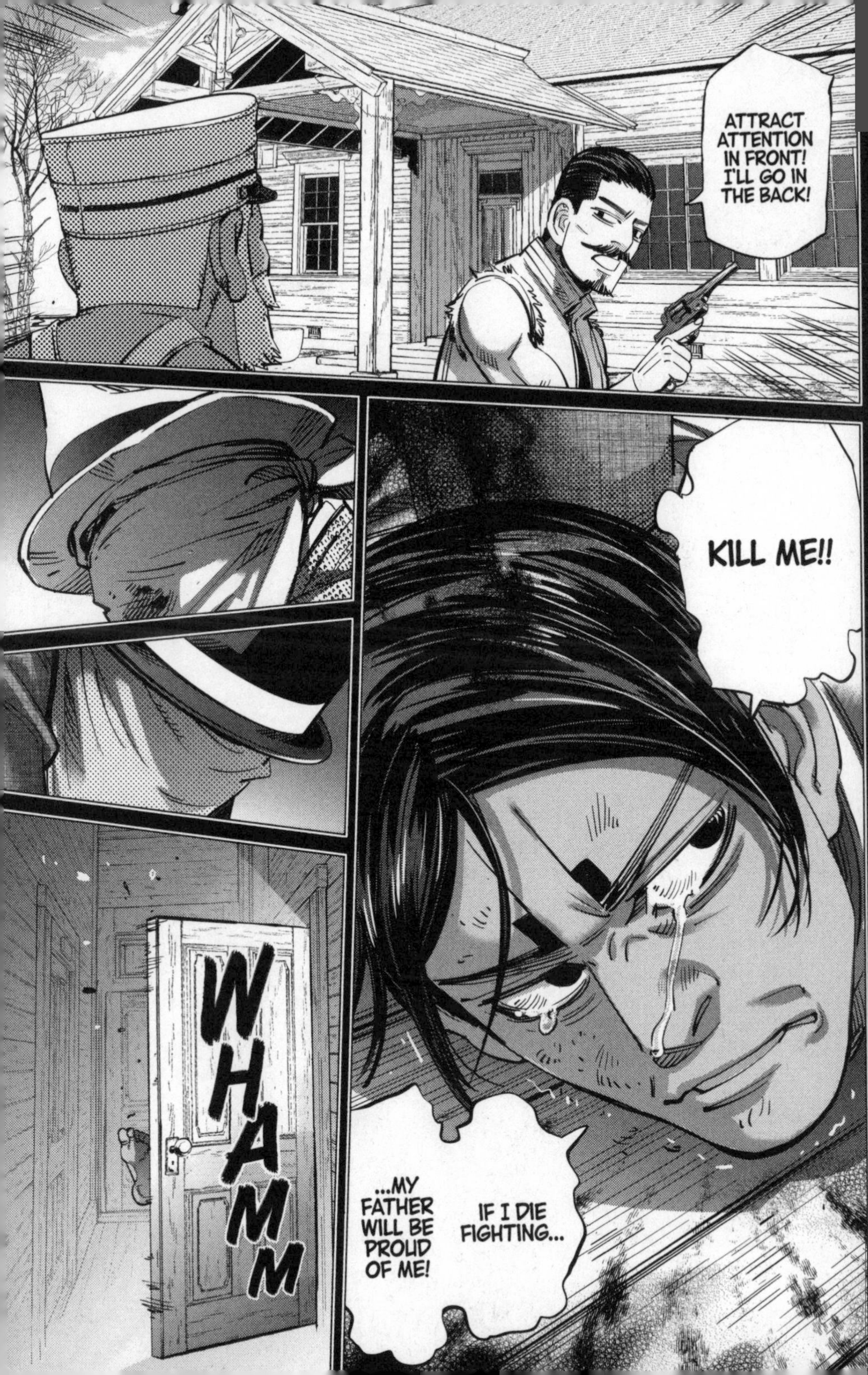

ATTRACT ATTENTION IN FRONT! I'LL GO IN THE BACK!
KILL ME!!
IF I DIE FIGHTING...
...MY FATHER WILL BE PROUD OF ME!
WHAMM

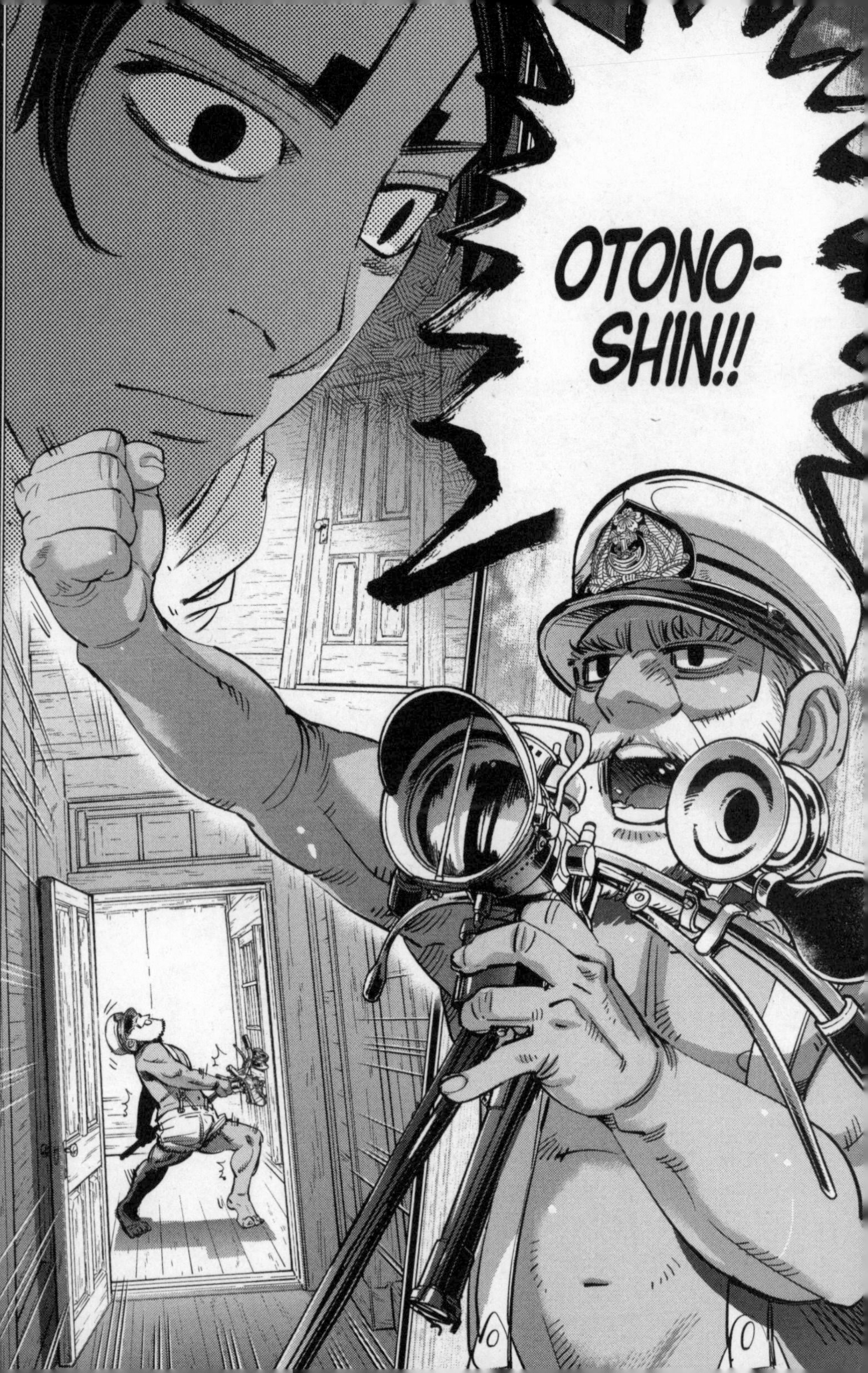
OTONO-
SHIN!!

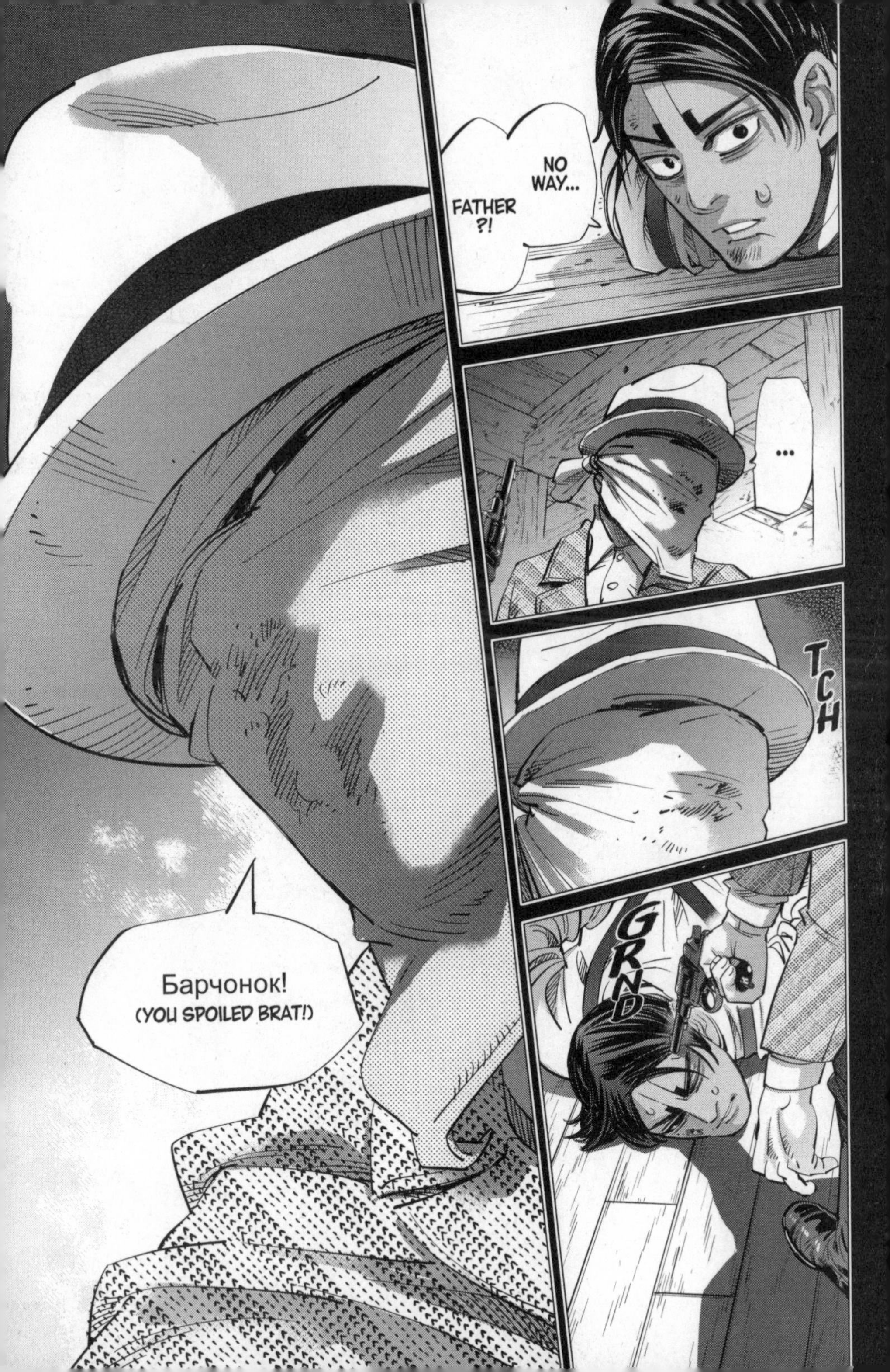
NO WAY...
FATHER ?!
...
TCH
GRND
Барчонок!
(YOU SPOILED BRAT!)

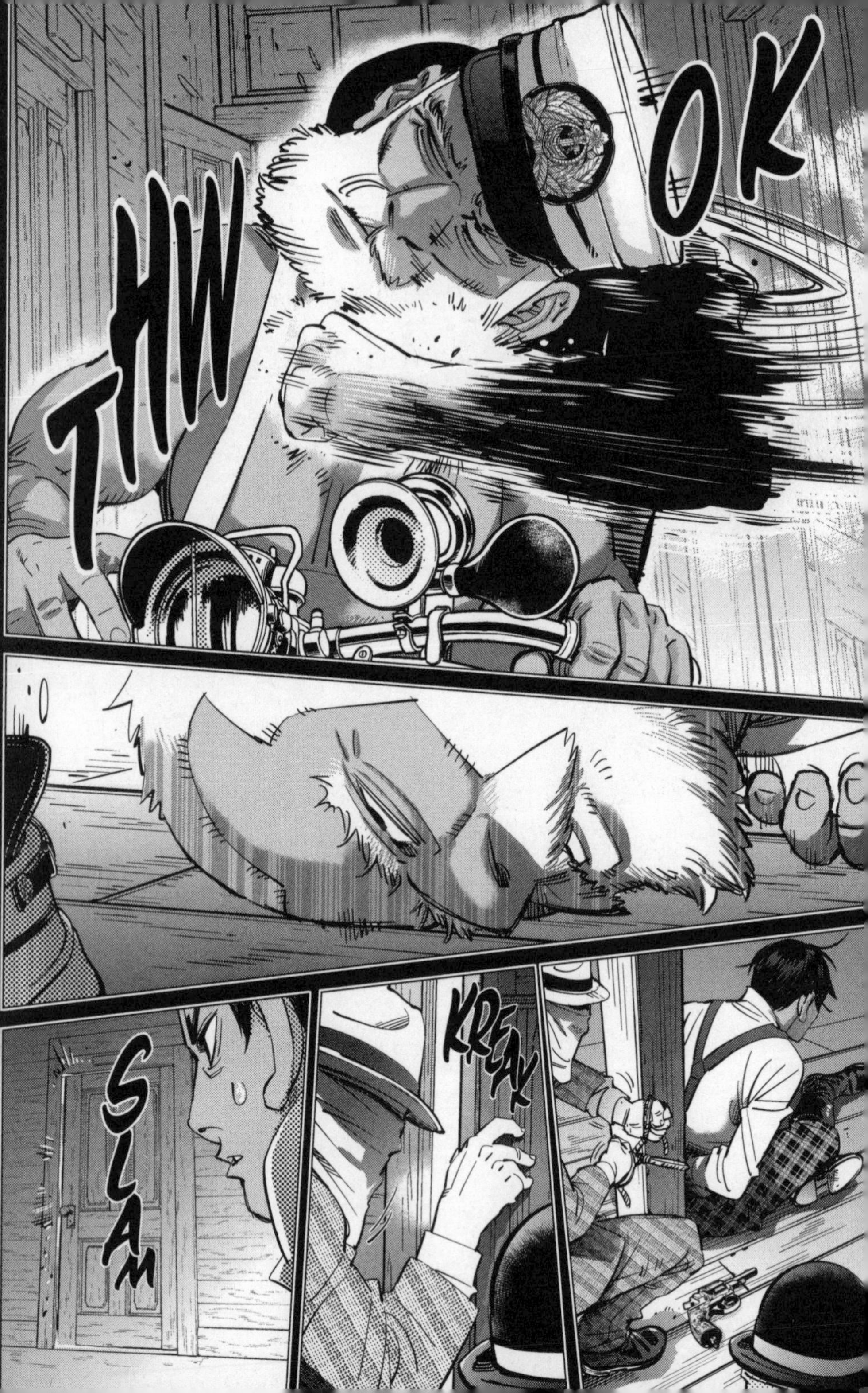
THWOK
KREAK
SLAM

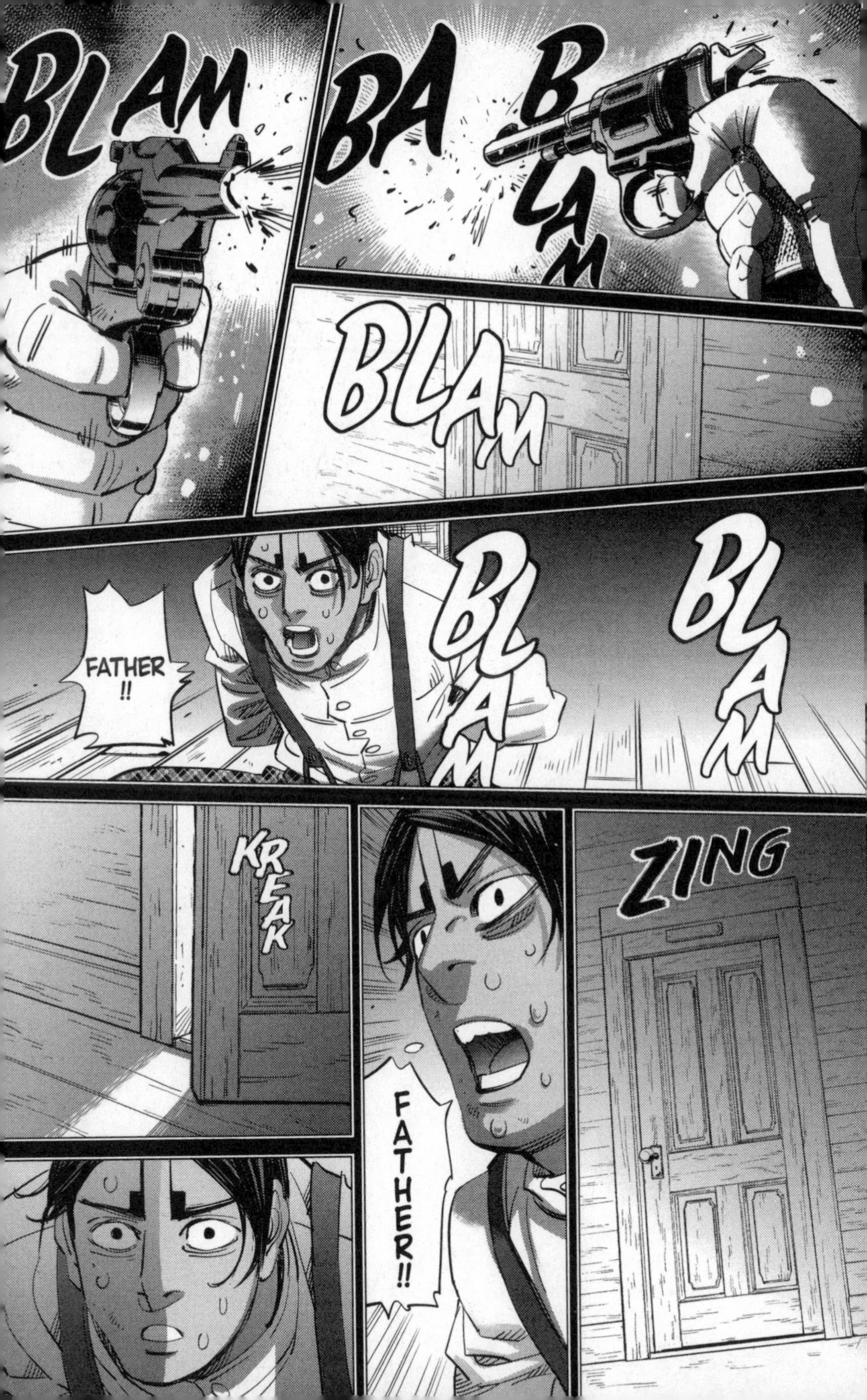
BA
BLAM
BLAM
BLAM
BLAM
BLAM
FATHER!!
ZING
FATHER!!
KREAK

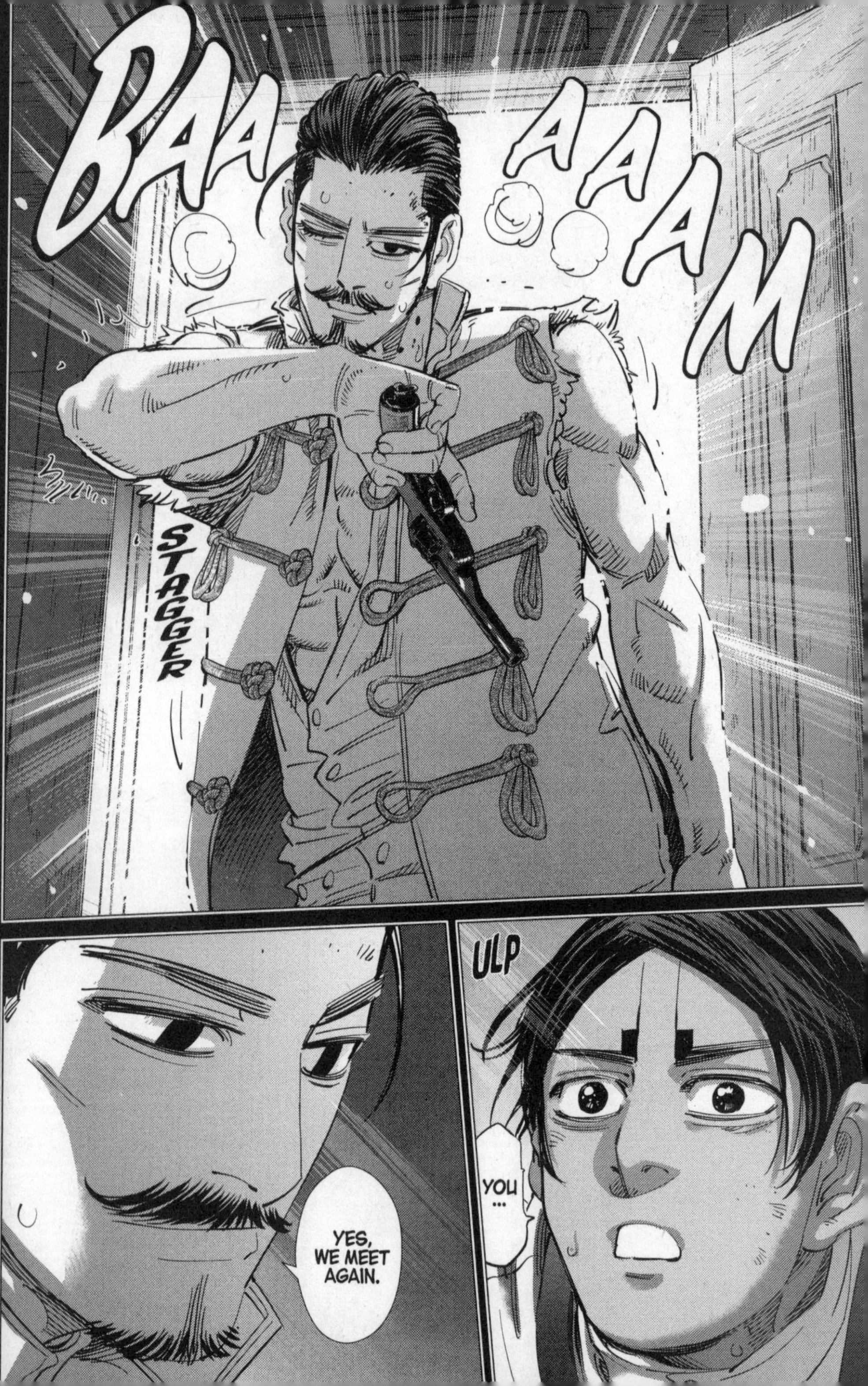
BAAAAAAM
STAGGER
ULP
YOU...
YES, WE MEET AGAIN.

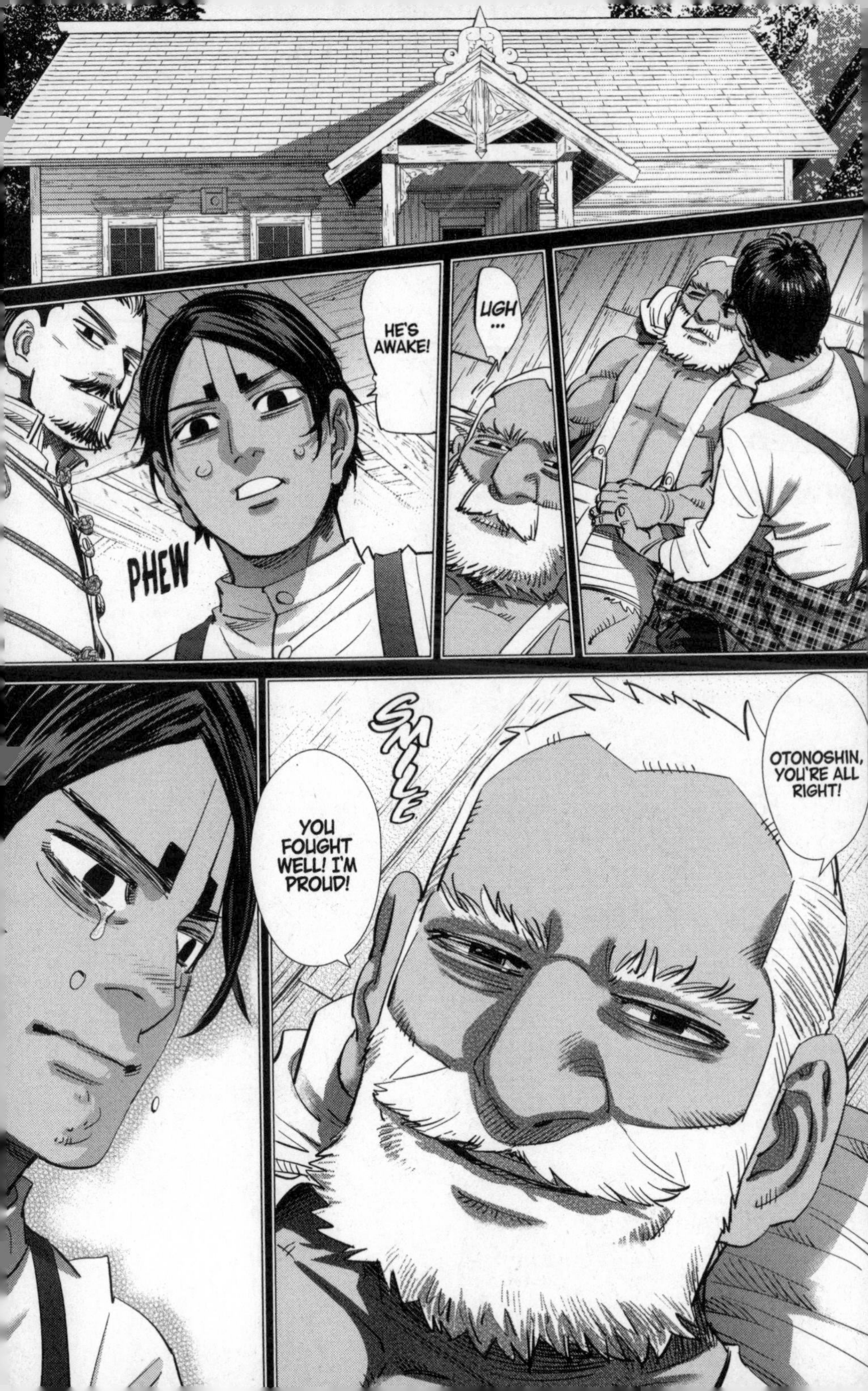
UGH ...
HE'S AWAKE!
PHEW
OTONOSHIN, YOU'RE ALL RIGHT!
SMILE
YOU FOUGHT WELL! I'M PROUD!

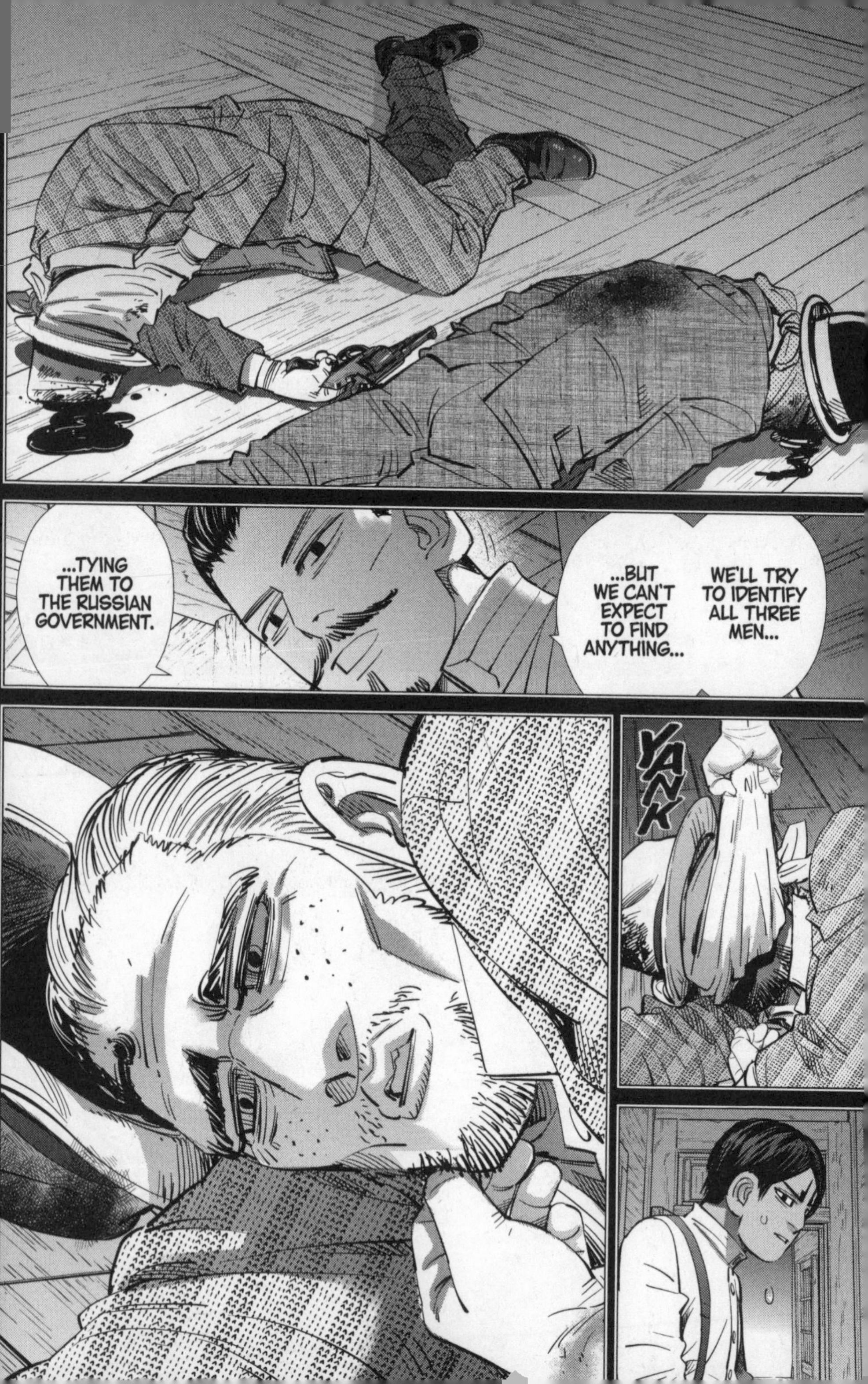
WE'LL TRY TO IDENTIFY ALL THREE MEN...
...BUT WE CAN'T EXPECT TO FIND ANYTHING...
...TYING THEM TO THE RUSSIAN GOVERNMENT.
YANK

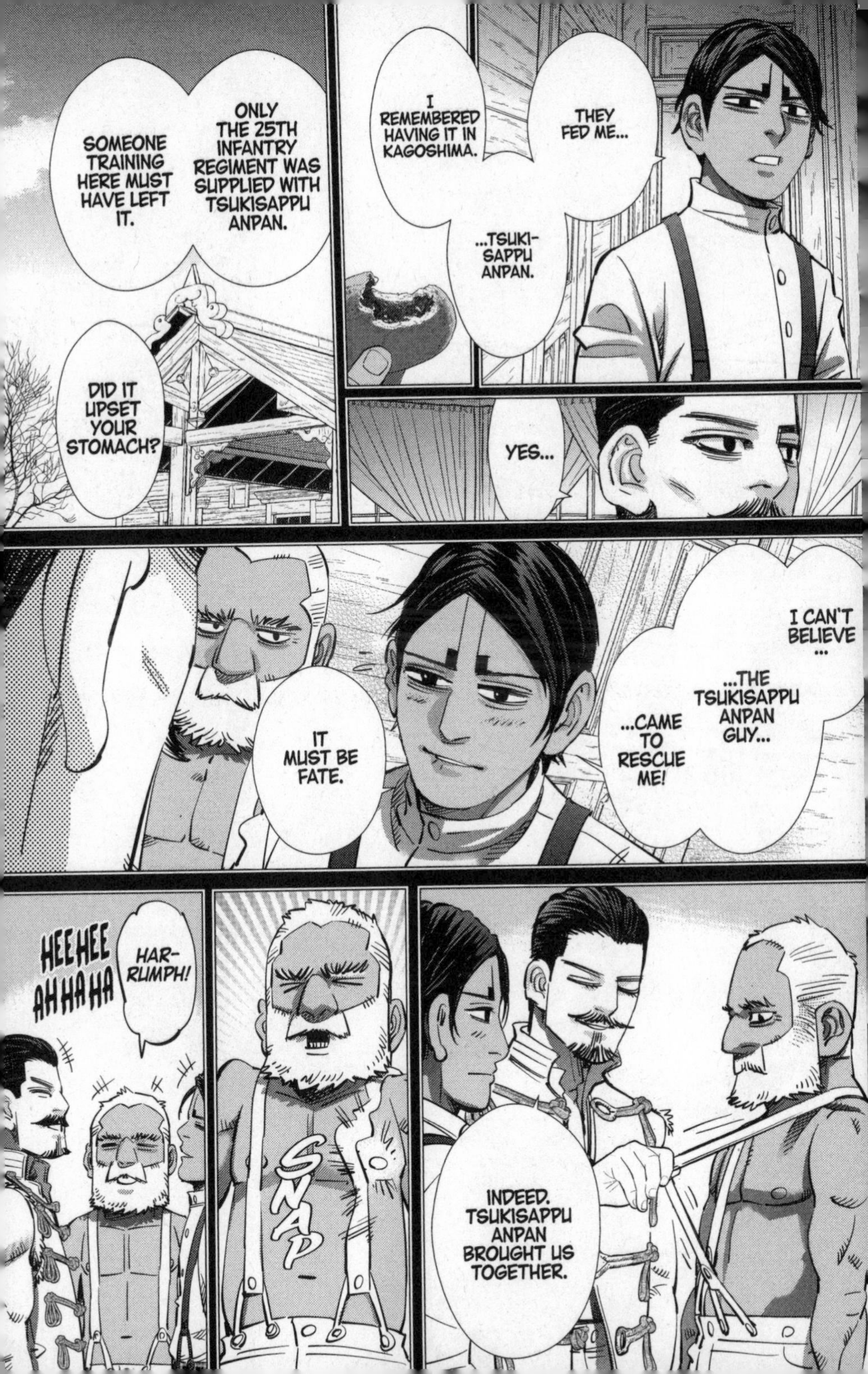

THEY FED ME...
...TSUKI-SAPPU ANPAN.
I REMEMBERED HAVING IT IN KAGOSHIMA.
YES...
ONLY THE 25TH INFANTRY REGIMENT WAS SUPPLIED WITH TSUKISAPPU ANPAN.
SOMEONE TRAINING HERE MUST HAVE LEFT IT.
DID IT UPSET YOUR STOMACH?
I CAN'T BELIEVE...
...THE TSUKISAPPU ANPAN GUY...
...CAME TO RESCUE ME!
IT MUST BE FATE.
INDEED. TSUKISAPPU ANPAN BROUGHT US TOGETHER.
SNAP
HAR-RUMPH!
HEE HEE AH HA HA

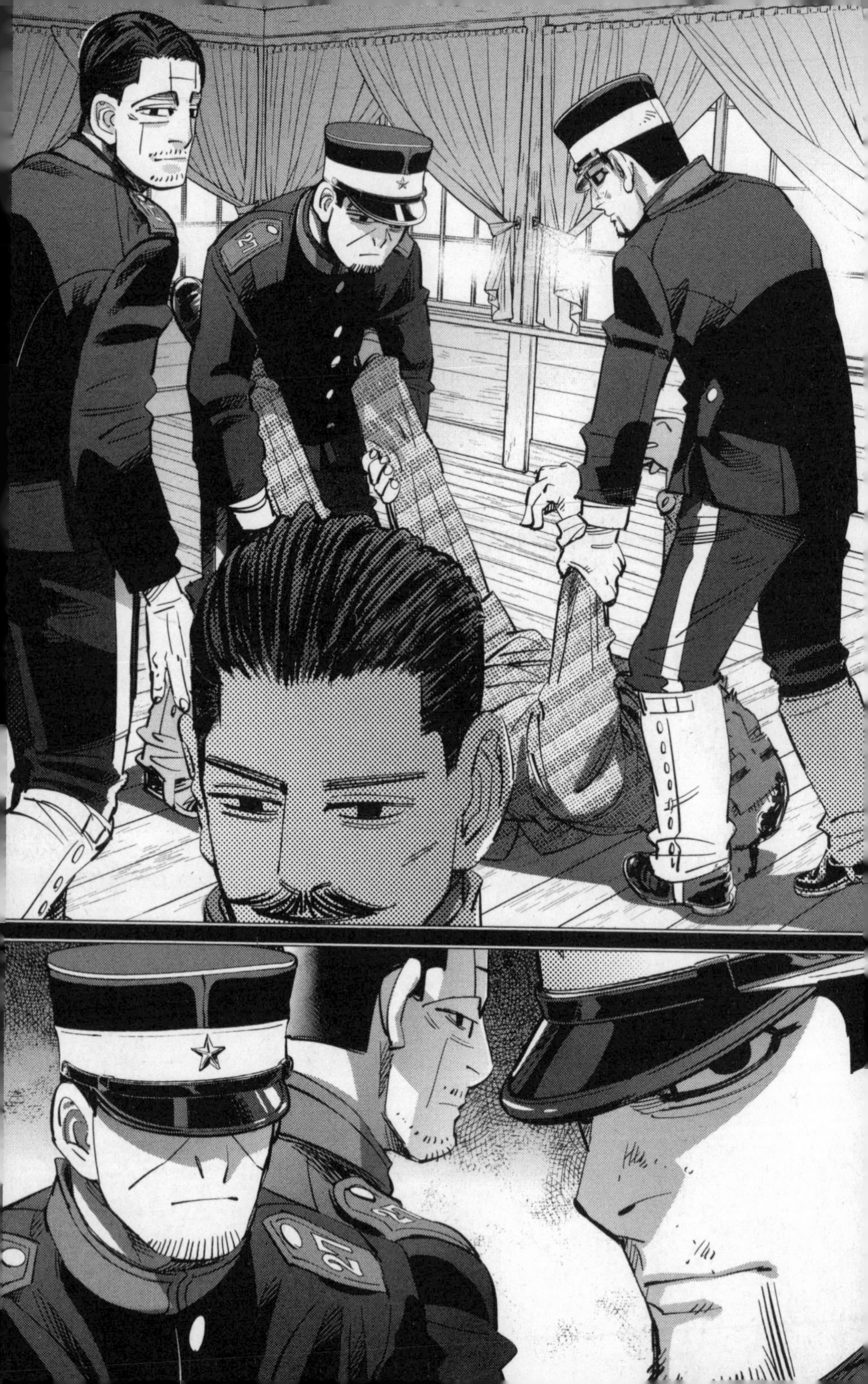

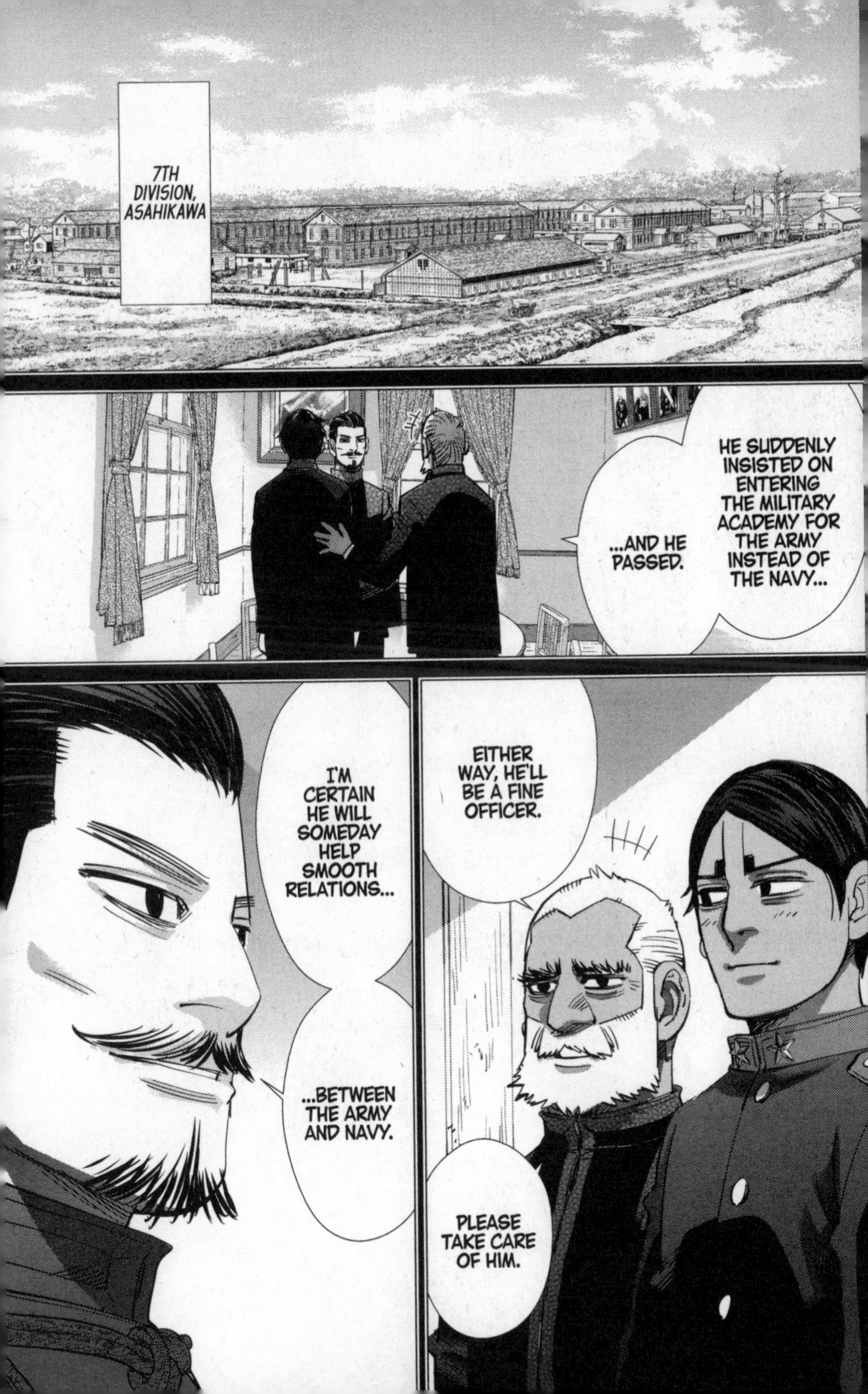
7TH DIVISION, ASAHIKAWA
HE SUDDENLY INSISTED ON ENTERING THE MILITARY ACADEMY FOR THE ARMY INSTEAD OF THE NAVY...
...AND HE PASSED.
EITHER WAY, HE'LL BE A FINE OFFICER.
PLEASE TAKE CARE OF HIM.
I'M CERTAIN HE WILL SOMEDAY HELP SMOOTH RELATIONS...
...BETWEEN THE ARMY AND NAVY.

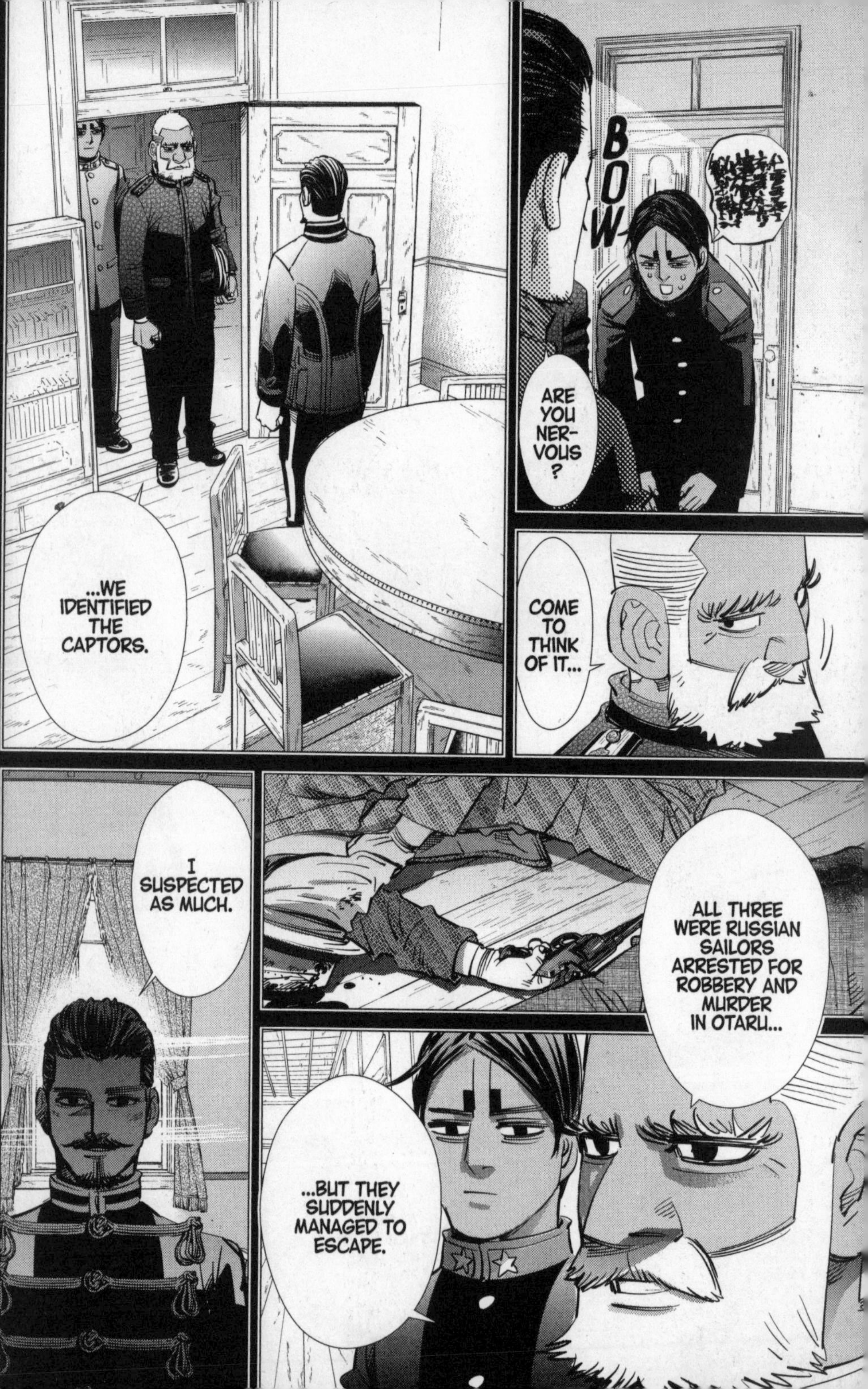
BOW
ARE YOU NERVOUS?
COME TO THINK OF IT...
...WE IDENTIFIED THE CAPTORS.
ALL THREE WERE RUSSIAN SAILORS ARRESTED FOR ROBBERY AND MURDER IN OTARU...
...BUT THEY SUDDENLY MANAGED TO ESCAPE.
I SUSPECTED AS MUCH.

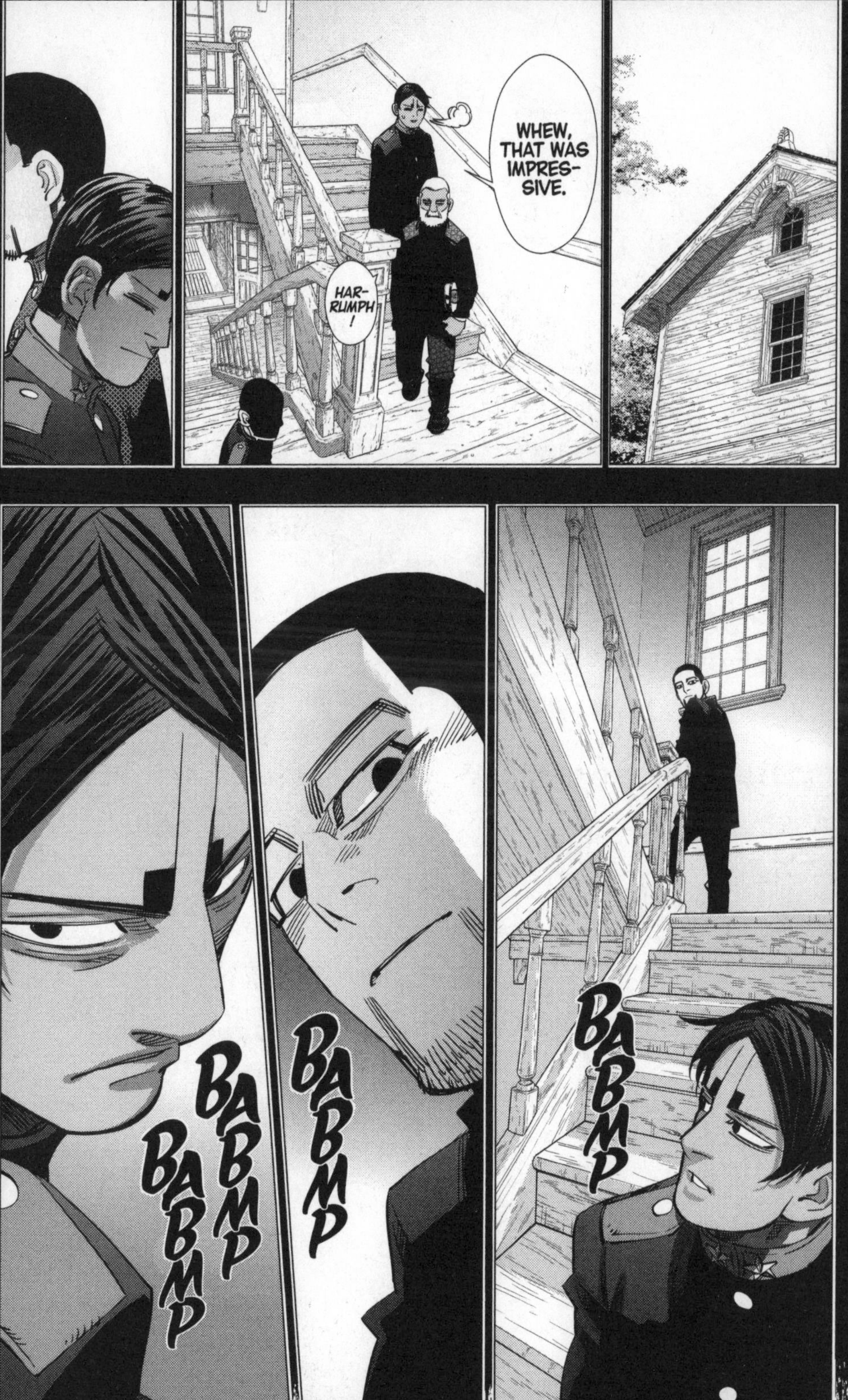
WHEW, THAT WAS IMPRES-SIVE.
HAR-RUMPH!
BABMP
BABMP
BABMP
BABMP

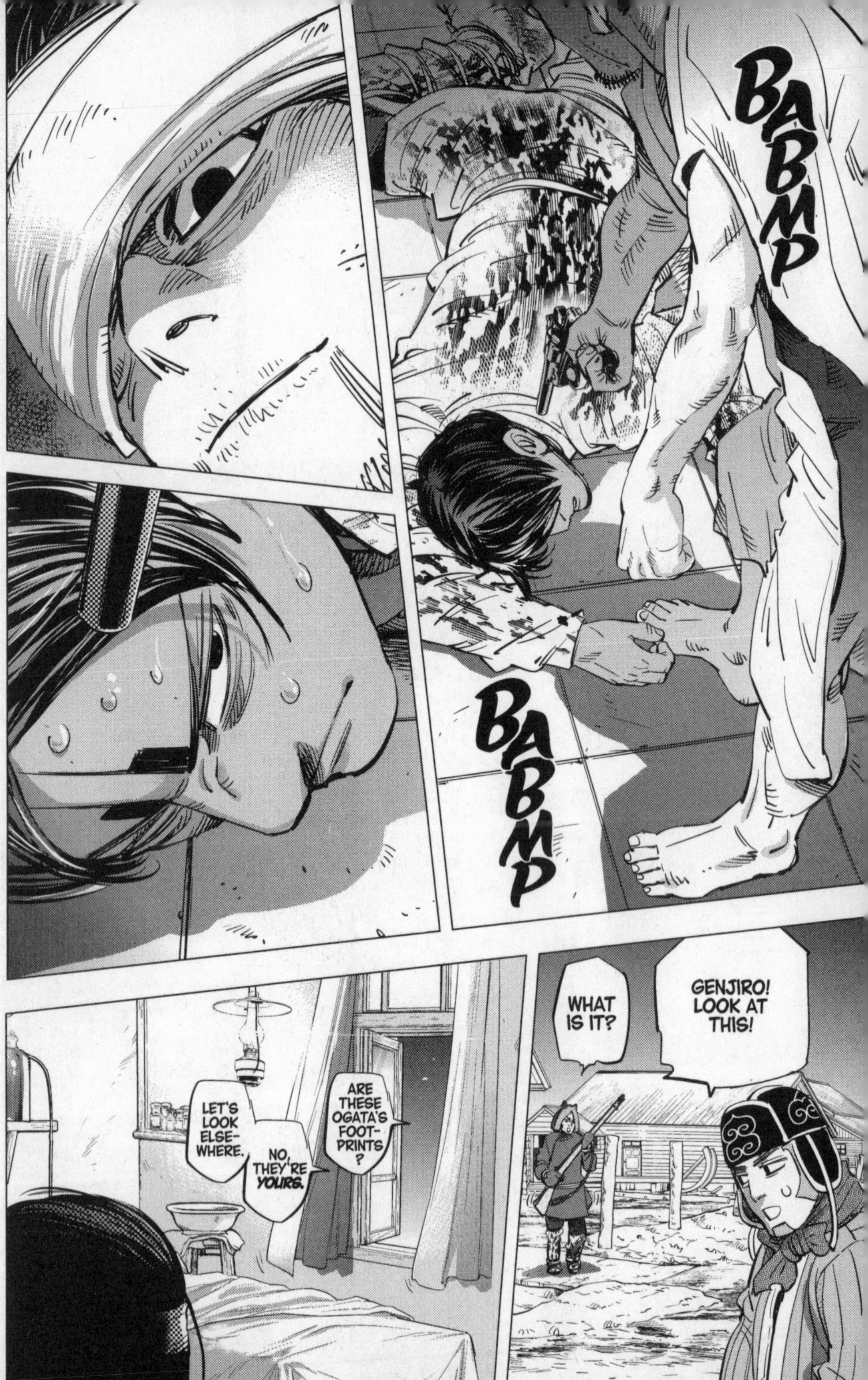
BABMP
BABMP
GENJIRO! LOOK AT THIS!
WHAT IS IT?
ARE THESE OGATA'S FOOT-PRINTS?
NO, THEY'RE YOURS.
LET'S LOOK ELSE-WHERE.

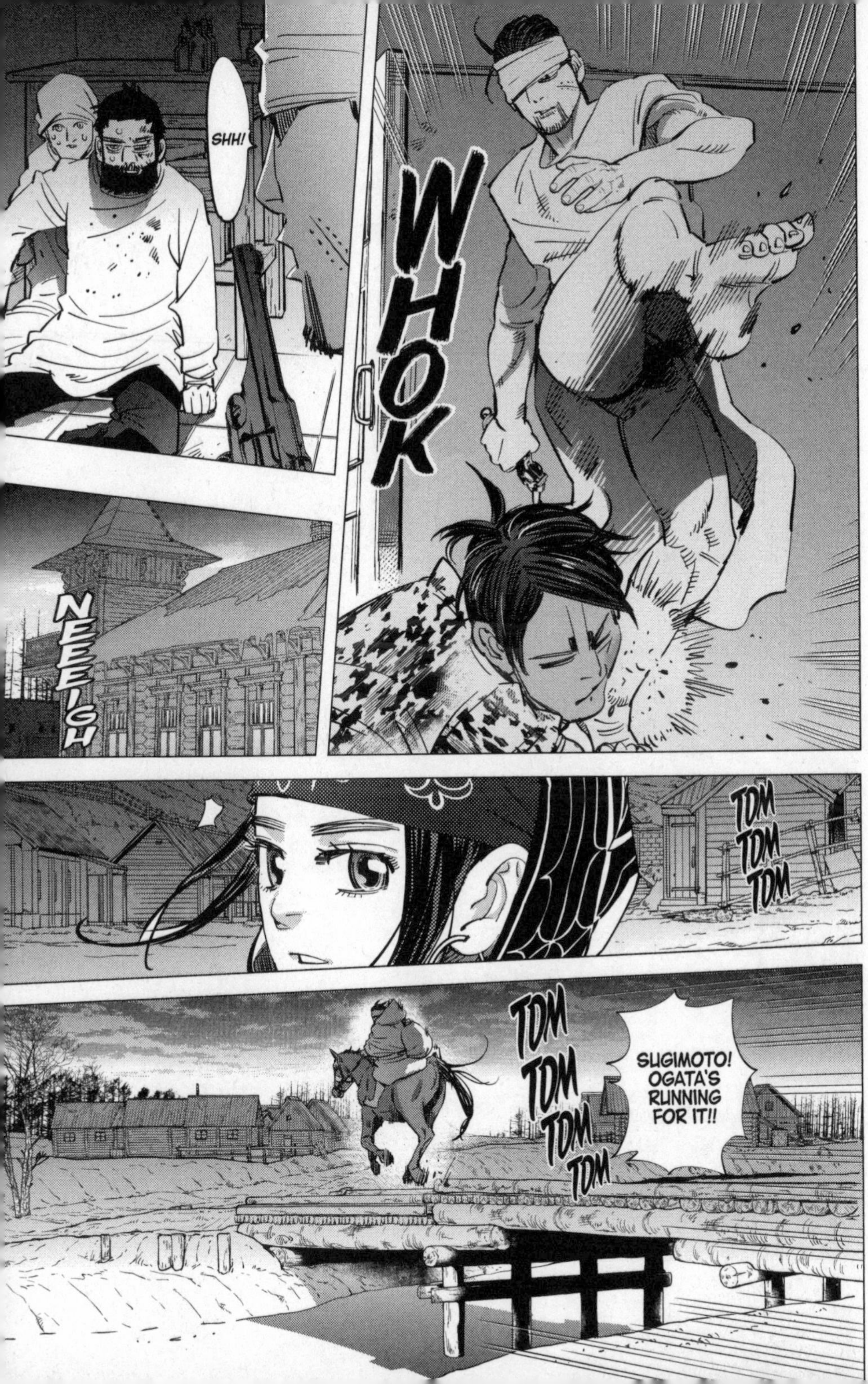
WHOK
SHH!
NEEEIGH
TDM TDM TDM
SUGIMOTO! OGATA'S RUNNING FOR IT!!
TDM TDM TDM TDM

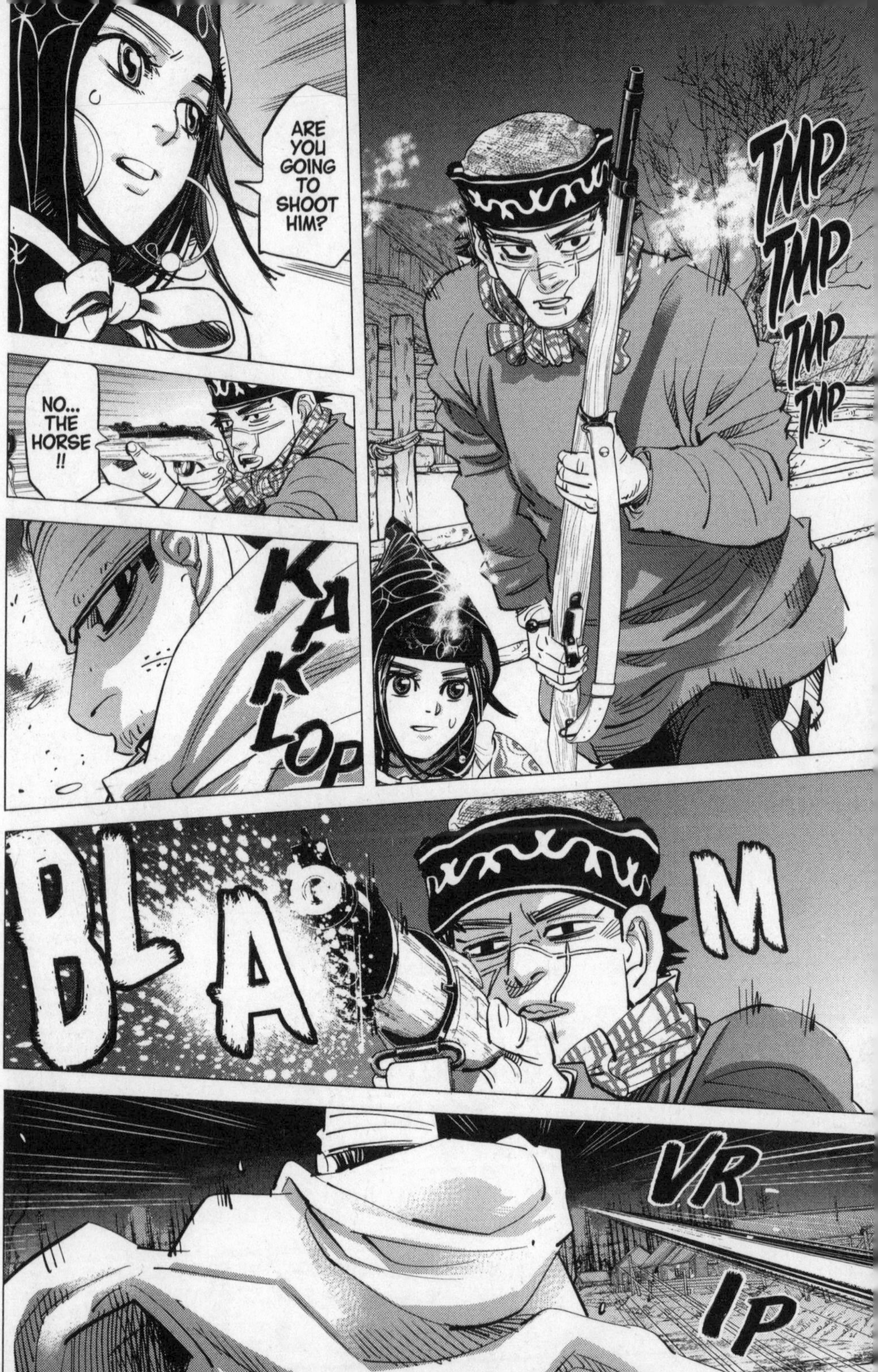
TMP TMP TMP TMP
ARE YOU GOING TO SHOOT HIM?
NO... THE HORSE !!
KAKLOP
BLAM
VRIP

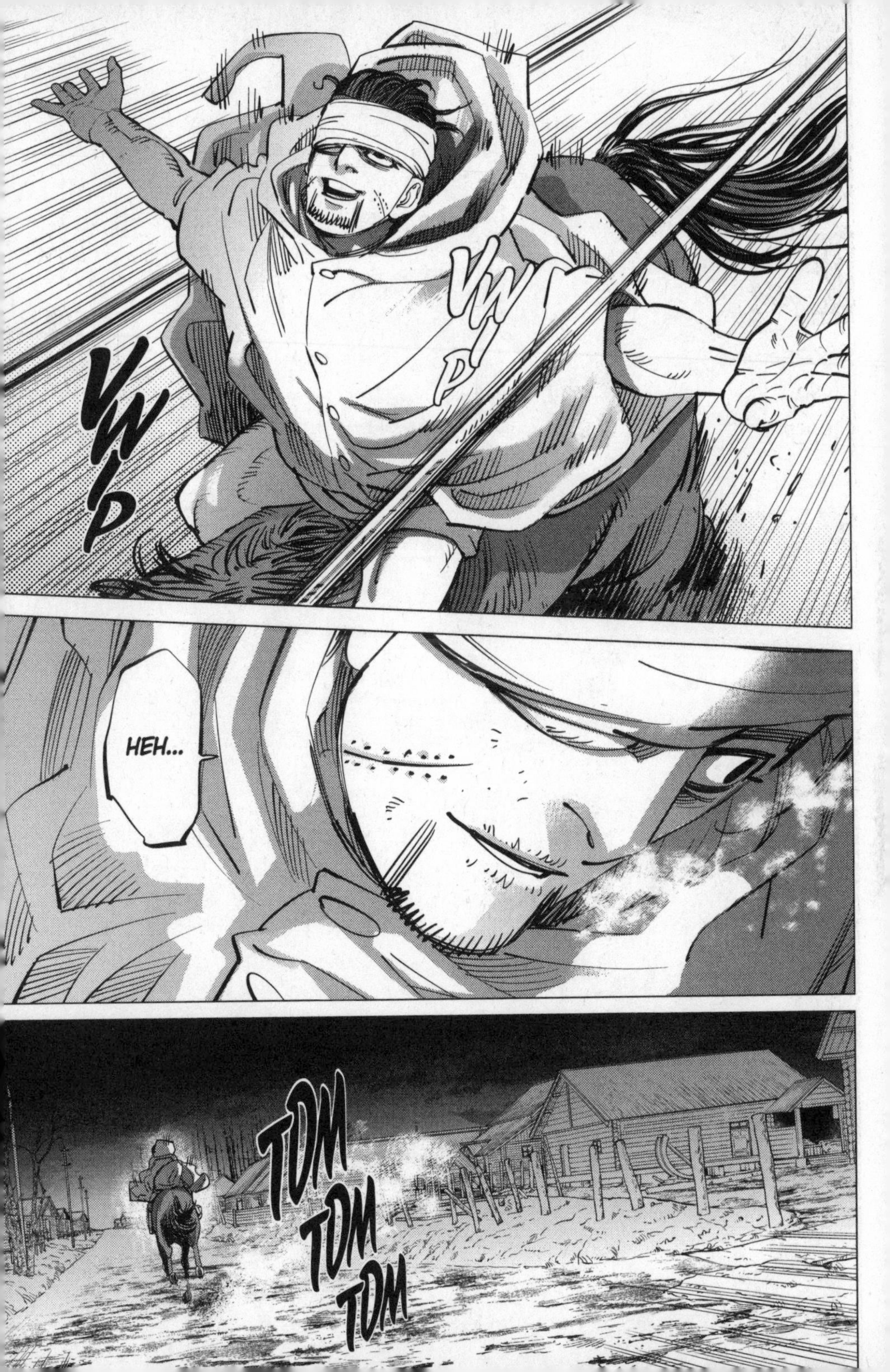
VWIP
VWIP
HEH...
TOM TOM TOM

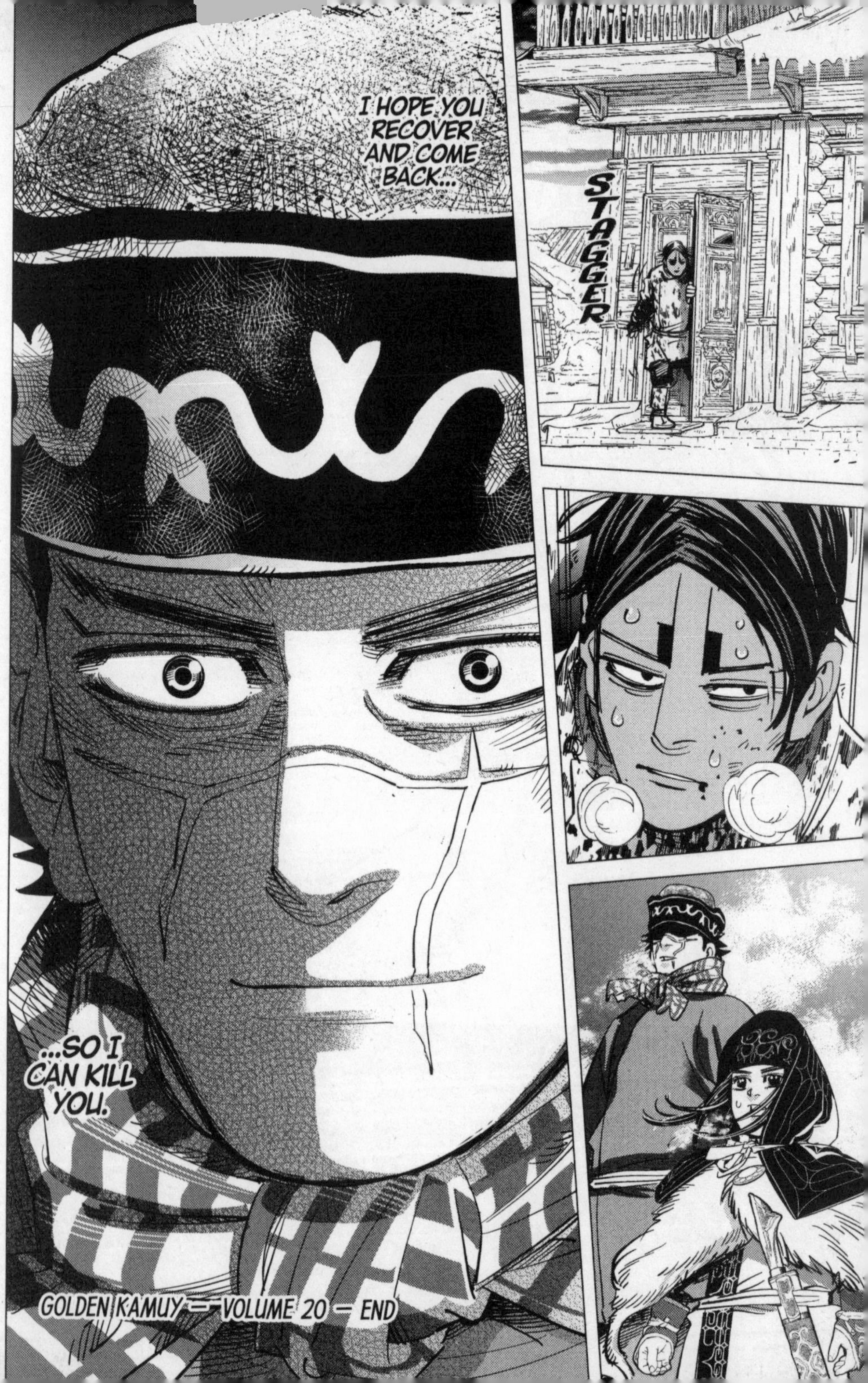
STAGGER
I HOPE YOU RECOVER AND COME BACK...
...SO I CAN KILL YOU.
GOLDEN KAMUY — VOLUME 20 — END

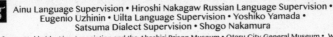

Ainu Language Supervision • Hiroshi Nakagaw Russian Language Supervision •
Eugenio Uzhinin • Uilta Language Supervision • Yoshiko Yamada •
Satsuma Dialect Supervision • Shogo Nakamura

Cooperation from • Hokkaido Ainu Association and the Abashiri Prison Museum • Otaru City General Museum • Waseda University
Aizu Museum • Kazunobu Goto, • Botanic Garden and Museum, Hokkaido University • National Museum of Ethnology •
Nibutani Ainu Culture Museum • The Ainu Museum • Moon Kabato Museum • Kushiro City Museum • Atsuyo Hisai •
Tatsuhiro Tokuda • Shigeharu Terui • All Japan Federation of Karafuto • Tokyo National Museum • Sakhalin Regional Museum •
Shiraishi Hidetoshi • Masato Tamura • Historical Village of Hokkaido • Asahikawa City Museum • Hokuchin Museum

Photo Credits • Takayuki Monma Takanori Matsuda Kozo Ishikawa

Ainu Culture References

Chiri, Takanaka and Yokoyama, Takao. *Ainugo Eiri Jiten* (Ainu Language Illustrated Dictionary). Tokyo: Kagyusha, 1994

Kayano, Shigeru. *Ainu no Mingu* (Ainu Folkcrafts). Kawagoe: Suzusawa Book Store, 1978

Kayano, Shigeru. *Kayano Shigeru no Ainugo Jiten* (Kayano Shigeru's Ainu Language Dictionary). Tokyo: Sanseido, 1996

Musashino Art University – The Research Institute for Culture and Cultural History. *Ainu no Mingu Jissoku Zushu* (Ainu Folkcrafts – Collection of Drawing and Figures). Biratori: Biratori-cho Council for Promoting Ainu Culture, 2014

Satouchi, Ai. *Ainu-shiki ekoroji-seikatsu: Haruzo Ekashi ni manabu shizen no chie* (Ainu Style Ecological Living: Haruzo Ekashi Teaches the Wisdom of Nature). Tokyo: Kabushiki gaisha Shogakukan, 2008

Chiri, Yukie. *Ainu Shin'yoshu* (Chiri Yukie's Ainu Epic Tales). Tokyo: Iwanami Shoten, 1978

Namikawa, Kenji. *Ainu Minzoku no Kiseki* (The Path of the Ainu People). Tokyo: Yamakawa Publishing, 2004

Mook. *Senjuumin Ainu Minzoku* (Bessatsu Taiyo) (The Ainu People (Extra Issue Taiyo). Tokyo: Heibonsha, 2004

Kinoshita, Seizo. *Shiraoikotan Kinoshita Seizo Isaku Shashin Shu* (Shiraoikotan: Kinoshita Seizo's Posthumous Photography Collection). Hokkaido Shiraoi-gun Shiraoi-cho: Shiraoi Heritage Conservation Foundation, 1988

The Ainu Museum. *Ainu no Ifuku Bunka* (The Culture of Ainu Clothing). Hokkaido Shiraoi-gun Shiraoi-cho: Shiraoi Ainu Museum, 1991

Keira, Tomoko and Kaji, Sayaka. *Ainu no Shiki* (Ainu's Four Seasons). Tokyo: Akashi Shoten, 1995

Fukuoka, Itoko and Sato, Kazuko. *Ainu Shokubutsushi* (Ainu Botanical Journal). Chiba Urayasu-Shi: Sofukan, 1995

Hayakawa, Noboru. *Ainu no Minzoku* (Ainu Folklore). Iwasaki Bijutsusha, 1983

Sunazawa, Kura. *Ku Sukuppu Orushibe* (The Memories of My Generation). Hokkaido, Sapporo-shi: Miyama Shobo, 1983

Haginaka, Miki et al. *Kikigaki Ainu no Shokuji* (Oral History of Ainu Diet). Tokyo: Rural Culture Association Japan, 1992

Nakagawa, Hiroshi. *New Express Ainu Go*. Tokyo: Hakusuisha, 2013

Nakagawa, Hiroshi. *Ainugo Chitose Hogen Jiten* (The Ainu-Japanese dictionary). Chiba Urayasu-Shi: Sofukan, 1995

Nakagawa, Hiroshi and Nakamoto, Mutsuko. *Kamuy Yukara de Ainu Go wo Manabu* (Learning Ainu with Kamuy Yukar). Tokyo: Hakusuisha, 2007

Nakagawa, Hiroshi. *Katari au Kotoba no Chikara – Kamuy tachi to Ikiru Sekai* (The Power of Spoken Words – Living in a World with Kamuy). Tokyo: Iwanami Shoten, 2010

Sarashina, Genzo and Sarashina, Hikari. *Kotan Seibutsu Ki <1 Juki / Zassou hen>* (Kotan Wildlife Vol. 1 – Trees and Weeds). Hosei University Publishing, 1992/2007

Sarashina, Genzo and Sarashina, Hikari. *Kotan Seibutsu Ki <2 Yacho / Kaijuu / Gyozoku hen>* (Kotan Wildlife Vol. 2 – Birds, Sea Creatures, and Fish). Hosei University Publishing, 1992/2007

Sarashina, Genzo and Sarashina, Hikari. *Kotan Seibutsu Ki <3 Yachou / Mizudori / Konchu hen>* (Kotan Wildlife Vol. 3 – Shorebirds, Seabirds, and Insects). Hosei University Publishing, 1992/2007

Sarashina, Genzo. *Ainu Minwashu* (Collection of Ainu Folktales). Kita Shobou, 1963

Sarashina, Genzo. *Ainu Rekishi to Minzoku* (Ainu History and Folklore). Shakai Shisousha, 1968

Kawakami Yuji. *Sarunkur Ainu Monogatari* (The Tale of Sarunkur Ainu). Kawagoe: Suzusawa Book Store, 2003/2005

Kawakami, Yuji. *Ekashi to Fuchi wo Tazunete* (Visiting Ekashi and Fuchi). Kawagoe: Suzusawa Book Store, 1991

Council for the Conservation of Ainu Culture. *Ainu Minzokushi* (Ainu People Magazine). Dai-ichi Hoki, 1970

Okamura, Kichiemon and Clancy, Judith A. *Ainu no Ishou* (The Clothes of the Ainu People). Kyoto Shoin, 1993

Hokkaido Cultural Property Protection Association. *Ainu Ifuku Chousa Houkokusho <1 Ainu Josei ga Denshou Suru Ibunka>* (The Ainu Clothing Research Report Vol. 1 – Traditional Clothing Passed Down Through Generations of Ainu Women). 1986

Yotsuji, Ichiro. Photos by Mizutani, Morio. *Ainu no Monyo* (Decorative Arts of the Ainu). Kasakura Publishing, 1981

Yoshida, Iwao. *Ainushi Shiryoshu* (Collection of Ainu Historical Documents). Hokkaido Publication Project Center, 1983

Kubodera, Itsuhiko. *Ainu no Mukashibanashi* (Old Stories of the Ainu). Miyaishoten, 1972

Kubodera, Itsuhiko (trans.). *Ainu Minzokushi* (Ainu People Magazine). Dai-ichi Hoki

Inoue, Koichi and Latyshev, Vladislav M. (coed.). *Karafuto Ainu no Mingu* (Karafuto Ainu Folkcraft). Hokkaido Publication Project Center, 2002

Russia ga Mita Ainu Bunka (Ainu Culture as Seen by Russia). The Foundation for Research and Promotion of Ainu Culture, 2013

Russia Minzokugaku Hakubutsukan Ainu Shiryoten—Russia ga Mita Shimaguni no Hitobito (Russia Museum of Ethnology Ainu Materials Exhibition—Island Peoples as Seen by Russia). The Foundation for Research and Promotion of Ainu Culture, 2005

The Foundation for Research and Promotion of Ainu Culture (ed.). *Senjima, Karafuto, Hokkaido—Ainu no Kurashi* (Ainu Life on the Kuril Islands, Karafuto and Hokkaido). The Senri Foundation, 2011

SPb-Ainu Project Group (ed.). *Russia Kagaku Academy Jinruigaku Minzokugaku Hakubutsukan Shozo Ainu Shiryo Mokuroku* (Ainu Collections of Peter the Great Museum of Anthropology and Ethnography Russian Academy of Sciences Catalogue). Sofukan, 1998

Yamamoto, Yuko. *Karafuto Ainu—Jukyo to Mingu* (Residences and Folkcraft of the Karafuto Ainu). Sagami Shobo, 1970

Yamamoto, Yuko (author and ed.). Chiri, Mashiho and Onuki, Emiko co-authors). *Karafuto Shizen Minzoku no Seikatsu* (Lifestyles of Karafuto Natural Peoples). Sagami Shobo, 1979

Chiri, Mashiho. *Chiri Mashiho Chosakushu 3 Seikatsu-shi / Minzokugaku-hen* (Mashiho Chiri Collected Works, Vol. 3: Lifestyles and Ethnology). Heibonsha, 1973

Yamamoto, Yuko. *Hoppo Shizen Minzoku Minwa Shusei* (Northern Natural Peoples Folk Tales Compilation). Sagami Shobo, 1968

Yamamoto, Yuko. *Karafuto Genshi Minzoku no Seikatsu* (Lifestyles of Karafuto Primitive Peoples). ARS, 1943

Nishitsuru, Sadaka. *Karafuto Ainu*. Miyama Shobo, 1974

Kasai, Takechiyo. *Karafuto Ainu no Minzoku* (Folklore of the Karafuto Ainu). Miyama Shobo, 1975

Tanigawa, Kenichi. *Kita no Minzokushi-Sakhalin / Chishima no Minzoku* (Northern Ethnography—Sakhalin / People of the Kuril Islands). San-Ichi Shobo Publishing Inc., 1997

Takabeya, Fukuhei. *Hoppoken no Ie* (Houses of the Northern Regions). Shokokusha Publishing Co., Ltd., 1943

Abashiri City Northern Folkore Cultural Preservation Society. *Uiruta no Kurashi to Mingu* (Uilta Lifestyles and Folkcraft). 1982

The Foundation for Research and Promotion of Ainu Culture (ed.). *Zaidan Hojin Ainu Bunka Fukko / Kenkyu Suishin Kiko Shuzo Mokuroku 7 (Ishida Shuzo Kyuzo Shashin)* (The Foundation for Research and Promotion of Ainu Culture Collection Catalog 7 (Ishida Collection Old Collection Photograph). The Foundation for Research and Promotion of Ainu Culture, 2012

Uilta Society Museum Steering Committee (ed.). *Shiryokan Jakka Duxuni Tenji Sakuhinshu* (Museum Jakka Duxuni Exhibition Works Collection). 2002

Bird, Isabella L. (author), Kobari, Kosai (trans.). *Meiji Shoki no Emishi Tanboki* (Report on Emishi in the Early Meiji Era). Sarorun Shobo, 1977

Munro, N.G. (author), Seligman, B.Z. (ed.), Tetsuro, Komatsu (trans.). *Ainu no Shinko to Sono Gishiki* (Ainu Creed and Cult). Kokushokankokai, 2002

Batchelor, John (author), Tetsuro, Komatsu (trans.). *Ainu no Kurashi to Densho* (Ainu Life and Lore). Hokkaido Publication Project Center, 1999

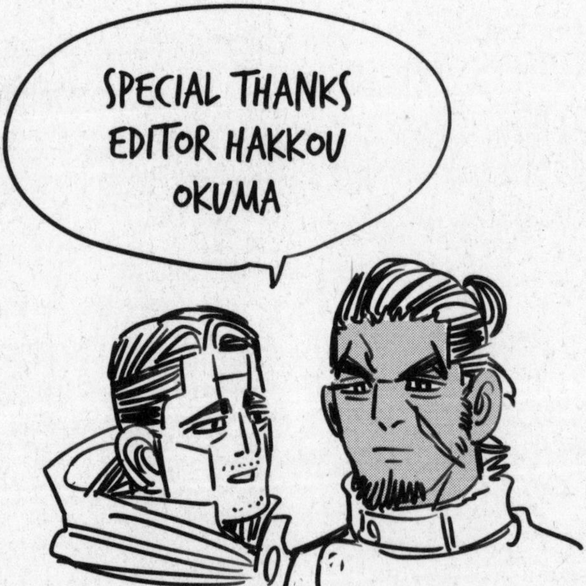
SPECIAL THANKS
EDITOR HAKKOU
OKUMA

Kanto or wa yaku sak no arankep sinep ka isam.

Nothing comes from heaven without purpose. —Ainu proverb

FUFUTO

NIVKH CLOTHING
MADE FROM
FISH SKIN

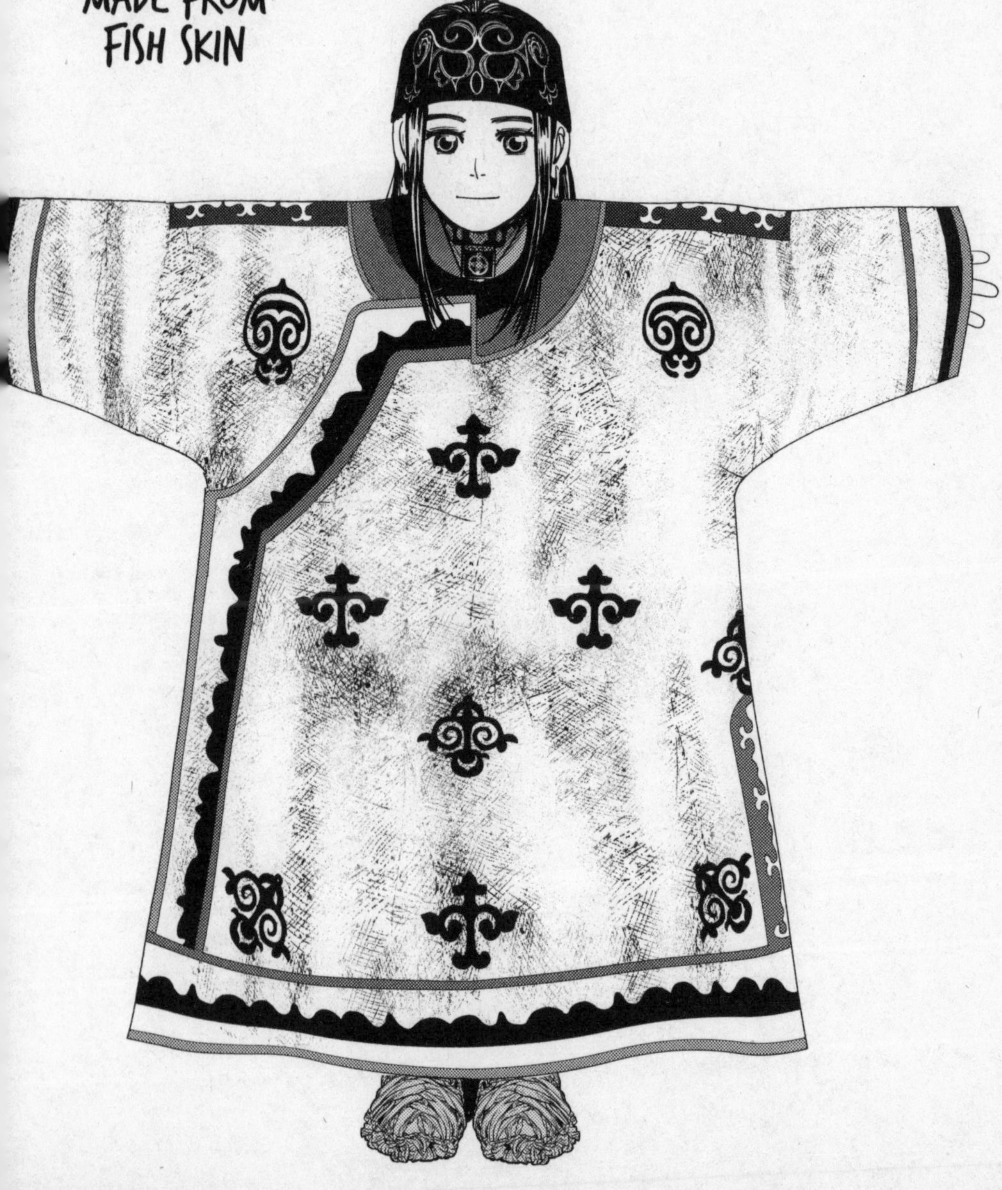

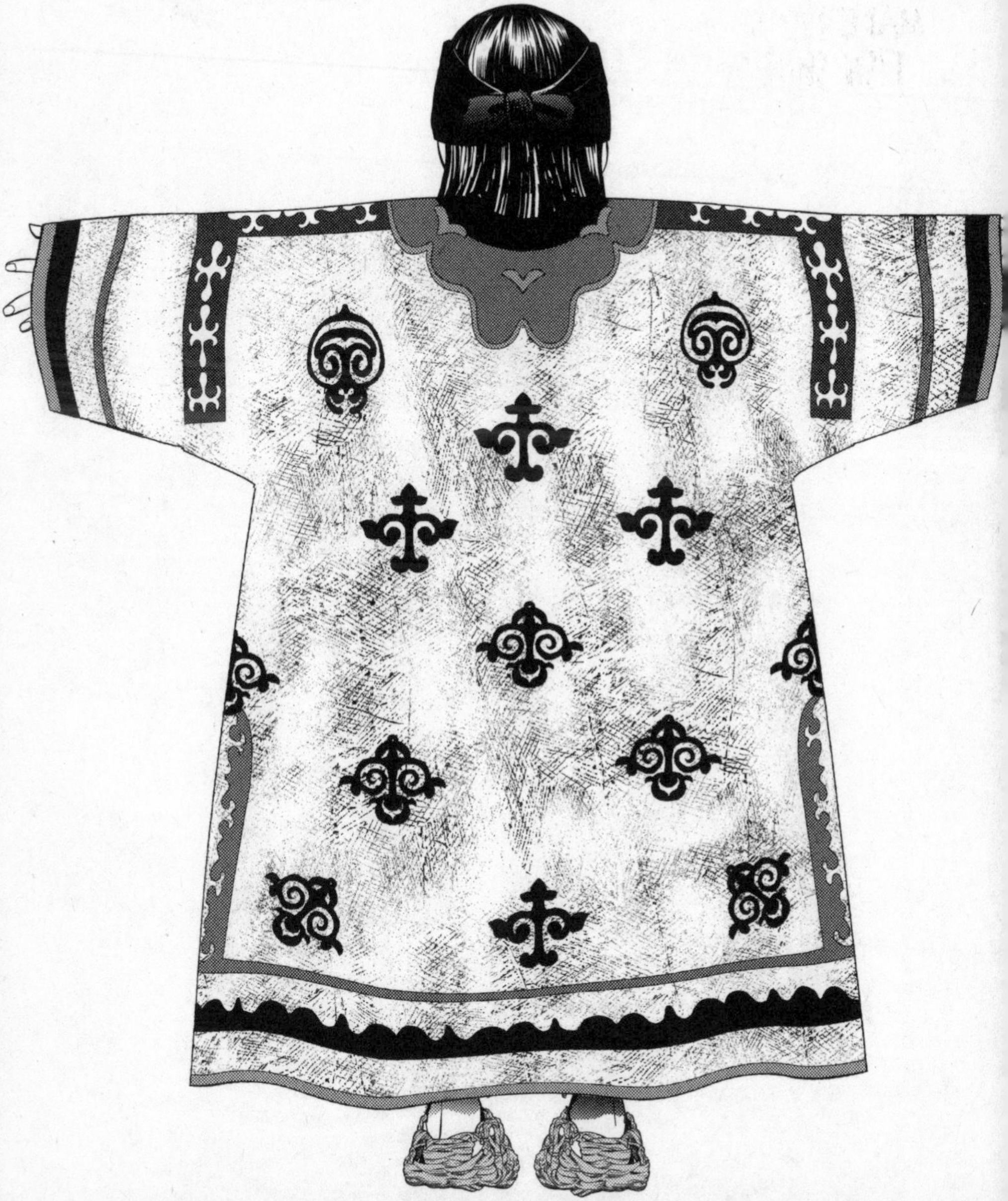

GOLDEN KAMUY

Volume 20
VIZ Signature Edition

Story/Art by **Satoru Noda**

GOLDEN KAMUY © 2014 by Satoru Noda
All rights reserved.
First published in Japan in 2014 by SHUEISHA Inc., Tokyo.
English translation rights arranged by SHUEISHA Inc.

Translation/John Werry
Touch-Up Art & Lettering/Steve Dutro
Design/Shawn Carrico
Editor/Mike Montesa

The stories, characters and incidents mentioned in this publication are entirely fictional.

Printed in Canada

Published by VIZ Media, LLC
P.O. Box 77010
San Francisco, CA 94107

10 9 8 7 6 5 4 3 2 1
First printing, February 2021

VIZ SIGNATURE

viz.com

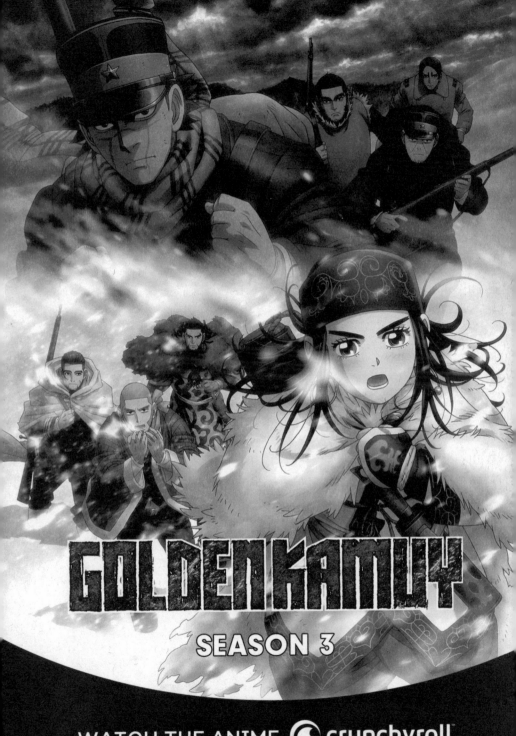

GOLDEN KAMUY

SEASON 3

WATCH THE ANIME ◖crunchyroll

THIS IS THE LAST PAGE.

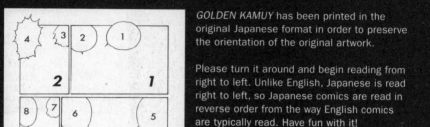

GOLDEN KAMUY has been printed in the original Japanese format in order to preserve the orientation of the original artwork.

Please turn it around and begin reading from right to left. Unlike English, Japanese is read right to left, so Japanese comics are read in reverse order from the way English comics are typically read. Have fun with it!

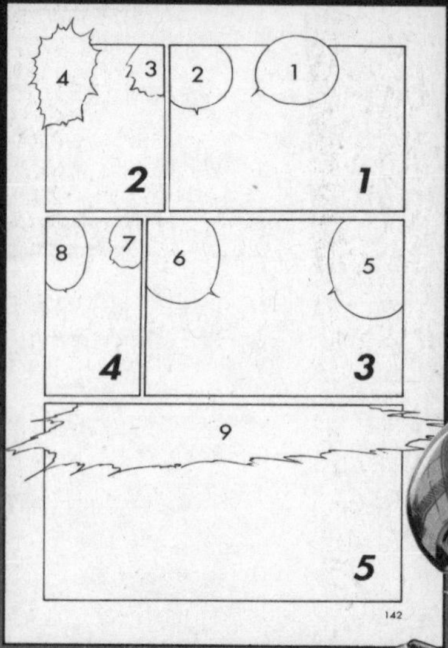
1
2
3
4
5
6
7
8
9
1
2
3
4
5
142

←Follow the action this way.

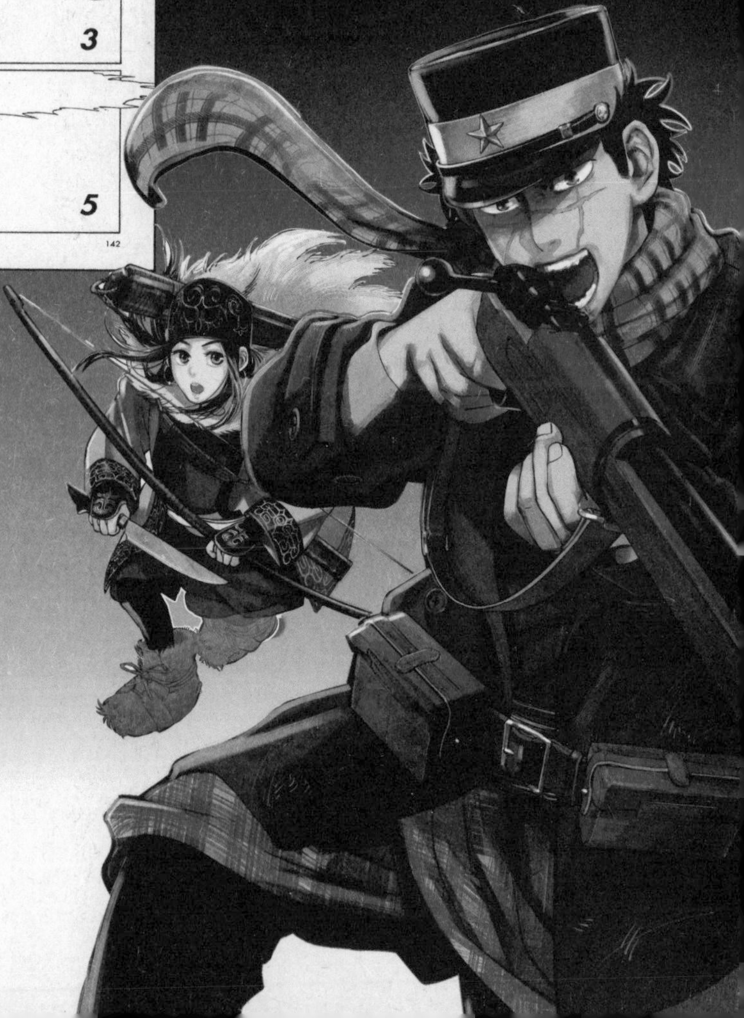